ANONYMOUS

in Their Own Names

DORIS E. FLEISCHMAN,

RUTH HALE,

AND JANE GRANT

ANONYMOUS
in Their Own Names

DORIS E. FLEISCHMAN,
RUTH HALE,
AND JANE GRANT

Susan Henry

Vanderbilt University Press   NASHVILLE

This book is printed on acid-free paper.
Manufactured in the United States of America

Excerpts from the Edward L. Bernays Papers, Manuscript Division,
Library of Congress, Washington, DC, are reprinted
by permission of the Library of Congress.

Excerpts from the Doris Fleischman Bernays Papers,
Schlesinger Library on the History of Women in America,
Radcliffe Institute for Advanced Study, Harvard University, Cambridge,
MA, are reprinted by permission of the Schlesinger Library.

Excerpts from the Jane C. Grant Papers, Special Collections,
University of Oregon Library, Eugene, OR, are reprinted
by permission of the University of Oregon Library.

Excerpts from the New Yorker Records, Manuscripts and
Archives Division, Astor, Lenox and Tilden Foundations,
New York Public Library, New York, NY, are reprinted
by permission of the New York Public Library.

Library of Congress Cataloging-in-Publication Data on file

LC control number: 2012003425
LC classification number: HQ759.H465 2012
Dewey class number: 306.872´30973—dc23

ISBN 978-0-8265-1846-0 (cloth)
ISBN 978-0-8265-1848-4 (e-book)

In memory of Janet Allyn Henry, Cathy Covert, and Kay Mills—

three extraordinary women who should have lived much longer,

and who continue to inspire, encourage, and guide me.

CONTENTS

ACKNOWLEDGMENTS

THESE BIOGRAPHIES OF THREE WOMEN owe the most to two men. Edward L. Bernays first sat down with me for several days of interviews at age ninety-four, then invited me back to his Cambridge, Massachusetts, home for two more long, interview-filled visits. Tremendously cooperative, he answered innumerable questions (some of them uncomfortable), offered me many photographs, and let me rummage through voluminous business records and personal materials in his home.

Heywood Hale Broun was equally generous with his time, memories, written documents, photographs, and hospitality. The dearth of archival material on his mother and father meant that without his unwavering help I could not have told Ruth Hale's story. Beyond that, he was so eloquent and erudite that I looked forward to visiting him simply to hear him talk, and occasionally to argue with him. He provided me with countless wonderful quotes.

Anne Bernays was an interviewer's dream: insightful, candid, vastly informative, welcoming, helpful in every possible way. Her sister Doris Held's different perspective on her mother and excellent guidance in understanding her also helped enormously. Camille Roman provided yet another perspective—that of someone who, as a young woman, was good friends with Doris Fleischman during the last decade of her life, and never stopped being grateful for their friendship. Two other friends, Eleanor Genovese and Carolyn Iverson Ackerman, helped me better understand Fleischman's Cambridge years.

Richard Hale, Ruth's brother, was close to her, so I was delighted when his daughter, Melissa Hale Ward, set aside a full day to talk with me. But I hadn't anticipated what a rich font of family history she would be, or the trove of useful materials she would gather up for me to borrow. Her other unexpected gift was helping me schedule an interview with—and later come to know and admire— Richard's third wife, the magnificent Fiona Hale.

My interviews with Ed Kemp let me tell the remarkable story of Jane Grant's papers finding a home in the University of Oregon Special Collections, even as he helped me better understand William Harris and the Grant/Harris marriage. Harris died before I could thank him for preserving and donating those papers, but fortunately I can thank Special Collections manuscript librarian Linda Long for repeatedly going out of her way to help me make the best possible use of them. I am indebted, as well, to numerous archivists and other staff members in the Manuscript Division of the Library of Congress, the New York Public Library Manuscripts and Archives Division, and the Schlesinger Library on the History of Women in America at Harvard University's Radcliffe Institute for Advanced Study.

My sister Marcy Alyn has avidly cheered me on ever since I first nervously flew off to interview Bernays in 1986. A talented graphic designer, in 2011 she also devoted a great deal of time and energy to arming me superbly well to fight for the best possible book cover. We won, Marcy. Inside, the quantity and high quality of the book's illustrations owe much to the efforts of Patrick Hale, Anne Bernays, Lesli Larson at the University of Oregon, and Dariel Mayer at Vanderbilt University Press.

No friend believed in this book more than Kay Mills, or did more to help me write it and get it published. I will always mourn her unexpected death in early 2011. Many other friends were stalwart in their support and helped in crucial ways, particularly Lori Baker-Schena, Barbara Cloud, Hazel Dicken-Garcia, Terry Hynes, Karen List, Zena Beth McGlashan, and Rodger Streitmatter. My heartfelt thanks to all of them, and to Eli J. Bortz at Vanderbilt University Press. I was lucky that my unusual manuscript made its way into his hands, for he was enthusiastic about it from the start, edited it with skill and sensitivity, and never ceased to be exceedingly knowledgeable, supportive, and patient.

INTRODUCTION

"My name is the symbol of my own identity and must not be lost"

> The woman who wishes to be famous should not marry; rather she should attach herself to one or more women who will fetch and carry for her in the immemorial style of "wives"; women who will secure her from interruption, give her freedom from the irritating small details of living, assure her that she is great and devote their lives to making her so.
> —Psychologist Lorine Pruette, "Why Women Fail," 1931[1]

ALL THREE MARRIAGES WERE UNEXPECTED.

Edward L. Bernays had so often and persuasively declared he never would marry that his family was convinced the name Bernays would not be passed on to the next generation, since he had four sisters but was the only son. In reaction, soon after his sister Hella wed Murray Cohen in 1917, Cohen legally changed his name to Murray C. Bernays so their children would keep the name alive. Newspaper coverage of the unusual name change spread the story of Hella's brother's vow to remain single. Among those who knew the story well was her brother's friend Doris E. Fleischman, the first person he hired—as a writer and his office manager—in 1919 when he set up a business offering a new service he called publicity direction. He quickly realized her skills were invaluable but was glacially slow to acknowledge the growing romantic attraction between them, and only in the face of an ultimatum from Fleischman did he reconsider his vow.

Ruth Hale, too, had adamantly declared she never would marry. This did not interest newspapers, although in early 1916 her friend Heywood Broun's engagement to Russian ballerina Lydia Lopokova was the subject of a *New York Times* news story. Three months later Lopokova broke off the engagement and Broun began to focus his attentions on Hale. Smart, tenacious, sharp-edged, and argumentative, Hale could not have been more unlike his exotic, delicate ex-fiancée, even as she was strikingly different from Broun in both personality and accomplishments. When they first met in 1915 he had a low-status job as a sportswriter for the *New York Tribune*—where he was known for his light touch with words, geniality, and laziness—while she was a writer for the Sunday *Times* and had been one of the country's few women drama critics.

Jane Grant had no objections to marriage but she was finding life as an exceedingly popular single woman so enjoyable that marriage must have seemed a tame alternative. Her suitors included Harold Ross, whom she had met in Paris at the end of World War I when he was editing the *Stars and Stripes*, the newspaper for

U.S. servicemen, and she was performing for some of the same troops as a volunteer entertainer. After the war she returned to her New York job, and he overcame his strong dislike for the city to take an unpromising editing position there so he could be near her. That proved to be more difficult than he had anticipated, however, because not only was she dating many other men, but his sparse social skills placed him at a competitive disadvantage.

Fleischman and Bernays married in 1922, Hale and Broun in 1917, Grant and Ross in 1920. The men then went on to extraordinary professional success.

Bernays has sometimes been called "the father of public relations," for the business he founded was instrumental in transforming press agentry into a new field marked by complex campaigns that could shape trends and change habits and attitudes. The high fees paid by a long, impressive list of clients attest to the effectiveness of some of the firm's strategies. In his 1996 social history of public relations, author Stuart Ewen concluded that Bernays "left a deep mark on the configuration of our world."[2]

Broun was a phenomenon. From the mid-1920s through the 1930s—a time when newspaper columns were a dominant force in molding public opinion—he was one of the country's most popular, influential, and generously paid columnists, and one of the best-known journalists. By 1929 his nationally syndicated column was estimated to have one million readers, many of them drawn to his humor and idiosyncratic, engaging "voice," as well as to his passionate protests against social, political, and economic injustices.

In 1925 Ross plunged into an immensely challenging job as the founding editor of a new type of magazine: a sophisticated, humorous weekly targeting upscale metropolitan readers and New York advertisers. Despite its unconventional concept and excruciatingly difficult birth, within a few years the *New Yorker* was both a financial and critical success. It flourished under Ross, even during the Depression, and by the end of World War II was widely regarded as one of the country's best and most influential magazines.

Bernays, Broun, and Ross have long been lauded as media innovators, their accomplishments chronicled in hundreds of articles and books. With very few exceptions, though, writers have failed to recognize a fundamental reason for the success of these three remarkable media ventures: each man had an uncredited collaborator.

When Bernays and Doris E. Fleischman wed in 1922, she legally became his equal partner in the firm that bore—and would always bear—his name alone, bringing to the partnership skills and sensitivities that complemented her husband's and were as crucial as his to their business's prosperity. Adept at anticipating audience responses, methodical, practical, a superb listener, she proved to be the ideal collaborator in developing campaigns that "sold" clients through actions and appeals based on understanding the needs and desires of the clients' publics. More than anything else, the couple's synergistic relationship explains why the firm thrived for forty years.

Ruth Hale began helping Broun handle the demands of his job immediately after their 1917 marriage when they both were Paris-based reporters covering World War I. In the following years she helped him to form and improve his columns, and to write many other articles (some of which she finished for him), by guiding him in saying more and saying it better. At the same time, this woman who had always been a rebel and activist prodded and inspired him to be much braver at the typewriter, fostering his transformation into a crusader and defender of the underdog. "Ruth was conscience and Heywood was the voice of conscience," their son wrote.[3]

Jane Grant did so much to help Ross research publication options, envision the *New Yorker*, obtain financial backing for it (several times), form its staff, and keep it operating during its perilous first year that two decades later he admitted, "There would be no New Yorker today if it were not for her."[4] Nor was that the end of her involvement, for during World War II she led a fight to reform the magazine's business office, then spearheaded the creation of a small-format edition for overseas troops that exposed hundreds of thousands of servicemen to the magazine and helped it nearly double its circulation after the war.

Anonymous in Their Own Names consists of separate but intertwined biographies of these three women whose work was invisible in their own time and has remained invisible to countless authors who have detailed their husbands' accomplishments but could not "see" the crucial contributions of their wives. Their invisibility is ironic given that they were feminists who kept their birth names when they married as a sign of their equality with their husbands and repeatedly battled the government and societal norms to continue using their names.

Still, they carried out their most important work anonymously—masked by their husbands' fame, which they helped create.

They also created an organization to help other women keep their names, inspired in their efforts by Lucy Stone, the nineteenth-century women's rights activist who was thought to have been the first American woman to keep her surname when she married. Her declaration, "My name is the symbol of my own identity and must not be lost," became the motto of the Lucy Stone League, founded in 1921 by Hale and Grant and revived in 1950 by Grant and Fleischman (also a 1920s member). The league was one of a small number of U.S. feminist organizations during the 1920s and the 1950s, making it important beyond its advocacy of this one cause.

The cause itself seemingly was simple. Women took their husbands' names by custom, not law; it was perfectly legal for them to keep their birth names. So the league educated them about their rights, and pressured government officials and businesses to accept the names women chose. During its early years, extensive newspaper coverage of league activities helped it succeed in its "education" goal, as evidenced by more women keeping their names (which led to still more news coverage, especially when the women were famous). Those numbers never were large, however, and resistance from employers, bank managers, hotel clerks, voting registrars, and passport office administrators—to cite just a few examples—often made using their birth names a frustrating struggle. As a result, the league carried out numerous but only sporadically successful campaigns to persuade opponents to change their policies.

The symbolism explicit in Lucy Stone's words helps explain opposition to the league as well as media interest in it. A married woman who kept her birth name was asserting her independence and equality within marriage, her identity not just as a wife but as a productive person with wider goals, even her entitlement to the rights and freedoms men enjoyed. In short, she was threatening. Espousal of this cause, a 1924 *Philadelphia Inquirer* writer observed, "is a manifestation of that restless, not to say turbulent, spirit that animates the 'new woman' in these days."[5]

Broadly speaking, "new women" sought economic, social, intellectual, and political equality with men. Resisting the restraints of conventional domestic roles, they were likely to be employed, and to hope that their work would provide not only financial independence but self-fulfillment. The "new woman" label dates from the 1890s and was used more and more in succeeding years as women's push into the wider world intensified. Hale (born in 1886) and Fleischman and Grant (both born in 1892) were part of a powerful push in the 1910s, and their professionally productive lives and success in overcoming obstacles make them excellent examples of that decade's new women.

Although raised in an extremely traditional upper-middle-class Manhattan home ruled by a controlling father, Fleischman worked as a *New York Tribune* women's page reporter and in a range of publicist positions until, during the three years prior to her marriage, she helped create one of the country's first public relations firms. Hale's determination to escape the small, insular Tennessee town where she was raised spurred her to obtain increasingly better jobs as a reporter and drama critic in Washington, D.C., Philadelphia, and finally New York. Grant fled rural Kansas for New York at age seventeen, hoping for a singing career but ending up as a poorly paid *New York Times* stenographer and eventually advancing to hotel reporter—a progression that was interrupted in 1918 and 1919 when she performed for U.S. troops in Europe as a YMCA war volunteer. Newspaper work changed all three women's lives.

They all married relatively late—Fleischman and Hale were thirty, Grant was twenty-seven—and were confident that their careers would continue after they married. In this they were part of a trend, for the number of married women with white-collar jobs steadily increased throughout the 1910s and 1920s, and by 1930 more than 24 percent of the country's professional women were married. But what kinds of marriages did they have? Were they the egalitarian partnerships that many new women hoped for? Post–World War I media were full of articles on the topic, and the biting words of Lorine Pruette that begin this introduction capture the disappointment women often expressed in them. Pruette had kept her birth name when she married a fellow psychology graduate student in 1920. Both earned PhDs and he conceded that she was smarter than he was, but he denigrated her work, his career took priority, and she divorced him in 1932 after a decade of unhappiness.

Fleischman, Hale, and Grant had the advantage of marrying men who respected their professional accomplishments, wanted them to continue their careers and keep their names, and, in the case of Bernays and Broun, did important work for the Lucy Stone League. But in other ways the marriages firmly followed a patriarchal pattern, for the men refused to participate in any of the responsibilities traditionally shouldered by married women, leaving their wives to handle the couples' personal lives and run their complicated households.

Those responsibilities included overseeing social lives that were extraordinarily busy, particularly during much of the 1920s when they seemed to be constantly entertaining large gatherings of people in their homes. So many high-spirited visitors were in and out of the Grant/Ross brownstone, for example, that neighbors decided they must be operating a speakeasy and reported them to the police. Still, the three women's greatest domestic challenge was managing their problematic marriages. Living with their quirky, talented, highly demanding husbands required bottomless reserves of adaptability, resilience, and patience, as well as acceptance of the men's negligible involvement in raising their children.

None of this means the marriages didn't work. Despite their many difficulties, they worked well in essential ways. Undeniably, too, the relationships were stunningly successful from the standpoint of the media ventures the couples collaborated to produce—but these also were high-stakes marriages, with more to lose if they failed. And the burden of making them work fell on the wives, who had no role models for what they were doing. Yet many of their challenges and concerns will resonate with women today.

The three women are intriguing to examine together for many reasons, among them the contrasts in their marital strategies. Fleischman ceded almost all control within the marriage to Bernays and spent so much time with him at home and at work that they called theirs a "twenty-four-hour-a-day partnership." At the opposite pole was the Hale/Broun relationship, in which power was equally distributed and husband and wife were only intermittently together, even living in separate apartments for several years. During most of their marriage Grant and Ross lived in a kind of commune where the distractions of other people kept them from being as emotionally engaged with each other as were Fleischman and Bernays or Hale and Broun, and which helped them stay together in spite of their clashing personalities.

Some of the results of those strategies may surprise readers. For example, the bargain Fleischman struck in her subservience to Bernays liberated her professionally. She had an exceptionally productive and fulfilling career, and in the late 1920s and early 1930s even became something of an authority on women's career options, editing a book and writing magazine articles on the topic. Her friends Hale and Grant were far less professionally successful, although for dramatically different reasons, just as they were strikingly dissimilar in their responses to their lack of professional productivity.

Comparisons such as these aid greatly in understanding—and learning from— the women's stories, with contrasts as revealing as trends. Certainly a crucial component of their stories is the work they did as their husbands' unacknowledged partners. As different as their work was, in all three cases it compensated for the men's weaknesses, and the women were alike in their motivations for doing it and in some of what they gained in return. This book documents that previously unrecognized work even as it traces the immense effects of the collaborations on other areas of the women's lives.

It also describes a fourth marriage, one that not only was radically unlike the other three and radically unlike most other marriages of its time, but still is far from the norm today. In 1939, a decade after reluctantly divorcing Ross, Grant married William Harris, a man who passionately embraced both her and her by-then-fervent feminism, and continued to do so for more than thirty years. (Ross seemed to never have been passionate about her, and he loathed her growing feminism.) The Grant/Harris marriage resulted in another successful collaboration, for in 1950 the couple founded White Flower Farm, pioneering at that time and to this day one of the country's most celebrated commercial nurseries.

As this love story (and much else) plays out in the second half of Grant's biography, readers may be struck by its reinforcement of a lesson brought home by the other three marriages: that maintaining even the most innately satisfying bond requires compromise, negotiation, and effort. It is a reminder, too, of the complexity of relationships between strong women and men, and the fascination such relationships hold.

Marriage always is an experiment. Yet a combination of factors—their professional partnerships being one of the most important—made these couples especially reliant on trial-and-error learning and other kinds of experimentation. They were tested often, and it is hard not to marvel at their creation of new variations within the institution that they hoped would make it work better for them. As Hale wrote in 1926: "If it is true that the married state is the most beneficial of all those yet devised for adult human beings to live in, it must certainly be made sufficiently pleasant and spacious to contain them."[6]

PART I

Doris E. Fleischman

CHAPTER 1

"I just knew she was the brightest woman I'd ever met"

THE WOMAN WHO WOULD HELP invent the field of public relations and make headlines for keeping her birth name after she married was born on July 18, 1892, into a highly traditional upper-middle-class family ruled by Victorian values. Rigid, authoritarian, and unemotional, Samuel E. Fleischman was a successful New York City lawyer who exerted firm control over his reserved, compliant wife, Harriet Rosenthal Fleischman, and their four children.[1] Much later, their second-born child admitted that her parents' marriage had strongly affected her expectations of her own. "Independence was something I yearned for, but hopelessly," Doris E. Fleischman wrote. "My mother's attitude showed me the futility of any struggle. She was completely docile, never argued with Pop, always followed his wishes."[2]

Doris, too, always followed his wishes, so she was fortunate that he believed she should "do something" with her life. "He was completely conservative in everything but his attitude toward women working," she explained.[3] Her education at the elite Horace Mann School prepared her well for Barnard College, where she most enjoyed her English, philosophy, and psychology classes, and played on three varsity sports teams. At home, she wrote fiction and poetry, practiced the piano every day, and studied singing with a teacher who encouraged her to consider becoming an opera singer (a suggestion she rejected because she knew she would feel uncomfortable performing in public).[4]

Despite these successes, she remembered feeling "bewildered" when, as she was about to graduate from Barnard in 1913, her father asked her what she planned to do next. She knew little about the world (in part because he had censored her reading) and felt unqualified for any career. After rejecting most of her initial ideas, he told her, "I would like you to do social welfare work of some kind." This probably was a reflection of his own interests; his *New York Times* obituary noted that he "was an active supporter of many Jewish charities." But his daughter's first job—as a fundraiser and publicist for a New York charitable organization—does not seem to have been very satisfying work, for she never mentioned it when she later wrote about this period of her life. Instead, she always claimed her employment history began in 1914 when she joined the *New York Tribune*—a job she accepted only after asking her father's permission.[5]

Her beloved older brother Leon was a reporter at the *New York World*, but it was Edward L. Bernays who helped her make the contact that eventually led to her *Tribune* job interview. She first met Bernays when she was in high school, then ran into him more often after he graduated from Cornell University in 1912 and moved into his parents' new apartment located around the corner from the West 107th Street Fleischman home. She and his sister Hella had been friends when they both attended Barnard.[6]

Like Fleischman, Bernays did not immediately find his true calling. His discovery began in early 1913 when he and a friend were editing a small medical magazine and received a physician's unsolicited glowing review of the play *Damaged Goods*, which dealt with a taboo subject—syphilis and the need for educating the public about its dangers. They knew the review would be controversial but published it anyway. Then, hearing that a well-known actor was interested in producing and starring in the play, they contacted him and rashly offered to underwrite a New York production. This was despite the likelihood of problems from the city's censors, who earlier had shut down a George Bernard Shaw play about prostitution.[7]

To raise the money they had promised and add respectability to the venture, Bernays created a Sociological Fund Committee. For a four-dollar donation, contributors to the fund would receive a ticket to the play and, he argued, the satisfaction of supporting a battle against prudishness. After he persuaded notables like John D. Rockefeller Jr. to join the committee, checks totaling more than $4,000 arrived and newspapers ran stories about the planned production. The morning after its sold-out debut, one paper's editorial page announced that the play had "struck sex o'clock in America," and it subsequently was performed in Washington, D.C., for members of Congress.[8] But these events had an even more important effect on Bernays. As he later explained, "I had had so much pleasure from what I had done that I said to myself, 'This is what I want to do.' I became a press agent."[9]

He spent the next five years publicizing Broadway plays, actors, musical performers such as Enrico Caruso, and—during three years that he said "taught me more about life than I have learned from politics, books, romance, marriage and fatherhood in the years since"—Diaghilev's Ballets Russes. This kind of work offered "one thrill after another," he said, and he loved doing it. Indeed, his own success was as exciting to him as the glamour and sophistication of the performing arts world. He not only knew what he wanted to do but had learned he was very good at it.[10]

Still, in June 1918 he happily stopped this work to join the many journalists, press agents, and advertising people being recruited by the U.S. Committee on Public Information (CPI). Headed by George Creel, this huge propaganda operation was extraordinarily effective in building nationwide public support for this country's World War I efforts and for spreading U.S. government views to the rest of the world. Bernays worked out of the CPI Foreign Press Bureau's New York office until, when the war ended in November, he went to Paris for the Versailles Peace Conference as part of the official press mission.[11]

The CPI has been widely credited with vividly demonstrating the power of organized, well-funded public opinion manipulation. The general public increasingly was aware of this power, as were businesses and other organizations. Certainly many of the people who worked for the CPI, Bernays among them, were struck by its effectiveness.[12] He also was affected by his experiences at the Peace Conference. "Paris was swarming with ethnic entities that had been promised independence," he explained, "and I couldn't help but notice the tremendous emphasis the small nations of the world placed on public opinion." Mesmerized by "this world picture emphasizing the power of words and ideas," he vowed that when he returned to New York in March 1919 he "would go into an activity that dealt with this force of ideas to affect attitudes."[13] His exposure to "the broader theater of world affairs" profoundly changed him, he wrote. "I knew that musical and theatrical press agentry and publicity would not satisfy me."[14]

His CPI connections soon resulted in publicity contracts with two organizations that were unlike his prewar clients. On March 20, 1919, the Lithuanian National Council hired him to help in its efforts to obtain American support for recognition of the country as an independent republic, and ten weeks later he began working for the U.S. War Department's campaign for the reemployment of former servicemen. He initially operated just as he had as a theatrical press agent—out of his clients' offices or his parents' home—but in late July he felt confident enough to rent his own office space and hire his first employee, Doris Fleischman.[15]

"The best move I ever made in my life"

At that time fleischman had much less to show for the preceding years than did her new boss, although five years earlier she would have had every reason to anticipate career success that would match his own. In mid-1914 she had begun working as a reporter for the *New York Tribune* women's page, which already was well-known for its extensive coverage of the women's suffrage movement. It was an exciting place to work, especially when, the next year, the department moved from isolated top-floor offices down into the city room, and women's news became part of the paper's "general schedule."[16]

In long feature stories Fleischman interviewed people ranging from suffrage leaders to actresses, from male politicians to working-class single women, from women entrepreneurs to social reformers. A particular pleasure was traveling to San Francisco to report on the Women's Peace Conference at the 1915 Panama-Pacific International Exposition. And she was, she believed, the first woman to cover a prizefight for a major newspaper. (Fearing she would be hurt, her father would only let her go if he accompanied her. In her story she described him sitting by her side near the ring in Madison Square Garden.)[17] She was promoted to assistant women's page editor and then to assistant Sunday editor, and her weekly pay jumped from the fifteen dollars she had made as a reporter to twenty-two dollars.[18]

Her work often put her in contact with people and events she would never have otherwise encountered, and it not only introduced her to feminism but gave her a chance to call attention to women's problems and the women working to solve them. Those experiences likely opened her eyes to a world she had known little about and inspired her to do things she would not previously have done. Thus this young woman whose fears of singing in public had kept her from considering opera as a career went on to proudly perform in area amateur theatricals, and someone who had scant knowledge of the world when she graduated from college was, in 1917, thrilled to march in the first Women's Peace Parade in New York City.[19]

She obviously enjoyed her job and was confident in her ability to do it well, yet she left sometime in 1916.[20] Her reasons are a mystery, made more difficult to unravel because she and Bernays consistently maintained that she stayed at the paper for three more years. He still held to that story three-quarters of a century later, only conceding her earlier exit after much prodding, and professing no knowledge of the reasons for it.[21] One of her close friends in the 1970s with whom she occasionally discussed her early career (never admitting that she left the *Tribune* early) subsequently speculated that Fleischman was forced to give up the job for family reasons.[22] Imprecise as it is, this interpretation makes sense.

In 1916 she was living at home with her parents, her pretty, popular younger sister Beatrice, and her younger brother Ira, whose health had been weakened by childhood scarlet fever. Her mother was remembered by others as warm, caring, gentle, and much loved, but Doris was not close to her, and in later writings she faulted her for poorly preparing her for married life. In those same writings she lauded her father as wise and strong. She made it clear that he controlled much of her life, laying down strict rules about what she must and must not do. He was, in the words of his granddaughter Anne, "taciturn, unsmiling—a disciplinarian with no shade of gray in his thinking." Fleischman almost never disobeyed him (although, knowing he would disapprove, she simply didn't tell him when she used tickets Bernays had given her to attend a performance of *Damaged Goods*).[23] He was by far the most powerful force in her life, and she would have left the *Tribune* if that had been his wish.

Only a sketchy picture can be drawn of her professional life following her departure from the newspaper. She seems to have mainly done freelance writing, publicity, and fundraising, and to have carried out what she called a "historical survey" for the Baron de Hirsch Fund, a philanthropic organization.[24] One client for which she apparently did considerable work was the New York Dispensary, a clinic serving the poor. She later called it "a terrible place," possibly referring to her experience there rather than the clinic itself.[25] None of these jobs seem to have been very satisfying, and they certainly were a step down from the *Tribune*. So she must have been delighted when Bernays offered her a full-time position in July 1919.

Bernays always asserted that she came to him directly from the *Tribune*, which kept him from acknowledging an important reason she was the first person he hired: she had previously worked for him as a freelance writer. A careful examination of his Lithuanian National Council and War Department work reveals that she wrote press releases for him in the spring and early summer of 1919 before he opened his own office.[26]

In those months she was looking for freelance assignments and his work was extensive enough to require help. In addition to organizing promotional events for the Lithuanian organization, he had agreed to provide it with six weekly press releases, which often called for substantial research. His War Department work was more sophisticated and complex, involving the production of programs, slogans, and many press releases. Because he had both clients' releases typeset, bound into pads and sent to newspapers, he also had to work closely with printers and mailers. And he was well compensated, earning $150 a week from the Lithuanian National Council and $100 a week (plus a large expense budget) from the War Department.[27] So he could afford to pay a freelancer.

As the summer progressed, he also realized he could afford to rent his own office. He found three rooms on the fifth floor of an old building at 19 East Forty-Eighth Street that he thought would meet his needs, and moved in on July 28, 1919. That same day, he hired Fleischman to serve as a writer and as what he called the "balance wheel of our operation." This was, he later declared, "the best move I ever made in my life."[28]

Certainly she was a logical choice. Nonetheless, his decision to immediately hire a woman, and to quickly turn over considerable responsibility to her, was unusual at a time when many men were uncomfortable with professional women and unappreciative of their intellectual capabilities. He knew Fleischman was a good writer, but he could have simply continued using her as a freelancer. And although he had, as he put it, "dropped in from time to time and been a casual member of the crowd" that sometimes gathered at the nearby Fleischman home, he did not know her very well. For eight years, he had been so busy with his work that he had had little time for anything else. "My publicity jobs filled my 24 hours a day," he remembered. "I did not miss the absence of an organized social life, because my work provided my pleasures."[29]

But he was at ease with women, in part because of his home life. He had always been close to his mother, Anna Freud Bernays (she was Sigmund Freud's older sister). He thought she favored him over his sisters, describing her as an "all-pervasive and beneficent influence" who "solved all my problems" and compensated for his ongoing difficulties with his remote, exacting, temperamental father, Ely Bernays (whose younger sister Martha was married to Freud). A grain exporter, Ely Bernays usually provided well for his family, but even Fleischman noted that his children "seemed to fear him long after they were grown."[30]

Anna Bernays always remembered her own father's favoritism of her brother Sigmund. He paid his son's way through medical school but she had to earn her living in Austria as a nursemaid.[31] Raising her five children in America, she would only talk with them in German (so it became their second language), yet she read not only a German-language newspaper but the *New York Times* every day. In addition to being well informed, she was unconditionally supportive of her only son—something that was particularly important to him in 1913 when, despite his father's strong disapproval, he decided to become a theatrical press agent.[32]

Looking back, Bernays thought his upbringing with two older and two younger sisters helped account for his positive views of women. "The fact that these four sisters were no different mentally from me must have made me recognize that women were just as smart as men," he said. He admired each sister's later accomplishments, which included translating psychology books from German into French, becoming a noted expert on government and economics, and serving as the executive secretary of an important women's organization.[33]

As for Fleischman, Bernays remembered, "I just knew she was the brightest woman I'd ever met."[34] Beyond that, he hired her knowing she had skills he lacked. Writing was not his strength, yet she was a fast writer (and typist) as well as an excellent editor. A perfectionist, she did extensive rewriting when she had time. And she promptly helped him set up his new office, then hire a secretary (at thirty dollars a week), a mail clerk (at twenty-five dollars a week), and an office boy (at twenty-five dollars a week). Fleischman's salary was fifty dollars, but when Bernays later hired his sister Hella's husband to do research and some writing, he paid him seventy-five dollars a week.[35]

Fleischman went on to blame herself for not asking for a higher salary (she actually had initially told him she would work for no less than forty-five dollars). She had little grasp of the value of money, she explained, since she lived at home and her father had always supported her. The money she earned "was extra and unimportant."[36] That for three years she had had no full-time job, and probably only modest freelance income, also may have led her to give scant consideration to her salary when she was offered this new position.

In fairness, it is possible that she would not have asked for more even if she had carefully considered her options. A 1921 book about professional women noted that salaries for "experienced publicity consultants" were "around $50 a week, and are said to be about 10 per cent lower than those for men."[37] A 1920 book describing careers for women quoted a "director of one publicity agency" as saying that women "freelance workers" could earn from fifty to a hundred dollars a week.[38] And when she left the *Tribune* in 1916, Fleischman had been making twenty-two dollars a week.

Bernays struggled with what to call his new business. Finally, with Fleischman's help, he settled on "Edward L. Bernays, Publicity Direction."[39] His 1919 client list included numerous theatrical clients, the Lithuanian National Council, and the War Department, as well as the American Civil Liberties Union, Best Foods Company (for which he helped launch a new salad oil), and the Federation for the Support of Jewish Philanthropies (which was conducting a large fundraising drive). With ten full- and part-time employees at the end of December, he calculated that since March he had earned about $11,000.[40]

"Prepared for your free publication by our Doris Fleischman"

HIS LARGEST CLIENT DURING HIS first year in his new office—and the one for which he went on to work the longest—was the book publisher Boni & Liveright. Fleischman seems to have played a role in obtaining this client, since it was her brother Leon who urged the firm's founder, Horace Liveright, to hire Bernays. After working as a reporter at the *World* and then the *New York Telegraph*, in 1919 Leon was brought into the company as a vice president and its secretary and treasurer. According to Bernays, Leon insisted that Bernays, who was hired that fall, "could give the firm and the authors an imaginative type of publicity other publishers had not dreamed of using, that this would sell books and upgrade the list of authors by attracting good new ones."[41]

Liveright was a daring young publisher who was willing to gamble on unknown authors and controversial books. He had recently signed a few established authors like Theodore Dreiser, but he also was anxious to publish works by Greenwich Village intellectuals who had been ignored by rival publishers.[42] "Other publishers deplored him, some envied him, and all had to admire his list," wrote book historian John Tebbel. "If Liveright did not invent the literary renaissance of the '20s, he was at least its chief conductor."[43] And he was enthusiastic about shattering the old, staid molds of book publishing as well as the musty conventions of bookselling. He had, in Bernays's words, "faith in aggressive publishing." Bernays, in turn, was "eager to try out our strategies and tactics on books." He believed "books would respond more quickly to our techniques than almost any other commodity."[44]

During their yearlong campaign, Bernays and Fleischman focused on expanding the book-reading public beyond the narrow audiences previously identified by most publishers. They prepared an attractive catalog highlighting the most important books—those that they predicted would be discussed wherever "men and women, who are interested in life and the books that express life, gather"—and bombarded three hundred bookstores with weekly circulars on different books. Newspapers throughout the country were sent both a continuous stream of short press releases and about a hundred features related to Boni & Liveright books.[45]

In what Bernays said was an application of a technique used in his government CPI work, these one-thousand- to fifteen-hundred-word features were offered as exclusives to one newspaper in a town.[46] Editors first received brief synopses of the pieces that had been "prepared for your free publication by our Doris Fleischman, who was until recently on the staff of the *New York Tribune*, and by other experienced feature writers." They returned postcards indicating those they wanted, which then were mailed to them.[47]

A small number of books were singled out for special publicity efforts. One was Christopher Morley and Bart Haley's satire on Prohibition, *In the Sweet Dry and Dry*. Numerous features and shorter releases were sent out, and a "booklovers tavern" was created in New York's Majestic Hotel, whose bar had been closed by Prohibition. Books by Boni & Liveright authors replaced liquor bottles behind the bar (where Bernays's sister Hella and a friend held forth), and some of these authors—as well as the president of the New York County chapter of the Woman's Christian Temperance Union—were in attendance at the well-covered opening of the "tavern." The event kicked off a campaign to turn "corner saloons" in ten medium-sized towns into bookstores. It also led to the creation of the American Council for Wider Reading, which was devoted to encouraging people to spend more time reading.[48]

This work was a good example of an often-used technique that Bernays variously labeled "the overt act," "created circumstances," and "the created event." As he explained it in his own first book (published by Boni & Liveright in 1923), with these kinds of activities the public relations practitioner "is not merely the purveyor of news; he is more logically the creator of news."[49] Working for Boni & Liveright, "I studied each book not as literature, but to find ideas that might be emphasized to increase public interest in the volume," he later remembered. "I then looked for a current news idea that could be correlated with the ideas I had isolated. Then I tried to dramatize these ideas."[50]

The campaign for *Iron City* by M. H. Hedges illustrated another technique—the "segmental approach"—that Bernays and Fleischman repeatedly used. This strategy, Bernays said, required the practitioner to "subdivide the appeal of his subjects and present it through the widest possible variety of avenues to the public."[51] Set on a college campus, *Iron City* dealt with wide-ranging issues that Fleischman "subdivided," writing features with titles such as "Can the College Woman Love?," "The Insecure Tenure of the College Professor—How He Is Pried Loose from His Job," and "Big Business and the American College—What Will Happen When the Two Are Divorced?" One feature even asked the question, "Are the Children of College Parents Puny?"[52]

Other releases connected the book to current news events, including fall 1919 strikes in the coal industry and a later strike by professors at the Carnegie Institute in Pittsburgh (the book portrayed a professors' strike). Author Hedges was asked to identify professors who would be willing to talk with newspaper reporters about issues raised in the novel, letters extolling the book were written to teachers' unions, and the Stutz Motor Car Company and Chicago's Marshall Field & Company (both prominently mentioned in the book) were approached in the hopes that they would cosponsor publicity efforts.[53]

Another effective strategy was the association of specific books with well-known people—whether or not they had any real connection to the books. For example, to call attention to Adriana Spandoni's *The Swing of the Pendulum*, a novel about a professional woman and her lovers, Fleischman wrote releases that profiled contemporary women activists. Many newspapers' women's pages ran the stories. Similarly, anarchist writer Hutchins Hapgood's novel, *The Story of a Lover* (written anonymously), was publicized with quotes from movie stars like Mary Pickford and Lillian Gish, who had supplied Fleischman with their definitions of love. The book sold eleven thousand copies in six months.[54]

No doubt much of this steady stream of publicity was ignored, and not everything they tried was successful. Bernays admitted, for example, that although the Majestic Hotel's "booklovers tavern" received extensive coverage in New York newspapers, *In the Sweet Dry and Dry* was not mentioned in any of the articles.[55] Yet certainly excitement was generated for some titles that otherwise would have received little attention, and sales increased when promotional materials especially resonated with editors.[56]

Bernays, though, had a larger goal than selling Boni & Liveright books. He wanted to sell American publishing on the value of book promotion, and already was making his case in a March 1920 *Publisher's Weekly* article in which he argued that his campaigns helped expand the general market for books.[57] Much later, intellectual historian Ann Douglas came to a similar conclusion. They "made sellers out of books that were not natural sellers," she said, and in the process they proved that it was possible to "*create* receptivity and revenue."[58] Other publishers noticed these effects and began to adopt more dynamic sales techniques aimed at broader audiences, even as new companies devoted to publishing books for previously neglected markets were born. Bookselling changed.[59] By the end of the 1920s, observed book historian Tebbel, "Publishers were at last convinced of the value of promotion and publicity, much more so than they had been before the war, and for the first time they were willing to spend money on it."[60]

"Atlanta is breathing easier now"

BERNAYS LATER WROTE, "My work with Liveright presented a divide between what I had done—my press agentry, publicity, publicity direction—and what I now attempted to do: counsel on public relations." He and Fleischman had given a lot of thought to the best way to describe the work they gradually were doing more of in 1920, and together they coined the phrase "counsel on public relations" to describe what they saw as a new, more important service: "giving professional advice to our clients on their public relationships, regardless of whether such advice resulted in publicity." They changed the firm's name from "Edward L. Bernays, Publicity Direction" to "Edward L. Bernays, Counsel on Public Relations."[61]

Their collaboration in developing that phrase was typical of the way they worked together. From the very beginning—when neither of them had a title—they had discussed clients with each other, combined ideas, jointly developed campaigns, and divided up the work according to each person's strengths. It was Fleischman's writing ability that initially mattered most to Bernays, but another strength soon proved important in establishing the new firm. An excellent listener, she had a gift for quickly understanding people. One reason she did well at the *Tribune*, Bernays thought, was that her interview subjects often felt comfortable enough to open up to her. She was empathetic, attentive, and a perceptive judge of people.[62]

These qualities were crucial to their success in carrying out their most challenging 1920 work. In early May, the National Association for the Advancement of Colored People hired them to stage a campaign for its national convention in Atlanta, planned for late May and early June. This would be the first NAACP convention ever held in the South, and the decision to meet there was controversial among the organization's members. Atlanta had been the scene of fierce race riots in 1906, lynchings and mob violence had increased since that time, and antagonism against local NAACP chapters had grown in other southern states.[63]

Hurriedly brought in after the regular NAACP publicity person became ill, Bernays and Fleischman were largely ignorant about the problems faced by African Americans, particularly in the South. And because the convention would begin soon, they had to act quickly. Their only instructions were to get as much good publicity as possible into southern newspapers (most of which previously had shown little support for the NAACP). Otherwise, they were on their own.[64]

While Bernays stayed in New York to work with northern media, a week before the convention began Fleischman traveled by herself to Atlanta. They knew little about the situation and the city, so her job was to be the advance person—to "probe the territory from the standpoint of public opinion" and also, Bernays said, "to make arrangements for news coverage and to try to assure that some top Georgian political figures would attend our meetings so that we could publicize the sanction our cause was receiving in Atlanta by their presence."[65]

Bernays explained that one reason he gave Fleischman this assignment was that he thought she would be able to avoid antagonizing the individuals she was trying to persuade to take actions they would have preferred not to take. At the same time, he believed many of the people she encountered would like her.[66] And her innocence meant that "no one could possibly mistake her for a propagandist for Civil Rights in the South."[67]

She first met with the city's mayor and the state's governor. According to Bernays, after the governor warned her that he thought whites were likely to cause trouble, she asked him to put the National Guard on reserve, which he did by phone as she sat in his office. Still, neither he nor the mayor ultimately agreed to attend the convention (although the mayor did send an official welcome to be read to the attendees).[68]

She had more success when she next met with men at Atlanta's daily newspapers and wire service bureaus. They all agreed to either cover specific meetings themselves or write reports based on news releases they received. The *Atlanta Constitution*'s city editor both consulted with Fleischman on how to cover what was for him an unusual event and asked her to provide stories on individual meetings and interviews with key participants. All of these media went on to provide substantial positive coverage.[69] "Their calm and matter-of-fact handling helped to make the community accept this invasion from the North quietly," Fleischman noted.[70]

But having received no NAACP briefing on the likely situation in Atlanta, she was, Bernays said, "oblivious to the dangers of her mission."[71] Indeed, it was only many years later that she learned from NAACP assistant secretary Walter White that bodyguards had accompanied her each time she left her hotel. Branded a "nigger lover" by some whites, she also failed to notice the men who threw pennies at her hotel window and, when she walked through the hotel lobby, at her feet. She did not realize they were telling her they thought she was no better than a prostitute who sold herself for pennies.[72]

Bernays met her in Atlanta for the convention and together they worked out a plan to guide their work that week. After deciding on a "publicity platform" with three themes they would stress, they set about "preparing copy for the newspapers under constant deadlines."[73] Mary White Ovington, the NAACP chairman of the board, was impressed with their technique, which she said essentially was "to make friends with the reporters and do all their work."[74] And even as they worked constantly with reporters from southern newspapers, they sent frequent press releases by telegraph to papers in New York and Chicago.[75]

The situation always was tense for conference attendees. A press release Fleischman wrote after the convention's conclusion expressed relief that "Atlanta is breathing easier now . . . and so are the delegates," one of whom told her she felt as if she had been "sitting on a volcano."[76] The success of their own efforts must have made Bernays and Fleischman breathe more easily too. Ovington remarked with surprise "how fully and correctly the *Atlanta Constitution* reported our meetings," and Walter White wrote Bernays to tell him that "the amount of publicity secured, largely through your efforts, was greater than at any other of the ten conferences preceding, although all of those conferences were held in northern cities."[77]

The convention also had strong personal meaning for Fleischman. When the meetings were over and she and Bernays met members of the NAACP's northern delegation at the city's railroad station to return to New York, she insisted on joining the black delegates in the Jim Crow sleeping car.[78] Forty years later, she said of her Atlanta experience, "No work I have ever done has had so deep and lasting an effect on me."[79]

"I'm not happy unless I do it myself"

HER ASSIGNMENTS FOR THEIR OTHER clients (including Boni & Liveright) were much more routine, but she worked hard writing and strategizing with Bernays. Describing herself during those early years as having "a nose for news and a steady compulsion to write," she often wrote from fifteen to twenty stories a week, then took them to newspaper offices and tried to get them placed. Bernays said she was good at placing because if editors told her they wanted changes, she was able to quickly modify a story for them on the spot.[80]

Clients added in 1920 and 1921 included several theatrical producers and performers, *Good Housekeeping* and *Cosmopolitan* magazines, Cartier jewelers, the Waldorf-Astoria hotel, and the Dort Motor Company.[81] Their "first big business client," in Bernays's words, was the U.S. Radium Corporation, which hired them in 1920 to promote radium's luminous properties for commercial use as well as its application in cancer therapy. Fleischman's stories had titles like "The Royal Jewel of Today," "Radium Becoming a Household Aid," and "Radium Bank for Those Who Bank on Radium." This last story described a service their client had established at their suggestion: a national radium bank that made the element easily accessible to physicians treating cancer patients (and in the process called attention to radium's medical value).[82]

Fleischman's work did not end with writing and strategizing; she also was the firm's office manager. She interviewed all job candidates, established schedules, charted the work being done for clients, kept the books, and paid bills.[83] One of the few surviving memos between her and Bernays from this time nicely illustrates the complexity of these responsibilities. Probably written in early 1921 when she planned to briefly be absent, it brought him up to date on their campaigns for four key clients, explained the work others in the office had been assigned, and detailed payments received and bills due. She said monthly vouchers had not yet been checked, but "Please do not do anything about this until I get back, because I'm not happy unless I do it myself."[84]

She likely took care of most of the details in 1921 when they moved from their three cramped rooms in an old building to newer, larger, more attractive quarters at a "prime address" next to the elegant Ritz-Carlton Hotel on Forty-Sixth Street and Fifth Avenue. With the move, she gained her own office, rather than sharing a crowded space outside Bernays's office with other staff members, as she had previously.[85] Apparently their staff stayed the same size it had been in late 1919, when Bernays had ten employees.[86]

The size of their staff may not have increased but their income certainly did. Rates for most clients were about seventy-five dollars a week when they set up their first operation, but by the early 1920s they were able to charge some clients as much as $12,000 a year (although most contracts were for shorter periods).[87] They seem to have had no trouble affording nicer quarters in a better neighborhood, especially since their business continued to expand. Clients added in 1922 included Macy's department store, the Hotel Association of New York (which hired them to publicize New York as a friendly place to visit), the Venida Hairnet Company, and numerous performers and event organizers.[88]

Occasionally Fleischman was in charge of entire small campaigns. For example, in January 1921 she helped plan, carried out the publicity for, and worked closely with the organizers of two charity fundraisers. (Her earlier fundraising work no doubt made her very familiar with these kinds of activities.) The first event was a musical review presented by the Cardiac Committee of the Public Education Association. The other, for which she obtained excellent advance coverage, was a concert at Carnegie Hall to benefit the Babies Hospital of New York.[89] All surviving press releases for the latter activity are identified as coming "From Doris E. Fleischman, 19 East 48th Street." They contain no reference at all to Bernays.[90]

She obviously was the contact person on these two campaigns, notwithstanding Bernays's unwavering assertions that she never had client contacts.[91] Indeed, there is no doubt that during the firm's early years she had at least a small number of these contacts.

In another example, in 1922 she made the initial contact and then met with the publisher of *American Agriculturist* to plan a campaign for his weekly magazine. Her notes from the meeting show that, among other things, she suggested ways of attracting more young readers through new kinds of stories and the formation of boys and girls clubs, proposed a more scientific-sounding name for the magazine's testing department, advised that more articles be run about new patents (since this might encourage new advertising), and recommended that well-known public officials be solicited for articles, which in turn could be widely distributed to media organizations and interest groups.[92]

It seems very likely that she had these kinds of meetings with additional clients for which written documentation has not survived. Still, her client contacts clearly were limited in importance and number, and they were to end completely in a few years. This was despite her extensive knowledge of public relations tactics and demonstrated competence in working with media people outside the firm. Yet only a few clients ever worked directly with her.

Instead, after Bernays met with a client, he sat down with Fleischman and told her about the meeting. Then they brainstormed—identifying critical issues, speculating on outcomes, critiquing each other's ideas, talking through strategies, exploring alternatives. As he put it, "I had the advantage of [Fleischman] having a mind that I thought was as good as mine and that I could always play with" in campaign development. They began strategizing together soon after he opened his first office, he said.[93]

"Feminism has created a new romance"

ONE REASON SHE THRIVED after she joined Bernays was that she actually had been progressing toward that job ever since she graduated from Barnard in 1913. She brought to her new position values, skills, and determination that had steadily been developing, and by 1919 she was a different person than she had been at her college graduation. At that earlier time, she was neither psychologically nor practically prepared for a career, seeming to know as little about her strengths as she did about the world. Despite these constraints, though, she soon found work.

In her later writings about this period of her life she emphasized her father's involvement in her early employment, picturing herself as someone who simply did what he wanted her to do (and only under circumstances that were acceptable to him). She never acknowledged her own desire to pursue a career, and never gave herself credit for the resolve and effort that her progress no doubt required.

Her father did initially urge her to find a job, but this seems to have been something she would have chosen to do without his urging. Thus, even though she had no desire to be a secretary, she enrolled in a secretarial school (which she didn't enjoy attending) to learn typing.[94] And she took the initiative in obtaining her *Tribune* position. All Bernays did was ask a friend who was a women's page reporter at another newspaper to advise her. When the two women met for lunch, Bernays's friend recommended that Fleischman introduce herself to the *Tribune*'s women's page editor and offer to write a story for her. That story—about a wealthy woman who had sponsored a labor meeting at her estate—led to her job offer.[95] She was very productive at the paper and in a relatively brief time was promoted twice.

Equally revealing is the work she did that she did not want to do. Her first job as a fundraiser and publicist for a charitable organization was so unsatisfying that she never listed it in any descriptions of her work history, yet she stayed there for about a year. This surely helped her hone her writing skills, and without that experience she might not have been offered the *Tribune* job, which she went on to love. Giving it up in 1916 undoubtedly was painful, but that didn't stop her from searching out freelance writing and fundraising assignments during the next three years, including some (at the New York Dispensary) that she apparently disliked.

Her persistence would be unremarkable if she had needed to work to support herself, but that was not the case. During all this time her father "continued to pay my way through life," she wrote, and she took so little notice of her *Tribune* salary that she once went three months without remembering to cash her paycheck.[96] Her earnings may well have been important in showing her (and perhaps her father) that she could do work that was valued by others, and she likely was pleased when she no longer had to go to him for spending money. But her primary goal was not to make money. She was working for other reasons, and in the process developing a strong work ethic that would benefit her future employer.

All the same, she must have been concerned that pursuing her goals lessened the likelihood that she would marry. Growing up, she could not have avoided knowing that middle-class employed women made many men uncomfortable. A 1904 *Good Housekeeping* article her mother might have read described a survey of five thousand men who were asked what qualities they most and least desired in a potential wife. Near the top of the list of least-desirable qualities was "career minded-ness."[97] Eight years later in a *Harper's Bazaar* article, Inez Haynes Gilmore, a successful writer, lamented that her "professional career" made her an "alien to this world" because it "puts me beyond the reach of the average woman's duties and pleasures."[98] Indeed, in 1910 only 12.2 percent of American professional women were married. The figure continued to rise, but by 1920 it was only 19.3 percent.[99]

Ironically, Fleischman's commitment to having a career increased the probability that she would continue to live at home, under her father's control. That had to be a sobering prospect, for he permitted her little freedom. She described him as having "a chilling contempt for most of my friends" as well as veto power over which young men she could see. He simply had to declare someone "not a suitable companion" for her to obey. And what she called his "forbidding manner" continued even when she was twenty-nine years old and spending time with someone who had been declared suitable. Bernays remembered that when he visited her at her home in 1921, her father always made him leave at 11 p.m.[100]

Another restriction was self-imposed. Fleischman later confessed that in college she had avoided studying too hard for fear "of seeming intelligent and losing boyfriends."[101] "You had to pretend you were ignorant" in talking with young men, she recalled. "If you had any ideas you had to slip them in through the conversational back door." Decades after it happened, she could not forget a "tall, dark man" she said she had "adored" and who also had found her appealing, until "one day I forgot my role and talked seriously about a new book. He left me forever."[102] The modesty that others would find so striking during the rest of her life may well have been rooted in her early reluctance to reveal her intelligence to men.

By the end of 1919 she faced a kind of double stigma in terms of changing her marital status: she had a satisfying job where she was making more money than she had ever made before, and her sharp mind was evident in the work she was doing. Both could be expected to bruise male egos. Within a year, however, she realized she was in love with a man who valued both her intelligence and her professional capabilities.[103]

Earlier she had written about a similar kind of fictional scenario in one of her press releases for a Boni & Liveright book, Adriana Spandoni's *The Swing of the Pendulum*. "Feminism has created a new romance," her piece began. "It is the romance of the new affection, nurtured in the fertile ground of interest between the woman who works and the man who works with her." The book's heroine had three lovers, all of whom she had met at work. There, Fleischman wrote, she was an "abrupt, unsentimental" woman who succeeded in attracting "the passionate loyalty of the three men who saw enough of the eternal feminine to satisfy them, beneath the shiny crust of efficiency."[104]

The topic seemed to inspire her. She wrote a three-page release that was full of emotion but gave little information about the book's plot and characters, focusing instead on the wider theme of the attraction between "new women" and the "intellectually congenial men" they met in their workplaces. "The new woman is here, patently. But she has not yet been accepted by the middle classes," Fleischman admitted. And workplace romances had long faced societal disapproval. Still, "the idea of choosing one's mate from among one's co-workers, instead of from a galaxy of dancing partners, will appeal quickly to progressive young women."[105]

When Fleischman wrote that release in early 1920 she was spending a good deal of time with Bernays. He awkwardly described their relationship this way: "During our days spent together in the office as professionals—we felt each other's presence. In the evening, as friends—we talked, dined together, walked and experienced the excitements of the sidewalks of New York." He noted the convenience of the relationship, since after their evenings together, "It was simple to take her home. We lived around the corner from each other." Yet much as they enjoyed each other's company, he stressed, "I did not believe the relationship was growing closer."[106]

Looking back, Fleischman admitted they both had "fallen in love with wrong people so often" that they could not put much faith in either "instinct or wisdom" in their romantic choices.[107] But after working for Bernays for about a year, she knew she was in love with him, and at some point she told him. He may have told her he also loved her, but when she brought up the subject of marriage, he said he would not marry her.[108]

That should have been no great surprise. Not only had she long known he did not want to marry anyone under any circumstances, but in 1917 newspaper readers in New York and Chicago could have learned about his resolve in stories that ran after his sister Hella married Murray Cohen. The bridegroom had legally changed his name to Murray C. Bernays so that the couple's children would keep the Bernays family name alive, the stories said. This was necessary because the bride had three sisters whose children would bear their husbands' names, and "also a brother, Edward L. Bernays, who has expressed his intention never to marry."[109]

Working together must have been rather awkward after he rejected her as a marriage partner, particularly since by that time they had hired Murray Bernays (at a salary 50 percent higher than hers) as a writer and researcher. Certainly, though, Fleischman and Bernays continued to operate as a productive team, and they undoubtedly delighted in the firm's growing revenues and list of clients. Yet Fleischman was frustrated that their business progress was not matched by the kind of progress she desired in their personal relationship.

When Bernays wrote about that relationship many decades later, he never acknowledged his resistance to marriage, claiming instead that it simply took a long time for both of them to realize they should marry each other. This was his dispassionate description of how they reached their decision: "Two people had the good judgment at approximately the same time, by an unconscious process of weighing all the factors, to recognize that they were better suited to spend the rest of their respective lives together than with anyone else."[110]

He was correct in highlighting the importance of "good judgment" in his decision, but in reality they married because Fleischman was brave enough to challenge him far more vigorously than she ever would again. As she much later told her daughter Anne, in the spring of 1922 she bought a steamship ticket to Europe and left it on her desk at work where he could not miss seeing it. When he asked where she was going, she said, "If you're not going to marry me, I'm leaving."[111] He seems not to have known his heart very well, but surely he knew his business could not afford to lose her. They wed later that year.

CHAPTER 2

"I won the right by the device of understatement"

"INDEPENDENT" WAS THE SINGLE-WORD headline on many of the stories about Fleischman that ran in more than 250 newspapers in 1922. At Bernays's insistence, she had kept her birth name when they married, and after a brief ceremony at the Manhattan Municipal Building just before it closed at noon on Saturday, September 16, they took a taxi to the Waldorf-Astoria, where they had a suite reserved for their honeymoon weekend. He signed the register "Edward L. Bernays" and she signed "Doris E. Fleischman." On standing orders to notify the press of anything that might result in positive media attention, the hotel's assistant manager called newspapers to tell them that, for the first time, a married woman had registered there using her birth name. Theirs was a "newsworthy precedent," Bernays said, and the stories helped the Waldorf "become a symbol for modernity and the liberation of women."[1]

In truth, the couple set no precedent. The Waldorf had been permitting married women to sign their birth names in its enormous registration book for more than a year, and the new policy already had been described in a March 1921 *New York Times* article.[2] So why did the hotel call attention to the couple's actions? It no doubt had much to do with Bernays being its public relations consultant.[3] He thought he was involved in something newsworthy, so the hotel did its part to make it so. Moreover, it was Bernays's idea that Fleischman sign her birth name. He later admitted that she didn't care one way or the other.[4] She was doing what he wanted, not asserting her independence from him.

More happened that weekend that would be revealing of the couple's future life. Their parents did not attend the ceremony since they hadn't been told about it.[5] When it was over, Bernays immediately called his office to check for messages (Saturday was a workday). That evening, he left his new wife at the hotel and went off with a friend to the annual DeWitt Clinton High School alumni dinner. He later said he wasn't sure why he didn't cancel those plans, but he thought he probably wanted to show that "I was completely objective about marriage and that furthermore marriage was not going to affect me or change my life in the slightest degree." He spent Sunday morning happily answering phone calls from newspapers and wire services requesting photographs of Fleischman for their stories.[6]

He supplied two photographs. In both she wore a silk evening dress and a pleasant, confident half-smile as she stared directly into the camera. Many newspapers ran a brief wire-service story with the "Independent" headline over a cropped photo of her face and, underneath, two sentences: "Although she's married to Edward L. Bernays, New York lawyer [*sic*], Doris E. Fleischman, public relations consultant, refuses to be the second part of a Mr. and Mrs. partnership. She retains her maiden name and signs the hotel register accordingly."[7]

The couple was back in the office Monday morning. Fleischman said her tasks that day included outlining a public relations campaign for one client, writing a press release for another, interviewing cooks, and calling an employment agency about hiring a maid. In addition to worrying that she knew almost nothing about establishing and running a home, she was well aware that she would not be able to count on her new husband for help.[8] "I had taken the workings of a home for granted," Bernays explained. "The idea that I might share some home responsibilities never crossed my mind."[9]

At the end of the day they apparently each returned to their parents' home. While in his autobiography Bernays claimed they immediately moved into their own place, they could not have done so because (as he revealed in notes for his book) it wasn't ready.[10] This originally would not have been a problem since they had planned to keep the marriage a secret and remain with their parents until what he called "some undesignated future time."[11] Now, the event was very public knowledge, but they seem to have had no alternate plan. When he wrote about this time long afterward, though, he certainly would not have wanted to admit that—following such an unconventional start of their marriage—they went back to their parents.

On October 16 they moved into the Greenwich Village home they had leased and just finished renovating. Located at 44 Washington Mews on a narrow, cobblestoned street, it was the former stable of a Washington Square North mansion that sculptor Paul Manship had converted into an apartment facing a picturesque courtyard. On the bottom floor were a kitchen, dining room, and one more room they had added on. Upstairs were a small bedroom, a bathroom, and an enormous north-facing studio with high ceilings. Some decorations were by Louis Comfort Tiffany.[12] One newspaper story said their "quiet little street" attracted "the aristocracy of Greenwich Village," including many sculptors and painters.[13]

Around the same time they finally moved in together, a far more important change took place: they signed a legal agreement making them fifty-fifty partners in the firm of Edward L. Bernays, Counsel on Public Relations. According to Bernays, it simply seemed the logical thing to do, and was useful for income tax purposes. Asked why Fleischman was made an equal partner in the firm he had founded, rather than being allocated a smaller share of the business, he responded, "I think if a man is in love with his wife . . . he won't give her just 25 percent."[14]

Indeed, the strength of the couple's affection and admiration for each other was a striking feature of their partnership. When Bernays's uncle, Sigmund Freud, wrote to his nephew congratulating him on having "married your friend and helpmate," his words captured the essence of their relationship at that time.[15] They had known each other casually since they were adolescents and had been building a business together since 1919. In 1922 they both were mature adults who thought very highly of each other, enjoyed each other's company, and knew they worked exceedingly well together.

Still, writing more than thirty years later, Fleischman confessed to having been "psychologically and emotionally illiterate when I married." She had lived with her parents until her wedding day, and in those years had learned little about either marriage or running a home. It was assumed she would hire household help, as her mother had.[16] Her insecurity about homemaking was compounded by insecurity about the marriage itself. "I hoped to live happily ever after, but I wasn't sure, because Eddie had resisted marriage during years of courtship," she said. "I wasn't sure of him, and was afraid he might fall in love with another girl for a long time." She warned, "Many husbands do fall in love with someone else."[17]

Bernays apparently did little to dispel her uncertainty. His explanation for urging her to keep her birth name, for example, cited advantages for him, not for her. "I had an inner fear that marriage (although I wanted it fiercely with Doris) would take away some of my liberties as an individual if there were always a Mrs. added to my name," he wrote. "I wanted both the ties and the freedom."[18] He thought women he met socially would be more likely to talk with him if they didn't know a nearby woman was his wife, and asserted, "It's equally important to the man's independence to be treated not in terms of her but in terms of himself."[19]

In all likelihood, on her own Fleischman would not have even thought to keep her name. It also seems to have been solely his idea that the marriage initially be kept a secret (which was another reason for her not to take his name). Surely she would have much preferred being able to tell her friends and family about the wedding in advance and to invite them to the ceremony. Her father, whose judgments mattered tremendously to her, had to have been especially displeased. She was long past the traditional age at which women of her generation married, and now she was marrying a man she loved—but he was the only person she knew at the ceremony. This secrecy and his insistence that she keep her name were two ways he could control the situation, and perhaps also remind her that he was marrying reluctantly.

They would have been in complete agreement, though, that their marriage would be very different from those of their parents. They each had grown up with an uncompromising father who had absolute power over his children and his wife. Bernays wrote that in all the time he lived at home, "I never saw my mother cross my father." She was "constantly on the alert to prevent explosions of Father's temper." Fleischman called Ely Bernays "a famous disciplinarian" and explained that her own father controlled his family differently: "My father kept us in uneasy subjection by lowering the temperature of his blue eyes."[20] Both were acutely aware of their mother's lack of freedom and the dangers of marriages grounded in Victorian values, as their parents' had been. No doubt Bernays's earlier resolution never to marry was in part a reaction to the constraints his father imposed on his mother and his siblings.

"I conferred with her after the clients had left"

WHATEVER CONCERNS FLEISCHMAN HAD about her preparation for marriage, she should have felt confident that she had proven herself highly qualified as a partner in their public relations firm. And it must have pleased her that her job was changing significantly as a result of changes in their business. By 1922 their services went beyond attracting publicity for clients. Now they stressed their expertise in advising clients about actions that would improve their relationships with their publics and in interpreting both clients to their publics and publics to their clients. The measures they recommended would not necessarily result in publicity.[21]

Since they needed fewer press releases and had at least one other writer on the staff, Fleischman's skills as a writer, editor, and story placer became much less important. Instead, Bernays primarily took advantage of her abilities to conceive and develop programs for clients and to strategize with him. Far more grounded, practical, and organized than he was, she was very good at determining what would be required to carry out ideas as well as how people likely would react to different approaches. Bernays recalled, "I used to say to her, 'It's great to have a George Gallup right in the house.'"[22]

Fleischman took on an additional project around the time of their marriage that Bernays thought "may well have been the single most important activity in advancing our cause."[23] She began *Contact*, a four-page newsletter published three or four times a year for more than a decade. It was a compilation of summarized information and brief articles from popular and trade publications, accompanied by comments pointing out the power of public opinion and public relations. The material was presented in a straightforward manner within a conservatively designed format that was intended to give the impression of respectability and restraint. Sent without charge to about fifteen thousand people, *Contact* helped attract new clients while improving the visibility and image of their new field.[24] In Bernays's words, "*Contact* established us."[25]

Fleischman not only developed the idea for *Contact* but designed it, collected the material for it, wrote all the commentary, and oversaw the production of each issue.[26] Her reporting and editing background made her a logical choice for this project, but one other factor likely was important: since she didn't need to set aside time to meet with clients, she could take on other tasks. Ironically, the editor of *Contact* had no formal client contacts. Nor could she take credit for the publication, for her name appeared nowhere on it.

Bernays never acknowledged that she actually had been the contact person with at least a few clients before they married, always maintaining that such contacts would have made no sense because her ideas would have been discounted. Since "in 1922 a woman entering any profession other than nursing, teaching or social work was a novelty," few clients respected women as professionals, he argued. As for Fleischman, "She recognized immediately that her ideas might be treated as 'a woman's' rather than judged on their merits, so she decided early to withdraw from personal relations with clients. I conferred with her after the clients had left."[27]

In her own account, written thirty years after they signed their partnership papers, she offered a similar, if more biting, explanation: "Many men resented having women tell them what to do in their business. . . . If ideas were to be considered first in terms of my sex, they might never get around to being judged on their merits." She did ask herself, "Have I been a coward to withdraw from such active company? Perhaps I have."[28] Still later, in the final year of her life, she acknowledged that although she had never really believed she should have client contacts, "it may have bothered me subconsciously."[29]

Just as she had no formal client interactions—the most visible aspect of public relations consulting—so her equal partnership was not publicly acknowledged. After they married the firm's name remained Edward L. Bernays, Counsel on Public Relations. It probably is true, as he asserted, that she never asked him to include her name.[30] She did not seem to need public recognition, and it's hard to picture her asking the man who had founded the firm and was its public face to change its name.

He also admitted that her role was deliberately downplayed in order to "make the name 'Bernays' stand for advice on public relations."[31] This had become enormously important to him by the time of their marriage. He not only loved his work and loved being recognized for it, but even as he avidly promoted his clients and himself, he was selling this new field. As he put it, "Public relations would become a continuing free client."[32]

In 1923 he carried out two of his most significant early efforts to bring visibility and respectability to this free client (and himself). In February he began teaching the first university course on public relations. Later that year, his *Crystallizing Public Opinion*—this country's first book on public relations—was published.[33] It is likely that Fleischman helped him write it.[34] And on a few occasions when he was unavailable, she even (very nervously) taught his New York University course.[35]

"Professionally known as Doris E. Fleischman"

THAT SAME YEAR, FLEISCHMAN RECEIVED considerable attention for activities outside of her public relations work. In 1923 she planned her first trip to Europe, where Bernays wanted her to meet with some of the firm's government and business connections, and also get to know his psychoanalyst uncle. Despite having no desire to travel such a long distance so soon after marrying, "as a wife she did what was expected of her," Bernays remembered. "But why I wanted her to go is still a mystery to me. It may have been that I wanted to prove to myself that I was still independent."[36]

In preparation, she applied for a passport in her birth name. The State Department at first refused to issue it to her, but it did eventually offer a compromise, which she accepted. She would be identified as "Doris Fleischman Bernays (professionally known as Doris E. Fleischman)."[37] The government said this would "preserve whatever professional or commercial advantage which may be ascribable to the use by a married woman of her maiden name."[38]

It was an inadequate solution, and two years earlier Ruth Hale, the wife of newspaper columnist Heywood Broun, had turned down a passport with only somewhat-less-satisfactory language—"Ruth Broun (otherwise known as Ruth Hale)." But Fleischman's fight for similar wording resulted in many newspaper stories.[39] A press release from the Bernays office was the original source of most of them, but his involvement in this story differed from the strategy he had used to call attention to his new bride's Waldorf-Astoria registration. His office's name was nowhere on the release. Rather, it was identified as coming from the Lucy Stone League, and it gave as a contact person the league's secretary-treasurer, Jane Grant.[40]

The league had been founded in April 1921 by Grant and Hale (its president) to help women keep their birth names when they married and to persuade businesses and government offices to accept the practice, which was not illegal. Bernays had joined in June 1921, then promptly began doing pro bono public relations work for the organization. For example, his office produced the press release describing the culmination of Hale's 1921 passport fight.[41] Fleischman did not become a member until after her marriage.[42]

Bernays's motivations for joining this unconventional organization shortly after its birth are unclear. Since many of its officers and executive committee members were journalists or linked to the theater as press agents, playwrights, or reviewers, he may have known them from his earlier theatrical publicity work or more recent public relations consulting. He acknowledged that he had known Grant for almost a decade.[43] In his published memoirs, the only explanation he offered—after falsely claiming that he and "a reluctant Doris" joined together in 1921—was that he "liked the league's idea of protest and independence."[44] A hypothesis he wrote but did not publish was that this might have been "a rebellion against my domination by my father."[45] Whatever his reasons, he stayed involved for several years, serving on its executive committee and on planning committees for its annual dinners, which always attracted media attention.[46]

Fleischman did not contribute in these ways (although she probably wrote some of the league press releases produced by the Bernays office), and she joined only at his request. Yet as she faced obstacles to using the birth name he had urged her to keep, she likely developed more interest in the cause and felt connected to other women fighting for it. And perhaps she was further motivated to take on the State Department because her public relations work went unrecognized while her partner's name was well known. Here was one document on which she could assert a professional identity.

With the league's help, in mid-April 1923 she obtained the passport partially in her birth name. She sailed for Europe soon afterward, beginning a three-month journey through Austria, Switzerland, Italy, and France. Lonely without her, Bernays constantly sent her coded cables, so at every stop she had to search out the nearest post office. "She rushed there, then back to the hotel, spent hours in deciphering my dispatches and thought up answers to my foolish questions. I suppose this illogical method of keeping in touch made me feel we were closer together," he reasoned. "To demonstrate this affection was no chore for me. It almost wore her down."[47]

During her trip she carried out tasks for their American clients and visited Freud, bringing him a dozen tins of American coffee and a crate of fresh grapefruits. His effusive gratitude helped her even better understand the scarcities resulting from Austria's economic depression. Those scarcities already were much on her mind because her primary task throughout the trip was to investigate the European postwar business climate, which she did by interviewing government officials and business leaders.[48] She noted with pleasure that most of these people thought it unremarkable that she had kept her birth name. In all four countries, she said, "I found general acceptance of the principle that a young woman was entitled to her maiden name in ordinary business and social life."[49]

Such acceptance may have strengthened her resolve to fight for her name, just as being apart from Bernays, meeting with important people on her own, and traveling alone (which she said caused her no problems) probably gave her more self-confidence. The Lucy Stone League also was steadily gaining strength. In 1924 one of its key battles was over the right of married women to use their birth names on federal paychecks, and that campaign resulted in renewed media interest in the State Department's rule that married women could not receive passports solely in their birth names. The league, in turn, increasingly focused on this issue, and in 1925, in partnership with the National Woman's Party, it mounted a test case to challenge the rule.[50]

Their work began that winter after journalist Ruby Black applied for a passport in her birth name, rather than in the surname of her husband, Herbert Little, and her request was denied. She filed an appeal and was granted an April hearing before Secretary of State Frank B. Kellogg. At that hearing, where six league and National Woman's Party lawyers argued her case, Kellogg offered Black new compromise passport language, which she refused. He then agreed to present their arguments for abolishing the rule to President Coolidge. On May 1, 1925, Coolidge announced that he would consider the matter.[51]

While he was pondering it, writer Esther Sayles Root, who was a member of both the league and the National Woman's Party, agreed to the kind of compromise language Black had refused. In May, after Root married famous newspaper columnist Franklin Pierce Adams, she fought hard and eventually successfully for the passport identification, "Esther Sayles Root, wife of Franklin Pierce Adams." Her lawyers based their argument on the fact that Kellogg had offered Black the same kind of language. Adams's celebrity helped ensure widespread press coverage of Root's actions, which the National Woman's Party treated as a victory. This was no victory to the league, however, and it petitioned the secretary of state to grant married women passports with no mention of their husbands' names.[52]

Meanwhile, Fleischman was preparing for another European trip. As part of their work for a silk manufacturer, Bernays had landed a position on an official commission representing the United States at the International Exposition of Modern Decorative and Industrial Arts in Paris. The commission was charged with reporting to the secretary of commerce on ways American businesses could profitably use ideas from artists whose work would be shown at this enormous exhibition, where art deco design made its international debut. Fleischman and Bernays also would carry out work for a few clients and attend the many receptions and dinners they had arranged for the commission.[53]

Before the trip, Fleischman again tried to obtain a passport in her birth name, although she never explained why she decided to make another attempt after having won a partial victory two years earlier. No doubt the Lucy Stone League was encouraging all of its members to enter the battle, which it had helped make newsworthy that spring. It seems likely, too, that she had come to see a larger purpose in such endeavors. Bernays captured that purpose (and his own interest in it) when he wrote: "The issue of the securing of passports was ready made for public exploitation and for the focussing of public opinion on the whole question" of married women retaining their names.[54] It had a powerful public relations function.

Fleischman's actions also may have been influenced by her father's unexpected death in May 1924. (He collapsed after a heart attack while walking home from work through Central Park. One newspaper noted, "It was the first time in forty years that Mr. Fleischman had not arrived home at the same hour and his wife became alarmed by his absence.")[55] He had been the strongest force in her life until the day of her marriage. Since he was conservative in almost all his views, it is extremely likely that, like most men, he opposed the Lucy Stone League's advocacy. Fleischman never explained his response to her keeping her birth name (which, after all, was his name), but she did write that her brother Leon "was the only member of my family who approved."[56] She might well have found it easier to rejoin the passport fight once she no longer had to be concerned about her father's reactions.

In early June 1925 she was back at the New York Passport Bureau, where the "sneering clerk" refused to issue her the document under the name Doris E. Fleischman. When she protested, he told her to "write to the Secretary of State" and she quickly handwrote a note to him on her application. She recalled that in it she simply explained that she had never used any other name and argued, "Since it is apparent that the purpose of a passport is to establish identity, I assume you will not wish me to travel under a false name." Not long afterward a new passport with the name she had requested arrived in the mail. In this fight for a woman's right "to sign her own name under her own face," she wrote, "I won the right by the device of understatement."[57]

Thus she became the first married woman in the country to receive a passport solely in her birth name, an accomplishment that received substantial newspaper coverage when she sailed for France as well as when she returned to New York after her trip. One photo accompanying some of these stories was especially revealing. It showed a serious-looking Fleischman and Bernays standing together on the deck on an ocean liner. Her hands clutched her purse and gloves, while his displayed her passport for the photographer.[58]

"We were earning a good living"

THAT SAME YEAR A PROFITABLE CONTRACT with a large Czechoslovakian company led them to open a branch office in Vienna. According to Bernays, this was Europe's first American public relations office. After attending the Paris Exposition the couple had traveled to Prague to learn more about the company and meet its owner, who had approached them after reading *Crystallizing Public Opinion*.[59] Before they left for Europe, Bernays also had offered to carry out work there for American clients, particularly in Paris and London, where, he said, "our connections are as good, we believe, as they are in New York."[60]

Their firm was doing very well even though the field was so new that the types of services they performed still were unfamiliar to most businesses. Bernays sometimes recommended that potential clients read *Contact* and *Crystallizing Public Opinion* to better understand what they had to offer.[61] Thinking back to a client they added in 1924, he admitted, "I suppose $10,000 seemed to clients an appreciable expenditure for services not specifically defined and not generally recognized or accepted. He was really taking us on faith to a great extent. My records indicate that we were earning a good living."[62]

He and Fleischman had the resources to start a Vienna office in 1925 because they recently had signed several major new clients, including the Ward Baking Company, Indian Refining Company, Knox Gelatin, and Hart, Schaffner & Marx men's clothing. Contracts also had been renewed with two important clients—Cartier Inc. and Procter & Gamble—with whom they would have lengthy relationships.[63] By this time their standard rate apparently was $12,000 a year, with further increases during the rest of the 1920s.[64] In addition, to boost their profits, they now were charging for reimbursement of their out-of-pocket expenses, which sometimes were large, rather than absorbing them as part of their fees.[65]

Their rising income was reflected in their lives at 44 Washington Mews. An itemization of their 1923 personal expenditures showed them spending close to $30,000 that year (about $380,000 in today's dollars), including almost $3,000 for rent; $1,800 for gifts, flowers, and entertainment expenses; $1,500 for household furnishings and supplies; and $2,500 for Fleischman's clothes. Other records show that in the mid-1920s they spent heavily on costly furniture such as antique Italian tapestry chairs, an antique Italian refectory table, and an early seventeenth-century Flemish tapestry, which they bought at auction for $1,500. And even though a 1925 household inventory listed sizable sets of silver knives, forks, spoons, and serving dishes, two years later they purchased almost 250 silver eating and serving utensils (including a dozen fish forks and fish knives) from Cartier.[66]

They had two servants—a cook and a very capable "houseman" on whom Fleischman relied heavily. She had realized from the day she married that she would need to hire experienced household help because she knew so little about running a home. Growing up in a family that had always had servants, she could remember only three times when she had set foot in the kitchen. "My own lack of training," she reasoned, "was based on the assumption that someday I was going to be second-in-command in a home, with hired help to take over most of my duties."[67]

She always knew she would get no help from Bernays, but she could not have known that her job as hostess would be as demanding as it quickly became or that her other nighttime entertainment options would be so limited. Bernays admitted, "Our social life kept us so busy at home or at the homes of friends that little time remained to explore many additional points of interest in New York." He also noted that despite Fleischman's love of music and the theater, "my previous participation in the theatre and the music world made me rather allergic to both," so they never went. In his words, "Doris had to forgo, and apparently willingly did, the enjoyment of these two arts. She exchanged them for the hectic kaleidoscopic segments of New York flowing in and out of our home."[68]

It is debatable whether this was a fair exchange, but it certainly resulted in many interesting people coming to their home. "Hardly an evening passed without guests for and/or after dinner," he recalled. "We worked all day and talked and played all night." Although he maintained that "it happened naturally without planning or purpose," extensive planning must have been required to entertain as many as forty guests at a time.[69] Bernays recalled that their visitors typically included "writers, publishers, musicians, artists, psychologists, doctors, scientists, uptown socialites, stock brokers, bankers, politicians and businessmen," and they sometimes stayed until 3 a.m.[70]

The couple seemed to take particular pleasure in mixing people from different professions and interests. One night, for example, they invited glamorous film actress Leatrice Joy to meet Federal Reserve Bank statistician Carl Snyder, then added a novelist, a painter, a lawyer, and a Broadway press agent to the mix. Similarly, Bernays described an animated dinner-table conversation between, among others, former prerevolutionary Russian prime minister Alexander Kerensky, psychoanalyst Sandor Ferenczi, and a young associate editor at *Harper's Bazaar*. Among the guests who dropped by after dinner and joined that night's discussion were a correspondent from the *London Daily Mail*, a *New York Times* editor, another psychoanalyst, a women's clothing designer, and New York Democratic Party strategist Belle Moskowitz.[71]

According to Bernays, others who regularly came to the house during the mid-1920s included numerous journalists and press agents; writers Konrad Bercovici, Hendrick Willem Van Loon, and Henry James Forman; lyricist Howard Dietz; poet Sara Teasdale; Zionist Organization president Chaim Weizmann; and charismatic mystic Georgi Gurdjieff. Fleischman also made sure that her brother Leon as well as Beatrice and Martin Untermeyer—Fleischman's sociable sister and her businessman husband—received frequent invitations. Topics of conversation seem to have been wide-ranging, covering everything from art to politics to religion to economics to philosophy to international affairs.[72]

As for the size of their gatherings, Bernays declared, "Doris liked six people at one time; I liked forty-six. We compromised on thirty or forty."[73] The compromise was all hers, but she seems to have been uncomplaining about the extra effort this kind of entertaining required. One of Fleischman's strongest lessons from her mother—who had constantly acquiesced to a rigid, demanding husband—was that she should never complain. Complaining was a weakness.[74]

Fleischman once wrote that as a wife she was guided by "the basic philosophies instilled into women." Specifically: "A woman must please her man. A woman must keep housekeeping difficulties from her husband. A woman must smile and smile."[75] In her case, she said, "It has been easy for me, in a way, to keep ideas of difficulty and trouble from my husband, because I like him."[76] And it was particularly easy for Bernays to ignore her difficulties because he had decided that, as he put it, "women must be born with a catering gift." Such tasks came naturally to women, he thought, but he lacked their talent. Indeed, the effort of simply setting out drinks for a few guests left him "ready for a rest."[77] Fleischman seldom rested.

"We talked public relations on the rare evenings when we had no guests," he fondly recalled, noting that she thought it very reasonable that he would want to spend any free evenings this way.[78] She, in turn, described him as someone who "would burst if he couldn't talk about his profession at home," and said she wondered what other couples who didn't share a profession found to talk about over dinner.[79] Yet she had a much wider range of interests than he did and might well have enjoyed discussing a few of them with him after she left the office. Evidence that his intense focus on public relations sometimes became wearing for her can be found in a note, signed "love and kisses," that she left for him when they were living at Washington Mews. "Please don't bring your work home every night," she wrote.[80]

"I am not as dedicated to improving the world through public relations as Eddie is," she acknowledged many years later. "My attention is far from concentrated on work after I leave the office. I like relaxation and diversion." Her pleasures included reading poetry, listening to classical music, and going to movies and the theater (although she lamented that she "never seemed to go"). When she was with others, she said, "I love talking good talk to a few people at a time. Better still, I like getting to know them one at a time."[81] By leading the kind of life Bernays preferred, however, she limited her chances for such relaxation and diversion.

They proudly and often described their relationship as a "twenty-four-hour-a-day partnership," but he was by far the dominant partner. Fleischman's published and unpublished writings show little resentment of his position, which she pictured this way: "Eddie's word is final and he casts the deciding vote in our partnership. I have elected him Chairman of the Board and Executive President in our personal life, where he decides where we shall live and when we shall diet, and in our public relations office, where he was the boss even before we were married."[82] Their unequal distribution of power and responsibility seemed logical to her. "As far as I'm concerned," she gratefully explained, "double partnership has made it possible to do the jobs I am expected to do as a woman without conflicting with his [Bernays's] idea of my professional duties."[83]

"Facing intelligently the special problems that may confront women"

THEIR EVER-EXPANDING CLIENT LISTS attest to her dexterity in carrying out her "professional duties." Clients added in 1927 and 1928 included the Luggage Information Service (in one campaign they tried to persuade people to travel with more clothes so they would need more luggage), a camera manufacturer, a large fabric company, and the Dodge Brothers automobile company.[84] "February 1929 was the busiest month thus far in my nine-year-old career," Bernays pointed out. Among the many clients for which they carried out campaigns were Cartier, Procter & Gamble (their soap sculpture contests helped promote Ivory soap), the Ward Baking Company, and the Paris fashion designer House of Worth. Fees received that month totaled a little more than $16,500, with profits of almost $12,000. "That was not considered too bad for a young man, 38 years old, adventuring into an untried, unknown field," he bragged.[85]

In addition, he published two books in rapid succession. First he compiled and edited *An Outline of Careers: A Practical Guide to Achievement by Thirty-Eight Emi-*

nent Americans, which came out in 1927. The "eminent Americans" who provided chapters included a Chase National Bank vice president writing on banking, the president of Union Theological Seminary on the ministry, and the board chairman of Scripps-Howard Newspapers on journalism. Bernays wrote about public relations and Fleischman contributed a final chapter titled "Concerning Women."[86] He subsequently admitted that the book's primary purpose was "putting public relations on a parity with other careers."[87]

Similarly, he wrote *Propaganda*, published the next year, to build his authority in the emerging field—the same reason he had written *Crystallizing Public Opinion*, which did not sell well (although it went on to become a landmark work). *Propaganda* received much more attention than the earlier book, but most of it was negative. By 1928 the government's failure to achieve its idealistic World War I aims had left many Americans disillusioned and blaming "propagandists" for U.S. entry into the war. That same year, cynicism over big businesses' propaganda efforts intensified when government hearings revealed how utility companies had carried out elaborate media campaigns that helped them cover up corruption while earning enormous profits. Bernays did stress the need for high ethical standards in the field, but he was unlucky in the book's timing and unwise in both his title choice and strong advocacy of social control. Public relations, his "continuing free client," was not well served.[88]

Fleischman no doubt helped him with *Propaganda*, but she also was busy with a book of her own during this time. In 1926 she began working on *An Outline of Careers for Women: A Practical Guide to Achievement*, which she compiled and edited.[89] It was like Bernays's 1927 *Outline of Careers* except she had to work much harder to identify accomplished women and persuade them to write chapters advising women readers on how to succeed in their fields.

It took more than a year simply to line up her contributors. After writing to myriad organizations and individuals for suggestions, she contacted the recommended women and often was turned down because respondents were too busy or thought they were unqualified to write a chapter.[90] Yet she continued to pursue even reluctant women, sometimes with notable success. For example, she asked Eleanor Roosevelt, then the finance chairman of the Women's Activities Committee of the New York State Democratic Party, to write about women in politics. Roosevelt declined since, she said, "I do not consider politics a career for women at present. But then I do not consider them an end in themselves for men either." Fleischman persevered, stressing, "we are eager to tell them [readers] the truth," and Roosevelt did write a chapter.[91]

Once she assembled her authors, Fleischman's work intensified. In 1927 and 1928 she contacted her contributors often, constantly prodding them to meet deadlines, add information, clarify points, and make corrections. Her considerable diplomatic skills are much in evidence in surviving correspondence about the book. She even had to fight to sign her birth name on her contract with her publisher, who had specifically instructed her to sign as Doris Bernays. She sent it back signed Doris E. Fleischman, explaining, "My conscience did not allow me to sign this under an alias."[92]

With forty-three chapters on women's opportunities in very diverse fields—not just nursing and social work, but architecture, law, civil engineering, and journalism, among others—*Careers for Women* was published on November 23, 1928.[93] In addition to Roosevelt, other well-known women contributed chapters, including film actress Norma Talmadge, activist physician Sara Josephine Baker, novelist Gertrude Atherton, and cosmetics entrepreneur Helena Rubinstein.

Fleischman, of course, wrote a chapter on public relations, which began by announcing that "no traditions have grown up against women's participation." Still, she called attention to "the necessity of facing intelligently the special problems that may confront women" because of "prejudice that remains in many men's minds." She was clear on women's best response: "This is usually combatted by convincing men by intelligent handling of problems, and not by slaying the dragon of antifeminism."[94] She knew women—such as her friends Ruth Hale and Jane Grant—who were fiercely fighting that dragon. But lacking their zeal as well as their weapons, she recommended against entering the battle.

Her "Concerning Women" chapter in Bernays's 1927 book on careers had been less sanguine about women as a whole, whom she characterized as a "handicapped occupational group." They were partially to blame for their problems in securing good jobs, promotions, and pay, she asserted, since too often they lacked ambition or confidence in their worth. Her advice on how best to deal with male prejudice was similar to what she would write in her own book the next year, but her wording was more revealing of her personal situation. "A woman must, first of all, and continuously thereafter, be able to sell the idea that she is important in spite of her sex," she warned. Hearing her boss say, "'She is a fine woman, but my clients won't take advice from a woman' is an idea that absorbs a great deal of her effectiveness." As a result, "her force must be doubled on any given problem."[95]

"Her insight and judgment are better than mine"

THE 1925 PHOTOGRAPH TAKEN when the couple sailed for France might serve as a quick snapshot of their ongoing personal and professional relationship. It was an important news story (not just one hyped by Bernays) when Fleischman received a passport in "her own name." Still, she stood next him in the photo, and he held her passport. Yet the document was hers, earned by what she called "the device of understatement," and she kept her name for another three decades despite societal disapproval. She could not have done so without Bernays's strong support for—not to mention pleasure in—her efforts, which he felt benefited him as well as her.

He benefited infinitely more from her public relations skills. By the time they married she already had demonstrated that she deserved to be made an equal partner in the firm. Then, as their business changed and they carried out more complex, sophisticated campaigns, her value increased. He was an expert at publicity, but once their work advanced beyond publicity he needed someone with whom he could develop new approaches, especially someone who had excellent ideas of her own. Their complementary abilities and personalities help explain the highly productive synergy of this enduring collaboration.

They had very different strengths. He saw himself as a scientist, theoretician, and philosopher. Anxious to apply techniques and ideas from the behavioral and social sciences to public relations, he loved developing principles, thinking broadly, intellectualizing. Two historians of public relations aptly noted some of the most conspicuous qualities of his mind and personality. Scott Cutlip described Bernays as "a man who was bright, articulate to excess, and most of all, an innovative thinker and philosopher of his vocation."[96] Similarly, he was called "the most important theorist of American public relations" by Stuart Ewen, who relied heavily on *Crystallizing Public Opinion* and *Propaganda* to describe the field's underpinnings. Yet Ewen also noted the "customary bombast" of those writings.[97]

Far more methodical and pragmatic than her dynamic, confident collaborator, Fleischman helped him translate his broad ideas into workable strategies. She also was devoid of bombast. She did not call attention to herself but did pay careful attention to other people and could understand them quickly. Their daughter Anne, who observed that her father often had trouble reading people accurately, called Fleischman his "personal antennae for judging people."[98] He admitted that "her insight and judgment are better than mine."[99]

With strengths such as these she might well have contributed even more to the firm if her responsibilities had included client contacts. In his chapter on public relations careers in his 1927 book, Bernays even had maintained, "Theoretically, there is nothing in this profession that a man can do that a woman cannot do."[100] Certainly there seemed to be nothing Fleischman was incapable of doing. What, then, really explains her invisibility? Anne Bernays offered a forthright answer: "He didn't want her to get the credit."[101] It also is a persuasive answer. Bernays was an expert self-promoter who loved both his work and being recognized for it. He was unlikely to willingly share credit if he could avoid it. Sharing credit with a woman in an era when professional women were not widely accepted would have been even more problematic. At the same time, if his partner had been a man, he would have been forced to give him credit.

"My father had persuaded his wife to stay in the background so as not to risk, he explained, being seen as a pushy female with ideas—a threatening and sometimes deadly combination, toxic to the male," Anne wrote. And since Fleischman was "temperamentally a shy person," Anne thought "the arrangement was okay with her."[102] Pondering her lack of client contacts as she was struggling to write her autobiography in the early 1950s, Fleischman came to similar conclusions. When she first joined with Bernays in 1919, she remembered, "I decided that I would not try to compete with men because the hurdles were too great." She confessed, though, "I surrendered without having seen an enemy. I wonder if I would try to avoid all conflict with men if I were to begin today."[103]

She avoided conflict with Bernays not only in their business but at home. "The only intelligent point of view I brought to my marriage was that it would be very stupid of me to try to change Eddie in anything. I liked him as he was," she declared.[104] He was a tremendously energetic, forceful person. With a keen mind of her own, in areas outside of her marriage she was not a docile woman. Yet her intelligence and ability to quickly understand other people must have helped her realize how difficult it would be to oppose him with any consistency. Instead she did a superb job of recognizing and meeting his needs.

Many of her own needs were met in return. She lived and worked with a man she thought was wonderful—and who thought she was brilliant, plus admirable in many other ways. Although most clients did not know about or appreciate her work and talents, he clearly did. He also made it possible for her to have what would be an extraordinary (if little recognized) public relations career. And their business success allowed them to live very well. Indeed, their standard of living was further elevated in March 1929 when they leased diplomat W. Averell Harriman's thirty-two-room mansion at 8 Washington Square North, facing directly onto the beautifully maintained Washington Square Park.[105]

They needed more space because Fleischman was pregnant and their daughter was due to be born in April. Still, her pregnancy did not slow her down; as before, she "worked all day and entertained all night," Bernays said. Eventually noticing she was tired, in early March he insisted that she join his mother for a two-week vacation at an Atlantic City hotel. (Interestingly, she did not go off with her own mother.) Having been attending a course for expectant mothers at Teachers College, she brought along a half-dozen books on prenatal and infant care to study.[106]

During her absence Bernays learned the Harrimans were divorcing and their four-story mansion, located around the corner from 44 Washington Mews, might be available for rent. He immediately called Harriman, was invited over to inspect it, and signed a three-year lease the next day. Fleischman would not see its interior rooms until she was preparing to move in.[107] But that did not seem to bother her. Unsurprisingly, given her work ethic, she had a very different grievance in a letter (addressed, "Dear dear Boss") she sent to him from Atlantic City. "There are 2500 idle people in this hotel," she lamented. "And *there* [in New York] is my little office. I am stultified. Please send me something to do."[108]

Fleischman probably was in her early twenties when
she donned conservative clothing and posed for this portrait.
Courtesy of Edward L. Bernays.

Fleischman, around 1920, working at her desk in a corner of the cramped quarters that first housed the firm of Edward L. Bernays, Counsel on Public Relations. *Courtesy of Anne Bernays.*

Fleischman and Bernays dressed for a night out, probably in 1923. *Courtesy of Edward L. Bernays.*

Fleischman and Bernays in Paris at the 1925 International Exposition of Modern Decorative and Industrial Arts. She sailed for France carrying a new passport that identified her by her birth name. *Courtesy of Edward L. Bernays.*

This lovely 1927 pencil-and-wash portrait of Fleischman
measures about two feet by three feet. The artist was Mary
MacKinnon, a well-known magazine and advertising fashion
illustrator. *Courtesy of Edward L. Bernays.*

For three decades Fleischman and Bernays often hosted two or three dinner
parties a week. Here, around 1940, Fleischman talks with dinner guests at a
party in their enormous apartment at the Sherry-Netherland Hotel on Fifth
Avenue. *Courtesy of Edward L. Bernays.*

Fleischman looks a bit dubious about her husband's enthusiasm for her in this photograph taken in the mid-1940s at an evening event in their home. *Courtesy of Edward L. Bernays.*

Fleischman as she typically dressed for work, around 1950. Most of her many hats were custom-made (after several sittings) by Mr. John, whose clients, the *New York Times* noted, "included stars of film, stage, opera and the society pages." *Courtesy of Edward L. Bernays.*

The equality of their professional partnership is evident in this late-1950s photograph of Fleischman and Bernays in one of the rooms of the elegant East Sixty-Fourth Street brownstone that they bought and converted into offices in 1944. *Courtesy of Edward L. Bernays.*

When this photograph was taken in 1969, Fleischman and Bernays had lived in Cambridge, Massachusetts, for eight years. She gave up much that was important to her when he decided they should leave New York. *Courtesy of Edward L. Bernays.*

CHAPTER 3

*"Keeping up the appearance
of independence"*

WHEN FLEISCHMAN WAS ABOUT to give birth in April 1929 and
checked into a fashionable maternity hospital—later described by a police-reporter
friend as "that swank Stork's Retreat on Park Ave. where they use Chanel No. 5
to sterilize potties"—she immediately ran into trouble.[1] As Walter Winchell recounted in his syndicated newspaper column, "there was great excitement" because
"Mrs. Bernays absolutely refused to register under her marriage tag." Trying in
vain to persuade her to change her mind, "the hospital authorities argued that it
was embarrassing to them to have to announce that a child had been born to a
Miss Doris E. Fleischman."[2]

The embarrassments continued after daughter Doris Fleischman Bernays's
birth certificate was filled out. Since the new parents' last names were different,
the New York Department of Health required that the certificate be stamped "illegitimate." On seeing the document's bright red stamp (which he described as
being about five inches long and three-quarters of an inch high), the same friend
remembered asking the clerk in charge of records the reasons for it. He said the
clerk told him, "Mister, when a record comes here and bears a different name for
the father and mother, we mark the child a bastard. A nicer word for the record is
ILLEGITIMATE. I don't make the rules."[3]

Bernays responded with a letter to the department's assistant registrar firmly
asserting that their child was "duly born in wedlock." Fleischman had kept her
birth name when she married "in accordance with the law and her own desires,"
he wrote. The U.S. government had issued her a passport in that name, and that
was the name she used on her federal income tax forms. Surely it must be clear that
"under the circumstances, to file any report under any other name would be in
error."[4]

Not only did the department order the stamp removed but it ruled that in the
future any married woman who kept her birth name would be permitted to have
that name recorded on her child's birth certificate.[5]

Even as he made their case to the city's bureaucracy, Bernays was planning his
daughter's future. His letter to the Department of Health was promptly followed
by a much shorter one to a prestigious Manhattan private school. In the first paragraph he asked that his daughter be admitted to the school "at the earliest age at
which you take children." The second and final paragraph read, in its entirety: "I

do not know what prerequisites there are for entrance. Doris Bernays is the grand niece of Professor Sigmund Freud. It is a bit difficult to give much further information about her since the child is only ten days old."[6]

Fleischman was even busier than Bernays was, both before and after her daughter's birth. One arduous task when she was eight months pregnant was supervising their move to the enormous house at 8 Washington Square North. They immediately started entertaining in their new home, although on April 8 they had to hurriedly cancel their usual Sunday-evening dinner party when she unexpectedly went into labor. Ten guests whom they had been unable to reach with cancellation phone calls arrived anyway and enjoyed a formal dinner hosted by their butler.[7]

Home from the hospital, Fleischman began charting her daughter's daily progress in a notebook, recording not only her height and weight but details such as the times she slept and awoke, when she cried, how much formula she consumed, when she smiled. The new mother clearly was consulting her many childcare books, for she paid close attention to the infant's developmental progress. Noted, for example, was when she first followed her mother with her eyes but without sound clues (June 16), her puzzled discovery of her own hands (July 4), and (after she grabbed a rattle hanging on the side of her bassinet) her "first definite coordination of eye, hand and ear" (August 1).[8] A June 21 note—"Smiles when nurse smiles"—highlights one reason Fleischman sometimes could step back and examine her daughter analytically: a "nurse" (today we would call her a nanny) lived with them.[9]

They hired a second nurse in October 1930 when their daughter Anne was born.[10] Her birth received newspaper attention of another kind because an inaccurate story circulated that she would be given her mother's surname. The Associated Press reporter seemed to think this had something to do with her famous relative, since an article from the wire service began, "A grandniece of Sigmund Freud, Vienna psychologist, is to be known by her mother's maiden name."[11] The connection may have been triggered by the fact that Anne was named after Bernays's mother Anna, who was Freud's sister. This seemed to please Freud, for he sent his new grandniece a handwritten postcard on which he bade her "welcome as a new output of life."[12]

Fleischman was fortunate to have experienced paid help in caring for her newborn and infant daughters, but this still must have been a hectic, demanding time, particularly since Bernays provided no help at all, as he freely admitted.[13] In this way he was similar to his own father, who he suspected never once set foot on the third floor of the family's house where his five children had their bedrooms. In his memoirs, Bernays was careful to first note that as a child "I spent little time with my father" before going on to explain, "My own personal relations with my children when they were small were sketchy. That was their mother's domain."[14]

He more candidly captured his obliviousness to Fleischman's concerns and responsibilities as a new mother—as well as his own priorities—in this recollection of the time immediately following the birth of his first daughter in the spring of 1929: "Adjustment to the baby, when she came, was easy. I suppose it helped that the burden on Doris wasn't so great that it took her away from me."[15]

"Will it light? Will it burn?"

HE COULD NOT HAVE AFFORDED her absence for very long, for 1929 proved to be an especially important year for their business. Among the campaigns they carried out that year were two for which the firm's founder would be known for the rest of his life. They went on to become—literally—textbook examples of how public relations operated. But more important at that time, they called attention to their firm and testified to the value of its services (and high fees), helping Bernays and Fleischman attract still more clients during the Depression, which soon would cause severe problems for many other businesses.

In 1929 the American Tobacco Company was one of their largest clients, paying $25,000 a year (the equivalent of about $310,000 today) for them to be available for whatever work the company's volatile president, George Washington Hill, wanted them to undertake. Hill was "obsessed" with increasing the number of women who smoked Lucky Strike cigarettes, Bernays said, and in November 1928 they launched their first campaign for him. Based on the slogan "Reach for a Lucky instead of a sweet," it touted Luckies as a dessert substitute that would help women stay slim. After they carried out a second campaign with a similar theme, Hill came to them in early 1929 with a new challenge: "How can we get women to smoke on the street? They're smoking indoors. But damn it, if they spend half the time outdoors and we can get them to smoke outdoors, we'll damn near double our female market."[16]

Knowing that this would require weakening the social taboo against women smoking in public, at Hill's expense Bernays consulted a psychoanalyst, who told him that for some women cigarettes were symbols of emancipation, or "torches of freedom." The phrase inspired the couple to create an Easter Sunday event in which ten debutantes smoking Lucky Strike "torches of freedom" joined the traditional parade of fashionably dressed New Yorkers strolling down Fifth Avenue. Most debutantes came in response to a telegram signed by the firm's secretary (who did not identify her employer) urging them to take part "in the interests of equality of the sexes and to fight another sex taboo." A newspaper ad with a similar message signed by Ruth Hale was used to build media interest. Shortly before Easter, press releases were sent out, a photographer was hired, and the women were coached on what to do and say.[17]

Newspapers loved the story. It ran nationwide, often on page one, and editorial writers assisted in keeping it alive with their (usually negative) responses, such as the one from the Indiana editor who grumbled, "It is always a regret to me to see women adopt the coarser attitudes and habits of men." No wonder reports soon followed of women smoking on the streets of cities and towns throughout the country.[18]

Fleischman and Bernays had many more ideas for increasing cigarette sales to women. One proposal focused on making cigarettes seem like a household necessity. As part of the plan, mailings would be sent to people who advised homemakers. Writers of etiquette columns, for example, would be encouraged to make their readers aware of "the need for having a supply of cigarettes on hand in the

home, and to the social error inherent in the hostess who fails to provide cigarettes for her guests."[19] Changing direction, they next developed a plan "to create
a vogue for smoking through celluloid cigarette holders," which might make the
habit more appealing to women. Thousands of holders would be distributed to
"groups who can be influential in bringing public attention to this fashion," such
as film industry publicists. They would give them to their well-known clients, who
might be photographed smoking with the holders, and "these pictures will get to
the papers through the usual channels."[20]

In February 1929, as the couple was envisioning ways to break the taboo
against women smoking outside their homes, a new client hired them to carry out
a very different kind of campaign. General Electric, which had long been criticized
for its monopolistic practices, asked them to handle its public relations for Light's
Golden Jubilee—the celebration of the fiftieth anniversary of Thomas Edison's invention of the incandescent light bulb. Thanks to the shrewd efforts of automobile
magnate Henry Ford, who idolized Edison, the October 21 event would take place
at his Greenfield Village near Detroit, where he was building a technical school
and museum to honor Edison. During the celebration President Herbert Hoover
would dedicate the new facilities and Edison would speak to a worldwide radio
audience.[21]

Edison was a hero to many, Bernays among them. He relished the assignment
and used it to burnish his own reputation along with his client's. This helps explain
the immensity of the campaign they developed. It included sending out innumerable press releases as well as feature stories on myriad specialized topics, organizing
a speakers bureau, producing a "plan book" of activities for local public utilities to
carry out, holding media information luncheons, soliciting Edison tribute letters
from luminaries like Albert Einstein, and asking the post office to issue a com-
memorative stamp. Bernays also made several trips to Detroit to confer with Ford
and his staff, and became heavily involved in some details of the jubilee itself.[22]

In a snowball effect, their activities stimulated others. "Everybody was joining
in the procession," Bernays remembered. "Universities offered lectures on Edison
and the implications of his discovery. Educational groups conducted essay contests. Museum heads arranged exhibits that would illustrate the history of light."
And there was much, much more. Celebrations, for example, were held in Europe,
Japan, and South America. A press release describing Edison's favorite flowers led
to a new dahlia being named the "Thomas A. Edison" at the American Dahlia
Society's annual Madison Square Garden flower show. George M. Cohan wrote
a song, "Edison—Miracle Man," and waived his royalty fee so that it could be
widely performed.[23]

National and international media coverage of Edison's accomplishments and
the upcoming jubilee snowballed as well. By October 21 interest was intense, and
live coverage of the event on the NBC and CBS radio networks attracted enormous audiences. In the evening's high point, the frail eighty-two-year-old Edison
reenacted his triumph of fifty years earlier. While he was connecting two wires to
light the carbon-filament globe, listeners heard an announcer anxiously ask, "Will
it light? Will it burn?" Front-page stories about the celebration ran in countless

newspapers the next day, and newsreel coverage soon played in movie theaters. Bernays happily concluded, "I had succeeded in my most elaborate public relations assignment."[24]

His public relations accomplishments were substantial, but of course Edison's iconic status was most responsible for the campaign's success. Beyond that, Bernays neglected to note that this assignment was not his alone; it was his and Fleischman's. She was his partner, yet the public credit went solely to him. And the spotlight shone even more brightly after the celebration, when he was approvingly credited for his jubilee work in articles running in magazines such as the *Nation*, the *New Yorker*, and *Atlantic Monthly*, and later in books. This was no accident, for he had called attention to his activities whenever possible.[25]

Fleischman benefited from his visibility because it helped attract more business to the firm, but it also further masked her own contributions. Still, it is possible to identify some of her probable responsibilities in the 1929 campaigns for General Electric and the American Tobacco Company based on knowledge of her strengths and of the work she carried out in earlier campaigns.

Because they had only seven months to promote Light's Golden Jubilee, they had to quickly develop and set in motion many different, often simultaneous plans. And the campaign's focus on Edison and his inventions meant they had a plethora of resources on which to draw as well as approaches they could pursue. At the same time, their "audiences" were enormously diverse, ranging from major newspapers to public utilities to community groups. They needed to be both imaginative and practical, to deal with the unexpected even as they applied lessons from past work, to rapidly solve problems while taking advantage of fortunate coincidences.

Fleischman's superb organizational skills surely were crucial in managing this elaborate, ever-changing campaign. She likely coordinated their multiple activities and charted their progress. As the campaign became more reactive—responding to requests, capitalizing on actions taken by others—she may well have been responsible for monitoring these efforts and making sure they stayed on track. Bernays would not have been very good at this. More significant, no doubt, was her role as his creative collaborator. With scant time to test out ideas and so much happening simultaneously, they had to quickly analyze options and likely outcomes, all while staying flexible enough to change their strategies in response to new developments. Frequent brainstorming with each other must have been indispensable in all of this. Together, they excelled in carrying out their most challenging campaign yet.

Their 1929 work for the American Tobacco Company was vital to their business for other reasons. They had never before been hired by someone as willing as George Washington Hill to spend large sums on campaigns—or as difficult to deal with, or as driven to increase sales of his product. In addition, this well-paying client had signed a one-year contract that they hoped would be extended, so they needed to prove themselves. (They did. It was renewed every year until 1936.)[26] Bernays was excited about that first contract, he wrote, because "I felt that the relationship would bring other corporate giants to me."[27]

Although less complex than their concurrent work for Light's Golden Jubilee, their campaign to increase the sales of Lucky Strikes to women was demanding because it required them to constantly propose new ideas and then, in spurts of intense activity, execute those that interested Hill. Here, too, inventive, efficient collaboration between Bernays and Fleischman would have been vital.

She brought particular strengths to this campaign because she was a woman and also because, unlike Bernays, she was a smoker. (He pressured her to quit, but this was one of the few things she would not do to accommodate him.)[28] And since she was far better than he was at understanding people and interpreting their actions, he would have needed her insights and guidance in his dealings with the abrasive Hill. Describing the American Tobacco Company president, one public relations historian wrote, "No counselor nor ad agency ever had a more difficult, temperamental and eccentric client."[29] Without Fleischman, Bernays could not have so successfully humored and placated Hill, nor developed the campaigns that persuaded him to continue renewing his company's lucrative contract.

"I was used to being rich"

BARELY A WEEK AFTER THE CELEBRATION of Light's Golden Jubilee, the stock market crashed, setting off the Great Depression. By 1932 more than one hundred thousand businesses had failed, and between a quarter and a third of the American workforce was unemployed.[30] Yet the firm of Edward L. Bernays, Counsel of Public Relations prospered. In 1931 their client fees totaled over $98,000 and their profits exceeded $60,000—the equivalent of more than $800,000 today. By 1935 their profits had increased fivefold.[31] Throughout the Depression, "my father continued to make piles of money," his daughter Anne remembered. "His P.R. services, like those of bankruptcy lawyers, were considered by many businessmen and institutions to be not a luxury but a necessity. I was used to being rich."[32]

After her October 1930 birth, Anne was brought home to 8 Washington Square North. Near the front door, one newspaper reported, "the brass name plate on which Miss Fleischman's maiden name appears with that of her husband, has long been pointed out to strangers."[33] The century-old brick mansion had thirty-two rooms, including, on the first floor, three enormous ones with eighteen-foot ceilings: a music room, a drawing room with a Carrara marble mantelpiece and crystal chandelier, and a dining room complete with a huge wall safe for their silver. Through a grand entryway, a curving mahogany staircase eventually reached the top floor with its eleven bedrooms for servants. The immense kitchen was in the basement, along with a maids' dining room, houseman's bedroom, butler's workroom, and "cold room" with an icebox and vegetable racks. A dumbwaiter connected the basement and first floor.[34]

In 1932 they left Greenwich Village for the Upper East Side and remained there for three decades. Their first apartment filled the entire twenty-seventh tower floor of the Sherry-Netherland Hotel on Fifth Avenue across from Central Park (its duck pond lay directly below their living-room window). Anne called the park "our front yard" and played there often, also enjoying the fact that this was a favorite hotel of movie stars visiting New York.[35]

Among the residents of the building at 817 Fifth Avenue, where they moved in 1936, was film actress Gloria Swanson. Anne sometimes encountered her in the elevator, remembering "a beautiful woman with blue-black hair and severely chic hats with a full-face veil." They remained at that address—"one of the few luxury buildings whose management was willing to rent to Jews," Anne said—for three years, living in an eleven-room apartment that was most notable for its twenty-five-foot-long living room and a dining room that looked like a tropical rain forest, thanks to an artist Fleischman hired to paint brightly colored birds and exotic flora on it walls.[36]

After briefly returning to the Sherry-Netherland, in 1941 Fleischman and Bernays bought a three-story double-width house with an ornate exterior at 163 East Sixty-Third Street. Its second-floor living room, which ran the width of the house, featured an eighteen-foot ceiling, a wall of mullioned windows, a balcony at one end, and, at the other, a fireplace big enough to stand in. Imported antique black oak panels lined the walls of the ground-floor library and dining room. All three rooms looked out over a forty-foot-wide backyard landscaped with bushes and trees.[37]

Some of the art in their home also was impressive. Their walls displayed oil paintings by Jules Pascin, Raoul Dufy, and Paul Burlin, a drawing by André Derain, and an unsigned Paul Cézanne watercolor. Much more valuable, according to an 1937 insurance appraisal, were two thirteen-inch-tall polished marble sculptures of women's heads by Elie Nadelman. (In 1917, when the artist was an impoverished Polish immigrant, he had wanted to marry Bernays's sister Judith but her father had made her break off the engagement.) For a while, a glass case holding the mummy of an Egyptian princess was a prominent feature of their living room. One of Bernays's auction finds, it made Fleischman uncomfortable and she finally persuaded him to relocate it to the conference room next to his office.[38]

Their 1929 move from a converted stable to a mansion had given them many additional rooms to furnish, and by 1937 they had numerous beautiful pieces. These included a walnut Steinway baby grand piano, a pair of upholstered mahogany Chippendale chairs valued at $2,500, a large number of English and Italian antique tables and chairs, and several couches and loveseats upholstered in silk velour.[39]

One of the first things Fleischman did after completing the move in the spring of 1929 was to hire a cabinetmaker to build an eight-foot-long, three-pedestal mahogany table with matching chairs.[40] "Our dining table was large enough to seat twenty-two people comfortably," she wrote, "and Eddie and I saw to it that all these places were filled at least three or four times a week." Wearing formal dinner clothes, they sat down to meals that might begin with a delicate fish pudding and end with a soufflé, all accompanied by wines and Champagne. Another twenty or so guests often arrived around ten o'clock and stayed for a buffet "midnight feast." Fleischman estimated that during most of the time they lived at 8 Washington Square North, almost 150 visitors ate at her home each week.[41]

They continued these dinner parties after they moved to the Upper East Side, where soon they also were hosting much more informal buffet-dinner Sunday-evening gatherings that were popular. In addition, they typically attended one or two parties at other people's homes every week, so there were only a few nights when they ate at home alone with their daughters. Since they tended to talk about their work then, the meals usually were rather dull for Anne and Doris. But they were encouraged to attend their parents' parties and remembered them as being tremendously stimulating. "I could see the fun of using your intellect," Doris recalled. "All the people were interesting," Anne said. "It was almost like a salon."[42]

"Authors, musicians, politicians, newspapermen and women, poets, with a sprinkling of businessmen, were the best mixture," Bernays declared. And he had happy memories of overhearing animated interactions between guests: a painter and a National City Bank vice president finding they had common views about art; a photographer, her inventor-husband, and a newspaper's foreign correspondent worrying about developments in England; an Arctic explorer and a psychiatrist sharply disagreeing; a playwright sparring with a humorist; the editor of a business magazine and the managing editor of *Variety* sharing their opinions about Broadway plays. "The men and women who spent evenings discussing, debating and prognosticating often met for the first time at our home," Bernays noted.[43]

In the summer their entertaining moved to the countryside where, for more than a decade beginning in 1928, Bernays insisted on renting what Fleischman called "pretentious monsters." Set on expanses of land as large as a hundred acres, all of them were huge—as many as thirty rooms—and she wrote that "one looked like Westminster Abbey" and another "like an Italianate castle on the edge of a large private pond." Their owners, she noted, were "delighted to share their burden" of maintaining these costly estates during the Depression by renting them out.[44]

Her own burden certainly was substantial. She called summers in the country "moving" rather than vacations, in part because of the effort required to transport and reorganize her household in a new "monster" each year.[45] Once there, she ended up serving as a "hotel keeper, caterer and traffic manager," she said, for Bernays had "conceived it his duty and avocation to book all beds and boards." Some guests stayed for a week or two, forty more might come just for a Saturday, and another "fresh, hungry and active" group would arrive on Sunday. At one estate, "guests and three-course picnic lunches had to be transported to and from the large pond on a rutted road through acres of private forest." At others, "swimming pools in the front yard simplified my planning. I only had to provide lunch, cocktails, dinner and maid service."[46]

Without servants she could not have begun to meet the needs of her guests and her own family, whether at country estates or at home in New York City. When she and Bernays first moved to their Washington Square mansion they hired seven servants—"two in the family and five in help," as she put it—but this number quickly proved insufficient, so the staff grew to "four in the family and nine in help."[47] Included were a butler, cook, kitchen maid, upstairs maid, houseman, waitress, laundress, two nurses, and a chauffeur. Bernays recalled that they had between seven and thirteen servants at a time throughout the 1930s and 1940s.[48]

Their chauffeur remained with them until World War II gas rationing made it impossible to operate a car. One of his morning tasks was driving daughters Doris and Anne to school, beginning with the City and Country School—to which, two weeks after her birth, Bernays had written requesting Doris's admission. (They each started attending at age four, apparently after their parents followed the standard application procedures.) But once they were older the girls began asking the uniformed driver to stop their Cadillac several blocks from the school's entrance, Anne explained. "Mortified by the possibility of being recognized for what we were—extremely rich kids, far more so than the other rich kids who attended this private school—we would get out and walk the rest of the way."[49]

"It seemed as if everything functioned perfectly"

THE CHAUFFEUR RETURNED TO PICK UP Bernays and take him to work. About an hour and a half later, he did the same for Fleischman. Their offices remained on East Forty-Sixth Street from 1921 until around 1930. Their next, larger offices were in the Gaybar Building adjacent to Grand Central Terminal, and by 1933 they had added auxiliary offices a short subway ride away at One Wall Street, next to the New York Stock Exchange. A move in 1942 took them to 9 Rockefeller Center. Two years later their final move was into an elegant three-story brownstone they had purchased and converted into offices. Located at 26 East Sixty-Fourth Street, it was close to their East Sixty-Third Street home, from which they could walk to work and where, Anne wrote, "Manhattan's poshest neighborhood surrounded us quietly."[50]

On arriving at work, Bernays and Fleischman operated very differently. He was in constant motion: carrying out two phone conversations at once with a telephone at each ear; rapidly dictating letters and reports to secretaries; surrounded by staff members as he came up with ideas and jotted down notes; talking animatedly with clients in his office or, more often, out meeting with them in their offices or other places, and increasingly in other cities. "He was the wheeler-dealer, always connected to other people," Anne said. Fleischman, in contrast, spent most of her time either alone or with Bernays, and often was writing. She usually stayed in her own office, happy to be free of distractions, or even worked at home.[51]

Her preference for solitary work helps explain why her contributions to their business did not lessen after her daughters were born. "He wanted the children properly taken care of," she explained. "We were able to work out great elasticity of schedules and functions and I did a good deal of home work, fortified by a direct wire between home and office."[52] This "great elasticity" was a key reason she was able to spend summers in the country. She could work efficiently by herself and talk through campaigns with him on the telephone as well as when he came out on weekends, no doubt carrying work for her.

Ironically, it was while enjoying a Sunday dinner with friends on the lawn of the palatial Westchester County home they had rented in the summer of 1933 that they became convinced of the real threat posed by Adolf Hitler. He had come to power a few months earlier and some of their friends at dinner dismissed him as a crank who would not hold on for long. But one guest was a newspaper foreign correspondent just back from Germany, where he had met at length with Nazi minister of culture Joseph Goebbels. Their friend's account of what Goebbels told him about his strategy, Bernays said, made it clear that "the attack on the Jews of Germany was no mere emotional outburst of the Nazis, but a deliberate, planned campaign."[53]

One morning five years later, eight-year-old Anne, still in her pajamas, walked into her parents' bedroom and saw something she had seen only once before: her mother crying. Her face "streaked with tears," Fleischman ignored Anne, so she asked her father what had happened. Germany had invaded Czechoslovakia, he told her, and war looked imminent.[54]

For many years they had been sending money to Bernays's Austrian relatives to aid them in difficult economic times, and they had offered to help several of them immigrate to America. But when Hitler annexed Austria in March 1937 they especially worried about getting Freud and his family out of the country. Along with many others in the United States and England, Bernays wrote to people he thought could help. As a result of these combined efforts, Freud received some protection from Gestapo persecution, and in April 1939 he was allowed to leave for England.[55]

Bernays's obligations continued, though, because he signed many affidavits for Jews who were allowed to immigrate to the United States only if they had a guarantee that the affidavit signer would be responsible for their welfare if they couldn't find work.[56] He also paid refugees' transportation costs. But when yet another request from a relief committee arrived in March 1941, he couldn't help but remark, "What annoys me a bit is that the more these relatives delay, the more it costs me to help them." Then, after quickly adding, "Naturally I shall pay Paula's passage," he asked, "Can we get her out before the Polish deportation measures catch up with her?"[57]

High fees and new clients helped make this kind of generosity possible. Among their big business clients added in the 1930s were General Motors, the Pullman Company, Bank of America, RCA, Allied Chemical & Dye, and Great Northern Railroad. Their highest yearly fee at this time apparently was the $60,000 paid by Bank of America. They also reduced and sometimes waived their fees for nonprofit organizations and the U.S. government, for which they regularly worked during the Depression and the war. Then the prosperity and increased business competition that followed the war's end helped them attract still more clients.[58]

They could afford to purchase the best for themselves and their daughters. Fleischman wore Ferragamo shoes and Cartier jewelry, and carried Mark Cross handbags. Most of her dresses came from Bergdorf Goodman, selected by a personal shopper who had them ready for her to stop by and pick up. After the war, she paid fifty or sixty dollars for hats—which she wore at the office—custom-made by Mr. John. Their construction required multiple consultations, and Anne thought it actually was these mindless talks with Mr. John that her mother most enjoyed.[59]

At home, Anne said, they could "have repairs made as soon as something was torn, broken or leaking," and Fleischman's address book was full of names of people who provided services ranging from delivering ice to replacing lost or damaged silver or lace. A man came by every week just to wind the clocks. The household's food was delivered after Fleischman called the neighborhood market in the morning. She chatted with the grocer and butcher about what she needed and what they recommended, then placed her order. When they lived in the Sherry-Netherland, she often ordered the family's dinner from the hotel kitchen—a waiter delivered it under a silver-plated dome—even though they had their own kitchen and a cook.[60]

Servants took care of many tasks, and others were delegated. Their household bills, for example, were paid by their office bookkeeper. Still, Fleischman was a perfectionist in charge of a complex household, and her solution was to organize every possible aspect of it. The servants each received a daily schedule, divided into fifteen- or thirty-minute intervals, showing their duties and the amount of time each task should take. Thus on Fridays one of their maids, Catherine, could expect to spend three-quarters of an hour cleaning the library, a half hour washing the lunch dishes, and an hour and a half laundering the fine table linens and Fleischman's underwear. She would be on duty to answer the first-floor telephone and doorbell between 12:30 and 3:00 p.m.[61]

The cook's schedule was particularly important. It included a daily meeting with Fleischman, who said she divided food purchases into three categories: food for staff, for her children, and for guests. She calculated that nine servants ate about 180 meals a week (counting days off), so she planned four weeks of their menus at a time, made out a "purchasing schedule," and mailed her order to a market. Staples were ordered at the same time and stored for future use. "In this way," she wrote, "I crammed all my steady customers into a morning's work once a month."[62] Dinners for guests required more elaborate menus, and these meals could be problematic since Bernays had a habit of inviting colleagues home at the last moment. "She had to scramble then," her daughter Doris said, pointing out that this was in an age before freezers. "But fortunately she already had most of the organization in place."[63]

Her daughters did not think Fleischman was overly stressed by this work. Her real problem, they said, was that she was determined to make sure Bernays knew nothing about all she had to do. She let him think the house ran by itself. This explains why she came into the office later than he did—waiting until he left for work before she ordered groceries, met with the cook, called repair people, and organized other aspects of the household. "She protected him from all these things," Doris explained.[64]

Her success seems to have been complete here. "To our guests and me it seemed as if everything functioned perfectly and painlessly," Bernays wrote. "Possibly it was a painstaking job for her. She never mentioned it to me if it was."[65] He admitted, too, that he provided no help in running their house or looking after their constant guests, nor could he remember ever giving an order to a servant.[66] He even observed, "My father was completely aloof from all household matters, and I doubt he ever was in the kitchen or cellar. Acquired characteristics are not inherited, but I followed my father in these respects for many, many years."[67]

Raising their daughters also was entirely her responsibility, but she was insecure about her ability to do this well so she frequently consulted her many child-care books. Influenced by these experts, she and Bernays agreed that they would try to be permissive, open-minded parents. When Anne hatched a chicken as part of a school project, for example, she was allowed to bring it home and raise it in a spare bathroom. And Anne and Doris appreciated their mother's solution to the problem of caring for them after school once they had outgrown their governess. She hired spirited Barnard College students to take them on outings and to appointments, and to look after them at home until she returned from her day at the office.[68]

But they did not appreciate her refusal to help them learn any domestic skills. Fleischman strongly faulted her own mother for teaching her nothing about cooking and housework, yet she was no different with her own daughters. "She imparted in me no domestic knowledge. I felt this was a mystery—one that other people knew but I wasn't going to find out about," Doris said. "When I married I had to start absolutely from scratch." Nor were the girls encouraged to learn on their own. "The kitchen was off limits," Doris recalled. "I wasn't supposed to go in and bother the cook." Fleischman, Anne wrote, "warned me away from the kitchen and from doing any chore that didn't require a college education." Typing was one of these since she said it would only prepare them for dead-end secretarial jobs. "If they find out you can type you'll be stuck there forever," she told them. Her response to Doris's desire to take a typing course was that she would have to pay for it herself out of her allowance.[69]

"A victorious career is the goal"

IN OTHER WAYS, THOUGH, FLEISCHMAN was an excellent guide. Perhaps her most important lesson to her daughters was on the value of developing their minds and using language well. She had a remarkable vocabulary and even made up words. It took her only a half hour to do the *Saturday Review* Double-Crostic in pen. In conversation, she was clever, interesting, and—despite her innate shyness—good at verbal sparring.[70] As Anne explained, "In a room of twenty-five or thirty people, she would be the one you'd stop and listen to because she was extraordinarily sharp."[71]

Bernays even quite dramatically applauded her wit in the presence of others. Anne remembered many times during parties at their home when her mother said something particularly clever or discerning and her father reacted by exclaiming, "Write that down!" When Fleischman, of course, did not, he extracted a notebook and wrote it down himself. "He was genuinely pleased and proud of her," Anne observed, "but he also was saying, 'Look at how smart I was to choose her.'" He knew what she had said reflected well on him.[72] In any case, her daughters saw the worth of a woman's verbal dexterity.

She also showed them the pleasure of reading. Unlike Bernays, who, as Anne put it, "never read anything but books that threw light on the management of group dynamics," Fleischman read widely and constantly. Especially fond of fiction (she loved mysteries) and poetry, she also was fascinated by how things worked so read nonfiction books on scientific and medical topics, and even scientific journals.[73]

Nor could Anne and Doris have had a better model for the professional success a perseverant woman could attain. They always were very aware of her public relations work, which carried over into dinner-table conversations. And despite remaining far in the background while Bernays basked in the spotlight, her visibility increased slightly in 1931 and 1941 when she published two articles about women in public relations in *Independent Woman*, the magazine of the National Federation of Business and Professional Women's Clubs.[74]

She also undertook a far more complicated, time-consuming writing project during what must have been one of the most demanding periods of her life. In the last months of 1929—even as she was a first-time mother with an infant daughter, and working intensely with Bernays to publicize Light's Golden Jubilee and please the president of the American Tobacco Company—she was researching and writing a series of articles for *Ladies' Home Journal*. The magazine had just begun a new department, "Women in Business," to provide information about women's career opportunities. Fleischman's 1928 book, *An Outline of Careers for Women*, must have been testimony to her expertise on this topic, for she wrote three of the department's earliest articles, published in January, March, and April 1930.[75]

Her January article was the most substantive and passionate. After faulting most working women for being "job-slaves" rather than pursuing careers, she analyzed the reasons for their lack of ambition, then offered practical advice on how readers could overcome assumptions and habits that held them back. Perhaps thinking about her own daughter, she noted that little girls seldom were asked what they wanted to be when they grew up, nor did businessmen take their daughters to work, "proudly hoping the pretty child will some day take over their duties." On her own, then, it was up to a girl "to start when she is young to consider herself seriously as a future worker."[76]

Her March and April articles primarily discussed specific professions, including their entry-level requirements, pay, and the kinds of work carried out. In discussing almost every field, she noted the difficulties women faced as a result of sex discrimination, but she encouraged readers to find the profession that best matched their interests and abilities, and in which they could excel. She reminded them that "not a job, but a victorious career is the goal."[77]

The next year she wrote about a much broader subject in *America as Americans See It*, a book created to explain Americans to Europeans. Fleischman was in good company, for other contributors included Upton Sinclair, W. E. B. Du Bois, and Robert E. Sherwood. Her chapter, "Women: Types and Movements," offered a well-researched picture of the wide range of ways American women work and live, and their struggles during the Depression. She provided particularly sympathetic, detailed descriptions of the lives of farm women and those married to poorly paid laborers, stressing that only "a small fringe" of women are wealthy, although there might seem to be many more because their "social activities are sprinkled like sugar" over the pages of newspapers. Tellingly, she also declared, "American women are popularly supposed to be very powerful. There is a great deal of truth to that assumption, although individual women, biologically and psychologically, yield to male dominance and authority."[78]

She was less able to escape the biases of her socioeconomic class in her 1946 *McCall's* article, "You Can't Get Help," which argued that the shortage of domestic workers was a grave problem for the women of America.[79] Following her analysis of the reasons fewer and fewer people were willing to become servants, she laid out a plan for making this work more appealing. Among her recommendations were a forty-hour workweek, increased pay, and written contracts. Yet she exaggerated the extent to which American women relied on (and could afford) household help and was far from realistic in her prediction that vast numbers would be forced to leave their jobs in order to take care of their homes if the shortage continued.

She also wrote fiction—at least one short story in 1926, three stories in the 1930s, and five more in the 1940s.[80] None of this work ever was published, but it clearly was a kind of writing she put great effort into and loved doing. As a result, it mattered to Bernays as well, and his involvement in one of these pieces typifies the way he dominated their relationship.

In 1945 she completed a fifty-thousand-word story about nuclear war titled "The Last Strike." She seemed to care deeply about the subject and the manuscript, which she subsequently radically condensed in response to reviewers' critiques. After sending copies of the first and second versions to editors he knew, in July 1947 Bernays had the fifty-six-page manuscript set in type. Three thousand copies were printed, and some of those were sent to still more editors.[81] Four months later, Fleischman admitted to one person who had received a copy that the project was out of her control. "Eddie isn't telling me at this point what he is going to do with the piece," she said. "I have been trying for a year and a half to convince him not to do anything at all."[82]

In spite of the aggravation his actions caused her, Bernays seems to have been motivated by genuine concern for Fleischman, who must have been disheartened that her earlier publishing success had not continued. She had published only two articles since 1932, and the first of those, her 1941 piece on women in public relations, was unpaid, while the other, her *McCall's* article, ran half the length of her original manuscript. She had failed to sell at least two other article ideas in the mid-1940s, and all of her fiction remained unpublished.[83] Understandably, he hoped to turn things around with "The Last Strike."

"I want to abandon the struggle against the married name"

FLEISCHMAN CAME UP WITH A better solution, inspired by a 1943 *American Mercury* article by Jane Grant titled "Confession of a Feminist." In it Grant explained why she cofounded the Lucy Stone League in 1921, kept her birth name through two marriages, and still was fighting hard for women's rights.[84] Fleischman apparently took the article with her when she and her daughters vacationed on Nantucket in the summer of 1948. Bernays stayed behind in New York, and in late July he wrote to his sister Judith, telling her what he'd learned about how the three of them were spending their time. He described his daughters' activities, then reported: "Doris is so bored that, I gather, she works three or four hours a day writing a piece on why feminism and a Lucy Stone name haven't worked after twenty-five years."[85]

That piece became "Notes of a Retiring Feminist," published in the *American Mercury* in February 1949. It began with an account of Fleischman's 1925 efforts to obtain a passport in her birth name—but said nothing about the significance of her success—and continued with a string of amusing stories about embarrassments and problems her name had caused her. Throughout, she expressed doubts over the purpose of keeping her name. "We feminists wanted our own personalities, wanted to throw off the ascendancy of the male," she wrote. But all she had succeeded in doing was "keeping up the appearance of independence."[86]

Contrasting herself with Ruth Hale, for whom retaining her name had been "an act of passion," Fleischman confessed to having had "no emotional involvement in what I believed was a good principle." In retrospect, she wrote, "I am inclined to think I entered too lightly this nominal obstacle race that has lasted 26 years with few stretches of clear running." And on the last page she made a startling announcement: "I want to abandon the struggle against the married name. I'd like to be Mrs. Edward L. Bernays."[87]

Yet the article's byline read "Doris E. Fleischman (Bernays)," with the magazine citing "the formidable confusions surrounding her name" to explain its awkwardness. Indeed, that byline revealed something of her own formidable confusions and mixed feelings, as did her signature on the correspondence related to her article. The letters she sent to some two dozen readers who wrote to her praising both the article and her decision to take Bernays's name were, with a very few exceptions, signed Doris E. Fleischman. Similarly, her own firm's press release about the article referred to her throughout as "Miss Fleischman."[88]

Equally confusing are her reasons for announcing to a large national audience that she would take her husband's name. Her daughters thought her birth name had decreasingly been a problem in the 1940s, and they emphasized the pleasures it had brought her. They remembered her being proud of her name, as was Bernays. "It made her singular," Anne explained. In addition, she was wildly inaccurate when she wrote, "My children, my parents, my friends have consistently refused to Miss me." As far as Anne knew, "Everybody called her Miss Fleischman. Everybody."[89]

Bernays admitted that, contrary to what Fleischman wrote in her article, receiving bills, bank statements, and other mail from businesses in an incorrect name didn't inconvenience her. When that happened, someone in their office simply called and straightened things out. Similarly, Anne believed that most of her claims of worrying over friends' and family members' discomfort with her name were untrue. Anne might be embarrassed to introduce a new friend to "my mother, Miss Fleischman," but she thought her mother enjoyed any resulting puzzlement over her marital status and said to herself, "that's their problem, not mine."[90]

Anne remembered reading "Notes of a Retiring Feminist" when it was published in 1949 and thinking, "You're revising history."[91] Much later, when she and her husband, Justin Kaplan, were writing a book about names, she read the article again and concluded that its author had used "not terribly convincing anecdotal material" as a "rationale for abandoning (a harsher word would be 'betraying') her own cause."[92]

Arguably an equally serious problem with the article was that Fleischman gave herself no credit for advancing her cause. Readers never would have known that partially as a result of what she did in 1925, married women could receive passports in their birth names. Instead, she portrayed her actions as inconsequential and quickly forgotten, expressing amazement that when she sailed for France with her new passport, "newspapers the next day actually ran the story and pictures of this event."[93] (She neglected, too, to note that her own public relations office had sent press releases to those newspapers alerting them to her departure.)

When she briefly described her problems with her daughter Doris's 1929 birth certificate, she said nothing about how the matter was resolved or the Health Department's ruling that in the future, a married woman would be permitted to sign the name she had been given when she was born on her child's birth certificate. Nor did she explain how unusual her actions were. Historian Una Stannard discovered that "Lucy Stoners tended to use the title Mrs. when they became pregnant," and few attempted to use their own names on their children's birth certificates. "It took a woman of great fortitude to go to a hospital to have a baby as Miss," Stannard concluded.[94]

Fleischman had to have been proud of these kinds of accomplishments, and of retaining her birth name for so long. This required a certain amount of bravery and must have sometimes been challenging, particularly since at that time new acquaintances almost always were introduced to each other with the honorific titles of "Miss," "Mrs.," or "Mr." But in her article she did not address difficulties of real substance, instead describing the kinds of problems caused by perplexed hostesses and inaccurate financial statements—problems she exaggerated. In the process she made herself look weak and somewhat silly, rather than like "a woman of great fortitude."

She seemed not to know how to explain why and how she had kept her name. But she likely did know that if she wrote an engaging response to Grant's *American Mercury* article, she had a good chance of it being accepted for publication in that popular mass-circulation magazine. And once she had decided to announce she was giving up her name, she almost inevitably had to profess that keeping it had been unimportant to her and of no consequence to other women.

The end result was an article that sometimes was inaccurate and never did her justice. But it did, in its way, capture her ambivalence about her name not only at that time but in the coming years. Although she could not have known it in 1949, she actually would continue using her birth name for several years. And others would continue using it even longer. As Bernays acknowledged, "She was called 'Miss Fleischman' until her death by many people."[95]

CHAPTER 4

"Whatever your job is, you do it"

OF ALL THE RESPONSES FLEISCHMAN received to "Notes of a Retiring Feminist," surely the most surprising was an invitation to help revive the organization she had disparaged in her article and that had been dormant for more than two decades.

A year after her article was published, she opened her mail and found a note from Jane Grant. "There is a movement afoot to revive the Lucy Stone League," Grant wrote, and "since the new enthusiasm appears to be in part due to your much discussed piece I feel that you might be interested in such a project." Would Fleischman like to come to a meeting to discuss a possible rebirth? "I would love to come," she promptly replied, and on February 16, 1950, she joined about a dozen former members at Grant's home. After voting in favor of revival, they elected Grant president and Fleischman vice president. Less than two weeks later, Bernays produced a development plan for the group.[1]

As his plan recommended, the new league was launched at a hotel "press luncheon" on March 22. Fleischman was one of the four speakers.[2] News stories and opinion pieces about the organization's revival and its first campaign (to permit married women to use their birth names on 1950 census forms) ran throughout the country for the next two months.[3] Seldom noted in those stories, though, was a key change in the league's goals. As a March 23 press release explained, it would not only work "to protect the rights of married women to use their own names," but planned to "concern itself with all civil and social rights of women."[4]

This broadening of its goals made the league a good match for Fleischman's own interests. Always using the name Doris E. Fleischman, she wrote letters, chaired committees, helped organize events dealing with women's issues, and was the league's representative, including at a Washington, D.C., national conference on women's pay.[5] Sometimes serving as the organization's spokeswoman, she seemed pleased to be in a position from which she could draw attention to matters that concerned her. One of those concerns was that too many young women were limiting their aspirations and opportunities. "The younger generation of women just wants to be wives," she told a reporter. "They're trying to escape their fears by marrying and looking for safety in the home. It isn't there."[6]

Despite her earlier declaration that she was going to take her husband's name, she did not do so in her league activities. And because some of those activities gave her newfound visibility, they actually helped her become better known as Doris E. Fleischman. She certainly could have carried out her work as Doris Fleischman Bernays since, as its March 23 press release stated, the league's members were "women and men who favor the right of married women to keep their own names, even if they themselves do not practice it." The organization's stationery identified some advisory council members as "Mrs." rather than "Miss," and about a quarter of the membership used a "Mrs." title, some with their husbands' first names.[7] Indeed, when Fleischman's sister Beatrice joined in 1951, the minutes listed her as Mrs. Martin Untermeyer.[8]

Yet Fleischman never used any other surname, even though this would have been a chance to begin establishing herself as Mrs. Bernays. Clearly she was less committed to changing her name than she had claimed to be at the end of her 1949 article. If this really had been important to her, she probably would not have gone to that first meeting at Grant's home. She did go, and as she spent more time with other members from the 1920s, she may have better appreciated some of the reasons she had kept her birth name for so long.

Most of those who attended that first February meeting probably came as much to get together with women like themselves as to advance Lucy Stone's cause. These middle-aged feminists and professional women must have felt like members of a very endangered species in postwar America. They had every reason to share Fleischman's worries that the current generation of young women was "looking for safety in the home," and to regret that other hopes from the 1920s had gone unrealized.

At the same time, most of them were highly accomplished. Founding members of the revived league included political activist Doris Stevens, judge Anna Kross, novelist Fannie Hurst, and physician Mildred Clark. That the companionship of women such as these was one of the things Fleischman most valued about her league membership was evident to her daughter Anne, who was appointed "junior advisor" in an effort to draw much-needed younger women to the organization. At the meetings Anne remembered, the women got together at each other's homes, drank Manhattan cocktails, and let down their hair. They shared much more than their concerns about sex discrimination, she said. "They sat around and schmoozed."[9]

Fleischman's emotional connection to other members must have made it harder for her to leave the group. She announced her resignation in a November 3, 1952, letter to Grant, explaining only that "my commitments as far as the eye can reach are so strenuous that I cannot find any possibility of working for the Lucy Stone League." The next day, Grant received a one-sentence letter signed by Bernays's office manager. It read: "Mr. Bernays tenders his resignation as of this date as a member of the Lucy Stone League and will ask you, please, to remove his name from all printed matter in connection therewith." A letter from Anne arrived in early January. Much more gracious than her father's, it gave "pressure of other activities" as the reason she was resigning, then ended by saying, "Thank you so much for letting me join and find out about the very real problems confronting the women in America."[10]

Fleischman and Grant unquestionably had some kind of serious falling out. Money may have played a role. In January 1952 Fleischman loaned the organization $100, which Grant seemed to assume was a gift. On October 20 Fleischman asked that it be repaid. It quickly was, and the league's annual meeting was held in her home on October 30. Her resignation letter followed immediately. She hardly needed the money (and the league did), so her request for repayment may have signified a larger problem, for in December four more members resigned.[11] And in late November Fleischman received a letter from member Eleanor Nicholes that pointed to discontent in the group. "Yours was a voice of skepticism which paralleled my own," Nicholes wrote. "I should greatly regret the League's over-extending itself or, at the very least, becoming a shrill gadfly organization. I know that I will miss your presence at the meetings."[12]

"My most important role"

THEY PROBABLY WERE IRRELEVANT TO her decision, but Fleischman was honest in telling Grant that she was busy with other "commitments" when she resigned. At that point she had been working on a book manuscript for three years without finding a publisher. Her agent had submitted an outline of an autobiographical book plus four sample chapters to Houghton Mifflin, and Fleischman made revisions based on editors' critiques, but in August 1950 her rewritten proposal was rejected. During the next two years, four other publishers either rejected it or discouraged further discussions about it. It was August 1954 before she finally signed a contract with Crown Publishers. The next May—after six years of using her birth name on everything related to the manuscript—she informed Crown that "the author's name is to appear as Doris Fleischman Bernays." *A Wife Is Many Women* was published in December 1955.[13]

No doubt a key reason she had a hard time finding a publisher was that her book's topic was something she was very poorly qualified to address: women's problems in caring for their families and homes. She recounted incidents from the lives of her friends, from her own married life, and especially from her childhood to show the many jobs wives must carry out, also proposing solutions to some of the problems she'd identified. Her main theme was that wives are "amateurs" in their domestic work, something she most frequently established by telling stories of her own ignorance and mistakes. And despite being the country's foremost woman public relations practitioner, she seldom mentioned her job. Instead, she called being a housewife "my most important role" and described herself as "an 'average woman' whose housewifely problems are common to average women."[14]

Those claims were made by someone who had always had servants and never cooked or done housework, so her examples of her own problems typically involved things like taking her daughters shopping for school clothes at Bonwit Teller or trying to remember the food allergies of famous friends who were coming to dinner at her home. Much in the book called attention to her high income and social status. And perhaps understandably, given her lack of "average" domestic experiences, she fabricated numerous incidents from her life.[15]

Her writing did not compensate for these flaws. Most chapters lacked clear direction, paragraphs tended to consist of strings of barely connected thoughts and incidents, and her points often were unclear. This disorganized, stream-of-consciousness style matched the way she presented herself. Too often she appeared naive, ignorant, inept, confused, and slow to learn—in many ways the opposite of the highly intelligent, witty, sophisticated woman she actually was. As a friend who read drafts of several chapters wrote in his critique, "Here, I submit, is the consistent testimonial of a first-class mind trying hard to be less significant than it can be."[16]

The book did feature one confident, knowledgeable, clear-thinking person: Bernays. He appeared frequently, always knowing the right thing to do, decisively answering her questions, understanding things that baffled her. She labeled him "perfect." Calling Fleischman "an exemplar of deference and even reverence for her husband," one book reviewer noted that "in fact, 'Eddie' emerges as quite the hero of the piece."[17]

She seems to have originally planned to write a very different book. Early notes, drafts, and correspondence indicate that she first began working on an autobiography that would quite systematically describe stages of her own life. She also read and took extensive notes on some of the research about women that was being carried out by scholars in fields such as sociology, psychology, medicine, and history, apparently intending to combine this kind of information with her own story.[18]

The book she actually wrote, however, was a haphazard treatment of a topic with which she'd had very limited personal experience. At the same time, *A Wife Is Many Women* captured the veneration of motherhood and traditional sex roles that was taking hold in middle-class America at that time, and later would be called the feminine mystique. In both popular and scholarly literature, family life was idealized and arguments that women were truly fulfilled only by motherhood and domesticity prevailed. As the birth rate skyrocketed, so did the number of sources offering expert childcare advice, which almost uniformly recommended that mothers stay home with their young children and remain physically available to older ones. Discontented homemakers were advised to work harder to find fulfillment in their domestic lives.[19]

With a few notable exceptions, the feminist rejoinder was moderate—advocating, for example, better training for homemakers, or treating them with more respect so that they would find their work more satisfying, or encouraging them to accept the prevailing domestic ideology but also develop other interests.[20] Fleischman made similar points in her book, although not very wholeheartedly. She also took issue with popular writers who criticized wives and mothers for their failures. Women, she repeatedly maintained, did their best under difficult circumstances.

Writing more than two decades later, the authors of a scholarly study of the American women's movement in the 1950s and 1960s turned to Fleischman's book as a contemporaneous source and observed that she had "responded to the antifeminist climate by glorifying the many roles that women filled in the modern family." And her position as a successful professional known for keeping her birth name gave her words additional impact, they believed: "Such testimonials from women who had once identified as feminists contributed to the impression that feminism was old-fashioned and irrelevant to women in the postwar world."[21]

As part of her extensive research Fleischman read best-selling books that were influencing Americans' views of women's roles.[22] Her scant firsthand experience with traditional domestic life made it inevitable that these sources would influence her thinking. Examining successive drafts, it is easy to see how the values they expressed crept into her writing and led her to deny her professional success even as she exaggerated her domestic ineptitude. Beyond that, these popular books may have affected her in the same way they affected some other women readers: by making her doubtful or defensive about some aspects of the way she had lived her life.

This helps explain why in her own book she frequently reaffirmed her subservience to her husband while maintaining that it made her happier than is very likely. Similarly, she recounted incidents and conversations with her daughters that never took place but helped her give the impression of an intimacy and involvement with them that did not exist. And she described finding pleasure in carrying out homemaking tasks that she never undertook.

Just as her wholehearted involvement in the revived Lucy Stone League contradicted key points in "Notes of a Retiring Feminist," so did much that she wrote in her book contradict the league's feminist advocacy, not to mention her concerns that young women were "trying to escape their fears by marrying and looking for safety in the home." She previously had been ahead of her times in many ways, but here she seemed to be trying to place herself solidly in the mainstream.

Given its contents, she could not have used her birth name on her 1955 book, but that was her name on a chapter in a very different kind of book published that same year. *The Engineering of Consent* was a collection of readings on public relations nominally compiled and edited by Bernays, although he admitted that Fleischman did as much of the necessary work as he did. She also wrote nearly all of one chapter, titled "Themes and Symbols." The book stressed the application of social science methods to public relations, and her chapter reinforced that objective, providing a cogent, methodical, well-organized explanation and analysis of the uses of themes and symbols in different contexts.[23]

The clarity and authority of her chapter testify to the confidence she felt as a public relations practitioner at that time. Indeed, the decade following World War II was an excellent period for her professionally. The firm was thriving and she was very productive, seeming to find a large amount of satisfaction in her work.[24] Yet something she did in the 1950s that she would be proud of for the rest of her life involved refusing work. Vice President Richard Nixon, preparing to run for president and hoping to improve his image, wanted to hire them. But she had had distasteful encounters with him and strongly objected to his politics. "Unless we're in the poorhouse," she told Bernays, "we can't go in this direction." They turned him down.[25]

"She didn't skip a beat"

THE STABILITY OF HER PROFESSIONAL life must have helped her deal with changes and challenges in her personal life. In less than a decade she faced two serious health scares. The first was circulatory problems that had been greatly aggravated by her pack-a-day smoking habit. In the late 1940s her doctor told her that if she didn't stop smoking he might have to amputate one of her legs. Bernays had tried to get her to quit for years—even resorting to tactics like throwing her cigarettes in the toilet—but she had continued. Faced with this new threat, though, she quit cold turkey.[26]

In May 1956 she was diagnosed with breast cancer and had a radical mastectomy. Bernays was tremendously worried, but Anne remembered visiting her mother in her hospital room soon after the surgery and never hearing her say a word about any discomfort, pain, or other problems. She was spared having to undergo chemotherapy and before long was doing almost everything she had done before her surgery. In Anne's words, "She didn't skip a beat." She felt confident that she was cancer-free and wasn't about to let what she'd been through slow her down.[27] As in her response to her doctor's ultimatum on her circulatory problems, she took stock of her options, did as much as she could on her own, and asked for no sympathy.

She did have one substantial task to carry out in the year before her surgery: supervising yet another household move. In mid-1955 they sold their three-story East Sixty-Third Street house (at a large profit) and moved into a seven-room apartment at 480 Park Avenue, still close enough to their offices to walk to work. Apartment life was easier for her because the building's management took care of much of the maintenance work she had had to supervise in the past.[28]

The main reason they moved was that a large home was even less necessary now that their daughters had gone off to college—Doris to Radcliffe, Anne to Wellesley before transferring to Barnard—graduated, begun careers, and married, both in weddings staged in their cavernous living room. In 1951 Doris married Richard Held, a teaching fellow and PhD candidate in psychology at Harvard. Three years later Anne married Justin Kaplan, an editor for art books publisher Harry N. Abrams. "My father produced the entire wedding, relying on his assistant, my mother, to supply the less important props," recalled Anne, who was not consulted on any detail or even told in advance about some of them. So she was surprised to be informed at the last minute that a five-year-old cousin she had never met would carry her train, and even more surprised when she entered the living room on her father's arm and found that the man sitting at their Steinway baby grand piano playing the wedding march was the cousin's father, Erich Leinsdorf, the conductor of the Metropolitan Opera Company's orchestra.[29]

Once her daughters were married, Fleischman's opportunities to develop close bonds with them further diminished. Her regret over never forming such bonds is evident in *A Wife Is Many Women* and in her unpublished notes for the book, where she consistently described mother-daughter relationships that were almost the direct opposite of reality. For example, she wrote that Anne sought her advice on how to make a fluffy omelet, which she proceeded to explain to the delighted teenager, and she told of giving both girls a detailed demonstration of how to wash dishes. Similarly, she described long discussions about love and sex with her daughters and sometimes their friends.[30] One displeased reviewer commented, "I dare say that few if any right thinking American mothers in any generation would have handled and discussed sex with a daughter in the manner she claims to have done."[31]

The reviewer need not have feared, for such discussions—whether about sex or cooking—never took place. Mother and daughters did not confide in each other, nor could Fleischman have advised them on domestic tasks since she didn't know how to do them. She also provided little specific guidance to help them prepare for careers. "There was an implicit message that I would have a profession," Doris said, "but she never gave me any career advice."[32]

Nonetheless, just before Anne married, her mother did offer two pieces of advice that "she fervently believed," Anne said. "One was that in an argument with your husband, he's always right. Another was that men always sleep with their secretaries."[33] Many years later, Fleischman told a friend that not long after her own wedding she had come home for lunch unexpectedly and caught Bernays with another woman. Fleischman ran out in anger but he rushed after her and persuaded her to stay in the marriage.[34] Still, he frequently flirted with attractive women, and both daughters suspected him of having at least one later affair. Doris thought this was particularly likely in the late 1940s.[35]

In this context, Fleischman's stated intention in her 1949 *American Mercury* article to begin identifying herself as "Mrs. Bernays" makes a bit more sense, as does her need to assert the importance of her role as a wife in the book she began researching that same year.

A chronology of the book's production prepared by their office reveals Bernays's heavy involvement. It shows, for example, that he constantly corresponded with Fleischman's agent and publisher about publication details, orchestrated an elaborate promotional campaign, wrote the jacket copy, and worked with artists on the book's cover.[36] The first cover design he approved was a drawing of a large man's hand pulling strings attached to small female figures representing the "many women" (and the many jobs done by wives) in the book's title.[37]

The publisher wisely rejected the idea, but it accurately captured Bernays's dominance over Fleischman as well as her portrayal of their relationship in her book. Thus in a chapter about women and money, she wrote, "I knew how much Eddie earned, because I was his partner in public relations and ours was a joint bank account. But I didn't feel that I owned half the money, or any of it. The money, I felt, and still feel, belongs to him, and it is generous of him to let me use it for myself."[38] Yet this was not money he earned; they earned it together.

"Some man has always bossed me," she confessed on another page. "My father and brother, whom I obeyed instantly, set the pattern of my attitude toward men, an attitude slightly tinged with awe." She had "profound feelings that men should rule."[39] Underneath her submissiveness, however, was a strength she could not disclose in her book. As her daughter Doris put it, "Whatever she did, she did knowing what she was doing. She was a tough-minded woman. She wasn't pushed around."[40] And even as she let Bernays "rule," he made her feel valued and praised her often. "He really admired the quality of her mind," Anne said. "He made a fuss over her."[41] He also wholeheartedly encouraged her writing efforts and did everything he could think of—probably more than she wanted—to boost her book's sales.

As part of the book's promotion, Fleischman appeared on radio and television programs and spoke to varied organizations, including, in late January 1956, the Woman Pays Club.[42] The club had been formed in 1919 in imitation of New York's famous all-male Dutch Treat Club by professional women who wanted to spend time together. (In early 1921—before the Lucy Stone League was founded— members passed a resolution advocating "the use and retention of their own names.") Fleischman originally joined in 1927 but later let her membership lapse.[43]

She was invited to rejoin soon after her talk and became heavily involved in the club. Among its more than one hundred members were numerous artists, musicians, writers, and women working in the theater, broadcasting, and film. They met biweekly at Sardi's for lunch and listened to speakers or occasionally performers, such as singers from the Metropolitan Opera. In a typical program, a panel of four women—an attorney, an obstetrician, a decorator, and a theater producer— discussed ways of fighting prejudice against women in their professions.[44]

Fleischman was elected publicity chairman in mid-1958 and served tirelessly for two years. She sent out press releases, compiled the monthly newsletter, and worked on many club programs under president Caroline Simon, an attorney who became New York's first female secretary of state in 1959. Then in mid-1960, to her great pleasure, Fleischman was elected to a two-year term as president.[45]

"I've learned you can do it"

YET SHE HAD TO LEAVE these women behind in late 1961 when she and Bernays moved to Cambridge, Massachusetts. Sadly explaining that she "found it impossible to get to New York except on rare occasions," in February 1962 she resigned as Woman Pays Club president.[46] They had said they were moving because they wanted to retire, and to give Bernays more time to finish his memoirs, but Fleischman had had little voice in the decision. "She would be acceptable to anything I wanted," he stressed, so he hadn't felt he needed to ask what her preferences were.[47]

He also seemed to give little thought to all she gave up when they moved. Among her greatest losses were her friends, not only those in the Woman Pays Club but other strong, interesting, accomplished women who led lives similar to hers. Her daughter Doris described them as "a phalanx of feminists and successful professionals"—women she saw often and from whom she gained sustenance.[48] Left behind, as well, were a career she loved and an extremely comfortable life in the vibrant city that had been her home for almost seventy years.

Bernays gave up much less. A loner who rarely cooperated with other public relations professionals and tended to alienate them, he had few close friends. And although his firm still was doing well, he had lost some longtime clients. Much larger firms, meanwhile, were attracting the kinds of big clients that once had come to him. Moreover, while he once had hoped to eventually turn the business over to Anne, he had known for several years that she had no interest in it.[49]

Yet their decision to leave New York and settle in Cambridge is puzzling. They actually did not completely retire, and Bernays later admitted he had already completed most of his memoirs by the time they moved.[50] Neither of them drove, and getting around the Boston area without a car was problematic. Neither of them flew, so trips of any distance took time. Both daughters lived in Cambridge with their husbands and children, but Fleischman and Bernays were not very close to them.[51] They may have hoped that physical proximity and more free time would help them become closer.

Their first challenge in the new city was finding a house. Since few were for sale that met Bernays's standards, they rented until August 1962, when they paid $80,000 for a nine-room house surrounded by a half-acre lawn at 7 Lowell Street. (They celebrated the purchase with a party for forty-five guests.) Fleischman had much preferred a smaller house they could have bought in the same fashionable neighborhood, but he wanted a place where they could have large parties. Thus they ended up owning a hundred-year-old, oddly designed, high-maintenance Victorian with huge downstairs rooms. Her primary pleasure there was sitting in the yard.[52]

Her life was more difficult because they had no servants and, as in New York, it was her responsibility to make sure the household ran smoothly. When she first moved to Cambridge she didn't even know how to make a cup of coffee, so domestic tasks had been a real challenge, she told an interviewer in 1973. "But I've learned you can do it. Whatever your job is, you do it." She more happily described one of her morning rituals: "Every day at six o'clock I have breakfast with my husband and tell him about a new invention. I keep inventing all the time."[53]

In addition, she developed a skill that pleased her immensely, although she was never able to use it. In the summer of 1965 she took fourteen driving lessons in one month, passed the state's driving test, and received her license. She was proud of having it and looked forward to driving their blue Cadillac, but Bernays soon told her he didn't want her to drive. After initially hiring a driver for their car, in the 1970s they primarily switched to taxis, using a few Cambridge Cab Company drivers they liked both to transport them and to carry out small errands for them.[54]

This restricted mobility did not keep them from continuing their public relations practice, for instead of retiring they operated a scaled-down business out of their home. Each had a second-floor office that opened onto a large room where a secretary worked, and they hired temporary workers (often graduate students) to perform necessary research. Any programs they developed that required still more resources were handed over to a local public relations firm, which carried out their plans.[55]

Most clients were from the Boston area, but they traveled by train to serve others. In 1968, for example, they were hired by a community college near San Francisco to determine ways it could attract more students and better serve the surrounding area. From 1970 to 1974 they did extensive work for the U.S. State Department's Bureau of Cultural and Educational Affairs, helping develop programs aimed at improving relations with other countries. Other paying clients in the 1960s and 1970s included the Brotherhood of Railroad Trainmen, the U.S. Department of Commerce, and the Department of Health, Education, and Welfare. They also did considerable pro bono work for groups such as the National

Library Association and the Massachusetts Society for the Prevention of Cruelty to Animals.[56]

Another unpaid campaign turned out to be their greatest contribution to Cambridge. In 1964 the state legislature proposed building underpasses to speed up traffic on Memorial Drive, a tree-lined highway along the Charles River. If the $6-million project went through, the historic riverfront would lose some of its tranquillity, traffic would swell on the faster-moving road, and a strand of sycamore trees would have to be chopped down so the road could be widened.[57]

Bernays and Fleischman organized the Emergency Committee for the Preservation of Memorial Drive, coining the slogan "Save the Sycamores" to focus on the trees rather than the highway. Interest groups ranging from Harvard administrators to parents concerned about the loss of their children's riverside playgrounds were persuaded to protest the project, and a clever media event was planned. During one well-publicized week, "a patrol of twentieth-century minutemen," as the *New York Times* called them, watched over the sycamores in the predawn hours, prepared to sound an alarm if trucks carrying lumberjacks appeared. The alarm, reporters were told, would be a whistle blown by a patrol member under the window of a nearby Harvard housemaster. Alerted by the whistle, the housemaster's wife would telephone picketers, who would rush to the scene and place themselves in the trucks' path to stop the trees' destruction. The trucks never arrived and the underpasses never were built.[58]

Fleischman also occasionally carried out pro bono work by herself. For example, in the early 1970s she analyzed a Boston music school's problems, drew up a development and fundraising program for it, and was the sole contact person.[59] But as in New York, she did not interact one-on-one with paying clients—except, apparently, in emergency situations. One public relations person who worked with them in Cambridge remembered, "Eddie could get a client totally mad, but in ten minutes Doris could get them back. She was totally gracious."[60]

"She really understood me"

EVEN THOUGH BERNAYS WAS NO more inclined to share the spotlight than he had been in New York, two of his efforts to draw attention to himself benefited Fleischman. They had barely settled in Cambridge when he began cultivating invitations to speak to college and university classes, and at other academic events.[61] It was a smart move. He craved attention and acclaim but had fewer opportunities to publicize his achievements once he was "retired" and living far from the city where he had been so well-known. Fortunately, the concentration of higher education institutions in the Boston area offered many possibilities for visibility, and his long career gave him much to talk about.

Academic exposure would help him further solidify his reputation as a founder of the field while building his case that he was important enough to be part of the curriculum when public relations was addressed.[62] He didn't let up on his other self-promotion efforts, even bombarding the *Boston Globe* with so many press releases about himself that an editor ordered anything from him to be discarded unopened.[63] By speaking to academic audiences, though, he could better secure a prominent spot for himself in public relations history.

He began his efforts in the early 1960s at Boston University's School of Public Communication, where he spoke often and participated in other activities. He usually wanted Fleischman along on his campus visits, and as a result she met Helen Wiebe, the wife of Gerhart Wiebe, dean of the school. The two women shared a high level of mental energy and were close friends for about a decade, until the Wiebes retired to Costa Rica in the early 1970s.[64]

Similarly, when in the fall of 1966 Bernays was asked to speak to a class at Babson College in nearby Wellesley, Fleischman accompanied him to a preclass dinner where she met economics professor Frank Genovese and his wife. Eleanor Genovese initially doubted she would have anything in common with this considerably older New York professional woman, but Fleischman quickly warmed to her and the two became good friends.[65] While Genovese had not had a career, Fleischman valued her intelligence and success as a mother of five children, also seeming to identify with her as someone who had to live in her husband's shadow.[66]

These two women were among the few Fleischman was close to during the 1960s, for she faced the legendary New England reticence and insularity that tended to make newcomers feel unwelcome.[67] She, in turn, was not always diplomatic in her interactions with local women. She tried joining a few traditional women's organizations, like the Women's City Club of Boston, but the relationships were short-lived because she tended not to be very tactful in presenting her good ideas for helping the groups. She also had contempt for the volunteerism that motivated most of the organizations' members, and disliked the fact that these intelligent women did not have careers. In fact, she met few local women of her generation who had had careers.[68]

In 1970, however, she was well rewarded when she made an effort to meet women very unlike those who had disappointed her. The previous year a small group of women had come together to address a common need: they were searching for journalism jobs after leaving the workplace to raise families. As college students many had been members of Theta Sigma Phi, a national society for women journalism majors. Besides student chapters, Theta Sigma Phi had alumni chapters that provided valuable networking opportunities for women journalists, who at that time were prohibited from joining the major professional organization for journalists, Sigma Delta Chi. In 1970 the local group was chartered as a Theta Sigma Phi alumni chapter—the only one in the Boston area—and voted to broaden its membership by admitting nonalumni.[69]

At the first meeting she attended in the fall of 1970 Fleischman met women who must have seemed vastly different from her. Most were much younger than she was and either recent college graduates or still shouldering heavy family responsibilities. With far less (and less impressive) work experience, they were trying to enter the kind of professional world she had left behind in New York. "We were all struggling," one member recalled. Yet Fleischman connected quite strongly with them, joining the chapter and enthusiastically participating in monthly meetings, where members knew her neither as Bernays's wife nor as someone who needed to brag about her past. Caroline Iverson Ackerman, one of the chapter's founders, noticed that most members regularly talked about their past work but Fleischman almost never did.[70]

Rather than talking about herself, she helped and encouraged other members by giving them career advice, helping them ascertain their strengths and find ways to emphasize them, and listening with sympathy to their concerns. She took particular pleasure in counseling student members, and when they told their friends about her, still more young women searched her out for career help.[71] As she described it, "There is almost not a day passing when some young woman doesn't come in and say can I give her some advice. And I love to do it."[72]

Yet it was a young woman helping Fleischman that led to one of her most satisfying Cambridge relationships. Since Bernays wouldn't let her drive, she needed transportation to Theta Sigma Phi meetings, and member Camille Roman, who had just graduated from the University of Michigan and was working at a small newspaper in nearby Quincy, volunteered to drive her. Soon, despite their fifty-year age difference (and almost as vast a class one), an extremely close friendship developed.[73]

Roman spent a great deal of time at 7 Lowell Street and sometimes was hired to work on the couple's projects. Fleischman took her under her wing, becoming involved in both her professional and personal life even as she told Roman more about her own life than she probably told anyone else. Something she would not discuss, though, was *A Wife Is Many Women*, which she was unhappy to learn Roman had read. "She wanted to disown it," Roman said.[74]

As the two of them talked about countless other subjects, Roman appreciated how carefully Fleischman listened and how well she understood her. She often shared lessons from her life and career, and provided her young friend with good guidance. Roman had had previous public relations–related experience by the time she arrived in Boston, but working for Fleischman and Bernays was invaluable in honing her skills. "I was like a student soaking up everything," she remembered. She did so well that Bernays urged her to continue in the field, but Fleischman had much better career advice. She told Roman she thought she would be happiest if she wrote and taught. After earning a PhD in English, she went on to very successfully do both.[75]

Fleischman always had been a superb listener who was discerning about people and sensitive to their needs. Anne recalled a time she introduced her mother to one of her friends, who talked with her only briefly, but Fleischman was able to tell him he would be wise to make a particular career change that would take him in a very different direction. "She really understood me," he told Anne.[76] "She had a wonderful knack of just concentrating on you when she talked with you," said Eleanor Genovese, describing how Fleischman encouraged her and boosted her confidence. "She made you feel that you were important and could do anything."[77]

Her ties to women one and two generations younger than she was seemed to serve yet another function. In New York she had not had close, confiding relationships with her daughters, nor did she have these kinds of relationships with them when they lived nearby in Cambridge. Even though they went on to enter fields that were two of her loves—Doris became a therapist and Anne a novelist—she never showed much interest in their work, just as she had not discussed possible careers with them when they were girls.[78]

That she presented such a different, fictionalized picture of these relationships in her 1955 book is poignant evidence that she wished she had been a more helpful, understanding mother. This desire was clear to Anne, who once wrote that although her mother "was neither warm nor affectionate" with her, "I knew, from the way her eyes had always followed me, that she wanted desperately to be both and simply didn't know how."[79] Yet Fleischman eventually was able to offer warmth, mothering, and guidance to women who had not known her previously, and only a few of whom ever knew her well. Her professional expertise helped her connect with them in ways she had not been able to connect with her daughters.

"I always knew he respected her"

SOME OF THESE FRIENDSHIPS PLAYED a role in Fleischman being honored for her earlier professional accomplishments—an irony given her reluctance to discuss them. Her work with the local Theta Sigma Phi chapter led to the first honor. In 1972 savvy members who were searching for a way to give the fledgling chapter more visibility nominated her for one of the national organization's prestigious Headliner Awards, given each year to outstanding women in communications. She was selected, then presented with the award—accompanied by significant media attention—at the organization's Houston convention. The four other recipients included UPI White House correspondent Helen Thomas and novelist Eudora Welty.[80]

In 1977 she received a local honor that sprang from similar motivations. Babson College, which recently had begun both accepting women students and awarding honorary degrees, was hoping for high media visibility when it awarded honorary doctor of law degrees that spring. Economics professor Frank Genovese and his wife, Eleanor, knew Fleischman and Bernays well by this time; he nominated them both and they were selected. He said there was no question in his mind that they were equally deserving, and he knew this husband-wife team would publicize the college's coed enrollment. As expected, Bernays made sure local media covered the event.[81]

Fleischman's connections with the organizations that honored her also were the basis for two competitions intended to help women like those she had come to know in Cambridge. Both contests received financing from the Edward L. Bernays Foundation, which had been established in 1946 to fund scholarships, awards, and projects. The small grants usually were intended as seed money and often advanced social causes in areas such as civil rights.[82]

The first competition, announced in 1974, was cosponsored by the foundation and Women in Communications Inc. (formerly Theta Sigma Phi; it had been renamed in 1972). It offered a $1,000 award for "the best plan to aid women in communications in achieving parity with men." The contest was a huge undertaking that involved numerous mailings, a great deal of administrative and clerical work, and considerable expense. Its nine judges of the finalists' entries included *Ms.* magazine publisher Patricia Carbine, writer Elizabeth Janeway, and *Philadelphia Inquirer* assistant managing editor Dorothy Jurney.[83]

Three years later the Bernays foundation cosponsored another contest, this time with Babson College. It awarded a $3,000 prize for the best five-thousand-word essay outlining a "practical program to achieve economic justice for American homemakers." Frank Genovese was the competition's administrator, and among its seven judges were the presidents of Radcliffe and Wellesley colleges and a U.S. congresswoman. Like the Women in Communications competition, this one was labor-intensive, carefully orchestrated, and heavily publicized.[84]

With both contests, Fleischman hoped to make a difference by addressing issues that had long concerned her. It was Bernays, however, who commanded the foreground in these efforts. He almost completely controlled the competition to advance women journalists—telling others what to do and how to do it, running meetings, allocating money, giving speeches. She worked as hard as he did, but he was in charge and even presented the award.[85] The pattern was the same in the "economic justice for homemakers" competition. He directed it, gave the orders, dominated the interviews, and was one of the award presenters (Fleischman was not).[86]

None of this could have surprised her, nor could she have thought it meant he didn't appreciate and admire her. He continued to praise her to others and even to credit her for her excellent ideas in their public relations work. "I always knew he respected her," said Eleanor Genovese, and she recalled many times when he was talking about their earlier work and told listeners, "Doris did this." Since she was modest, private, and not very self-revealing, their Cambridge-area friends typically learned far more about her abilities and achievements from him than from her.[87]

He thought many things about her were wonderful, including her creative writing, which she continued to do in Cambridge. In the mid-1960s she started a new novel; she said its woman protagonist was "a cross between Virginia Woolf, Marcel Proust and Steve Allen."[88] A decade later she still was working on that manuscript and also had returned to another novel she had started in New York.[89] Yet her poetry seemed to matter the most to her. She spent more time on it than she had previously, composing it in a little notebook that she carried around with her. Bernays sometimes drew small illustrations for the poems.[90]

In 1977 he persuaded her to let him oversee the publication of twenty-two of her poems in a small vanity-press book titled *Progression*. The poetry was hers, but otherwise this was his project. He made all the publication arrangements, sent press releases about it to newspapers, and mailed countless copies to people they knew.[91] Fleischman said the book was published "despite my protest—a kind of invasion of privacy." Still, she admitted to being "delighted at the response."[92]

Worsening arthritis had made the physical act of writing much more difficult by the time *Progression* was published, and other medical problems—including debilitating angina, severe hearing loss, and cataracts—further weakened her.[93] But for someone who had declared in *A Wife Is Many Women* that one of her dreams was to have "a portable electric typewriter in every room," writing was too important a form of expression for her to give up.[94]

Thus in March 1980 she began her last writing endeavor, a journal. Her first words in it were "I will write something every day." Typing was impossible and at first writing in longhand wasn't much easier, but before long she was explaining, "I think I know why I'm able to do all this writing. My hand used to hurt so severely that I always gave up after a few sentences." She had thought it through, she said, and "made up a therapy" by using "traction and all digits" in the bathtub. "It works! Hooray."[95]

The journal is a revealing record of how mentally vigorous she remained. She often wrote about news events (and had harsh words for both President Reagan and former president Carter). Frank Genovese was coming to lunch on April 19, she wrote, and "we have promised each other to discuss socialism—I want to know how we can put its virtues in the capitalist system." In another entry she described helping Bernays with a magazine article he was working on. "We've talked it over before writing," she noted, and now he was going to read his draft to her out loud since he had used a typewriter font that was smaller than she was able to read. But because "editing from vocal reading is quite difficult," she was glad he was "very good about accepting critical comments."[96]

Her deteriorating health also can be charted in her journal, although she chastised herself for writing too much about her problems. And she was delighted to note improvements, such as when, in mid-April, new eyeglasses after cataract surgery improved her vision so much that it "changes my outlook on life." But she was constantly in pain, took myriad medications, and for more than a year had to keep a tank of oxygen nearby. Indeed, the last sentence of her final journal entry reads, "I'm going to go up and get some oxygen."[97]

The journal was one of the few places she admitted having serious health problems. She seems to have barely mentioned them to people outside her family, and one friend was shocked to arrive at her house for lunch and find her lying completely incapacitated on the couch but unwilling to discuss why she could not move.[98] Daughter Doris remembered that physical complaints were one of the few taboo dinner conversation topics when she was a child; her mother used to say, "no clinic at the table."[99] Fleischman had always lived by the credo that women should never complain about their problems, and she adhered to that credo to the end.

One of the last interviews she gave was to a *Christian Science Monitor* reporter interviewing her and Bernays for a series of "Valentine's Day Love Stories" published on February 14, 1980. When asked about their public relations work, Bernays said, "Doris had all the bright ideas," although she responded, "I had all the wild ideas." As for the secrets of their long-lasting marriage, she told the reporter, "Love has been the big thing in my life. . . . It actually interferes with what I want to do." Then she said of her husband: "I think it's the same for him. But he doesn't let love interfere with his life. He is all business."[100]

In early April she pondered in her journal how, given her unrelenting physical discomfort and the "dreadful state of the world," she could feel happy. She decided, "It must be because I love Eddie. He's nearly always cheerful, active, helpful." Later in the month, after admitting, "I've had a bad week," she noted, "I get along as long as Eddie continues kind, thoughtful and patient—and trying to spare me from effort and pain."[101]

He looked after her attentively and usually uncomplainingly for two more months until she died on July 10 following a massive stroke. On her death certificate, her occupation was identified by the phrase she and Bernays had coined together in 1920: "counsel on public relations."[102] It was a reminder that, just as (despite the title of her 1949 article) she never retired as a feminist, so she never retired from this field she helped found.

PART II

Ruth Hale

CHAPTER 5

"She totally conquered where she came from"

AT AN EARLY AGE RUTH HALE REBELLED against life in Rogersville, Tennessee, the small, racially segregated town in the northeastern corner of the state where she was born on July 5, 1886. She seems to have almost always been at odds with her mother, Annie Riley Hale, even though she adored her father, James Richards Hale, an amicable lawyer who also raised and traded horses. And she was very fond of her two brothers, Shelton, born in early 1891, and Richard, born almost two years later.[1] Ruth's given name (later described by her son as "squashily feminine") was Lillie Ruth, and in typical southern fashion she was called by both names. She hated the two names together and soon showed how poorly they suited her.[2]

At first the family lived very comfortably. They could afford to have servants, and a photograph of their house shows a large, gabled, two-story Victorian surrounded by land. But their circumstances abruptly changed in the spring of 1897 when Shelton and Richard were sent to stay with relatives while Ruth and her mother watched over a very ill James Richards Hale, who died in early April.[3] Annie Riley Hale was left with no immediate source of income, sons ages four and six, and an unhappy ten-year-old daughter. In addition to missing her father, Ruth chafed at the town's rural insularity and resented the restrictions of southern "ladylike" behavior, such as being forbidden to sing in her natural contralto voice and forced to read too much by Sir Walter Scott. Still, she found numerous ways to defy the community that she later labeled "a basket of snakes," such as by being the area's first female to ride astride, rather than sidesaddle.[4]

Her mother returned to teaching high school mathematics, as she had done before her marriage, and no doubt was relieved when in late summer 1899 Ruth left for Roanoke, Virginia, to enroll in the Hollins Institute and live with an aunt, who probably paid her tuition.[5] Its catalog provides evidence that the school offered a rigorous education, making very plausible its claim that since its founding fifty years earlier it had sent more graduates on to higher educational institutions than any other school for girls in the state.[6] Ruth attended for two years, mainly taking basic college preparatory classes, and graduated in the spring of 1901. After initially struggling with Latin, she earned mostly Bs in her first year. Her grades were higher in her second year, when she excelled in French.[7]

In 1902, at age sixteen, she entered the Drexel Academy of Fine Arts in Philadelphia to study painting and sculpture, living with cousins in the area while she was there.[8] The aunt with whom she had lived while attending the Hollins Institute—imagined by Ruth's son as "one of those elderly autocrats who wear cameo brooches like medals"—had sent her north with these words: "If you have any trouble up there, Lillie Ruth, you just tell them that you're the niece of Miss Richards of Culpepper County, Virginia, and everything will be all right."[9]

Everything may not have been all right, for she left Drexel after two years. She moved to Washington, D.C., in 1904 and began her journalism career as an eighteen-year-old society reporter for the Hearst Bureau, perhaps later writing for the *Washington Star*.[10] Based on the drawings and small sculptures he saw, her son thought she had real talent as an artist, so her reasons for leaving art school are unclear. It may be that the costs became prohibitive. At the same time, the Hearst Bureau job was an excellent opportunity for someone so young and inexperienced, and its location may have been appealing since her mother had found a teaching position in Washington and was living there with Shelton and Richard.[11] Ruth almost certainly lived with and helped support them, as she often would do later.

In 1908 she returned to Philadelphia, this time for a better job as a drama critic at the *Public Ledger*. She occasionally covered sports too, making her one of the country's first women sports reporters. Richard, who already was earning a tiny income as a singer, remembered that she took him to hear his first operas when he visited her during his Christmas and Easter breaks, and paid for his summer vacations in Atlantic City.[12] It also probably was in Philadelphia that, with astonishing discipline, she completely shed one vestige of her Tennessee upbringing: her southern accent. Aided, surely, by frequent theater attendance, she taught herself flawless "stage English," with perfect diction and no trace of regionalism. She was so successful, her son said, that "there was never any hint of Rogersville" in her speech, even when she was frazzled. As he put it, "She totally conquered where she came from."[13]

That conquest no doubt helped her make her most important move—to New York City. In 1910 she began working as a drama critic at *Vogue*, which had recently expanded in size and may have been hiring more writers as a result.[14] The next year Richard joined her in the city after receiving a scholarship to attend Columbia University. She paid for his singing lessons and took him to operas, plays, and dance performances. "Doors and windows onto arts and letters continued to be opened to me by my wonderful sister," he recalled. She also sent money to Shelton when he has attending the University of Pennsylvania and then Harvard Law School.[15] Thus she helped her brothers obtain educations superior to her own.

Possibly following a period as a *Vanity Fair* drama critic, in 1915 she was hired as a writer for the Sunday *New York Times*.[16] (There she may have run into Jane Grant, who was working as a stenographer in the society department.) One of her assignments was to compile the "Hundred Neediest Cases" for the paper's annual Christmas appeal. When the local charities that had been asked to submit cases could only come up with about eighty, she found the remaining cases herself by going to family court sessions and obtaining the names of impoverished families. She was proud of her initiative but the *Times* was not, since these families might be difficult to locate. They were rejected, and she had to go back to the charities to get names and addresses of less-needy families.[17]

"The weapon of a woman's sharp tongue and facile pen"

HER MOTHER, MEANWHILE, THRIVED AS a widow free from the confines of Rogersville, where she had firmly controlled her mild-mannered husband and two of her three children. Characterizing her as "a steamroller," her granddaughter thought "she must have been as tenacious with her husband as she was with her children."[18] She was used to taking charge and fortunate that when her husband died she had a profession to which she could return. After briefly teaching in Nashville, Chattanooga, and Knoxville, by 1902 she had settled with her young sons in Washington. She stayed there for several years, not only teaching high school mathematics but also operating a research bureau for legislators and speechwriters.[19]

That was a logical endeavor for someone who was well informed and had strong opinions. In 1899, for example, she had written a logically reasoned, carefully researched—and highly racist—letter to the *New York Times* outlining her solution to the "race problem." She proposed that "the careless, rollicking, water-melon eating, funeral-enjoying darky" stay in the United States and serve his Caucasian superiors, while "his educated and ambitious brethren" should move to Africa and found "a new home and self-government for the colored race." She believed "this would afford a safety valve for the discontent of the negroes, and the most legitimate escape from 'the white man's burden' in this country." A *Times* editor apparently was impressed with her argument, for her long, two-column piece ran not as a standard letter but by itself under a four-deck headline.[20]

This was not her only cause. She proceeded to address many others in more than a half-dozen books, myriad articles and pamphlets, and countless speeches. Theodore Roosevelt was an early target; she had self-published two books about him by 1912. One, *Rooseveltian Fact and Fable*, seems to have received considerable attention. An advertisement for it quoted reviews from several major newspapers, including one from the *New York World* declaring that a "little Southern woman, apparently harmless, has essayed to measure the slender lance of her deftly shaded sarcasm, the weapon of a woman's sharp tongue and facile pen against the Big Stick."[21]

Five years later Woodrow Wilson was in her sights. In September 1917 she was the keynote speaker at a Hartford, Connecticut, mass meeting of a group opposed to U.S. involvement in World War I. After she made "seditious utterances and denunciatory remarks against President Wilson," the *New York Times* reported, the police stopped her speech and arrested her. Audience members then rushed to the stage, "chairs being overturned and benches thrust aside in the dash toward the speaker." Trailed by a crowd of sympathizers, she was brought to police headquarters.[22] Before long the U.S. district attorney announced he would not prosecute her, much as he would have liked to. "I regret that there is no statute of the United States known to me on which could be based a successful prosecution," he explained. But her words "bordered on criminality, and were intensely unpatriotic."[23]

The *Times* noted that in her speech, "She claimed her constitutional right to criticise the President and that because she was his personal friend, she could say what she pleased."[24] On being shown the *Times* article, her grandson remarked, "She certainly shared Wilson's well-known bigotry." As for any friendship she thought she had with the president, he surmised it would have been secondhand through Shelton, who had graduated from Harvard in 1916 and become Supreme Court justice Oliver Wendell Holmes's law clerk for the 1916–1917 court term. He then served as the assistant secretary of the U.S. War Trade Board and joined Wilson as part of the American delegation at the Versailles Peace Conference. In 1919 he moved to New York City with his wife, Susan Evarts Hale (the granddaughter of a former secretary of state), and joined a local law firm.[25]

Shelton's death in September 1920 launched his mother on her most passionate crusade. He was her favorite child and his achievements were remarkable, particularly given his humble Rogersville roots. At that time each Supreme Court justice had only one law clerk, so the positions were prized, and Holmes was unusual in his commitment to mentoring his clerks. "As a group, these men achieved extraordinary levels of professional success," one scholar concluded, and "Holmes played a large part in that success."[26] But three years after his clerkship, Shelton died at his wife's family's Vermont home, where he had gone to recover from unsuccessful brain surgery five months earlier.[27] One of his wife's cousins remembered, "During his long, terrible illness there was a war between the families as to his care, and I don't know which acted the more crazily."[28]

The loss set Annie Riley Hale forever against the medical establishment, and she spent more than two decades researching, speaking, and writing about topics ranging from the advantages of vegetarianism to the dangers of vaccination. She managed to sell many articles about what she benignly called "medical reform" to health magazines and wrote two books on the subject. A review of *Medical Voodoo*, her cleverly titled antivaccination book, predicted that it "will arouse a lot of controversy in days to come; and it will not be cool."[29]

Exceptionally smart and energetic, relentless and absolutely sure she was right, she influenced her children in essential ways. "Her basic keenness and her basic confidence were her legacy to Shelton," her grandson wrote. Her legacy to Richard, his daughter thought, was "her ferocious belief in independence—in doing what you believed in, no matter what anyone said." This helped him muster the courage to drop out of Columbia to tour with a respected acting company as an understudy in 1914, and afterward to doggedly pursue a career as a singer and stage and film actor.[30]

Yet Annie Riley Hale's greatest influence was on her daughter. As Ruth later would do with her own son, her mother made her into a voracious reader. She was required to read every day throughout her childhood, and her appreciation of the value of the written word must have grown when she later saw how the research Annie Riley systematically undertook gave her remarkable expertise in the wide-ranging areas she devoted herself to writing and speaking about. By example, her impressively self-taught mother showed Ruth how to learn on her own, something she went on to do with great success through varied and constant reading.[31] Ruth also inherited much of her mother's zeal, tenacity, intelligence, verbal dexterity, unwillingness to compromise, and willingness to offend. But she did not inherit the older woman's social and political views, most of which she adamantly opposed.

Their deepest and longest-lasting differences were about feminism. Incensed by women's fight for suffrage, in April 1913 Annie Riley vigorously expressed her opposition in testimony before the U.S. Senate committee considering a suffrage constitutional amendment. Six months later she traveled to Knoxville to represent the antisuffrage position at Tennessee's first public debate on the issue, and to call for a meeting to form a state antisuffrage society. She spoke at the subsequent meeting but her organizing efforts were unsuccessful and no Tennessee antisuffrage society was formed until 1916—the same year she self-published her antisuffrage book, *The Eden Sphinx.*[32]

In its more than two hundred pages, she contended that women already had obtained all necessary legal and economic rights without suffrage, while suffrage advocacy "confuses and obscures the issue, by permitting woman to think her ineffectiveness due to lack of political power." Rather, "her lack of power—where such lack exists—is due primarily and fundamentally to her failure to master the requirements of her woman's job of mothering," she maintained. "When women learn responsibility in *their* tasks there will be enough responsible *male* voters, lawmakers and governors, to keep the Ship of State off the rocks!"[33]

The book "must be counted among the sprightliest and cleverest that have appeared on either side of the controversy," wrote a *New York Times* book reviewer who was impressed with its author's talent for "making a pungent criticism or letting fly a shaft of ridicule." Her strengths as a writer—regardless of her views—were best summed up by the reviewer's conclusion that *The Eden Sphinx* "shows that she had read much and widely on both sides of the question and also that she possesses a nimble and lively pen."[34]

In her book she repeatedly reminded readers of just where women's priorities should lie. "Woman's greatest happiness and true destiny center in the simple life of home," she wrote. "The only reason her home occupation ever lacks dignity or interest is her failure to *put intelligent thought into it.*"[35] Nonetheless, her own "intelligent thought" was devoted elsewhere. By 1912 she had left her Washington teaching job, moved to New York, and was living with Ruth and Richard. Ruth probably provided most of her support.[36] Presumably, too, it was money from Ruth, and for a while Shelton, that financed the publication of her books and her numerous trips to speak in places like Hartford and Knoxville.[37]

Richard's wife remembered him complaining that when he lived with the two women, "Ruth was out encouraging women's freedom and Annie Riley was saying women should go back to the home, while Richard was at home doing the cooking."[38] Contradictions did not bother her. Indeed, after teaching her children to assert their independence, she became financially dependent on them. After writing that a happy home life was a married woman's "true destiny," she went on to add enormous stress to her daughter's marriage and home life. After crusading against women's right to vote, once women won that right she voted regularly and in 1932 ran as a candidate for California's U.S. Senate seat. "Doubts did not disturb her sleep or her thought," her grandson observed. This was her "one great advantage over her daughter, an advantage that made her unbearable but invulnerable."[39]

"Fine, daring, rather joyous and independent women"

EVEN AS HER MOTHER WAS writing a book declaring women "the weak link in the human chain" and calling feminists "peeved disciples of sex grouches," Ruth was attending meetings of Heterodoxy, a feminist women's organization formed in 1912. She may well have been one of its twenty-five charter members, for in 1912 she already was good friends with Marie Jenney Howe, the reformer and suffrage organizer who was the group's founder and who, like her, had arrived in New York two years earlier.[40] Certainly she was an early member of the group, which would remain important to her for the rest of her life.

Heterodoxy has been called the American organization where "feminism found its first full expression" because its members advocated liberation from all forms of sex discrimination. While most previous women reformers (including those in the suffrage movement) had stressed women's duty and power to improve society, feminists were fighting to obtain all the freedoms men had.[41] The term was new when Heterodoxy was formed, and the group played a key role in defining it by organizing the county's first feminist mass meetings on February 17 and 20, 1914. On February 17, a dozen women and men delivered ten-minute speeches on "What Feminism Means to Me." Three days later, when the subject was "Breaking Into the Human Race," seven speakers addressed seven key women's rights, including the rights to work and to organize. Howe, who led both meetings, explained at the second one, "We intend simply to be ourselves, not just our little female selves, but our whole, big, human selves."[42]

Writer and activist Mabel Dodge Luhan described her fellow Heterodoxy members as "fine, daring, rather joyous and independent women." Above all, they were "unorthodox women, that is to say, women who did things and did them openly."[43] Every other Saturday afternoon, about three dozen of them met at a Greenwich Village restaurant for what one member called "loud talk and simple feasting," debating topics ranging from free love to socialism to psychoanalysis to modern art.[44] Their guest speakers were "all kinds of thinking women," remembered journalist Rheta Childe Dorr. "They told us how and why they had written a particular book, painted a particular picture, advocated this or that reform, had a baby under twilight sleep, bobbed their hair, or voted for Debs."[45]

Their feminism was a strong bond, but members were remarkably diverse in their other concerns and in their personal and professional lives. Thus, among the best known early members were writer and economic theorist Charlotte Perkins Gilman, psychologist Leta Hollingworth, actress Fola La Follette, lawyer and social activist Crystal Eastman, and Dr. Sara Josephine Baker, director of the New York City Bureau of Child Hygiene. Hale's many good friends from the group included suffrage leader Doris Stevens, actress Margaret Wycherly, and writers Zona Gale, Alice Duer Miller, and Nina Putnam.[46]

Like Hale, most Heterodoxy members had had long fought against the narrow values and expectations of their families and communities.[47] Outsiders for much of their lives, they now were free "simply to be ourselves," as Howe put it. The company of these self-sufficient "unorthodox women," these "thinking women," must have fortified Hale and helped her better cope with living and working in a large, fast-paced northern city very different from any other place she had lived.

They would have been an excellent source of professional support, for more than half of the group's members were writers or editors. Many wrote for newspapers or magazines, or were book authors. Some were playwrights, while still more were actors, were press agents for actors or individual theaters, or had other jobs connected to the theater.[48] Hale had been one of the country's only female drama critics when she was at the *Philadelphia Public Ledger*, and even a decade later there were just a few in New York.[49] After previously having little contact with women who did what she did, it must have been revitalizing to know so many Heterodoxy women in related fields. And it is possible that her 1915 move from reviewing plays for a magazine to writing for the Sunday *New York Times* was eased by advice from Rheta Childe Dorr or Alice Duer Miller, both at the *New York Tribune*.

The *Times* was a notoriously difficult place for women and Hale's job there may not have been a good fit, for she left sometime in 1916, changing careers again to become a press agent for Broadway producer Arthur Hopkins.[50] She was highly qualified for the position, which had to pay more than she was making at the *Times*, while the support of Heterodoxy friends working in the theater may have helped her decide whether she should take a job that was less prestigious than newspaper or magazine work.

If she had needed to be prodded to accept the offer, those friends could have reminded her that it was one of the best jobs in the field. Most other theatrical press agents were like Edward L. Bernays, carrying out only short campaigns for clients while always looking for new ones. "The press agent depended on fraternizing to learn what was really happening on Broadway" and obtain leads to possible new clients, he had discovered. Every opportunity for media attention had to be pursued since "newspapers provided a daily showcase that indicated the effectiveness of a press agent." Actors or producers often decided to hire a press agent for one-shot campaigns after they "found out who was behind the item or picture in the newspaper that indicated a press agent's handiwork and got in touch with him."[51]

Hale's job would be much more substantive and less hectic, for it required promoting the plays of only one producer, and he was highly regarded. In addition to being prolific, Arthur Hopkins was widely praised for his taste, intelligence, and ability to nurture talent.[52] Hale's friend from the *Times*, drama critic Alexander Woollcott, likely was among those who encouraged her to take the job, for he called Hopkins "the best producer in America."[53] A later *Times* drama critic, Brooks Atkinson, wrote that Hopkins "revolutionized Broadway by taking the drama seriously." After a breakthrough 1914 success, Atkinson said, Hopkins "proceeded to revitalize classics and produce plays that the old Broadway would not know what to do with."[54]

Hopkins surely felt fortunate to hire someone with several years of experience as a drama critic. (In contrast, Bernays's knowledge of the theater was limited to what he had learned from his clients and from "fraternizing.") Hale's background would have helped her rise to the standard of the ideal theatrical press agent as envisioned by Atkinson. "The press agent who not only can write but who also has artistic and intellectual understanding is a gift from the gods," he explained. "Many of the finest productions need to be promoted not merely from the box office point of view but as works of art that have significance to the theatre."[55]

Her firsthand knowledge of how newspapers operated probably was equally valuable, and her son had no doubts that she worked well with drama editors. "She was smart enough to know what would appeal to them," he noted, and could be extremely persuasive, thanks to her logical mind and verbal dexterity. "She marshaled her words as carefully as she pronounced them," as he put it, and listeners tended to pay attention when she talked.[56] Yet writing and placing stories was only part of her job, for producers' press agents also had to please the people involved in a production, particularly the major actors.[57] Here, too, her son thought she did well. As evidence, he pointed out that John Barrymore, one of Hopkins's frequent leading men, was fond of her, "and I don't think he liked a whole lot of people."[58]

Normally she "used language with assurance and grace," her son wrote, but that was not the case the afternoon Barrymore caught her sleeping in the auditorium during a rehearsal and "rushed backstage to make up his hands with a set of warts, carbuncles, and claws so that, standing behind her, he could wake her by touching her face with them." Her response to this rude awakening probably was not quite what he had expected: "On that occasion Ruth was supposed to have used words even Barrymore had never heard."[59]

"He seemed ungraduated in the truest sense of the word"

SHE WAS IN A MUCH better mood one day in July 1915 when she and Alice Duer Miller, her good friend from Heterodoxy, attended a baseball game at the Polo Grounds. (Miller's husband seemed a bit wary of Heterodoxy, describing its members as "unusual and dangerous women.") An avid baseball fan and popular *Tribune* columnist, Miller knew that one of her paper's sportswriters, Heywood Broun, was covering the game. So when the women decided they would prefer to watch it from the all-male sanctuary of the press box, they walked up the steps to the box's entrance and asked if they could join him. Too polite (and perhaps too intimidated) to say no, he invited them to sit next to him while he reported the game for his paper and served as official scorer, a responsibility that rotated among the sportswriters.[60]

Probably drawing on her own occasional sports reporting experience in Philadelphia, Hale questioned some of his calls and told him she did not think very highly of his baseball writing, even though he had a reputation as one of the city's better sportswriters. Still, he liked her forthrightness, they became friends, and soon she was encouraging him to accept a job as a *Tribune* drama critic. Apparently his interest in the theater, ability to write amusingly, and penchant for dramatic prose (which Hale thought overblown in his sports reporting) had persuaded editors to offer him the position.[61]

His first review ran in mid-August and he enjoyed Hale's company in the months that followed. Yet he had a new distraction that fall: Lydia Lopokova, a delicate, vivacious Russian ballerina who had joined the experimental Washington Square Players to obtain acting experience. Smitten when he reviewed an October play in which she had a role, Broun arranged to be introduced, fell in love, and single-mindedly courted her. "They must have looked like some Aesopian pairing of a bear and a bird," his son imagined, "the big man, made even larger by a voluminous and shapeless fur coat, bending adoringly over the vivid, tiny little woman." He bravely proposed in early January 1916 and she blithely agreed to marry him at some vague time in the future.[62]

Later that month she was invited to join Diaghilev's Ballets Russes, which was arriving in New York to begin its first American tour. Bernays, who was handling the tour's publicity, remembered watching Broun and Lopokova together at the Century Theater before and after her performances. He thought "they demonstrated their attachment unmistakably." But in April, when the tour ended and the group returned to New York, Lopokova broke off the engagement. She told Broun she had fallen in love with Randolfo Barocchi, Diaghilev's secretary-manager, and would stay with the company when it sailed for its Paris home base. (She went on to a successful career, an unhappy marriage with Barocchi, and, following their 1925 annulment, an exceedingly happy marriage with economist John Maynard Keynes.)[63]

Broun and Hale remained friends during this time and she may have sometimes provided help with his reviews, but after a while he knew he wanted to see her more often.[64] Perhaps her strength, intelligence, and combativeness were newly appealing in light of his experience with the soft, exotic, capricious Lopokova. And like him, Hale was on the rebound from an unsuccessful romance, although its details are unknown.[65]

Still, they were an improbable match. Their backgrounds were as different as their personalities. Born in 1888, Broun was raised in an upper-middle-class New York City home, the third of four children (a brother died in childhood). His mother, Henrietta Brose Broun, had wielded authority since she was a girl. After her mother died when she was a child, her well-off father placed her in charge of his household, and at age twelve she was serving as his hostess at formal dinners. Heywood Cox Broun, the self-absorbed man she married, ran a profitable printing business before becoming a successful wine merchant. He prided himself on being a top pistol marksman, an expert billiards player, and one of the city's best dressers. Finding life at home not as appealing as life at his club, he sometimes stayed there for months at a time.[66]

His son Heywood received excellent elementary and high school educations at the Horace Mann School, where his classmate Doris Fleischman remembered him clowning on the stage during the graduation ceremony.[67] In 1906 he headed off for what should have been another excellent education at Harvard. His parents told him they expected him to do even better there than his older brother Irving, but he had a hard time taking his classes seriously, and he was not invited to join the staff of the *Crimson*. As his own son put it, "He failed in almost every goal in college, including the basic matter of getting a degree." He did improve his poker playing through frequent practice, however, and he made sure he saw most Red Sox home games.[68]

When after four years he had not managed to pass the freshman French class that was a graduation requirement, his father refused to finance his education any further. Instead he used his connections to help his son get a job as a reporter at the *New York Morning Telegraph*, the city's least-reputable newspaper. Sometimes called "the chorus girl's breakfast," it devoted most of its resources to covering vaudeville news and the racetrack. Broun lasted almost two years, pleased that his poker playing continued to improve in games both there and at the *Tribune*, his next employer. He began on the copy desk and eventually advanced to sports-writer. This undemanding job where he could draw on his affection for the subject and ability to write amusingly suited him well, and he was doing it quite happily when he met Hale in 1915.[69]

At that point he had essentially wandered through life, content but with little direction. Despite every advantage—from privileged economic circumstances to superior education to undeniable writing talent—he had mainly done what was easy or enjoyable, and he didn't have a great deal to show for it. There was little prestige in sportswriting and he had failed to obtain a Harvard degree. In his son's words, "He seemed ungraduated in the truest sense of the word."[70]

In 1915 Hale had much to show for her efforts, and had worked far harder than Broun had ever worked to get where she was. Her success had come despite obstacles that included a southern small-town upbringing, economic difficul-ties, and—perhaps the greatest impediment of all—her gender. Yet when she left art school at age eighteen she was offered a journalism job in Washington, even though she had few formal qualifications and women's choices in the field were ex-tremely narrow. Four years later she was in Philadelphia working as a drama critic, rather than on the society pages, and after only two more years she was hired for a still-better job in New York.

They were markedly different, too, in their academic backgrounds. Hale's high school education ended at age sixteen; she never attended a university and never regretted it. Broun always was bothered by his lack of a Harvard degree. And not-withstanding the many years he had spent at schools that were among the nation's best, he lacked the kind of intellectual inquisitiveness that Hale had. Superbly self-educated, she read widely and deeply, and absorbed a great deal.[71] This helps ex-plain why, in her early twenties, she was knowledgeable enough about the theater to become one of the country's few female drama critics. And her brother Richard credited her with serving as his guide in a new intellectual world. "Her knowledge of music and the fine arts opened his eyes," his daughter said. "She was his most important teacher."[72]

Hale's and Broun's financial circumstances also differed in fundamental ways. When Broun left Harvard in 1910 he not only returned to New York (and to a job arranged by his father); he moved back into his parents' home.[73] So he wasn't even financially responsible for himself, unlike Hale, who supported herself and helped support her mother and brothers. Economic pressure was one reason she had accomplished so much, while the absence of this kind of pressure was one reason he had little ambition.

"I decided he was the kind of person I wanted to marry"

ONE COMMONALITY WAS THAT THEY both had lived most of their lives with a strong-willed, sharp-edged mother who was quick to voice her disapproval. Her grandson called Henrietta Brose Broun "a razor blade" and "splendidly invulnerable," noting that her firm control over her household was based on her ability to "indulge her husband in the belief that he was in charge of things."[74] In this she was like Annie Riley Hale, who, he discerned, had "run the household in Rogersville in the traditional southern manner of authority disguised as deference." This let her "enjoy the fruits of tyranny without any of the criticism that sometimes embitter them."[75] She herself had carefully explained in *The Eden Sphinx* what was required for a woman to efficiently carry out her "home occupation": "She should know how to manage children, and she should know how to manage men."[76]

Mrs. Broun, however, had the advantage of a son who never fought with her, no matter how unkind her actions were. Thus he was silent even after she read what she thought was Alexander Woollcott's review of a new play, expressed delight at his clever description of John Barrymore's acting, was informed by Broun, "Mother, I wrote that line," and responded, "Well, it seemed so witty I guess I just assumed Woollcott had written it." He told that story often, his own son remembered, "with a persistence that revealed his hurt."[77] She frequently put him down, but he never responded with more than "a resisting smile," as his son characterized it.[78]

None of this worried Broun's father. "If someone had pointed out to Heywood Cox Broun that he was totally self-concerned and remarkably ungiving in emotional matters, he would have laughed comfortably and pointed out that his wife had a butler, a cook, and two housemaids, and that his children attended the best schools, proof positive that he was the best of husbands and fathers," his grandson wrote. "I never met a person so completely without guilt or self-examination."[79] Yet Hale was much more tolerant of him than of his wife. "She saw him as a charming rascal," her son said. And indeed, "He was an immensely charming guy as long as you didn't have to depend on him for anything."[80]

Mr. and Mrs. Broun's relationship hardly served as a recommendation for matrimony, but this was something their son increasingly desired even after Lopokova broke their engagement. Approaching thirty, he was still living at home with his parents, and there was much he found appealing about Hale. "He liked that she didn't hide that she was smarter than he was," his son said. "His mind was roving and creative, but hers was sharper, and he liked that sharpness." Thanks to his mother (and unlike most men of the time), Broun was used to strong, opinionated women. At the same time, he appreciated Hale's firm sense of direction. While he still did not know what he was capable of doing or most wanted to do, she knew who she was and what she wanted.[81]

She also knew what she did not want. In early 1917, for example, she told her brother Richard that she would never marry. Yet a few months later she agreed to marry Broun. Long afterward, trying to explain her decision to her son, the best she could do was to tell the story of sitting with Broun on a bench in Central Park and being approached by a chattering, begging squirrel. When she asked him to buy peanuts to feed to the squirrel, she recalled, "Sitting there, big and lazy in the sunshine, Heywood smiled and said, 'I tell you what. I'll give him a nickel and he can go buy his own.' At that moment I decided he was the kind of person I wanted to marry." Her son found the story unsatisfying, "like something made up later to explain something essentially inexplicable." But it was persuasive, he thought, in "its picture of Heywood substituting charm for effort."[82]

Charm certainly was one of his strengths, and he and Hale had many things in common professionally. Moreover, he had asked her to marry him when she was thirty, long past the age when southern women usually married. She undoubtedly understood that one reason she remained single was that most of the men she'd known would have thought Alice Duer Miller's husband's characterization of Heterodoxy members described her well. She was one of the "unusual and dangerous women." Whatever his concerns about danger, Broun was pleased that she was unusual.

That he was so unformed and unfocused also was part of his appeal, thought their son, who was convinced that these weaknesses in his father actually made him more desirable to Hale. As he explained it, in 1917 Broun was like the clay she had molded in art school. "She knew you could take that material and make General Sherman or a horse out of it. He was a big mass of soft clay that she could shape into something remarkable." She not only could see his potential but he had let her know he wanted to be shaped.[83]

And he had agreed to the kind of marriage on which she insisted. She would continue with her career. Their relationship would be one of equals. They would feel entirely free to go out by themselves, spend time with their own friends, pursue their own interests, live their own lives. She had worked too hard for the independence she had enjoyed for more than a decade to sacrifice any of it to marriage. In addition, as a mark of that continuing independence, she would keep her birth name.[84]

Her membership in Heterodoxy made her infinitely more knowledgeable about keeping her name than most women were in 1917. Three years earlier, when the group held its second feminist mass meeting in a packed Greenwich Village auditorium and seven speakers addressed seven key women's rights, one speech was titled "The Right to Her Name." That speaker was actress Fola La Follette (the daughter of liberal Wisconsin senator Robert La Follette), who had kept her birth name when she married playwright George Middleton.[85]

Many other members had kept their names and most, like La Follette, had established professional reputations under those names before they married. This was true of Hale as well. And she had every reason to believe she would become better known after her marriage, for she and Broun were primed to advance in their careers, thanks to the jobs awaiting them that summer. The United States had entered World War I in April, and Broun (no doubt with Hale's urging) had managed to obtain a position as a war correspondent for his paper. Similarly, after what must have been far more complex machinations, she had been hired as a reporter for the soon-to-be-launched Army Edition of the *Chicago Tribune.*

Both would be based in Paris, where they would, of course, need to communicate in the language each had studied much earlier, Hale at the Hollins Institute and Broun at Harvard. Fortunately for Broun, although he had repeatedly failed his French class, Hale had earned an average grade of ninety-six in hers.[86]

Their jobs started in early July and traveling to France would take time, so they could not wait long for their wedding. But planning the event proved more difficult than Hale had anticipated. She wanted a quick city hall ceremony, bereft of religious ritual, with a few friends as witnesses. This was not how Henrietta Brose Broun envisioned the long-awaited nuptials of her favorite child. She wanted the couple to have a "proper" religious ceremony in fashionable St. Agnes Episcopal Church on West Ninety-Second Street. As for Broun, his son was sure he "just wanted to get married without making anybody angry."[87]

To his relief and surprise, Hale gave in to his mother regarding the location of the ceremony, and a church wedding was quickly scheduled. She even consented to being "given away" by her brother Shelton, who traveled from Washington to do the honors. One of her friends from Heterodoxy, actress Margaret Wycherly, agreed to be the maid of honor, also lending the couple her limousine and chauffeur for their prewedding trip to city hall to obtain their license.[88]

Having compromised on the place and type of ceremony, however, Hale was adamant that it must be modified in three ways. First, she and Broun would not exchange wedding rings. She refused to wear one. Second, the bride's customary agreement to obey her husband would be struck from the service. Third, there would be, she asserted, "no goddamn music—no marching down the aisle to Mendelssohn."[89]

These rules having been agreed upon, on June 6 she set out for the ceremony with her mother and brothers, unaware that her future mother-in-law had heavily armed herself for one more battle at the church.[90]

CHAPTER 6

"A married woman who claims her name is issuing a challenge"

ENTERING THE BACK OF THE church at which she had grudgingly agreed to be married, the bride heard the opening chords of Mendelssohn's wedding march rumbling from the organ. The groom's mother, who had broken her word and hired an organist, sat in her pew and smiled. Her smile dimmed when the bride did not appear. Instead, into the second chorus, a messenger tiptoed down the side aisle to Henrietta Brose Broun and informed her that the bride was not going to move until the music stopped.[1]

Mrs. Broun resisted through another full repetition, then surrendered, dispatching the messenger to the organ loft. "In mid-bar the church was suddenly, eerily, silent and Ruth Hale came sternly down the aisle," wrote her son, picturing a scene that had been described to him many times. "It was the purposeful tread of the crusader as she marched toward the passive, perspiring man who was distributing placatory smiles to everyone in view."[2]

The edited service proceeded as she had planned. The word "obey" was never uttered, no wedding rings were exchanged, and she left the church determined to remain Miss Ruth Hale. Yet she still felt, her son said, that "by agreeing to show up at a foolish place to go through an outmoded ritual, she had led the enemy to doubt her resolution." At least the couple's best man, wit Franklin Pierce Adams, offered the wedding guests an apt description of the two main characters in the drama they had just witnessed. He pronounced Heywood Broun and Ruth Hale "the clinging oak and the sturdy vine."[3]

A few days later the newlyweds boarded a passenger liner that would take them far from their difficult mothers and to France, where Broun was to serve as a war correspondent for the *New York Tribune* and Hale as a reporter for the *Chicago Tribune*'s nascent Army Edition. They encountered the war even before they landed when a German submarine's torpedo barely missed hitting their steamer. Broun hastily left his poker game in the lounge and joined Hale. They donned lifejackets, rushed to the deck, and watched the ship's guns return fire as the submarine's periscope vanished underwater. Another passenger, railroad heir William K. Vanderbilt, was less interested in the activity. He "did not put on a life preserver nor did he leave his deck chair," Broun wrote in his first story for the *Tribune*. "He sat up just a bit and watched the whole affair tolerantly. After all the submarine captain was a stranger to him."[4]

The six months that followed in Paris were to be the happiest time in their marriage. After moving into a poorly heated apartment at 248 Boulevard Raspail near the Luxembourg Gardens, they began their new jobs.[5] Hale apparently helped launch the Army Edition, which debuted on July 4 with a goal of providing U.S. soldiers with news from home. Before long, however, it was selling well to American and British residents in Paris, perhaps because it not only reprinted the Chicago newspaper's stories sent to Paris (at great expense) by cable but ran its own war reports. Three factors did initially cause problems: paper was in short supply, the typesetters knew no English, and its editor, Joseph Pierson, knew no French.[6]

Hale's precise responsibilities are unknown, but she may well have been the understaffed paper's sole local reporter, and seems to have had some editorial and production responsibilities. Publishing fourteen columns of news every day, the Army Edition used the typesetters, type, and presses of Paris's *Le Petit Journal*, so pages had to be meticulously proofread to correct typographical errors. She would have excelled at this. As for her reporting experiences, Alexander Woollcott, her friend serving in the Army medical corps, wrote to an acquaintance that Hale "has been far nearer the front than I and can tell you many things I have never seen and may never see."[7]

Broun spent more time than she did near the front, although this former sportswriter and theater critic was an unlikely war correspondent. Disorganized by nature, hating guns, and squeamish around blood, he grew as a reporter even as he broke army rules, including those of dress. Accredited correspondents were supposed to wear neat officers' uniforms, but his was unkempt and topped by a black felt slouch hat. To circumvent the military censorship that infuriated him, he used the mails to send some of his reports to New York. He frequently wrote about the deeds and difficulties of ordinary soldiers, and often made it clear that he did not have a high opinion of the American Expeditionary Force leadership.[8]

When they weren't working, the couple found Paris life very agreeable, in part because friends from New York, including Franklin Pierce Adams and other journalists, were living in the city. The newlyweds' arrival was an excuse for many celebrations on the Left Bank, and Broun soon joined male friends for weekly poker games at a Montmartre bistro. Woollcott, who had taken a leave from his *New York Times* drama critic position and was stationed in a medical unit in the village of Savenay, spent time with them during what he called a "giddy series of Paris leaves," and was delighted when they visited him in Savenay. He was even happier when he obtained a furlough to stay with them over Christmas.[9]

But he was dismayed when they broke the news that they would be returning to New York after the holidays. Hale was six months pregnant with their son, who later was told they came back so he could be born in the United States and avoid citizenship problems. His own theory was that the army's complaints about Broun were most responsible for sending them home. He also believed his father had had enough of the war while his mother, already distrustful of medicine, may have been fearful of French doctors.[10]

At the same time, Broun's experience as a war correspondent meant he returned to his New York newspaper with strengthened credentials for advancement. With no such possibilities awaiting her, Hale left far more behind when they sailed in

January. Her son thought "those days in France were the last in which she felt in control of her own destiny and therefore happy in the enjoyment of that independence so fiercely wanted and yet so easily defeated."[11]

"She has a mind of her own (as well as a name)"

THAT SON, NAMED HEYWOOD BROUN but always called Woodie, was born on March 10, 1918. Hale's mother and mother-in-law criticized her for choosing Twilight Sleep as her anesthetic, but she said she was glad she did.[12] A combination of morphine and scopolamine intended to provide both partial pain relief and amnesia, Twilight Sleep was controversial. It could be extremely effective, but the correct dosage was difficult to determine and much could go wrong. Its strongest proponents were feminists who urged women to fight for access to this purported medical miracle and argued that most doctors' resistance was due to their insensitivity to women's suffering in childbirth. Hale found a doctor willing to administer the anesthetic, probably helped by her friend, Heterodoxy founder Marie Jenney Howe, who was a board member of the National Twilight Sleep Association.[13]

By the time of Woodie's birth Hale may have returned to her earlier job as a press agent for Arthur Hopkins. She certainly had done so by the fall of 1918, and she continued working as a theatrical publicist at least sporadically for three more years. In 1919 she was hired by Edgar Selwyn and in October 1921 by John Golden, both highly successful Broadway producers.[14]

Theatrical publicity jobs typically were cyclical or part-time since producers primarily needed press agents when plays were in production. They usually focused on placing stories in newspapers prior to and immediately following a play's opening, after which their tasks tended to be more routine until it closed.[15] This flexibility meant Hale could have worked around her responsibilities as a mother, which lessened appreciably in September 1918 when she hired eighteen-year-old Mattie Hester as live-in help. "Mattie learned quickly," Woodie later wrote, "and within another six months she could have taken care of me lovingly and capably during whatever working hours professional demands imposed on Ruth."[16]

Experienced theatrical publicists had little trouble finding work in 1920s New York, where there were some seventy theaters producing an average of 225 plays a year, as well as fourteen daily newspapers, most devoting substantial space to the theater.[17] At the top of her profession, Hale should have had her pick of good jobs. And she enjoyed working with people in the theater, some of whom remained her friends for many years. Yet in 1922 she apparently stopped doing this kind of work.[18] It must have been a comedown after all she had done in France. She had to want more.

She seemed on her way to something better in the summer of 1922 when she was hired by *Judge* to write its movie reviews, replacing the previous reviewer, Heywood Broun, who had been asked to write a sports column instead. Describing her qualifications, the humor magazine stressed her background as a *Philadelphia Pub-*

lic Ledger and *Vogue* drama critic, as well as her "press work" for "famous theatrical folk." It noted, too, "We believe Miss Hale is married," although it did not say to whom. And it ended by asserting, "She has a mind of her own (as well as a name) which she doesn't hesitate to make public."[19]

"Ruth Hale's Movie Page" ran weekly from August 12, 1922, through March 31, 1923. It took about a month for her to settle in and begin expressing her views in ways that might be useful to readers, and it was even longer before she found a movie she could praise. Yet her columns always were well informed and offered thoughtful analysis, and she shone when she was enthusiastic about a film or people involved in it. A clear problem, however, was that her writing was more complex, literary, and sophisticated than most of the rest of the magazine, as typified by a joke inserted as filler at the bottom of one of her columns: "*New Yorker*— Don't say Greenwich. It's pronounced Grennich. *Visitor*—Well, where in Grennich can I buy a sanich?"[20] Broun had no trouble writing light, broadly humorous columns, but this was not in Hale's nature.

Her interest in writing for *Judge* is understandable since its 1923 circulation was 250,000, the largest ever for an American humor magazine.[21] Her work had a large potential readership. But she must have known she did not belong there, and her column ended with no explanation, although she continued to contribute book reviews. She also reviewed books for the *New York World* and plays for the *Brooklyn Eagle*.[22] And for a brief period she was visible enough to warrant being singled out in an article in *Time*'s inaugural issue. She was, according to the magazine, a "slim, dark, eager" woman who "writes moving picture criticisms and book reviews" and "has a cleverness nearly as distinct as that of her versatile husband."[23]

The subject of that March 3, 1923, article was the Algonquin Round Table group, born in the early summer of 1919. Founding members present at its first lunch included Hale and Broun as well as two of their good friends, Woollcott, who was back at the *Times* as a drama critic, and Franklin Pierce Adams, by then a *New York Tribune* columnist. Also at that lunch (held to mock Woollcott) were two of Hale's publicist friends, John Peter Toohey and Murdock Pemberton, who came with his brother Brock, a former drama critic who had just been hired as Arthur Hopkins's assistant producer. Other founders were *New York Telegraph* reporter Marc Connelly and two more drama critics, George S. Kaufman of the *Times* and *Vanity Fair*'s Dorothy Parker—the only other woman charter member. She brought along her magazine's new drama editor, Robert Sherwood, and managing editor, Robert Benchley.[24]

In 1919 Adams was the group's most prominent member. His widely read column, written under the byline F.P.A., often recorded the remarks and activities of fellow Algonks, most of whom were not well known in 1919. Yet during the next decade many of them achieved significant success and fame, as did other New Yorkers who at some time were regulars at the table. These included composer Deems Taylor, artist Neysa McMein, lyricist Howard Dietz, and playwrights Charles MacArthur, Donald Ogden Stewart, and Edna Ferber. Charter members Connelly, Kaufman, Sherwood, and Benchley also became highly successful playwrights. Woollcott would become the best known of them all, thanks to an immensely popular radio program, his columns, a zest for the spotlight, and a flamboyant personality that helped make him a frequent subject of newspaper and magazine pieces, not to mention of Kaufman and Moss Hart's play *The Man Who Came to Dinner*.[25]

From the beginning, the Algonks' renown was helped along by the media attention they received. Members both wrote about each other and were a source of copious copy for other journalists, who quoted their (often well-rehearsed) witticisms. Their humor typically was irreverent, their put-downs as merciless as their puns were appalling. Part of the appeal of these almost-daily lunches was the camaraderie the diners found there and the strong affection many of them felt for each other. Still, their verbal swordplay was ferociously competitive.[26] "The dining-room corner was a hotbed of raconteurs and conversationalists," recalled comedian Harpo Marx. "But until I came along, there wasn't a full-time listener in the crowd. I couldn't have been more welcome if I had had the power to repeal Prohibition."[27]

Hale probably enjoyed these sessions more than Broun did because she was a better talker than he was and loved sparring with other good talkers. She also valued many of the women Algonks. The Round Table was "one of the few places where bright women and bright men got together," her son pointed out. "To be well received for your brain was important to most of the women there." Undeniably, the men made sexist jokes and eagerly admired attractive women who passed through their line of sight. But to Hale this simply was "firehouse behavior" that could not be changed and did little real damage. Equally important, her son said, she liked these men and liked being part of the group, "so she really did let it alone."[28]

Woodie remembered the Algonks well because he often spent time with them as a child. If there was no one to care for him at home and his parents wanted to go to the hotel for lunch, they rented a room for him there and let him order his favorite room-service dishes of chicken hash or oatmeal. A maid or bellhop would check in on him until, after his nap, he came down to the Rose Room to sit at the table.[29] "With my eyes at napkin level, I could see the exultation that gripped this improbable group of artistic arrivistes," he recollected, even as they "huddled around their table in bewilderment at their sudden eminence." Later, he understood that these adults had been "sophisticated innocents" who, "much to their surprise, exerted a powerful influence on American taste from 1919 until the onset of the Great Depression."[30]

"The layered little kingdoms of Eighty-Fifth Street"

HE SAW MUCH MORE OF them after May 1921, when Hale and Broun bought a brownstone at 333 West Eighty-Fifth Street that became an after-lunch gathering place for the group. The house also was the scene of weekly dinner parties (where their child was expected to converse interestingly with their well-read, highly verbal friends). And about once a month, the couple held a large party featuring a constantly replenished punchbowl of bootleg gin and orange juice. Guests included the core Algonks and a wide assortment of other friends, such as Jascha Heifetz, James Weldon and J. Rosamond Johnson, Edna St. Vincent Millay, Jules Bledsoe, Fyodor Chaliapin, Harpo Marx, and Ring Lardner. Additional visitors were in and out of the house constantly during the day, usually coming to see Hale. Her best friend, Dorothy Parker, was there often.[31]

The brownstone was an inviting place to visit and to live in. On the basement level were a nicely furnished dining room, poorly furnished kitchen, laundry room, and tiny bedroom for Mattie Hester, who had been uneducated and newly arrived from the rural South when she was hired in 1918. "Ruth taught Mattie to cook, she taught her to read, she taught her to be substantially a sophisticated person. And after she taught her to cook, I don't think Ruth ever boiled an egg," her son said. The highly adaptable Hester was the chaotic household's flywheel, not only taking excellent care of Woodie and creating (on a wood-burning stove) delicious meals for guests on short notice, but performing countless large and small, essential and trivial, routine and unusual tasks. She also had a deep friendship with Hale that enriched both their lives.[32]

Most socializing took place on the brownstone's first floor, which was Broun's floor. The heavy rolling doors dividing the one large room always were pulled back, creating an ideal gathering place with easy access to the kitchen via a dumbwaiter. The front of the room featured attractive, long triple windows and a green-tile fireplace, but it was dominated by an enormous electric grand player piano that was popular at parties. Visitors had to navigate around stacks of books on the floor and much other debris to get to the back area, which held Broun's massive bed and a table with his typewriter.[33]

When he wrote his column, his son remembered, Broun would "rise from the messy bed with its piles of open books, flattened out at various stages of completion, its baskets of letters, overflowing ashtrays, and crumpled covers," and begin typing, almost in a trance. "This done, he sent the model piece of personal essay art to his office and sank back into sloppiness, indecision, and the contemplation of all the problems outside of the easy job of journalism."[34]

The second floor was Hale's. On the back wall, over her bed, she had meticulously painted a squatting, three-foot-tall Aztec god. His body was green, he wore a red headdress, and he was thumbing his nose at the world. She called him her "defy"—her declaration of her defiance of authority—and loved that his gesture, seemingly so modern, was centuries old. The image, which she had copied from a photograph, said something about her discontent with her life, but she also meant it to be humorous. She was pleased, too, that it upset her mother.[35]

Her floor was furnished with a sofa, a delicate, heavily carved teak desk, and crammed bookshelves. More books were scattered throughout, and equally noticeable were ashtrays overflowing with the remains of the English Oval cigarettes that she smoked down to the end before immediately lighting another. Near the front windows, card tables held thousand-piece jigsaw puzzles, bundles of sharpened pencils, and grids for diagramless crossword puzzles (with no black boxes to indicate where words began and ended). These she restlessly spent more and more time solving in the succeeding years as she contemplated her own problems.[36]

The third floor housed her son's bedroom and the small, seldom-empty guest room that typically was occupied by an indigent artist or performer when Hale's brother or peripatetic mother wasn't staying there. Moderately successful as a baritone singer and actor, Richard Hale was charming, mild-mannered, and grateful for his sister's financial help, which included renting concert halls for his recitals. Other kinds of support were just as important, for she introduced him to influential people in the musical world and used her contacts to get him invited to parties where he knew he would be asked to sing. At these events, and the many times he sang at her parties, he gained exposure that led to jobs. But despite all he felt he owed his sister, his mother controlled him. And he insisted on assuming the thankless role of intermediary in the two women's never-ending battles that further disrupted the Hale/Broun marriage.[37]

Annie Riley Hale stayed with them out of economic necessity, her grandson explained, because "she did not make any money out of her endless campaigns against vaccination, vivisection, feminism, the economic policies of Theodore Roosevelt . . . and the mingling of the races." Yet not all of her causes were negative. She also waged what he described as "vigorous campaigns in favor of native American fascism and a diet free of white flour and animal flesh."[38] Her efforts truly were vigorous, for in addition to writing articles and books, she made speeches throughout the country (having particular success attracting audiences in California).[39] These trips kept her away from West Eighty-Fifth Street, but not for long enough. Woodie likened her to "a mosquito that bothers you and then comes back again. You never knew when she'd come buzzing in."[40]

Fortunately, he enjoyed most of the other people who stayed in the guest room on what was considered "his" floor. His uncle Richard was an affable companion, but the most welcome long-term guest was Ed McNamara. A former policeman turned rarely employed singer and actor, this Irishman cooked, cleaned, entertained, and generally was wonderful company. Woodie called McNamara "one of the two outside grown-ups with whom I felt the warmth of loving and being loved." The other was frequent visitor Paul Robeson. Although Robeson "had every right to be afraid of a genuinely unfair world," Woodie wrote, "in the years in which I knew him and worshipped him, he faced that world with a rumbling and confident joy."[41]

Not only did the child of the household have his own floor but his parents promised to always ask permission to enter his room. "When they asked, so quietly, 'May we come up?' they must surely have really been annoyed at the discovery that I had thrown a whole dressing-table set out the window, or traded my bicycle for a baseball," he recalled, "but no one would know it." He could only remember two times they raised their voices in anger at him. Yet perhaps the most striking symbol of their attempts at progressive childrearing was their insistence that he call them by their first names. They claimed this would make them equals.[42]

He, in turn, would try to become "the independent person they had wanted since they first set me on a telephone book at the dinner table and left me to deal with the witty dinner partners to my left and right." Although he eventually did become an excellent conversationalist, he always was unsure of how best to steer his way through what he called "the layered little kingdoms of Eighty-fifth Street," where, in reality, his parents offered him only a sham equality that sent contradictory, confusing messages.[43]

They did provide him with a superb caretaker and comrade in Mattie Hester. "I escaped the pressures of the first and second floors by clopclopping down the stairs to the kitchen where Mattie, to my pleasure, treated me as a very ordinary child," he remembered. She "blessedly made me forget that I had any obligation to be interesting."[44] Even as she offered him security, she was indispensable to his parents, and Hale made sure she knew that she deserved not only her high pay (thirty dollars a week plus room and board) but respect. Their guests, too, understood they should treat her well, something that did not please Annie Riley Hale, who also objected to the couple's many African American friends. "As far as she was concerned, Mattie hadn't even been freed by Lincoln," her grandson said, and his parents' devotion to her was yet another topic of arguments between his mother and grandmother.[45]

"Useful diversions"

Hester's "basement realm" was to the small boy "a kind of Switzerland compared to the chaotic kingdoms of the first and second floors." Those two floors captured his parents' efforts at independence. Theirs was to be a "new" marriage in which each partner's needs were equally important. Thus they entertained at home together but often went out separately, they seldom slept together, and during much of the time they were home they stayed on their own floors. It probably was Hale who insisted they both should feel free to have affairs.[46]

Their son explained: "They weren't happy but they were devoted. They tried to live apart as much as possible and needed each other very much. They disagreed about a great many important things and supported each other's beliefs."[47] Certainly they had friends with similar marriages—husbands and wives who were very unlike each other, had no intention of remaining faithful when they married, led quite separate lives, yet cared deeply about each other. Citing Mary Kennedy and Deems Taylor, Beatrice and George Kaufman, and Alice Duer Miller and Henry Wise Miller as examples, Woodie said "there were so many of those strange marriages at that time" that he barely noticed anything unusual about his parents' relationship.[48]

Irrespective of their philosophy on independence within marriage, sharp differences between Hale and Broun probably would have made it difficult for them to live in close contact for prolonged periods. She was tough-minded, strong-willed, disciplined, argumentative, and a perfectionist. Her mind was quicker and more logical than his. An omnivorous reader with excellent taste, she had little tolerance for mediocrity in literature or the arts. Once when a friend chastised her for lacking a sense of humor, she responded, "I thank God that the dead albatross of a sense of humor has never been hung around my neck." She actually was very witty and laughed often, but she rarely told jokes and was fundamentally a serious person who took herself seriously. And although she spoke extremely well, she wrote with difficulty.[49]

Broun was easygoing, shy, passive, and self-effacing. Despite his curious mind, he read in moderation. His tastes were middlebrow and he admitted, "I have never been able to learn the reasons for my enthusiasms." Far more sentimental than Hale, he loved telling jokes as much as he hated confrontation. Their son remembered "how powerfully she could wheel up the artillery of logic and facts until, deprived of every weapon save the sword of charm, he would twinkle his way out of the argument." But his father's greatest contrast to his mother was in "his non-precise approach to life that was embodied in his sloppy dress, sloppy speech, physical laziness." The one place he was not lazy was at his typewriter, where he wrote easily and often amusingly.[50]

Given these contrasts, it is unsurprising that they frequently were apart or surrounded by other people when they were together. In their son's analysis, "The waves of people washing through the house or lying agreeably stranded in the guest room were useful diversions."[51] He said the house almost always had visitors. They came to drink, talk, and play word games (at which Hale excelled) after Algonquin lunches; to drink, talk, and eat delicious dinners served by a handsome man in a white jacket; to drink, talk, sing around the piano, and listen to impromptu performances by people like Jascha Heifetz, Paul Robeson, and Richard Hale at parties; to drink, talk, and snack on leftovers after the theaters and speakeasies closed in the early morning.[52]

Ironically, the southern upbringing she despised helped make Hale a gracious hostess. Visitors were drawn to 333 West Eighty-Fifth Street not only by the good food and ample alcohol but by the company and conversation. Hale had beautiful manners and (like her friend Doris Fleischman) was an excellent listener. Much as she loved to argue, she believed it was important to treat other people well.[53] As her son wrote, "For all her fanaticism, Ruth exercised a charm that was an effective emollient for the abrasions she dealt out when being what she called straightforward and other people called frightening."[54] "When she chose to be charming," he explained, "she was overwhelmingly charming."[55]

He thought many people first came to the house because Broun was well-known and they liked him, but they came back because they wanted to spend more time with Hale. In addition to being welcoming and considerate of her guests, she was exceptionally articulate and had a huge vocabulary. Woodie called her "the best-informed person in matters pertaining to the arts that I have ever met."[56] Visitors could expect conversations with her to be lively and thought-provoking. "She didn't waste your time with clichés or well-worn ideas," he remembered. "She could speak interestingly about interesting things. She knew theater, she knew books, she knew all about the things that make up our culture."[57]

Broun wanted the "useful diversions" of these visitors as much as Hale did, but he played no part in the complex mechanics of the couple's entertaining. Similarly, he was uninvolved in running their household and raising their son. These obligations were Hale's, just as she was in charge of getting Broun through the day. He was a hypochondriac, suffered from innumerable phobias, had no sense of how much money he made or spent, was tremendously disorganized and forgetful, and needed help simply dressing (usually very badly) and going out into the world. In his son's words, "It was as if she had a very large child who had to be told what to do."[58]

Although Woodie faulted his father for his "avoidance of all responsibilities except those to his job," Broun certainly did meet those responsibilities.[59] Returning from France in early 1918, he resumed his old job as the *Tribune*'s drama critic until, a year later, he was promoted to the dual positions of literary editor and drama editor. He also wrote a regular Sunday feature on new plays and a thrice-weekly column called "Books," as well as sometimes reviewing plays, covering major sports events, and writing for the Sunday magazine. But he was best known for his column, which was retitled "Books and Things" after he began writing less about books (in part because that saved him the work of reading them) and more about himself.[60]

He claimed the change occurred when, facing a deadline but with "no novel or travel tome under my belt," as a last resort he wrote about his own life. Soon the managing editor told him, "Those casual pieces of yours are better than your book reviews," and he took this "ambiguous remark" to mean "it was possible to get paid for the very simple task of writing about yourself and you own experiences."[61] Thus Broun became what his son described as "the kind of colorful columnist–personal diarist who was to be the phenomenon of the twenties and thirties, the sort of person who one day talked about the world and the next about a birthday necktie."[62]

For all the job's advantages, it paid only about a hundred dollars a week, and he disliked working for a Republican paper whose conservative editorial stands he sometimes opposed in his column. So in August 1921 he moved to the *New York World*, the city's most liberal newspaper and one that its energetic executive editor, Herbert Bayard Swope, was determined to make more interesting and exciting. Among Swope's innovations was the page across from the editorial page where, as he put it, "I decided to print opinions, ignoring facts." His promise that the page's writers would have free rein in the topics they chose and viewpoints they expressed helped him attract Broun and, shortly afterward, Broun's friends Adams and Woollcott.[63]

Encouraged by Swope to be provocative, Broun agreed to write a column titled "It Seems to Me." He soon was earning a salary of $250 a week (equivalent to about $3,000 in today's dollars), thanks to the column's popularity and his additional work for the *World*, which in 1922 included theater reviews and a syndicated book column. Nor was that the full extent of his productivity. That same year, he wrote a weekly column for *Judge* and an article a month for *Collier's*, *Vanity Fair*, and *Atlantic Monthly*.[64]

Also in 1922, Broun and Hale both contributed chapters to *Nonsenseorship*, a collection of humorous essays subtitled "Sundry Observations Concerning Prohibitions, Inhibitions and Illegalities." They each made fun of Prohibition, but in ways that show the marked differences in their thinking, wit, and writing. Broun's chapter sounds much like "It Seems to Me." Mainly ruminations on the misguided reasoning behind public denunciations of a variety of pleasurable activities, the easy-to-read piece flows smoothly and features casually strung-together examples, nonstop gentle humor, and a mocking but congenial tone.[65]

In a chapter typical of her writing style and thought processes, Hale takes a very different approach. Her satire is much sharper as she describes how women always have expertly circumvented formal restrictions on their lives. "If the world outside the home is to become as circumscribed and paternalized as the world inside it, obviously all the advantage lies with those who have been living under nonsenseorship long enough to have learned to manage it," she argues. Now that it is illegal to buy liquor in America, she predicts that men will need women to teach them "how to live under prohibitions and taboos."[66]

Her piece is full of information on women's legal and societal barriers in areas ranging from birth control to serving on juries, and of historical and literary references. These, combined with an intricate, sometimes convoluted sentence structure, make it far more challenging to read than Broun's essay. For example, she asserts that, with their freedoms curtailed throughout history, "Women had to do all the outwitting and circumventing, all the little smart twists and turns, all the cunning scheming by which people snatch off what they want without appearing to, whereas men got their much or their little by prosily sticking their hands out for it."[67]

She clearly devoted far more care and thought to her chapter than Broun did to his, not only because writing was much more difficult for her but because she had more to say. As her son noted of her writing overall, "She wanted it to be perfect, so she put more and more ideas into it, and filled the bucket with more water than it could hold."[68] Still, here her approach is cleverer than Broun's, her humor more finely honed, her points wittier and more perceptive. At the same time, the appeal of her piece is narrower. Broun already had perfected an engaging, staccato writing style that easily drew the reader along. She lacked his light touch.

"Ruth Hale was looking over my shoulder"

EVEN MORE REVEALING THAN THE contents of the two chapters are the accompanying caricatures. Next to his chapter, a very large, rumpled, pleasant-looking Broun is shown cradling a jester's staff as his head breaks through the top of the frame, all over a caption reading, "Heywood Broun Finds America Suffering from a Dearth of Folly." Hale's chapter is illustrated with a smaller female figure confidently sitting atop a house that is about her same size, making her look enormous. Wearing a tailored, almost mannish dress and a serious expression, she holds a pair of fireplace tongs as a symbol of her power. The caption reads, "Ruth Hale as a XXth Century Woman Guarding the Home Brew." Yet no home brew is shown. All that can be seen, through a corner window, is a stout, cigarette-smoking man pounding on a typewriter.

Illustrator Ralph Barton probably simply meant to make a sly reference to Hale as Broun's wife (something unmentioned in the book) and to her assertive nature. But the image says much more, capturing a collaboration that was fully developed by that time, although few people were aware of it. Hale is shown not only "guarding the home"—that center of constant activity where her husband had no responsibilities—but also looming over his work. Barton actually was providing part of the explanation for why Broun was so prolific and successful.

For all his ease with written words, Broun never was able to accurately describe Hale's role in his work. The day after she died, he made this confession in "It Seems to Me": "A very considerable percentage of all newspaper columns, books and magazine articles which appeared under the name 'Heywood Broun' were written by Ruth Hale. I mean, of course, the better columns. And even those I felt I was writing on my own stemmed from her."[69] Driven by grief and guilt, he fell back on his gift for simplifying to make larger points. In the process he both exaggerated and told the truth, for unquestionably she wrote only a very small portion of what appeared under his name. What she did for him was far more complex.

He was accurate when he said his writing stemmed from her. Before they were married she pushed him to apply for the *Tribune* drama critic position despite his minimal qualifications, and probably helped him write some reviews. In France the challenges were much greater. Both of them were doing work unlike anything they had ever done before, even as they tried to quickly understand unfamiliar events in an unfamiliar country. Living together in a small apartment, they inevitably would have turned to each other for help. He later wrote, "When we met we were reporters, and I have never denied that Ruth Hale was the better newspaperman of the two."[70] She also was a much more focused thinker and far more disciplined than he was.[71] And once she was living with him, so more aware of his weaknesses—including his serious problems meeting deadlines—she would have been even more strongly motivated to help him.[72]

Whatever her specific involvement in his day-to-day reporting, it seems certain that she influenced one aspect of it. He often wrote critically about military censorship and American Expeditionary Force leaders, especially when he believed their actions were causing unnecessary hardships for the enlisted men whose perspectives he worked hard to include in his stories.[73] Unexpectedly, this admittedly timid man was becoming a fighter. It was the beginning of the kind of defense of the underdog and protest against the misuse of authority for which he would become legendary a decade later. And he could not have started down that path without Hale.

Part of her appeal to him was that she was an idealist and rebel. Their son noted that "Heywood would go to great lengths to avoid an argument while Ruth sought them out with the zeal of a missionary."[74] Broun's psychiatrist went on to label him "a 'phantophobe,' or one almost universally phobic," Woodie wrote. "Ruth could not allay all those fears, but with her determination she could help him fight them and remind him that whatever the cost he had a larger fight on his hands that would need his attention every day, the forwarding of his beliefs."[75]

In 1917 she undoubtedly objected as much as he did—if not more—to press restrictions, poorly planned and executed military operations, and disregard for soldiers' well-being. With his job at stake, he would not have protested perceived wartime wrongs without her approval. But she had to have gone beyond providing approval, particularly considering how forcefully she was to prod him into action a decade later, when, as one of their friends remembered, "It was Ruth Hale who, more often that not, buckled on Heywood's armor and sent him into battle."[76] Surely she helped forge that armor in France.

After they returned to New York in 1918 and he returned to reviewing plays, they lived with their infant son in a two-bedroom apartment at 200 West Fifty-Sixth Street. Broun's promotion the next year put him in a much more demanding job; he reviewed plays and books, did substantial additional writing for the *Tribune*, and directed the paper's theater and book reviewers. In contrast, although she had Mattie Hester to take care of Woodie and handle other household tasks, Hale was doing only sporadic and unchallenging theatrical publicity work.

This must have been when the couple's full-scale collaboration began. Much as Broun wanted to move ahead and was doubly motivated by the need to provide most of his family's financial support, he would have had trouble handling all of his *Tribune* responsibilities without help. He confessed to being basically lazy, once writing that his ambitions had been "seriously compromised by a monstrous inertia."[77] And he was notorious for missing deadlines. Even in an effusive eulogy for Broun after his death, a longtime admirer felt the need to note, "He was always late with everything."[78]

At first he probably most relied on her to help with his reviews. He could be an amusing book reviewer but tended to favor short books because he could read them rapidly, and he was not a very good judge of quality. "She knew what was first-rate and he didn't," their son observed. "He only knew what appealed to him, and what appealed to him was sentimental."[79] Tremendously well-read, Hale was conversant with works ranging from French philosophy to Irish classics to controversial new American fiction. Her judgments probably shaped both his book and drama criticism, even though he had written about the theater for so long that he would hardly have had trouble finding something to say in his reviews. Yet here, too, he had a weakness for sentimentality; her taste and insight were far superior. He also struggled with the next-morning deadlines of theater criticism.[80]

Woodie thought his mother contributed to his father's reviews in several ways: by recommending works, helping him understand them, talking through what he should address in writing about them, and finishing reviews when he was late. In addition, he thought she often suggested topics for Broun's freelance magazine pieces and probably finished some of them for him. She may even have written substantial portions, for he generally treated these articles as a low priority, and they did not require as distinct a "Broun voice" as his other writings.[81]

By early 1922 Broun was settled in at the *World*, still writing drama and book reviews but best known for "It Seems to Me." He needed little help in the actual writing of the column since this was something he could do quickly, in an almost transfixed state. It was the only work he consistently handed in on time. But Hale did help greatly in forming and improving columns. They bought every edition of every English-language New York newspaper and constantly discussed current issues. It was common for her to suggest column topics, for the two of them to talk through columns before he sat down to write them, and for him to ask her to critique them for such things as logic and organization before he handed them in.[82]

As he worked on his columns and other pieces, Hale "focused his vision," their son explained. "It's as if you get a new pair of glasses and can see better."[83] Using her "precise, surgical-knife mind," she taught Broun—who "had the mind of a surgical sponge that wipes up after the knife has done the operation"—to think harder, reason better, write more effectively.[84] As Broun himself put it in 1934: "I suppose that for seventeen years practically every word I wrote was set down with the feeling that Ruth Hale was looking over my shoulder."[85]

"Will keep her identity"

BROUN'S REPUTATION AND INFLUENCE GREW so quickly that in 1921 he was recognized with an entry in *Who's Who*.[86] His career was rapidly advancing as Hale's declined, and as she was helping him do the work that made him well-known. That same year, though, she began to attract attention for a different kind of work: her crusade for women's right to keep their birth names when they married.

She had been fighting for her own name since her June 1917 wedding, facing her first legal obstacle when she applied for a passport prior to sailing for France and could not obtain one as Ruth Hale. Back in New York the next year, she began researching women's legal rights by consulting with other married women who had kept their birth names and with women lawyers and male jurists, including federal judge Learned Hand.[87]

Hoping to visit postwar France in 1920, she again applied for a passport and eventually was sent one with compromise identification: "Mrs. Heywood Broun, otherwise known as Ruth Hale." She promptly returned it. In February 1921 her lawyer asked the secretary of state for a ruling on the matter, but this only resulted in the offer of another unacceptable compromise: "Ruth Broun (otherwise known as Ruth Hale)." In yet another try that fall, she asked to be identified as "Ruth Hale, wife of Heywood Broun." This request, too, was denied, and she was never to receive an acceptable passport.[88] "When the verdict went against her," Broun wrote, "she decided she would rather remain Miss Hale in America than be Mrs. Heywood Broun in any garden spot of the old world. It would have spoiled the scenery for her."[89]

Women's names were much on her mind in the summer of 1920 when she and Broun rented Woodie's temporarily vacant bedroom (he was staying at the beach with relatives) to their friends Jane Grant and Harold Ross, who had married that spring and were in urgent need of a place to live because of the postwar housing shortage. Grant, the *New York Times* hotel reporter, had impulsively decided to keep her birth name right after her wedding, and that summer the two women often talked about their shared problems in using their names. Ross once became so irritated by those discussions that he exclaimed, "Aw, why don't you two hire a hall?"[90]

Rather than hiring a hall, the following spring they invited a few like-minded women to meet with them in Hale's living room. Galvanized, these women invited still others to a meeting on April 28, 1921, during which the group voted to form an "organization to encourage women to retain their own names" and to name it after Lucy Stone, the nineteenth-century women's rights activist who had kept her birth name when she married Henry Blackwell. Adopting as their slogan her words, "My name is the symbol of my own identity and must not be lost," they elected Hale president and Grant secretary-treasurer.[91] Thirteen Heterodoxy members joined the Lucy Stone League, and several—including Fola La Follette, Charlotte Perkins Gilman, Crystal Eastman, and Zona Gale—served on its executive committee.[92]

Hale was a logical choice for president since she had just finished a successful campaign to persuade the Waldorf-Astoria to permit married women to register in their birth names, was engaged in a passport fight she was to lose, and had almost completed another fight for her name that she was to win. On May 14, 1921, she became the first married woman in New York City to have her birth name incorporated on a real estate deed. The deed to the West Eighty-Fifth Street brownstone she and Broun had just bought (for $28,500) was made out to "Heywood Broun and Ruth Hale, his wife." A subhead of the *New York Times* story about the document read: "Will Keep Her Identity."[93]

The primary purpose of the league was not to change laws (inasmuch as no law required a woman to use her husband's name) but to inform the public that American women had the legal right to use their birth names after they married. Women would be educated about their rights, and business and government policy makers would be pressured to let women use whatever names they chose. Thus extensive media coverage was crucial to the league's success, which explains why at the group's April 28 meeting four officers were elected: president, vice president, secretary-treasurer, and publicity director. In addition, many early members were journalists or press agents who well knew how to attract publicity.[94]

Hale took advantage of the attention her real estate deed received when, in her *Times* interview about the deed, she announced the time and place of the league's first public meeting. This may have increased attendance, but the main reason for the newspaper coverage the event subsequently received was the league's use of a powerful media-attracting device: celebrities. Popular actress Elsie Ferguson and playwright (and wife of actor John Barrymore) Michael Strange rose from the audience and asked Hale questions about using their birth names. Both women were members of the league's executive committee so hardly needed to make inquiries in public, but doing so helped put the story at the top of the *Times* theater page. Since most league dinners and public meetings featured well-known people debating whether married women should keep their birth names, newspaper stories inevitably followed.[95]

As the organization found more ways to obtain media coverage, interest in it and its cause grew. And as women read these stories and learned about their rights, more decided to keep their birth names and use them in legal transactions. Some of those decisions in turn became news, especially when the women were prominent. Growing familiarity with the league then helped make its subsequent activities—such as sending a lawyer to Washington to argue that Hale should receive a passport in her birth name—newsworthy.[96]

Magazines carried their own stories about women keeping their birth names. Probably the first, written by league member Signe Toksvig, ran in the July 1921

New Republic. The magazine's editor was Francis Hackett, Toksvig's husband and another league member. Since magazine writers had more time and space to develop their points, the league's defenders could make a stronger case, and those who opposed it had more to attack. So some magazines carried spirited arguments about the organization, giving it still more publicity.[97] Hale joined this fight when she answered a December 1921 *Bookman* article that criticized the league. "A married woman who claims her name is issuing a challenge," she wrote in her response. "It is a defiance, and as such is dealt with by society, under a hundred euphemisms, always with hostility."[98]

Francis Hackett used his position to help the league early on, but two other male members did far more. One was Edward L. Bernays, who joined in June 1921 and immediately began suggesting ways the group could increase its membership and attract more media attention. He attended meetings, joined its executive committee, had his office produce league press releases, and gathered the views of "opinion leaders" to use in campaigns.[99] His primary tactic, he said, was to stress conflict: "I recognized that if we articulated support for our viewpoint from leading liberals, their position and ours would be enhanced if we simultaneously played up the reactionary opposition to the movement."[100]

The other man who did much for the league was Heywood Broun. He began attending meetings in the spring of 1921 (he and Bernays usually were the only males present), joined its executive committee the next year, and often was one of the speakers at its public events, beginning with its first dinner in March 1922. His growing renown helped attract the media to these events, just as the fact that Hale was married to a well-known husband (whose name she rejected) helped make her league work more newsworthy. References to the league, its principles, and its campaigns also regularly appeared in "It Seems to Me," usually casually dropped into columns among other items or mentioned incidentally in accounts of Broun's everyday life (where Hale often was called "Miss X").[101] In this way he made the cause seem all the more commonplace.

"Heywood would pitch in for the Lucy Stoners at any time," his son said, contrasting him with Harold Ross, who "wouldn't do anything." Broun provided moral support for Hale and practical support for the organization, although that backing came at some cost. His parents were strongly opposed to the league, convinced that it was "some kind of radical madness." And many of his male friends—whose reactions were important to him—thought he was being henpecked. But he told them, "This is what I really believe."[102]

"The barbed-steel tether of dependence"

MUCH WENT WELL FOR HALE and Broun in 1922. The year began happily as they celebrated their first New Year's Eve at 333 West Eighty-Fifth Street, surrounded, as they so often were, by other people. Their party attracted some two hundred guests, among them best-selling British author H. G. Wells, who was not his mother's favorite visitor, Woodie recalled, because "he was always pinching her behind." But that night he was a popular attraction and signed autographs for Franklin Pierce Adams and other impressed visitors.[103]

As the year progressed Hale would have had many good reasons to feel hopeful about the turns her life was taking. She "appeared to be a rocket of energy and had soared successfully through a productive decade," Woodie wrote, apparently thinking about this time period. "Alert to everything that was happening, precise in speech and thought, she seemed a success machine in excelsis, ready to move into high gear at any moment."[104]

She had cofounded an organization that was fighting for a cause she cared deeply about. Newspapers and magazines were paying attention to the Lucy Stone League, more women were keeping their birth names when they married, and more businesses and government bodies were permitting women to use their birth names in areas they controlled. The league also kept her closely connected to other accomplished, dynamic women.

No longer a theatrical press agent, she was writing a weekly movie column for *Judge*. This could not have paid much but it gave her a byline and may have seemed to be taking her in a promising new direction. Even though she had given up the routine contacts with people in the worlds of theater and journalism that were a rewarding part of publicity work (and one of her strengths), she was working with interesting league members, more than holding her own with the ever-more-successful Algonks during long lunches, and socializing with stimulating people who frequently were in her home.

She also had more time to help Broun, who was thriving professionally and earning a sizable income. Surely this was of no small importance to someone who had watched her mother suddenly forced to provide for her children following her husband's death, who had left art school to begin working as a journalist at age eighteen, and who had supported herself (often while subsidizing other family members) for more than a decade. Now she had the freedom to turn down theatrical publicity jobs that would not challenge her. And the reputation she had earned from doing those jobs well, from her Lucy Stone League activism, and from her *Judge* column gave her enough visibility to warrant particular notice in *Time*'s March 3, 1923, article about the Round Table.

Yet her column would cease with no explanation four weeks after that *Time* article ran, she would publish little afterward, and the league would remain active for just a few more years. In contrast, Broun soon would be one of the country's most popular and influential newspaper columnists, while the woman who was unswerving in arguing that married women should be known by their birth names would continue to anonymously shape his work.

By 1922 the couple was inextricably caught in what their son called "the barbed-steel tether of dependence that held them together."[105] Although they increasingly would live separately, that tether would bind them all the more tightly in the years that followed. No wonder their son characterized them as "two complicated people who were desperately trying to hang on to each other even as their disparate natures were pulling them apart."[106]

He recalled a time during the summer of 1922 when those disparate natures were strikingly evident. The family was staying in a rented house in the Hudson Valley countryside when a thunderstorm approached. Afraid of innumerable things but especially of thunder, Broun fled to town. Hale remained in the house and was sitting in an armchair with Woodie on her lap when they heard a deafening sound, then watched a fireball hurl down an ungrounded electrical wire to the base of a nearby lamp, where it exploded. She did not move. Afterward, when the small boy asked why, she told him, "I didn't want you to be afraid. I thought if I wasn't afraid, you wouldn't be."[107]

The rest of her life would be marked by storms of other kinds as she took on new causes, continually battled to "keep her identity," and dealt with myriad disappointments. But she never stopped fighting. And few ever doubted her fearlessness.

Hale at age eighteen, around the time she left art school in Philadelphia and moved to Washington, D.C., to begin her journalism career.
Courtesy of Heywood Hale Broun.

In this 1918 portrait with her perplexed-looking infant son, Hale strikes a highly uncharacteristic sentimental pose. Manning Harris was the photographer. *Courtesy of Heywood Hale Broun.*

"This is the face with which Ruth defied [Secretary of State] Charles Evans Hughes and all the hosts who spoke of compromise," her son wrote, in describing this early-1920s portrait. *Courtesy of Heywood Hale Broun.*

Heywood Broun in 1922, his first full year at the *New York World*, where his column "It Seems to Me" already was one of the newspaper's most popular features. *Courtesy of Heywood Hale Broun.*

RUTH HALE AS A XXTH CENTURY WOMAN GUARDING THE HOME BREW

In this illustration accompanying Hale's humorous essay in the 1922 anti-censorship book *Nonsenseorship*, artist Ralph Barton—perhaps unknowingly—captured her role in Broun's work.

Highly regarded for his portraits of New York celebrities, Nickolas Muray
also was Hale's good friend, which may account for her letting a little
vulnerability show when he photographed her here. She was a chain smoker.
Courtesy of Heywood Hale Broun.

Heywood Hale Broun's parents began treating him like an adult at an
early age. He remembered, for example, that when he was too small to
reach the table at their frequent dinner parties, they boosted his chair with
a telephone book and "left me to deal with the witty dinner partners to
my left and right." He grew up to become an excellent conversationalist.
Courtesy of Heywood Hale Broun.

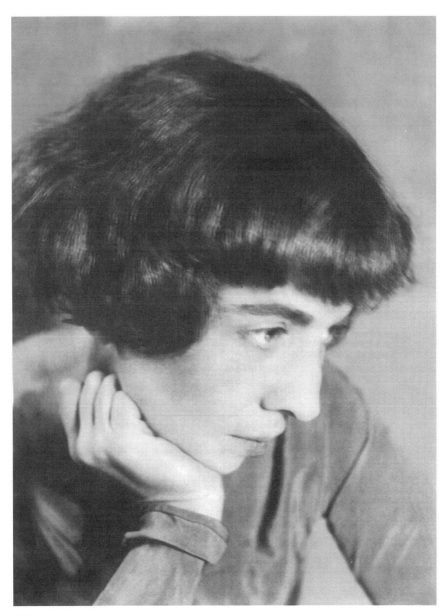

Hale looks thoughtful in this photograph, probably taken in 1928. The title of the magazine article it accompanied asked, "Has Modern Woman Disrupted the Home?" *Courtesy of Heywood Hale Broun.*

ANNIE RILEY HALE

The First Woman Candidate
FOR
United States Senator
From The State of California
and the
FIRST
MEDICAL FREEDOM
Candidate In History

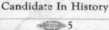 5

Rise Above Prejudice and Partizanry

REGISTER AS A DEMOCRAT BEFORE JULY 21st, and vote in
the August Primaries for the woman who is fighting the MEDICAL
TRUST, the MUNITION MAKERS, and the RACKETEERING
RULE of the lawless liquor trade.

VOTE FOR
ANNIE RILEY HALE

and for Medical Freedom, World Peace, Economic Reconstruction and Prohibition Reform

Annie Riley Hale, her daughter Ruth's constant adversary, was a
fervent antisuffragist. Yet she happily voted once women had that
right, and in 1932 entered the California Democratic primary,
hoping to become the party's U.S. Senate candidate. This two-sided
campaign card shows the idiosyncratic platform that helped her
attract more than 7,000 votes (versus the winner's approximately
262,000 votes). *Courtesy of Patrick S. Hale.*

CHAPTER 7

"It was a curious collaboration"

EARLY IN 1923 HALE DID something that would bring her great pleasure but seemed the height of folly. She bought ninety-four acres of infertile land—complete with an eleven-acre shallow lake, two dilapidated houses, and a barn—about eight miles north of Stamford, Connecticut. Inhabited by a family of squatters and several dozen chickens, the larger house was almost two hundred years old and sagging severely from age, neglect, and the rotting wooden pegs that (barely) held its hand-hewn beams in place. The second house was in almost as sorry shape. Broun thought this was a dubious investment and refused to contribute to its purchase, so Hale paid for it with her own savings, telling him he could visit as her guest. She was "buoyed by her delight in a place of her own," Woodie wrote, "a place where she hoped to achieve the deepest and most impossible of her dreams, independence."[1]

She immediately named it Sabine Farm after the Roman poet Horace's elegant retreat, although Woodie noted that "it looked as Horace's place must have looked after the Goths, Gauls and Vandals had passed over it several times." That spring, the squatters and chickens were evicted from the farmhouse and many of the interior walls dividing the first floor into tiny rooms were demolished, causing the ceiling to sag and necessitating the construction of expensive hidden supports. The resulting structure had six very small upstairs bedrooms and, downstairs, a medium-sized bedroom and a large living room with a huge stone hearth. Attached to the back wall was a kitchen shed with a cast iron kerosene stove, well-head, and dirt floor.[2]

In midsummer she moved in with Woodie and Mattie Hester, who said the kitchen shed reminded her of the kind of place she had come north to escape. Much was lacking, including electricity, indoor plumbing, and any source of heat beyond the fireplace. A hungry population of rats also was in residence. Nevertheless, Broun came to visit, as did Dorothy Parker, Ed McNamara, and other New York friends. Three more friends stayed in the barn for the rest of the summer, making the long walk to the house for meals that Hester somehow was expertly producing in spite of the unpredictable stove and necessity of drawing water from the well in a bucket. By summer's end Hale was certain that her purchase had been a wise one, and she added to her pleasure of proprietorship by naming her pond Hale Lake.[3]

It apparently was Broun's desire to visit Sabine Farm that led them to hire Earl Wilson in 1923. Phobic about the closed spaces of trains and too nervous to travel in a car driven by Hale (although she enjoyed driving and was proud of doing it well), Broun's solution was to hire a chauffeur. Wilson drove his tense passenger back and forth to Connecticut and delivered his columns to the Stamford Western Union station to be sent to the *World*. Later that same year he married Mattie Hester (who became Mattie Wilson) and moved into her West Eighty-Fifth Street room with her.[4]

He was not terribly busy as a chauffeur in the summer and did little driving during the rest of the year since Broun kept a cab driver on call in the city, so he soon became the family's houseman, a role for which he was perfectly suited. He had been raised in an African American middle-class Indiana family, attended college for a year, and, Woodie recalled, "had a rich baritone voice and the features of a leading man." He also was another patient, agreeable caretaker for the boy, helped in the kitchen, and served as a handyman. But he most enjoyed putting on a white coat and offering food and drinks to their famous guests, many of whose names he already knew.[5] They in turn were impressed with his good looks, regal bearing, and the fact that, as Woodie put it, "he was the only person in the house who met Ruth's standards of speech." Like her, he spoke perfect stage English.[6]

Around the same time Wilson joined the household, Hale decided it would benefit from one more addition. Still a bit of a country girl, she wanted a dog. At Manhattan's Speyer Animal Hospital she asked to see the most miserable, alienated animal available for adoption and was shown to a room where a large Airedale-like dog who had refused to eat for several days was whining and running in circles. She sat with him for hours while he continued running and whining, until suddenly he stopped in front of her and put his head in her lap. She brought him home.[7]

There "he signaled his fealty by pinning Heywood to a bed and growling in a menacing manner as an indication that no one was to touch his new friend," Woodie wrote. "Heywood, who was afraid of elevators, rooms too small and rooms too big, crowds, and cars, was surprisingly quite cool and brave in this dilemma." He remained motionless while the animal "debated tearing out his throat, and when Ruth got the dog off him, said nothing about getting rid of him." This proved to be to his advantage because in addition to being devoted to Hale and much loved by Woodie, the dog "provided him with a large number of columns."[8]

"By Ruth Hale"

HALE CAREFULLY WORKED OUT PLANS for shoring up, expanding, and furnishing her farmhouse. The earliest additions were a screened back porch and a kitchen with a cement floor, followed by a small bedroom off the master bedroom and a large enclosed front porch. An old upright piano was found for the living room. Still, the house stayed primitive in many ways, the most notable being its lack of indoor plumbing. Instead, there was a two-hole privy at considerable distance from the house, and people who wanted to bathe were welcome to bring soap to the pond. The hand pump soon added to the kitchen well made it somewhat easier to obtain water, which could be heated in a pot on the stove, but the kerosene smell was disagreeable. With no electricity, kerosene lamps provided light.[9]

Her solution to salvaging the smaller house was to let her good friend Murdock Pemberton, a theatrical publicist and fellow Algonquin Round Table founder, stay there for free. A closet handyman, he industriously fixed it up himself. Two other advantages of giving him the house were that Woodie enjoyed playing with his children and that Hale enjoyed verbal combat with him. He was a staunch male chauvinist, and "either Ruth would go up and have an argument with Murdock or Murdock would come down and have an argument with Ruth," Woodie remembered. Beyond that, he was cultured, interesting, and glad to be spending his summers in the country away from his unhappy marriage, all of which made him excellent company.[10]

Other good company moved into the area. At first her neighbors mostly were Norwegian truck farmers, but gradually more New Yorkers purchased or rented nearby houses and socialized at Sabine Farm. In this way she had her own circle of friends distinct from Broun's. Neighbors who visited often included dress designer Muriel King, composer Deems Taylor, reporter George Bye, painter Allen Sallberg, and drama critic Gilbert Gabriel, a close friend who bought the house across the road because it was so near Hale's.[11]

More remarkable was the continuous stream of New York friends who kept her tiny guest rooms (and often her barn) occupied. They came throughout the summer, despite the two-hour drive from Manhattan or the train ride to the Stamford station—"the last civilized thing they saw," Woodie remarked. Despite the mandatory nude bathing in Hale Lake.[12] Despite, as his editor Maxwell Perkins wrote to F. Scott Fitzgerald, land that was "a ruin of thickets, grass-grown roads, broken walls and decaying orchards."[13] Despite amenities so limited that after visiting for the day, the elegant manager of the Algonquin, Frank Case, complained to his daughter, "There is *one* towel hanging on a nail on the back porch, for *everybody* to use." And, he ventured, "*that* towel must have come with the house."[14]

They came, among other reasons, to play golf on the rocky terrain, to play word games and bridge indoors, to sing and play the piano (notwithstanding a few missing keys). Some even came for the nude bathing and the freedom from convention it demonstrated, although when actor Roland Young—described by Woodie as "one of the more reluctant strippers"—was struck by lightning in the lake, he questioned whether it would have happened if he had been wearing a bathing suit. Almost everyone came to escape from stress and worries, often helped by plentiful alcohol (the deputy sheriff was the local bootlegger), and to eat the excellent meals created by Mattie Wilson or Ed McNamara. He became famous for rapidly grilling dozens of "magic steaks" wrapped in salt and wet paper napkins, all while singing and pouring drinks.[15]

And they came to spend time with Ruth Hale. She greatly enjoyed fixing up Sabine Farm and entertaining there. Even though Broun was a frequent weekend visitor, she liked living apart from him in a place that was distinctly her own. Busier, happier, and livelier than she was in New York, she was an even more enjoyable companion and hostess.[16]

But this new enthusiasm did not make her more professionally productive. In April 1923, not long after she took possession of Sabine Farm, her *Judge* movie column ended after a thirty-four-week run. She published only about a half-dozen magazine articles during the rest of the decade, most of them personal essays.[17] An exception was an April 11, 1925, *New Yorker* Profile of one of her friends, birth control activist Margaret Sanger.[18]

At that point the two-month-old *New Yorker* was struggling to attract readers. After cofounding it with Harold Ross, Jane Grant was doing much to help it survive, including finding contributors. She likely recommended Hale to write what was at that time a new kind of magazine article, intended to provide a more intimate, anecdotal view of a person than was commonly offered.[19] Hale did this by focusing on Sanger's early life and using details, quotes, and contrasts to present a flattering picture of her controversial subject.

Because *New Yorker* Profiles never carried bylines, Hale's authorship went unrecognized. While working on it, though, she was writing something else where her name was prominently featured. For a six-month period beginning in November 1924, she wrote a weekly book review column called "The Paper Knife" for the *Brooklyn Eagle*. Set in double-column width, it often ran the entire length of the Saturday book page. She took good advantage of the space, usually reviewing at least three books and frequently providing context by discussing other books on similar topics or by the same author. Her conversational style kept her from sounding professorial or self-important, and there was a warmth to her writing that must have made its idiosyncrasies less jarring. Her voice was distinctive and at times self-deprecating, conveying some of the appealing aspects of her quirky personality.

She often was amusing. Reviewing a new collection of Thomas Hardy's essays, she called one piece "the only time Hardy ever smiled in all his recorded life." Amazed at her discovery, she wrote, "There it is, and no matter how many times you rub your eyes, there it still is." Equally amazed when Dutton finally published something by a diehard feminist, she explained that her wait for such a book had been agonizing since "they have, for years, sent me copies of their books on feminism. I believe that was in order that I should commit suicide." And she expressed homicidal tendencies when she judged one author to be so misguided that "I am whetting The Paper Knife and I want the scalp of Mr. Charles R. Brown."[20]

She also wrote about her own experiences. For example, in reviewing Walter White's novel about an African American physician who was lynched, she noted that, having been raised in the South where racism was endemic, she had struggled to try to overcome it in herself. A book about women's work reminded her of her wartime visit to a French munitions factory where burly male employees worked "at top speed" under the command of a cheerful, plump forewoman. This woman, Hale decided, was just like one of her southern aunts "who used to make both husband and son do all the work she didn't feel like doing herself." Such women, "without apparent power and with no overt prestige," slyly accomplished a great deal.[21]

The column was an ideal channel for her interests and abilities. She was able to draw on her exceptional knowledge of books and authors, and to express her views with confidence and wit. No doubt she enjoyed having her opinions matter to readers, authors, and publishers. And seeing "by Ruth Hale" at the top of the page every week must have been immensely satisfying.

Yet like her *Judge* movie column two years earlier, "The Paper Knife" stopped abruptly, with no explanation to readers.[22] And unlike her *Judge* column, which was strikingly out of place in that magazine, "The Paper Knife" seemed to work well on the *Brooklyn Eagle*'s book page. So its demise in March 1925 is a mystery—and perhaps a sad one, since more than seventy years later, her son was surprised to learn of the column's existence. She had every reason to be proud of it, but he couldn't remember her ever saying a word about it to him.[23]

She did talk with him about many other things. "From age seven or so I was either her confidant or her sounding board on a lot of subjects that are not normally in the preteen interest range," he wrote.[24] He didn't understand everything she told him when he was young, but he came to value their discussions "about ways of life, about philosophies, about ideas," as he put it, as well as the many times they talked about things like books, news events, and what he was learning in school. She respected his views and "really wanted to know what I thought."[25]

One of his longest-lasting lessons from those talks was the importance of holding firm to one's beliefs and acting morally. "She taught me that you should do things against your best interest because that's what honor means," he said. "You do them because you know they're right."[26] This often took courage, an attribute he had associated with his mother even before he was old enough to have serious conversations with her. Broun once told an interviewer that his very young son had showed him a picture of a huge lion and asked if he would be afraid of it. When Broun denied he would be, Woodie shouted, "Yes you would, too." Then to cinch his argument about the animal's ferocity, he declared, "Why even Ruth would be afraid of him."[27]

"That restless, not to say turbulent, spirit"

"MISS HALE WAS ESSENTIALLY THE intellectual type of reporter," fellow journalist Ishbel Ross wrote. "Her interests were much deeper than the superficial turn of event. She took up causes with the intensity of a crusader."[28] Yet although she increasingly helped Broun probe beyond "the superficial turn of event" in his columns, she had no job in which she could do the same. This surely is one reason she was so devoted to causes in the 1920s.

For much of the decade she worked with the National Woman's Party and its fiery leader, Alice Paul. Committed to achieving absolute gender equality, the NWP appealed to women who were impatient with the slow progress in women's rights after suffrage was achieved, and with the hundreds of state and federal laws that still restricted women. It was uncompromising in fighting for a constitutional equal rights amendment as the only way to eliminate all sex discrimination. And in an effort to attract more professional women as members, it set up occupational councils, whenever possible headed by well-known women. The actresses council, for example, was headed by Ethel Barrymore and the journalists council by Hale.[29]

Early in 1924 she was one of the founders of another group, the Women's Committee for Political Action, which advocated diverse economic reforms and sustained efforts to end war. One of the WCPA's first actions was to organize a Washington, D.C., conference in early May to "rally to progressive standards all women who put principles before parties or candidates." Hale was the final speaker at the mass meeting that ended the conference.[30]

She also was a frequent spokesperson for the Lucy Stone League, which in 1923 and 1924 was in the news for helping married women use their birth names on documents ranging from library cards to voter registration records to insurance policies. Other events drew attention to the organization, such as when prominent women like Edna St. Vincent Millay and Margaret Mead married and kept their birth names. This attention inspired more opinions—both positive and negative—about the league in newspaper stories and editorials.[31] "The idea that a woman loses her individuality unless she retains her maiden name after marriage strikes many persons as rather silly," the *Philadelphia Inquirer* argued. "It is a manifestation of that restless, not to say turbulent, spirit that animates the 'new woman' in these days."[32]

The league's first major defeat occurred in the fall of 1924. Earlier that year Marjorie Jarvis, a physician at a federal hospital, had kept her birth name when she married and requested that her paycheck continue to be issued in her name. When her request was denied and her lawyer appealed the decision, the issue was sent to the secretary of the interior, who asked for a verdict from U.S. comptroller general J. R. McCarl. In August he ruled that married women who were government employees must receive their paychecks in their husbands' surnames. The league condemned the ruling, as did many major newspapers. The *World* pointed out that McCarl "could have chosen no better method to fan the Lucy Stone agitation to a fine flame."[33]

No doubt at Hale's urging, in 1922 the National Woman's Party had added a married woman's right to keep her name to its Woman's Bill of Rights, and in 1924 its lawyer presented a brief in favor of Jarvis. Newspaper condemnations of McCarl continued, women organized to send a delegation to Washington, and the secretary of the interior informed Hale that the case would be reopened. But for unknown reasons Jarvis decided to drop her case and leave government service, so McCarl's ruling remained in effect.[34]

The controversy resulted in more publicity (much of it positive) for the league and drew new attention to the State Department's refusal to grant passports to married women in their birth names. Thus the main speaker at the league's annual dinner in January 1925 was Helena Normanton, England's first woman barrister as well as the first married woman to receive a British passport in her birth name. After she told her story at the dinner, Hale took the podium and announced that the league would sue the secretary of state over the passport issue.[35]

The NWP agreed to participate in the action and journalist Ruby Black agreed to be the test case. She applied for a passport in her birth name and appealed to the secretary of state after her request was denied; league and NWP lawyers argued her case that April. At her hearing she was offered compromise language of "Ruby Black, wife of Herbert Little," which she refused, and at a May 1 news conference President Calvin Coolidge announced that he would consider abolishing the State Department rule. Before he could decide, though, Hale's friend Franklin Pierce Adams married writer and NWP member Esther Sayles Root, and prior to leaving for her honeymoon in Italy she applied for a passport in her birth name. With the help of NWP lawyers who cited the offer to Ruby Black as a precedent, she obtained one as "Esther Root, wife of Franklin Pierce Adams."[36]

This was seen as a victory by the NWP but not by the league, which again petitioned for passports with no mention of husbands' names. In June Doris Fleischman received such a passport, and shortly afterward so did other women. This truly was a victory. Not only was the passport issue settled, but since the State Department had recognized a married woman's birth name as her legal name, other government bodies apparently would have to do the same. The league seemed to have succeeded in its goal of educating policy makers to the fact that no law required a woman to take her husband's name. American women, too, seemed to have been educated, for growing numbers were keeping their birth names when they married, and widespread media coverage had made "Lucy Stoner" and "Lucy Stone bride" familiar terms.[37]

Yet Comptroller General McCarl still refused to issue paychecks in women's birth names, and in late 1925 he threatened to fire women who married and did not change their payroll names. The next year several state and federal governmental bodies refused to let married women use their birth names on important documents, and in December 1926 the Copyright Division of the Library of Congress ruled that married women must apply for copyrights in their husbands' surnames. When Virginia Douglas Hyde, who had been copyrighting her poems and plays in her own name for twenty years, was informed that she would have to use her husband's name, she contacted Hale. Hale, though, referred her to the National Woman's Party, and after its protests the decision was overturned.[38]

Despite being credited with helping win this fight, the league was not directly involved. In fact, it very likely had ceased operating by this time, although newspapers still carried stories about the debate over women keeping their names.[39] In 1926 Hale even wrote a booklet titled "The First Five Years of the Lucy Stone League," which ended by pledging that the league would "continue its role as adviser and friend to all women who do want their own surnames."[40] Yet her scrapbook covering league activities contains no clippings after 1926, and Jane Grant's treasurer's reports show that the last membership dues were paid in May 1926.[41]

Conflicts between the two women probably caused the league's dissolution. In late April 1925 Hale wrote to Grant from Washington, where she was working on the passport case, and accused her to trying to take control of the group. "I am under fire considerably here," she said, "and I am standing it because I am still the president of the Lucy Stone League—however much you would apparently like to forget it." After objecting to changes that had taken place in her absence, she told Grant, "I could sit down and cry when I think of you as I first knew you."[42] It is a mark of how painful this falling-out must have been for Grant that much later, when she wrote a book about her life during this period, she said nothing at all about her league work.[43]

Hale's regret surely was profound. She was closely identified with the league and it had advanced a cause that mattered enormously to her. In addition, she lost not just an organization but a friendship. She and Grant had been real partners in founding the league, and in March 1925 one officer credited its high visibility to the combination of "the able journalism of Jane Grant and the courage and persistence of Ruth Hale."[44] Their complementary strengths had made them an effective team.

Hale remained a resource for women fighting to keep their names and continued her contacts with league members at places like Heterodoxy meetings. British activist Ella Winter was the guest speaker at one meeting, probably in 1928, and recalled being introduced to a "dark, small and brooding" Hale. "She's made a life's battle of her feminist views," Marie Jenney Howe told Winter. "I think she's harder and more aggressive than the others."[45]

The league's demise did free Hale to devote more energy to a very different cause—the fight against capital punishment. Her son traced this concern to her southern upbringing, explaining that among the many things she abhorred about the South were its toleration of lynchings and widespread support for capital punishment. She also knew Clarence Darrow, who often came to parties at her home.[46] One of the country's most active death penalty opponents, Darrow saved Chicago murderers Nathan Leopold and Richard Loeb from the gallows in 1924 through legal maneuverings and an impassioned plea about the uselessness and immorality of capital punishment. His success energized reformers, and in 1925 the American League to Abolish Capital Punishment was formed. Hale was elected treasurer in 1927.[47]

Her friend Marc Connelly remembered her being troubled by the death penalty in 1923. That summer Woodie had taken a vacation trip to California with a family friend and caught the measles. Hale set off by train to be with him, promising Broun to call him when she arrived. He waited and worried for five days, then received her telegram from Kansas City exclaiming, "Mrs. Clavering Must Not Hang!" Hale had gotten off the train and become involved in the trial of a local woman accused of murder. She finally arrived in La Jolla to discover that Woodie was confined to a darkened room because light was thought to cause eye damage to measles patients. So she sat outside the room and read to him through the door. [48]

She had a better-organized means of fighting for the cause once the League to Abolish Capital Punishment set up its New York headquarters two years later. The league shaped much of the country's abolitionist activity by developing and coordinating individual states' abolition efforts, publishing anti-death-penalty literature, and doing much more. Its executive committee included some of the county's best-known abolitionists. Lewis Lawes, the warden at Sing Sing Prison and a renowned death penalty opponent, was its chairman. His continual articles, speeches, interviews, and testimony to legislative bodies—even as he was forced to supervise prisoner executions—made him a visible and effective leader.[49]

Fiercely committed to this cause, Hale often traveled to Sing Sing to work with Lawes. At the prison she sometimes visited inmate Charles Chapin, the former *World* city editor who was serving a twenty-year sentence for killing his wife. Although he had edited the Sing Sing newspaper, Chapin preferred his assignment as the head prison gardener. He enjoyed showing Hale his lush roses and birdhouses, and arguing with her about capital punishment. This murderer who had not received the death penalty was convinced that it was a deterrent to murder.[50]

Unfortunately for abolitionists, many state legislators shared Chapin's opinion. The league never came close to getting an abolition bill passed in any state, and ended up having to combat efforts to reinstate the death penalty in states where it previously had been abolished.[51] Similarly, the National Woman's Party failed in its primary goal—passage of an equal rights amendment—and by the end of the 1920s women were finding it harder to keep their names. Indeed, they did so less often as more judges ruled that a husband's surname was a married woman's legal name, and as some states passed new laws prohibiting use of birth names.[52]

"It matters to me"

HALE, HOWEVER, WAS UNDETERRED in using her name. "Being Ruth Hale gave her great pleasure and jest," her son said, recalling that her personal crusade included returning invitations sent to Mrs. Broun and, when drapes she had ordered arrived addressed to Mrs. Heywood Broun, redirecting them to Broun's mother.[53] Broun's support also was unwavering, and in 1928 he explained Hale's commitment well in one of his columns. When people ask her why her name matters, her best answer is, "It matters to me," he wrote. "Some near and dear to her have suggested, 'Oh, can't you let it pass just once?' And she can't, nor can anybody with a cause afford to make exceptions."[54]

A drama critic who did not want his wife to keep her name showed much less admiration for Hale's resolve. Writing in the popular magazine *Liberty*, Percy Hammond called Hale "the principal martyr to the Lucy Stone cause" and pointed out that as Broun's wife "she might share more fully the joys of his prestige were she willing to sacrifice her own identity. But she will not. Rather than be vicariously glorified by another's headline, Miss Hale elects to lurk in the shadows of an independent obscurity."[55]

Her "independent obscurity" was undeserved since she had long been a key force in Broun's work. As Woodie put it: "She would have been who she was whether he existed or not. But he was very much her creation."[56] His tremendous popularity was largely due to "It Seems to Me," which he wrote quickly and easily. Yet before he sat down at his typewriter he had to think a column through, and this is where Hale came in. "Their intellectual relationship was very close," Woodie noted. "She would point out things and say, 'You really ought to write a piece about this,'" and they might talk through how the topic could be developed. Or if he already had an idea for a topic, he might come down to the dining room (their usual meeting place) and discuss it with her, then go back up to his floor and write.[57]

Beyond discussions about individual columns, "she supervised the rigor of his thinking," Woodie said. "It's not so much that she was looking over his shoulder while he was writing, saying, 'Say this, say that.' It was a general approach." While Broun tended to have trouble focusing and reasoning logically, "She was like some very good English teacher. The student's thoughts are his, but the teacher says, 'You could put this more sharply.' She didn't supervise individual columns. She supervised the totality of the way he went about thinking."[58]

And she influenced his work in a still deeper way, as Broun explained after her death. "It was a curious collaboration," he wrote, "because Ruth Hale gave me out of the very best she had to equip me for the understanding of human problems."[59] A shy man with countless phobias, he so clung to his upper-middle-class roots that in 1925 he proudly joined the exclusive Racquet and Tennis Club to which his father belonged.[60] Hale, in contrast, was a rebel and crusader, unyielding in her beliefs and eager to act on them. As she prodded and educated him, and his "understanding of human problems" deepened, he went on to become a crusader himself. In Woodie's words: "Ruth was conscience and Heywood was the voice of conscience."[61]

She also was entirely responsible for one of his jobs. When the Book-of-the-Month Club was formed in 1926, Broun was asked to join Henry Seidel Canby, Dorothy Canfield Fisher, William Allen White, and Christopher Morley on its selection committee. These five "eminent experts," the club's promotional literature explained, would identify "the best new book published every month," which would be sent to subscribers too busy to stay knowledgeable about new books on their own. The judges would meet once a month to determine the next month's choice as well as alternate subscriber options.[62]

The job paid about $5,000 a year and Broun liked the prestige that came with it. But he was a poor choice because, as his son put it, "basically, unless Heywood was writing his column, he was lazy and disorganized." Book club work required a kind of sustained effort he had never been good at, for he had to not only read up to ten "A" books but also look over the same number of "B" and "C" books to determine if any of them deserved to be added to the list of alternative selections. And the books arrived in a long, difficult-to-read galley format. "They flooded him with package after package," Woodie said, and he soon was overwhelmed.[63]

So he turned the job—and the checks—over to Hale, who had the patience and time to do it. She also, Woodie wrote, "had a better, more informed taste" than the other four selection committee judges.[64] Each month she read the nominated books, chose the best one for Broun to recommend, then the night before the judges' meeting spent several hours preparing him to talk about all the books under consideration. She coached him to defend his choice by pointing out its strengths as well as the weaknesses of the other books. "She would tell him, 'If they bring this up, you say this,'" Woodie explained. Their system worked because "she needed the money and he needed to get out of the work. Otherwise I think he would have resigned."[65]

The book club's management would not have easily accepted his resignation since he had been hired not so much for his knowledge of books as for his celebrity, appealing persona, and unique bond with his column's readers. The bond was strengthened by his habit of writing about his own life, and by his reputation for protesting large and small injustices and championing the underdog. Hale's critic Percy Hammond described Broun as "being gifted with the large heart of the humanitarian."[66]

He was so popular that in 1926, when he agreed to serve as a judge, the *World* was paying him $30,000 a year and his column was said to bring in fifty thousand extra readers.[67] By the end of the decade he was one of the country's most widely known journalists and best-paid columnists. His lawyer estimated that during most of the 1930s Broun made about $70,000 a year (the equivalent of more than a million dollars today) for his column and other work.[68] This was at a time when New York reporters were paid an average of $4,000 a year.[69]

The checks Broun signed over to Hale added up to more than the average reporter's pay, but this usually was her only income source, and it largely was used to maintain and improve Sabine Farm (indoor plumbing and electricity were added in 1928).[70] Otherwise she was financially dependent on Broun, and she called attention to the real costs of this kind of dependence in a 1929 magazine article. Warning that a woman who relied on her husband for financial support was risking "her own future happiness and liberty of action," she urged married women to find jobs. "Needing the money has nothing at all to do with it," she argued. Rather, the point is "to know that you are free and independent and can call your soul your own."[71]

That article probably was the last she ever published, and one of only three published after her *Brooklyn Eagle* column ended in 1925.[72] She remained active in both old and new causes (not all of them futile) and participated in public debates.[73] But her career was at a standstill while Broun's was flourishing, and her unhappiness and restlessness were obvious, even to a child. "When all the day's battles had been fought and Heywood's mind bent in some new and interesting direction," her son recalled, "there seemed to be a number, a terrifying number, of hours left over, and Ruth's second-floor living room became increasingly cluttered with card tables bearing puzzles, piles of cigarette butts, and boxes of Requa's Charcoal Tablets." The presence of this "stomachic," he wrote, "seemed to prove that idleness can roil up the digestion as badly as does executive strain."[74]

She was frustrated not only by the writing she was not doing but by her uncredited work for Broun, and the praise he received for it. As Woodie observed, she lived by Lucy Stone's words, "My name is the symbol of my own identity and must not be lost," but she was "losing it in the basic newspaper prerogative, the byline."[75] Even Broun, writing about her after her death, admitted that he "will always understand the inevitable bitterness of the person who projects herself through another."[76]

Yet she did it willingly. She never complained to her son about it, and he thought he understood why: in some ways she was a traditional nineteenth-century southern woman who "is a power but does not show the power," he said. "It was like Leola Mae Somebody who actually runs the plantation while everyone thinks her husband's doing it." Thus, "however unhappy she was, she got what she wanted—to run Heywood Broun."[77] It was worth it because "here's one of the leading journalists of the time and you're telling him what to think."[78]

It was worth it, too, because Broun's income allowed them to live well, even during the Depression, which left them untouched. They had two cars, two live-in servants, a laundress, and others who took care of tasks at their home. Hale bought nice furniture and wore nice clothes. They ran up large tabs at speakeasies and restaurants. Broun frequently gave money to Hale's brother and especially her mother, and to his own relatives. He also was very generous with friends as well as strangers, telling his son, "You give without asking what it's for."[79]

Plus, Woodie said, "No money was ever stinted on my education." From ages five to eleven he attended two progressive schools, Walden School and Hessian Hills. Then he boarded for three years at one of the nation's most expensive schools, the Arizona Desert School for Boys.[80] It was, he said, the first "educational institution that approved of my sprawling but extensive book learning," and he thrived there.[81] Hale made sure his book learning continued by sending him a box of carefully selected books every month. Thus at age twelve he found himself contentedly reading Aldous Huxley's just-published *Brave New World*. In a letter accompanying one of those boxes, she told him, "What's the use of having a son if you can't send him books?"[82]

Drinking and gambling used up even more money. In Woodie's words, "Their liquor bills must have been giant." He recalled that, like many of their friends, they began drinking before breakfast and continued throughout the day, starting a new drink every two hours or so. "They were never drunk and never sober. I never saw them under the influence of liquor because they spaced their drinks so that you wrecked your kidneys but never spoiled your speech." Certainly they were alcoholics, but they also considered drinking during Prohibition a form of protest against a law that was both unjust and corrupt, since bootleggers flourished.[83]

At the same time, Broun was "a compulsive and self-destructive gambler," Woodie said. He gambled at every opportunity—including at roulette, dice, and horse races—but most often played poker, where his losses were the highest. After he joined other Algonks in forming the Thanatopsis Literary and Inside Straight Club in 1921, games typically started at the Algonquin after Saturday lunch and sometimes ran until Monday morning. As the 1920s progressed and the stakes rose, games moved to the fashionable Colony Restaurant. When they rose again in the early 1930s, players migrated to the Long Island home of wealthy *World* executive editor Herbert Bayard Swope. It was the participation of Swope and other well-to-do Algonks, such as *New Yorker* publisher Raoul Fleischmann, that caused these table-stakes poker games to become so costly. Broun may have owed Swope $10,000 when he died.[84]

For Hale, acceptance of Broun's incessant gambling losses was part of the cost of their "free marriage." "You're free to sleep out, you're free to spend money any way you want," their son explained. "He was a gambler and she had to take him as he was."[85] That also meant accepting what Woodie called his "lazy living—not shaving, not getting dressed right, lying around. He was a peculiar person in that were it not for these moments of frenzy at the typewriter, he was slothful." Hale had to keep track of his deadlines, deposit his paychecks, pay the bills, make all decisions regarding their son, and much more. She was so used to this that she seldom remarked on it. "Most of us had agreed to treat him as an eccentric," Woodie said. "He was a big figure of fun, except that he was a figure of fun who was wielding a big club in world opinion."[86]

When his carelessness tested her limits, charm was an effective response. He once lost a huge sum gambling in Florida and telegraphed Hale asking her to send money. "Along with the cash she sent a long, angry, well-reasoned wire on the subject of financial fecklessness," Woodie remembered. "She showed me his reply, a wire that said 'Love, Heywood.'"[87]

"You're supposed to make sacrifices for lost causes"

HIS LARGEST, RISKIEST GAMBLE, though, was not at a poker table but at the *World* when he insisted on writing about the Sacco-Vanzetti case. Many liberals thought the shoemaker and fish peddler had been found guilty of armed robbery and murder in Boston primarily because they were foreigners and anarchists, and that evidence of their innocence had been ignored. After they were sentenced to death in April 1927, Hale went to Boston to work for the Sacco-Vanzetti Defense Committee. She wrote press releases, ran errands, provided food for fellow defenders, marched in demonstrations, and even helped make sure the *Times* ran Edna St. Vincent Millay's poem about the two men's execution. But unlike her friend Dorothy Parker, she was not taken into custody during a State House demonstration. When she went to bail Parker out, the *Times* reported, Hale "bemoaned the fact that she had missed being arrested." On trips home she talked with Broun and encouraged his defense of the condemned men in his column.[88]

The case was a turning point for Broun. "It would be overstating . . . to say that he made overnight a conscious decision which changed him from a light essayist to a fiery crusader," his son wrote, "but for the first time he ran into public apathy on a large scale and realized more vividly than ever before that injustice is not knocked out in one round."[89] Hale "was the pusher at that watershed," Woodie thought. "She told him he had to become earnest, to stop being this funny man, this charming fellow."[90] A reporter who asked him why he continued writing about the case said Broun's answer was simple: He did so "at the request of his wife, Ruth Hale."[91]

That summer a commission appointed by the Massachusetts governor upheld the men's conviction and death sentence. In response, the *World*'s editorial page, which had argued for clemency all along, only urged that the sentence be commuted to life imprisonment, and stressed that the law must be obeyed. Infuriated by this moderate stand by the city's most liberal newspaper, in early August Broun wrote three passionate columns condemning the commission's members and their decision. Only two columns ran. The third was replaced with a notice to Broun's readers that the *World*'s editorial board had "instructed him, now that he had made his own position clear, to select other subjects for his next articles." He resigned. The resulting circulation decline at the *World* and financial insecurity in the Hale/Broun household persuaded both sides to participate in long negotiations that led his return on January 2, 1928.[92]

Broun, meanwhile, also was writing a weekly column for the *Nation* magazine. There, four months after returning to his old job, he vented his frustration with the *World*. "Again and again the paper has managed to get a perfect full-Nelson on some public problem only to let its opponent slip away because its fingers were too feeble," he wrote. "It does not seem to me that the paper possesses either courage or tenacity." This time he was fired. The Scripps-Howard chain quickly stepped in with a job offer, which he accepted. It promised him complete freedom, more space, and even a larger audience, since the column would run in the chain's *New York Telegram*, in its other papers, and in syndication.[93]

Broun's place of employment was not all that changed in 1928. One spring morning, Woodie, who was formally known as Heywood Broun III (and "H. 3d" in his father's columns), came down to breakfast and declared, "From now on, I'm not Heywood Broun III, I am Heywood Hale Broun." That then became the name he consistently used. He explained, "I did it to get away from the 'third,' and also to honor her."[94]

Later that spring, Broun bought the house and property next to Hale's in Stamford. One reason, Woodie said, was that he was only a guest at Hale's place, "which was a big social center, and he felt kind of left out."[95] Now they could both spend summers in the country without living together. In May 1929 they separated even further. They sold their West Eighty-Fifth Street brownstone and moved to two apartments, hers on West Fifty-First Street and his seven blocks away on West Fifty-Eighth Street. Thus, in their son's words, "The uneasy balance of separate existence under the same roof, that strange, unnatural, substantially successful compromise, came to an end."[96]

Yet they never truly separated. "They were out of the house but still clinging together," Woodie said. "They leaned on each other like two towers who would fall down if the other one stepped away." She went to his place nearly every day, both to continue their professional collaboration and help him handle the practicalities of day-to-day life. They spent almost as much time together as they had previously, and for similar reasons.[97]

Hale even was his campaign manager in 1930 when he ran for Congress as a Socialist Party candidate on a platform emphasizing the need for federal intervention to relieve rising unemployment. His father's August death delayed the start of the campaign, but in early September Hale agreed to contribute her considerable organizational skills to it, even though Broun's Republican opponent was a woman, the incumbent Ruth Pratt. "Ordinarily I would not campaign against a woman," she told the *Times*, but "I believe Mr. Broun is a far abler feminist, a much more whole-hearted one."[98]

The National Woman's Party refused to endorse Pratt, a staunch opponent of the equal rights amendment, and Hale collected extensive NWP material to prepare Broun to support the ERA in a debate. "Of course, the old bum has this extraordinary charm which would enable him to take an audience away from a good opponent, and in a bad cause. But at this particular debate, he was on the right side, and he was equipped to prove it," she reported to an NWP officer after the event. "Primed to the last notch with both fact and theory," and using his "general all-around lovableness," he was the clear victor, she thought.[99]

Hale ran the campaign from its Algonquin headquarters. Her tasks included scheduling speeches and making sure Broun arrived at them, collecting donations, dispatching volunteers, and milking the endorsements from their celebrity friends. She worked hard even though she did not believe in socialism and knew Broun had little chance of winning (he received 6,662 votes; his two opponents each received more than 19,000). "I think it was important to him that she supported him rather than saying it was a dopey thing to do," Woodie said. And she probably didn't think it was dopey "because it was a lost cause, and you're supposed to make sacrifices for lost causes."[100]

Broun was not the only member of Hale's family to carry out a quixotic political campaign. After giving speeches in California for several years, Annie Riley Hale began staying there for longer stretches once the New York brownstone was sold, finally settling in Pasadena. In 1932 this woman who had fervently opposed women's suffrage entered the state's Democratic primary as a candidate for the party's U.S. Senate nomination and lost by a huge margin. She then ran for the Senate as an independent candidate on a platform that, according to the *Los Angeles Times*, "espoused pacifism, 'economic change' and medical reform." Broun helped finance both campaigns, no doubt pleased to keep his mother-in-law occupied and far away.[101]

Once Broun's campaign ended in November 1930, Hale could turn her attention to another project that had better odds of success. She had written the libretto for *The Venetian Glass Nephew*, a "little opera" in two acts that was scheduled to open on Broadway in February 1931. It was based on the novel of the same name by Elinor Wylie, a poet and novelist who died in 1928. In addition to having known Wylie, Hale may have been attracted to the project because of the novel's story, a fantasy about a young woman falling in love with a man created out of Murano glass. She transforms herself into porcelain so she can marry him, sacrificing herself for her fragile husband. Some thought the novel reflected Wylie's unhappiness with her marriage to writer William Rose Benét.[102]

A number of theatrical press agents and drama critics, including Hale's friend Robert Benchley, went on to write very successfully for the theater.[103] So she was in good company when she agreed to write the libretto for a fledgling company's planned 1927 production of the opera. That production was never staged, making the opera's premiere at the Vanderbilt Theater on February 23, 1931, all the more important to Hale. A *Times* reviewer wrote that her libretto "communicates the story ably and retains the flavor of the prose," although the opera itself was disappointing. But it was not poor reviews that closed the production after a week's run. Rather, a financial dispute between the producer and theater management led to its abrupt cancellation, and the producer never made good on his promise to reopen the show at another theater.[104]

That same year Broun launched a theatrical endeavor of his own. It was the offshoot of his earlier campaign to provide jobs for people who had lost them in the Depression. Called "Give a Job Till June" and fueled primarily by appeals in his column and a great deal of personal arm-twisting, it had resulted in the creation of about a thousand make-work positions. This success inspired him to set about creating jobs for unemployed members of the theatrical industry by coproducing a musical revue called *Shoot the Works*. He persuaded well-known writers and composers to contribute sketches and songs, and famous performers such as the Marx Brothers, Sophie Tucker, and Eddie Cantor to show up unannounced onstage. The show opened on July 21, 1931, and ran for eighty-nine performances, during which he lost $7,500 but dozens of actors, singers, and many others had steady work. Even the chorus girls were paid above Equity scale.[105]

"Nothing really would change in their own relationship"

AMONG THE CHORUS GIRLS was Connie Madison. Her husband, a successful Broadway dancer, had died shortly before the birth of their daughter, and she had moved back to her parents' Yonkers home to live with them, her young child, and her three sisters. Broun began courting her despite the complicated logistics involved. "She was bright and perky and funny—very funny," Woodie remembered, "but if she ever read a book, I never heard about it."[106] Her appeal was not just that she was pretty and vivacious. She also held Broun in extremely high esteem: "She never criticized him and thought he was wonderful."[107]

This attraction at first seemed unremarkable, for Broun had had many brief, conspicuous affairs. Hale's affairs had been fewer in number, probably more satisfying, and certainly more discreet. Her son was aware of only one at the time it was happening. In spring 1931—while Broun was getting to know Connie Madison during rehearsals of *Shoot the Works*—Hale drove out to visit Woodie at his Arizona school accompanied by an attractive younger man with whom he could tell she was romantically involved. "He was around a lot in Stamford, too," Woodie said. And much later, he realized she had had an affair lasting at least seven years with a married municipal judge. Among his kindnesses were ruling in favor of Hale in a traffic court dispute and giving Woodie a horse, which he kept in the barn at Sabine Farm.[108]

His parents were "devoted to the idea that a free marriage is when you're a pair but it's OK to go outside for sexual adventures," Woodie explained. They were quite vocal in their espousal of sexual freedom, and he did not believe their love for each other lessened after they separated. Indeed, one reason they separated was to help preserve their marriage. Perhaps it was in another effort at preservation that they moved once more in 1933, this time to two apartments in the same building at 1 West Sixty-Seventh Street, Broun's unit one floor above Hale's.[109]

His father thus "enjoyed the best of both worlds—sex with Connie and intellectual life with Ruth," Woodie thought.[110] "Connie was pert and pretty, lively and funny." Beyond that, "she was everything Ruth wouldn't like because she very much subordinated herself to him."[111] Delighting in the attentions of the famous, charming columnist, "Connie lavished adoration while Ruth gave him education." Woodie believed that left to itself the romance eventually would have ended, but Hale took it very seriously. Broun seemed not to notice how much it troubled her, and he was stunned in the fall of 1933 when she told him she wanted a divorce.[112]

He might have been less surprised if he hadn't been preoccupied with another cause. In early August he had written a syndicated column calling for the formation of a journalists union. Thoughtful and good-humored, it ended with his dream of "watching Walter Lippmann heave half a brick through a *Tribune* window at a non-union operative who had been called in to write the current Today and Tomorrow column on the gold standard." The piece had enormous impact, helping rally local journalists to the cause and prompting those in other cities to furtively begin organizing. He threw himself into the difficult process of forming the American Newspaper Guild and was elected its president in late 1933.[113]

He would spend the next six years running countless meetings, walking picket lines, testifying in Washington, and doing much else, all while facing adversaries not just in publishers' offices but within factions of the guild itself. He believed this effort—which eventually cost him his job—was his most significant and enduring work. It became the capstone of a life about which his son would write, "No man afraid of so many things ever accomplished so much. Few people as frightened as he kept their idealism and their optimism so shining and unscratched."[114] Although Hale supported his initial guild activities, "I think she realized he was committing suicide professionally," Woodie said. At any rate, "By that time everything was coming to a crisis. She had a lot of other things on her mind."[115]

One of those things was telling her son about the planned divorce. He, too, was stunned because, as far as he knew, none of his parents' unhappily married friends ever divorced. They lived apart, had affairs, and otherwise adapted while staying married. To him divorce was unimaginable.[116] His parents were taking this step because "Ruth, wishing to take up again her journalistic career, felt that this could be better accomplished if she were not operating in the shadow of Heywood Broun," he was told. "Nothing, I was assured, would change in their relationship with me. Nothing really would change in their own relationship."[117]

In November Hale traveled to Nogales, Mexico, and obtained a divorce on the grounds that she and Broun had been separated for five years. Their lives changed in so few obvious ways afterward that newspapers didn't discover what had happened for two months. In mid-January an Associated Press reporter revealed to Broun that "news of the quiet parting had filtered north" and asked him what the grounds had been. Broun said he wasn't sure, although he knew "we weren't mad at each other."[118]

But inexplicably and inexcusably, they made their "quiet parting" even more difficult for Woodie. Since 1929 he had moved between them when he wasn't away at school, staying variously at each one's apartment or Stamford home. Now, though, they told him they wanted him to decide which parent he would live with. When he protested that the old arrangements had worked fine and, in any case, this should be their decision, not that of a fifteen-year-old, they reminded him that the three of them were equal so they shouldn't impose their choices on him. Miserable after more failed protests, he finally decided that since Broun's apartment had an extra room, he would live with him. He later learned from his uncle Richard that his response caused Hale to weep for days. Yet his real error, Woodie realized, was that "I had not insisted on my right as the child to make them act like parents instead of colleagues."[119]

Trying to make up for the hurt, he spent more time in Hale's apartment than in Broun's. He was boarding at the Horace Mann School's Riverdale campus during the week and coming home on weekends, when he went down to her place almost every afternoon and they talked for a few hours. These were "long, intimate, satisfying talks," he remembered, and "we were closer than we had even been before." She gave him useful advice and showed she believed in him and trusted him. But her distress continued, as did Broun's. She knew the divorce had been a mistake. He had suffered a serious blow to his ego. They both drank more.[120]

In March 1934 Hale spoke at the memorial service for Marie Jenney Howe, held at the home of Alice Duer Miller, who had introduced her to Broun.[121] Later that spring the divorced couple moved into Broun's house in Stamford, "the excuse being that Ruth, needing money, had rented her place as an income-producing proposition," Woodie wrote. As they were moving, Woodie was preparing for a long summer vacation in Europe, his first trip out of the country. He had no trouble getting a passport as Heywood Hale Broun, even though that was not the name on his birth certificate.[122] His mother had had no such success when she simply wanted a passport in the name that was on her birth certificate.

Hale seemed fine when he left for Europe, but when he returned at the end of August he worried that she seemed "languid—like someone who doesn't care very much." He attributed this to her unhappiness over the divorce and the fact that it had done nothing to help her career. Her health quickly deteriorated, and in the early morning of September 18, Broun and her brother Richard rode with her in an ambulance to a Manhattan hospital. She died there a few hours later.[123] The cause of her death at age forty-eight was ambiguously listed on her death certificate as "general visceral congestion" and pleurisy, roughly translated as an infection of the intestine and an inflammation of the lining of the lung.[124]

Broun hadn't thought to wake Woodie to let him know they were rushing his mother to the hospital, so he woke to hear the news from Mattie and Earl Wilson. Broun called later that day to tell him Hale had died. After a silent journey into Manhattan with the Wilsons, Woodie met his father for dinner at the Stork Club. "Both of us did a good deal of drinking and talked about her a lot," he remembered.[125] Then they went back to Broun's apartment and he wrote his next day's column. It began, "My best friend died yesterday."[126]

PART III

Jane Grant

CHAPTER 8

"I meant to remain in the East once I got there"

VERY FEW YOUNG WOMEN, let alone those who grew up in rural America at the turn of the twentieth century, could have imagined they ever would encounter such a scene. Probably in 1915, when she was working as a stenographer in the society department at the *New York Times* and hoping to become a reporter, she begged the night city editor for an assignment and was sent to cover the annual stag costume party at an exclusive Greenwich Village men's club. She had expected a sedate dinner but was greeted instead, through a smoky haze, by drunken men. Some wore very little clothing, some impersonated newsmakers such as Teddy Roosevelt, some were dressed as mermaids and other mythic figures—"satyrs and fawns [*sic*], particularly popular, were vulgarly characterized," she noted.[1]

Her embarrassment and lack of reporting experience kept her from taking notes, but she did not flee immediately, as the night city editor no doubt expected her to do. She stayed to talk with the men, then returned to the *Times* and tried to write her story. "Uncertain about what to record of the things I had seen, I wrote and tore up, wrote and tore up," she recalled, until she was saved by the midnight arrival of the society editor, who listened to her account, then wrote the story himself.[2]

Despite her problems that night, he eventually assigned her to cover a much easier story—a wedding—for the society page, which proved to be the official beginning of her reporting career.[3] Perhaps he saw that her small-town midwestern background had helped her develop initiative and persistence that would take her beyond her simple clerical job. But he could not have seen that, a decade later, those strengths would help her cofound a sophisticated magazine about New York City.

Jane Cole Grant was born on May 29, 1892, in Joplin, Missouri, and spent her childhood in the tiny nearby mining town of Duenweg, where her father, Robert T. Grant, was an independent prospector. Her mother, Sophronia Cole Grant, stopped working as a schoolteacher because of ill health in 1890 and died in early 1899. After her father remarried two years later, the family moved to an eighty-acre farm near Girard, Kansas, that he had bought with his modest lead- and zinc-mining profits. He hoped to provide his family with middle-class comforts and his daughter with a better education, although Girard had only a three-year high school program.[4] This, she explained, was thought to be sufficient to prepare her for the one profession that was acceptable for women in her family: "They became schoolteachers until, if they were lucky, they got married."[5]

By moving to Kansas, Jane and her sister Edith also could be near their mother's father and stepmother. The couple had their own farm near Girard where the two girls were sent to spend their summers after their mother's death. Jane seems not to have been close to Edith, who was seven years older, attended boarding school, and married at age nineteen. But she much enjoyed the summer company of her older male cousins with whom she fished, climbed trees, wrestled, and rode horses bareback. She was fond of her grandfather as well, and had many aunts and uncles in the area.[6] Still, she could see the downside of her strong family ties. As she later wrote, "In my youth, everything pointed towards my following the pattern of my closely knitted family. Few of us had journeyed far from the arm of my patriarchal grandfather."[7]

Yet her father's experiences may have made him a believer in women's wider potential. Sophronia Grant was sixteen when she began teaching in Kansas schools; she taught for fourteen years, then served one year as a principal. Although deteriorating health forced her to retire, she still helped her husband run the general store that was part of his mining venture, and, as her obituary reported, "proved herself most capable as a business woman, having interests in the mining operations of those parts."[8] Thus she helped support her family for several years, even when she was in poor health and raising her daughters.

Her younger daughter's greatest advantage proved to be her voice. A popular singer at church events as a child, Jane said she "gained a reputation as a performer" and began to aspire to a singing career. She was on her way to realizing those aspirations when, near the end of her final high school year, her voice teacher arranged for Jane to audition for her own former teacher, Willie Warner, who was visiting friends in Girard after marrying and moving to a New York City suburb. Warner was so impressed with Jane's singing that she offered to take her back to New York for lessons and to let her live in her home. Robert Grant consented on the condition that after a year she would return to Girard and teach "voice." Her small inheritance from her mother would help pay her expenses, and he also would give her money.[9]

So in May 1909, the week after her graduation ceremony (at which she sang "Voce de Primavera") and just before her seventeenth birthday, she and Warner boarded a train to New York, where she would begin her studies. She had another plan as well. "At an early age I had decided against both teaching and marriage," she admitted. "In my secret heart I meant to remain in the East once I got there."[10]

"I knew I could count on them to help me"

HAD SHE BEEN WILLING TO ABIDE by her father's wishes, her experiences the next year would have been excellent preparation for a career as a small-town voice teacher. She took "voice culture" from a Swedish singer, learned some German at a local high school, studied harmony and music history with Warner, and practiced playing the piano. She enjoyed living in the Warners' comfortable home and was grateful for her twenty-five-dollars-a-month job as a soprano soloist at a Presbyterian church. But she lost that job after less than a year, and lost her father's funding when she informed him that she would not return to Girard.[11] In a birthday letter to her written shortly afterward, he sounded resigned to her decision, advising only that if she continued to "work and study for a few years and mingle in good society she will come out all right."[12]

Her problems the following year must have made her wonder if she really would "come out all right." Her mother's inheritance was long spent, she struggled to get small engagements at women's clubs and schools, and Willie Warner died unexpectedly. Before she died, though, she asked her cousin, Grace Griswold, to watch over Grant.[13] Griswold would prove to be a very different kind of savior.

An actress, Griswold put together "An Evening of Readings and Song" that she and Grant performed for small fees in nearby churches and schools. She also invited the younger woman to dinners at the homes of relatives, including her theologian brother, and to teas and other fashionable events. A favorite activity was attending the "Sunday evenings" held by banker and Shakespearean scholar Richard Purdy. These gatherings, Grant proudly noted, attracted "important statesmen, writers, theatrical personalities and socialites."[14] Little by little, she was learning about a new world, which would later become her world.

Griswold aided her protégé in another way by letting her live with her at the Three Arts Club, which Grant described as a "home for girls studying music, drama and art." (She qualified by being a singer.)[15] The move meant she likely paid little or no rent to live in Manhattan, rather than in a less-stimulating suburb, and benefited from getting to know fellow aspiring singers. She also met men who were drawn to the appealing young women who lived in the rooming house. Some of those men, she said, "were already beau-ing me, and I knew I could count on them to help me."[16]

She did need help, for even though she described herself as being determined to "dig in with a vengeance and no mistake," she was making little money and most of her singing jobs were unsatisfactory. She remembered: "I hounded musical agencies which booked me for clubs and horrible smokers; I sang in cheap restaurants with a female quartette, and on Sundays, at the Church of St. Mary the Virgin, I was a member of a choir." The final blow came when she spent fourteen unpaid weeks rehearsing in a musical comedy that never opened. After that experience she vowed "to undertake something more substantial than singing," despite knowing this meant she no longer would be eligible to stay at the Three Arts Club.[17] For the first time, she would have to search for a place to live.

She also needed a steady job, and her prospects looked very different than they had appeared the very first time she looked for work. Then she had been barely seventeen years old and unconcerned with women's highly restricted career opportunities. As she acknowledged, "That fact worried me not at all, for I could sing and I set myself to rise to fame." Now, however, she looked down from what she called her "perilous economic perch" and saw few occupational possibilities.[18] Evidently she did not think teaching was one of them, perhaps because this would have been difficult in a city that already had many women equally or more qualified than she was to teach music.

By November 1911 she was on her way to solving both her employment and her housing problems, for at that point she was living in a tiny apartment and attending business school in preparation for a job she'd been promised on completion of her courses. Although she was unaware of it, her father was subsidizing these changes. He had sent her a check for $150—the proceeds, he said, from selling her piano, which she had earlier asked him to do.[19] Yet on her next visit home she discovered her piano was still in his house.[20]

Those funds helped her manage until she began what was probably a low-level clerical job at *Collier's Weekly*. She stayed at the magazine from 1912 until 1914, but it must not have been a good experience since she never acknowledged working there when she described this period of her life in a book published in 1968. She claimed instead that her first full-time job was at the *New York Times* and that she took business school courses to qualify for that position.[21]

She claimed, too, that she went directly from the Three Arts Club to a room in a nearby house owned by Florence Williams, secretary to renowned *Times* managing editor Carr Van Anda.[22] At the earliest, the move occurred two years after she left the club. Still, it set in motion such vital improvements in her life that she may have preferred to ignore previous less-agreeable experiences when she told her story fifty years later. (In fact, she avoided discussing most of the unpleasant aspects of her life in the book.)

Williams was another person who went out of her way to help Grant, no doubt easily surmising that the young woman needed assistance. Grant admitted that when she first lived with Williams she was sewing for fellow boarders to make ends meet and "trying to subsist on the hearty breakfast she provided and occasional dinners I allowed myself [to buy] at the club."[23] Either she had lost her *Collier's* job or the pay was very low.

The *Times* secretary not only let her forgo rent payments until her situation improved but offered to help her get a job at the newspaper. She recommended her tenant to her boss, and, probably sometime during the first half of 1914, Van Anda offered her a position as a stenographer in the society department.[24] It paid too little but its security was appealing. "When you have rehearsed fourteen weeks in the chorus of a show to be let out before you reach Broadway; when you barnstorm in vaudeville, playing one week in four; when you have a whirl in cabaret as a member of a dancing team," she explained, "you look upon ten dollars a week not only as a lot of money but a steady anchor."[25]

Van Anda warned her from the start that she would never make more than ten dollars a week and never do more than record information telephoned in by people who wanted their activities reported in the society columns. She complained that it was a tedious job requiring "so little more than recording names and addresses, which had to be carefully spelled out, that I soon forgot the little shorthand I had hurriedly crammed into my head." No one thought to explain how the department filled its pages, but she determined on her own that it hinged on the families listed in *The Social Register*. This inspired her to study the book in her spare time, and to commit enough of it to memory that for years she was able to recite family lineages.[26]

Although confident that she had the necessary stenography skills, she had doubts of a different kind after she met some of the paper's reporters and editors. "I knew that I was associating with a group of well educated people," she said, and this meant "I had to know far more than I did." Griswold's friend Richard Purdy answered Grant's appeals for help and agreed to tutor her. Learning to write required writing often, he told her, so he made her write a one-page essay every day. In addition, he put together a reading list that exposed her to authors like William Shakespeare, Thomas Hardy, and George Meredith. She had read few serious books—"I had scarcely graduated from juvenile ones," she confessed—and when Purdy assigned her Victor Hugo's *Les Misérables*, "I feared I'd never finish that thick volume."[27]

As the essays she wrote for Purdy improved, she developed the confidence to take his advice and volunteer to do more work at the paper. Her department's editor, William F. Fauley, gave her rules that made it easier to take notes on telephoned information, then showed her how to rewrite her notes into the simple stories that filled most of the Sunday society page and for which he was paid space rates (although he did not share the money with her). Next he taught her how to make up the Sunday page, another of his responsibilities, and she took over much of this work as well. As she put it, "My avidity and capacity for work delighted Mr. Fauley—he saw he could profit by it."[28]

One night she was the only person working in her department when the phone rang not with a society announcement but with a request that a reporter be sent to cover the Salmagundi Club's annual dinner at its Greenwich Village headquarters. She had never done any reporting and knew nothing about this event, but she pleaded with the night city editor to assign her to it. He relented, sending her off to the stag costume party—a "bawdy scene" where inebriated men in "rakish costumes" were extremely pleased to see her. They thrust flowers from the centerpieces into her arms, she remembered, and "some of the more modest ones quickly made themselves presentable with napkins and tablecloths." Afterward she returned to the *Times* with a bounty of flowers but no notes, having forgotten to take any.[29]

The experience was telling in more ways than she realized. She thought it simply showed her early ineptitude, but it also revealed an ability to function in unnerving circumstances. Surely the night city editor expected her to make an immediate, red-faced exit that would provide amusement for the men waiting back in the city room. Instead, she was undeterred by the vulgarity she encountered, stayed at the event, and on her return to the paper tried to write a story. At the same time, she may have learned a useful lesson from the enthusiastic welcome she received from the upper-class men at the Salmagundi Club's headquarters.

"The situation suited me down to the ground"

SHE ALREADY WAS GETTING ALONG WELL with men in another place that most women would have found unnerving: the offices of the *New York Times*. While not as difficult a setting in which to remain composed as a stag party, the newspaper was heavily misogynistic. Grant's contemporary, journalist Ishbel Ross, wrote that *Times* publisher Adolph Ochs "felt about women on the staff as he did about features. They were not part of his conception of the perfect paper."[30] Not only were women unwelcome but swearing, gambling, and playing practical jokes—especially on Grant—were common, and the men enjoyed calling her by the nickname "Fluff." But she answered to her nickname and happily learned to swear (sportswriters and the athletes who visited them were outstanding teachers) and gamble (receiving particularly good instruction, she noted, in "the science of red dog and poker, as well as crap shooting").[31]

That this outgoing, attractive young woman adapted so well to this environment must have pleased many of her male colleagues. And in light of her considerable appeal and the scarcity of women at the paper, it is unsurprising that men tended to gather in her office while waiting for assignments. Van Anda once told Ochs that she was the "flypaper" who kept his staff in the building so he didn't "have to send across the street to the saloon any more when I needed someone in a hurry." Grant described how, rather than putting an end to their fun, the managing editor urged them to continue when "he would come upon us as we were huddled in a crap game . . . or executing the intricacies of the Fox Trot."[32]

Indeed, even as the men taught her to gamble and swear, she taught them to dance, and then became their dance partner at hotel ballroom dances, fancy dress balls, and clubs. And she did much more with them. Sportswriters took her to games, she attended the theater with drama critics, and after the night shift ended, she often went out to dinner with her colleagues. "The reporters at the *Times* were wonderful to me," she declared. "They furnished much of my sustenance and social life."[33]

Her job improved as Fauley began sending her to cover weddings and, when he was short on copy, to places where she might pick up stories. She went, for example, to the Hotel Knickerbocker in search of famous guests who might tell her about their plans, and to the Metropolitan Opera House "to get names of pillars of society who were attending the performance." A celebrity she encountered in both places was opera singer Enrico Caruso, who, Grant said, "was especially cooperative." The notoriously unaccommodating Caruso seems to have been motivated by more than a desire to see his name in the *Times*, for in addition to giving her autographed photographs and a gold amulet displaying his profile for her charm bracelet, he reserved orchestra seats at one of his performances for her and her visiting sister (his note said he hoped to see them afterward) and invited her to accompany him to a baseball game.[34]

Evidently the same enthusiasm, flirtatiousness, and amiability that pleased her *Times* coworkers helped her obtain some of her small stories for the society section. She was becoming proficient at using male power to her advantage. "All my associates were men and the situation suited me down to the ground," she later wrote of her years at the paper. "Men were old hat to me. I come from a large family of males. I knew their strength and their weakness and I was used to getting what I wanted from them." Her Kansas summers with her grandfather and cousins had taught her that most men are "kind and helpful if you know how to get 'round them."[35]

Yet she would not have been able to interact successfully with well-educated colleagues, guests at society weddings, and opera singers if not for Grace Griswold's earlier assistance in honing her social skills. Although she had been afraid to speak when Griswold first took her to parties and receptions, she explained that

"Grace would toss me into a group, ignore me for a time, then, if I continued silent she would pin a fishy eye on me until I talked." Gradually she learned to rid herself of her "homely western phraseology" and converse with people who were far more accomplished than she was. Even more gradually and to her surprise, she came to enjoy it. No wonder she asserted that the older woman's coaching was "the best course of lessons I have ever had."[36]

She grew noticeably, too, in her knowledge and appreciation of the arts as she took advantage of some of the privileges of *Times* employment. She was able to attend Metropolitan Opera performances at no cost, go to the opening nights of Broadway shows, and catch afternoon acts at venues like the Palace Theater. Similarly, the longer she worked at the newspaper the more knowledgeable she became about New York. She found herself in love with a city that, she said, not only was "warm and hospitable underneath the cosmopolitan veneer" but offered "adventure every hour of the day."[37]

She had become a young woman very different from the one who had timidly made her way down the long corridor to the newspaper's society department in 1914. Still, she remained a stenographer and was receiving only a ten-dollar paycheck, notwithstanding the extra work she was doing for Fauley. (In contrast, her good friend, drama critic Alexander Woollcott, was making sixty dollars a week.)[38] She asked her colleagues to help her increase her *Times* income and they showed her how to write new kinds of formulaic articles for space rates.[39]

They also suggested ways she could earn money by drawing on other talents. She had been such a hit when she sang and acted in a skit at the paper's annual dinner that senior drama critic Adolph Klauber wrote letters of introduction that helped her get auditions with theatrical producers. Next, Woollcott and another drama critic wrote a vaudeville act for her to perform with two male partners at a New Jersey theater. But none of these attempts at singing and acting was a success, leading her advisors to recommend that she concentrate on what they saw as her considerable strengths as a dancer. This time she did succeed after she teamed up with a professional male dancer and created new routines with him. They were booked as part of the floor show at a popular restaurant next door to the *Times*, which helped ensure that her applauding colleagues often were in the audience.[40]

"Week after week our engagement was extended and we were exploited in the papers by the management and our friends," she recalled. "At the end of 15 weeks we were still going strong." It made for a hectic schedule, however, since she had to start her *Times* shift at 1:00 p.m., leave at 6:30 for the dinner show, rush back to the paper immediately afterward, then leave at 11:00 p.m. for the late show, never arriving home before 2:00 a.m. Most mornings were devoted to rehearsals, sewing new costumes, or ballet lessons. "The days were getting hot, too, and I was getting tired and petulant," she acknowledged. "Mr. Van Anda was off on his long summer vacation, no longer there to act as a buffer, and Mr. Ochs again raised an eyebrow at my unconventional goings-on." Finally she was sternly told she would have to choose between the dance floor and the newspaper.[41]

Knowing that her dreams of theatrical success would be easier to give up than the extra money she was earning as a dancer (which doubled her income), she set out to obtain a raise. Fauley advised her to make her case by doing still more work, so she wrote as many as fifteen columns of copy a week for the society section. Then, armed with proof of her productivity, she went to see Van Anda.[42] He would pay her only two dollars a week more, but she accepted the offer, then augmented her salary by writing additional paid pieces for the *Times* and for a newspaper syndicate, even sometimes working as a "social press agent" for debutantes and brides. She'd decided to remain in a job that was rewarding in nonmonetary ways, having realized that "as time passed the excitement of newspaper work got into my bones."[43]

"Your ardent courtier, H. W. Ross"

NEVERTHELESS, SHE TRIED HARD to leave the paper following the U.S. entrance into World War I in April 1917, for she badly wanted to do war work overseas. Although her incessant reminders of her goal became something of a joke among her colleagues, she did succeed in getting letters of recommendation from *Times* executives and people outside the paper, and took the letters to Washington, D.C., where she hoped they would persuade an organization such as the Red Cross or Salvation Army to accept her as a volunteer. After being turned down again and again, she returned to New York, acted on a tip from one of the paper's reporters, and finally was accepted by the YMCA as a clerical worker in its Motion Picture Bureau.[44]

The primary organization responsible for providing recreation for the war's American Expeditionary Force troops, the YMCA operated hundreds of canteens and created entertainment units that performed at military bases, with films supplementing the live entertainment. It went on to sponsor more than eight hundred professional entertainers, and its operations required an extensive clerical force, composed overwhelmingly of women.[45] Thus, much as it bored her, Grant's office experience helped her go overseas. And, ironically, she would make more as a war volunteer—$108 a month—than she had at the *Times*.[46]

In September 1918 she sailed for France. Her first stop was the *Stars and Stripes* office in Paris where she hoped to visit her friend Woollcott, who had been working there since February and with whom she had been corresponding. But he had left for the front, so she continued on to her duties in Tours.[47] There her days were spent doing clerical work and tasks such as repairing and splicing films. At night she was sent to Y canteens to dance and talk with the enlisted men, which usually left her with bleeding feet and a mind numbed by dull conversation. Yet that did not deter her, after the canteens closed, from stopping at the officers' club to, as she put it, "dance and sing close harmony with old friends there." She later admitted that she had chosen Tours as her posting in part because an army colonel friend who was stationed there had told her she would have a good time at the club.[48]

Thanks to Woollcott, she was back in Paris in mid-December. He had pulled strings to get her transferred to the YMCA Entertainment Corps so she could sing in a three-person unit he was organizing to perform at nearby hospitals and camps. She hadn't seen him since July 1917, when he'd left the *Times* to join the army medical corps. In France he had compensated for his disappointment with his menial hospital chores and distance from the front lines by collaborating with actor Schuyler Ladd to produce a full-length drama for area soldiers. The show's success encouraged him to continue his entertainment sideline after February 1918, when the AEF was beginning the *Stars and Stripes*, its newspaper for American troops, and he was detached to become one of the four writers and two artists who would form the editorial core of the new weekly. Another of those writers was Harold Ross.[49]

Ross had traveled widely before the war. Born in Aspen, Colorado, in 1892, he moved with his family to Salt Lake City nine years later. An apprenticeship at the *Salt Lake Tribune* when he was a high school freshman taught him that he much preferred newspaper work to schoolwork, so he dropped out after his sophomore year and was hired as a reporter by another Salt Lake paper. He subsequently left for California where he hoped to become a "tramp reporter"—a freelancer who worked briefly at one paper, then moved on to another and another. These reporters were common in the West, and Ross had come under their spell at his hometown newspapers. He proceeded to find jobs in the Sacramento area, Panama, New Orleans, and Atlanta; by 1915 he was in San Francisco covering the waterfront for the *Call and Post*. He so relished this work and the city that he stayed for two years, not leaving until he enlisted in the army engineering corps shortly after the United States joined the war.[50]

As soon as he heard about plans to start the *Stars and Stripes* he put in for a transfer from his base in Langres. When his request was denied, he went AWOL, arriving at the paper's Paris offices just as its second issue went to press. The small, tired staff was so grateful for the appearance of this experienced reporter carrying his own portable typewriter that his transfer was approved. In addition to becoming a productive writer, reporter, and editor, he proved to have a gift for knowing what enlisted men wanted to read. And once peace came with the signing of the armistice in November 1918, the staff felt freer to rebel against their unpopular managing editor. He was removed, with Ross elected to replace him. Now Ross not only had to master the intricacies of production, editorial, and advertising but also had to carve out a new focus for the peacetime weekly. His strategies included running in-depth stories, interesting features, and personality pieces—in short, making the newspaper more like a magazine.[51]

Staff members socialized together, particularly on Saturday evenings at a Montmartre bistro where they gathered to eat and play poker. (This was the same café where Heywood Broun and his journalist friends had gambled the previous year.) Woollcott brought Grant along to a game shortly after she arrived in Paris, and her expertise in both poker playing and being the sole woman in a large group of men helped her settle in comfortably.[52]

She was the first woman ever allowed to sit with the players but her efforts to join the game itself were thwarted, so she decided to enjoy herself with the men who were not playing. This frustrated Private Ross, who had bribed the player sitting next to her to switch seats with him and seemed intent on monopolizing her attention. With a fellow reporter (Woollcott did not want to bother making the long trip), he escorted her back to her hotel at dawn. Yet he had little chance of monopolizing her in the future, given the appeal of the other men she met that night. "During the weeks that followed I saw quite a lot of these soldiers. I enjoyed them enormously," she remembered. "Scarcely a day passed that I did not lunch with at least two or three of them, and I would hang around the [*Stars and Stripes*] office when I probably should have been at a military hospital writing letters for patients."[53]

"I preferred the gang at the *Stars and Stripes*," she said, but she had her choice of other male companions, including "a dashing aviator" who searched her out when he was on leave and the "soldiers and officers whom I had encountered in the Y canteens and officers' clubs at Tours or Le Mans" and "were soon to find me in Paris."[54] Later, after she joined a professional unit formed to entertain occupation troops, so many men came to see her off when her train left for Germany that, she wrote, "The attention was embarrassing in view of the subordinate place I occupied with this professional group. I shared my flowers and presents, with which I was laden, with others on the train, and for days my companions and I enjoyed the largess."[55]

Ross's many duties at the *Stars and Stripes* did not keep him from pursuing Grant in person and by mail. In December 1918 he took her on an automobile tour of the Belleau Wood and Château-Thierry battlefields, signing his invitation, "Your ardent courtier, H. W. Ross," followed by a row of x's.[56] She saw him often until mid-February, when her entertainment unit broke up, forcing her to leave Paris. Grant, an accompanist, and a comedian had been performing material written by Woollcott that she said was very good, but they were disbanded when his superiors discovered he had failed to get official permission for the venture. So the YMCA sent her to the French coast to provide entertainment for troops waiting to depart for home. Her new five-person unit, she remarked, staged "some of the hammiest playlets ever put on paper."[57]

Meanwhile, Ross and Woollcott schemed to get her transferred back to Paris. In a letter detailing their efforts Ross told her, "I haven't laughed much since you left town. Funny coincidence, isn't it?"[58] As a result of the men's labors she was back in early April and began rehearsing with a professional unit organized by Woollcott's friend Schuyler Ladd to entertain occupation forces in Germany. She was to perform in skits and sing between the acts. The group would depart in a few weeks, but Ross used the time well. She noted: "He embarrassed me with corsages which I couldn't wear with my uniform and showered candy and perfume upon me. He took me to the theater and the opera, in fact, did many things not to his liking to please me, and marveled himself at this new manifestation in him."[59]

When they were together they discussed what they would do once they returned to the States. She knew she would go back to the *Times*, but he at first was adamant that he would never live in New York, calling it a "terrible place." His dream was to sail the South Seas like Jack London, whom he had met in San Francisco. After Grant wore him down with praise of the city, he decided to give it another chance. He had some publishing ideas he might pursue, he told her, and perhaps one of them "could be worked out by us, together."[60]

Since he would need a job in the intervening time, he listened carefully to the Butterick Publishing Company executive who came to Paris to try to interest *Stars and Stripes* staffers in starting a New York–based, magazine-style version of their newspaper aimed at returning veterans. Overcoming strong reservations, he agreed to be its managing editor (for $10,000 a year), persuaded six other staff members to join him, and sailed for New York in mid-May.[61]

Grant spent most of May and June performing in mess halls, theaters, and canteens as part of a "flying squadron" of entertainers assembled to distract bored, unhappy occupation soldiers who had expected to go home long ago and had little to do in Germany. True to form, she also found ways to meet "the important brass," as she called them. With officers "in a holiday mood," she confessed, "I, too, was in a mood for comfort, sightseeing and any fun that might come my way." She happily accompanied AEF officers on boat excursions up and down the Rhine, to elegant dances, on picnics in parks and scenic woodlands, to fine restaurants, to banquets in old German palaces.[62]

In late June a temporary impasse in the peace negotiations led to the removal of all entertainment units from Germany. After staying briefly in a disappointingly changed Paris, on July 12 Grant left for a French port from which she would sail for home. She no longer needed the Motion Picture Bureau identification card she had carried since September that classified her as a secretary. Instead, she now carried a YMCA Certificate of Release on which she was identified as an entertainer.[63] Overseas, as in New York, she had moved beyond her original position, ultimately doing work that pleased her far more than the duties to which she initially had been assigned. Here, too, the efforts of helpful men who were fond of her had been crucial to her advancement. And once again she had played almost as hard as she had worked.

"I meant to be independent"

GRANT AND ROSS CORRESPONDED while she toured with her YMCA group, but, she said, "My answers to his letters were casual and noncommittal. I meant to be independent when I reached New York." Similarly, her *Times* editor was the only person she informed of her return date. "Ross could hear I was home when I got there," she decided. Delighted to be back at the newspaper after a yearlong absence, she recalled that she "quickly fell into the old routine of work, dancing, gambling, general hilarity and bickering with Aleck [Woollcott]."[64]

She enjoyed herself even more away from her job. Once they knew she was home, ex-soldiers she had dated in France began to call, and often she was busy by the time Ross asked her out. Frustrated, he once exclaimed, "Don't you ever buy your own dinner?"—and in fact she seldom did. She later admitted to having been coy with him, "not only because I didn't want to seem too eager, but also because I didn't have too much difficulty finding other entertainment."[65]

Nor had it been difficult to find entertainment in the years before the war, thanks to her *Times* companions and the Three Arts Club visitors who became her "beaus." She also had at least two devoted boyfriends who sent her love letters after they went off to war in 1918. When she subsequently went off to her own war work, she thrived in the intensely male military world. Already an accomplished flirt, she had still more of a whirlwind social life in France and later in Germany, even receiving several marriage proposals (although she said she didn't take them very seriously).[66] She must have returned home newly confident of her appeal.

It's little wonder that Ross was attracted to her, but understanding why she was attracted to him is more difficult. Descriptions of his gangly, oddly proportioned body, widely spaced front teeth, uncontrollable hair, disconcerting mannerisms, and unfashionable clothes are legion. He looked "like a cowhand who'd lost his horse," claimed his friend Harpo Marx. *New Yorker* writer Janet Flanner recalled first meeting Ross around 1920: "His face was homely, with a pendant lower lip . . . he wore his butternut-colored thick hair in a high, stiff pompadour . . . and he also wore anachronistic, old-fashioned, high laced shoes, because he thought Manhattan men dressed like what he called dudes." He made an even more negative impression on Edward L. Bernays when the two men met at the 1919 Paris Peace Conference. Ross was "uncouth, uncultured, and he acted like a boob," Bernays said.[67]

Observers often took particular note of Ross's language preferences. His friend, humorist James Thurber, maintained that he had "a virtual inability to talk without a continuous flow of profanity." Flanner called him "the most blasphemous good talker on record." The *New Yorker*'s first managing editor, Ralph McAllister Ingersoll, described him as "nervous beyond belief" and painted this picture: "Wildly, with great sweeping gestures, he talked—with furious intensity, with steady unimaginative profanity. He had charm—and the vitality of a mad bull."[68]

Grant struggled to explain why she increasingly preferred Ross to her many other suitors. "After the first shock at meeting him, his widely spaced teeth, his unruly hair, his awkward habits only added to his charm," she wrote in her 1968 book. "He was a stimulating and unusual companion and I enjoyed being with him more than with any of the others." She was drawn to "his unbounded curiosity and forthrightness," she said. "His humor was spontaneous, off-beat, and his unusual point of view was refreshing." Even his language was forgivable: "He was as profane as a man can be—but he was never smutty. In the presence of women he was especially puritanical."[69]

That was the extent of her analysis of his desirability except for her description of her first impressions watching him play poker at the Montmartre bistro. As the game progressed he "displayed singular restlessness," Grant wrote. "Even among the eccentrics I'd known in the newspaper world I had not seen such arm waving, coin jingling and hair mussing." Still, "I had been told the night before that he had a reputation as a wit and was showing exceptional ability as the managing editor of the *Stars and Stripes*." Concluding that "he was really the homeliest man I'd ever met," she decided "he'd *have* to be good with that face and figure."[70]

She also might have identified significant commonalties in their lives. Both of them had spent their childhoods in mining towns, received skimpy educations, and, as teenagers, left their families to search for work in professions in which they had demonstrated talent at an early age. They were adventurers, gamblers, and outsiders who first met each other at a time and in a city where they were enjoying themselves enormously. The specifics of their careers had been widely divergent, following stereotypical male and female patterns. Yet they both had assertively created opportunities for themselves, and by 1919 both could be pleased with their journalistic accomplishments, different as they were.

In New York, Ross continued to energetically court Grant. His tactics were similar to those he had used in Paris: candy, flowers, tickets to the theater, boyish love notes, and talk of their compatibility—even though, she admitted, "Ross was not very articulate when he tried to be romantic." Since she loved the opera and symphonic music, he willingly went with her to concerts, but she soon realized he probably was tone-deaf and certainly was not enjoying the performances. Thus while she was engrossed in the music he would do such things as count the house and estimate the management's take, or add up the number of musicians and exclaim, "No wonder they make so much noise."[71]

He much more happily accompanied her on excursions throughout the city she was delighted to be living in again, letting her introduce him to places ranging from Coney Island to the Lower East Side, from Chinatown to the waterfront. She later described these journeys as "part of my campaign to sell New York to him, to make him like it as much as I did, so he'd have no regrets about the South Seas."[72] Her efforts were remarkably successful. In the words of Ross's biographer Thomas Kunkel: "Slowly, deliberately, Jane began to unlock New York for the insatiably curious Ross. His infatuation with the woman and the city advanced in lockstep."[73]

They experienced a very different facet of New York life in a West Forty-Fourth Street hotel's dining room that Grant initially visited with Woollcott. Her friend had returned to his *Times* drama critic position earlier that summer, and on her first day back at the paper in July he excitedly took her to lunch at what he called "our new eating place" in the nearby Algonquin Hotel. Although they were not there that day, a group of journalists and theater people often met at the hotel for lunch, he told her. He later invited her to join the Round Table.[74]

Woollcott was not her only connection to the group, for she had spent time with two of its founders—*New York Tribune* columnist Franklin Pierce Adams and *Vanity Fair* drama critic Robert Sherwood—in Paris when they were *Stars and Stripes* reporters. Her ties to two other founding members—theatrical publicist Murdock Pemberton and his brother Brock, a theatrical assistant producer—went back further, since she had first known them when they visited their art-student sister at the Three Arts Club while she was living there.[75]

Despite these connections, Grant probably would not have been welcome at the Round Table without Woollcott's recommendation. The group had no designated leader but it had originated as a result of an elaborate lunchtime practical joke played on Woollcott in the hotel's Rose Room. The participants had such a good time that they decided to return regularly for lunch, during which Woollcott usually presided. Young and unknown as most early Algonks were, they loved trying to outdo their companions with clever wordplay, then expanded their audience when they wrote about each other and when their witticisms were quoted by still more newspaper and magazine writers.[76] Grant lacked the wit to be a frequent accomplice in this kind of verbal jousting, yet her close friendship with Woollcott and background in the worlds of music and journalism must have let her take at least a minor role.

Even this role, however, would not have been feasible for a *Times* stenographer who sometimes wrote for the society page. Grant was fortunate that when she returned from France she was promoted to hotel reporter (and given an expense account and a small raise). Although far less accomplished than the other Algonks, she did have a regularly staffed position (most New York dailies had a hotel reporter) at a major newspaper. And she probably easily settled into the uncomplicated hotel beat, which required her mainly to interview famous visitors and cover conventions and similar events, with occasional reporting on hard news involving hotel patrons. The topics of her stories, she said, ranged "from suicides to cat shows."[77]

Certainly she was infinitely more content with her job than Ross was with his. When he arrived in New York late in the spring he immediately immersed himself in creating the *Home Sector*, the new magazine for veterans. It was difficult, stressful work, and when he wrote to Grant he complained, "I expect it'll kill me." His first issue, dated September 20, 1919, was followed by only three more before an eight-week-long printers strike shut them down. The publication dragged through the rest of the year and into early 1920, never sure of its focus as it faced both paper shortages and strong competition from the *American Legion Weekly*, the veterans organization's house organ that was trying to expand its readership.[78]

Stars and Stripes alumni in New York no doubt offered Ross their sympathy. Adams had returned to the city early that year and resumed his *Tribune* column, "The Diary of Our Own Samuel Pepys," a personal "journal" written in the Elizabethan style of the seventeenth-century diarist. His July 2 column told readers he had just had dinner with "A. Woollcott and H. Ross," as well as with two others Ross probably met for the first time that night, "H. Broun and Miss R. Hale, nee Hale" (Adams's joke on Hale keeping her name).[79] More often, Ross saw Adams, Woollcott, and Broun at Saturday-night poker games—a carryover of their Paris games—played in the Greenwich Village apartment where he lived with John Winterich, the *Home Sector*'s managing editor and another friend from the *Stars and Stripes*.[80]

Grant sometimes cooked for the two bachelors there, preferring their place to the cramped apartment she shared with a roommate. But even as Ross found more ways to spend time with her, she continued seeing other suitors. One night—following what she said were "a few rude remarks about an escort he'd seen me with"—Ross proposed, suggesting a six-month engagement. Responding "I don't want to be tagged for future delivery," she agreed to marry him, but only on the following Saturday.[81]

Ross thought an immediate wedding was a terrible idea. It violated his strong sense of social decorum; more important, he wasn't confident he would have a job in the near future. The *Home Sector* was folding after only twenty-three issues, having been absorbed by the *American Legion Weekly*. Ross had been asked to edit the expanded *Weekly*, again at a $10,000 salary, but he was reluctant to take the job.

Much as he supported veterans' causes and the legion, he did not want to edit a house organ. Still, he had no other employment prospects. How could he afford to get married right away?[82]

Grant, too, had thought about their finances. In France, with the help of Winterich and two other *Stars and Stripes* staffers, Ross had produced a booklet of soldiers' humor called *Yank Talk* that he sold for a franc. Its profits soared after the Red Cross bought fifty thousand copies, and he ended up clearing more than $3,000 on the project.[83] This nest egg, Grant explained, "served as a big talking point when Ross proposed marriage to me. It would be set aside as a starter for a home we would own."[84] She also insisted that if they wed they would live on her *Times* paycheck, supplemented by any additional money she could earn. Ross's salary, from whatever source, would be saved to fund what she called their "publishing dreams."[85]

Ross decided to accept the American Legion's offer since it would give him the job security he felt he needed to marry. After signing the contract on the morning of March 27, 1920, he left for the Twenty-Ninth Street Methodist church where he and Grant would be married early that afternoon.[86]

CHAPTER 9

"There would be no New Yorker today if it were not for her"

GRANT ARRIVED AT THE LITTLE Church Around the Corner wearing the slightly frayed cinnamon-colored silk dress she had bought in France and worn during many months of performing there and in Germany. It was a busy day for weddings so she and Ross went to the end of a line of couples standing outside the chapel. They were joined by Alexander Woollcott, their witness and the only person who knew about the wedding, which they had decided to keep secret until Ross felt more financially secure.[1]

Their turn finally came for a brief ceremony, after which they were briskly escorted to the exit and the church secretary handed Grant their wedding certificate, saying, "Congratulations, Mrs. Ross." Ross responded first. "Jesus Christ, I don't think I like that 'Mrs. Ross' stuff," he told Grant. "Maybe Ruth Hale's got something after all." Grant later admitted, "Until my wedding day, I had been frankly disinterested in Ruth's agitation. Never for a moment had I considered the possibility of losing my name."[2] With Ross taking the lead, they decided that when they revealed their marriage she would keep her name.[3]

Grant and Woollcott left for their *Times* jobs and Ross headed off to a meeting with his new employer. The trio met for dinner at the Waldorf-Astoria, then Woollcott put them on the train to Philadelphia, where he had reserved two nights for them at the Bellevue-Stratford Hotel, sure that they would encounter no one they knew there. They were back at work on Monday and returned to their own apartments and roommates Monday night.[4]

In late April they gave up the subterfuge, announced their marriage, and moved into a small suite at the Algonquin. Vowing to "give each other complete independence," they agreed that they would each have three weekly "nights off" during which they could do whatever they wanted. Ross knew he would continue going to his Saturday-night poker game. Without Ross as a roommate, John Winterich couldn't afford the rent on their Greenwich Village apartment so had moved to smaller quarters. The game now roamed between players' homes. Because Ross didn't dance and Grant loved dancing, she planned to spend some of her nights off with friends at dance clubs.[5]

Ross did play poker every Saturday night, but he was at a loss for what to do on his other nights. "He waited for me to arrange his social life," Grant said. And the first time she received a midnight phone call inviting her to go dancing, he complained that if she went out that late she wouldn't be able to function the next day. She responded, "Just because you used to take me home early was no reason I stayed there. I've been doing this for years." He said he'd worry about her all night. She left anyway, but his objections continued each time she planned to go dancing, so she went less and less. "It wasn't worth the struggle," she explained.[6]

Since their tight budget made it impractical to stay at the Algonquin for long, that summer they took Ruth Hale and Heywood Broun up on their offer to rent Woodie's temporarily vacant bedroom to them. Here Grant faced a different struggle. Their rent was modest but they shared the expenses of entertaining the innumerable visitors to the West Fifty-Sixth Street apartment. "My liquor budget proved to be definitely inadequate," she recalled. Lack of privacy and Broun's messiness were other disadvantages.[7]

Ross would have his own reasons to regret their summer with Hale and Broun, for it was then that the seeds were sown for something that would irritate him even more than Grant's midnight dance outings. After listening with growing impatience to the two women's many discussions about their problems with keeping their birth names, he facetiously suggested they hire a hall and publicly vent their grievances. This proved to be the extent of his involvement in the Lucy Stone League, which was launched the following spring when Grant and Hale invited friends who shared their concerns to a meeting in the same living room where the two of them had first talked. The small group voted to form an organization to help married women keep their names, electing Hale president and Grant secretary-treasurer.[8]

Early officers and advisory board members included the kinds of activist feminists Grant probably would never have otherwise known, and working with them inevitably affected her. She later acknowledged that before her involvement with the league, "I knew very little about the early feminist struggles. I had followed the activities of the suffragists with interest but it was not my cause." Once she was fighting for women's right to keep their names, though, she "soon worked up indignation over other feminine taboos."[9]

She began working with similar highly motivated women after she helped found the New York Newspaper Women's Club in 1922. Although originally envisioned as a social club, it quickly developed programs to provide mentoring and other career assistance, and to recognize newspaperwomen's achievements. Its top officers included some of the most prominent women journalists in the city, including Martha Coman of the *Herald* and Emma Bugbee of the *Tribune*. Heavily involved in the club from its formation—marked by a congratulatory telegram from President Warren Harding's wife, Florence—Grant chaired several committees and went on to serve as a vice president in 1927, 1928, and 1929.[10]

Associating with these women and with Lucy Stone League members must have helped compensate for the some of Grant's workplace trials. For years she had cheerfully endured the unbridled misogyny at the *Times*, but now she had to suppress her growing concerns with sex discrimination in America and at the paper. Even when she "began to see injustice at first hand," she later confessed, she stayed silent for fear of losing her job.[11] A quick look around the newsroom would have reminded her of her good fortune at having that job. By the early 1920s substantial opportunities had opened up for women at other New York papers, but they "felt it was hopeless to try their luck at the gates of the leading paper in the country," noted Newspaper Women's Club member Ishbel Ross. "Long after the Associated Press had welcomed women, the *Times* still regarded them with suspicion."[12]

Grant's cheerful endurance had helped her advance from society department stenographer to hotel reporter in just five years. It also had helped this high school graduate from small-town Kansas become knowledgeable about the city's social elite as well as familiar with some of the best of its performing arts, thanks in part to the invitations and free admissions that were among her employment privileges. Thus it was at the *Times* that her path to sophistication began.

In the summer of 1922 she took advantage of another perquisite: free transportation to and from France in return for covering the maiden voyage of a new steamship. Traveling not with Ross but with magazine illustrator Neysa McMein, a friend from the Round Table, Grant's first stop was Paris, where she met up with Woollcott and several of his friends, including novelist Edna Ferber. "We whirled around together, we ate ice or drank apéritifs outside the Café Nationale, we saw the Russian Ballet at the Opera in that first world tour which gave Scheherazade and Petrouschka to a bedazzled world," Ferber fondly recalled.[13] And Grant apparently learned how much she enjoyed traveling, for she would continue taking trips like this to places far from New York for almost five decades.

"Jane Grant separately and independently"

SHORTLY AFTER HER RETURN HOME, she and Ross used his *Yank Talk* savings to buy a decrepit double brownstone at 412 West Forty-Seventh Street in a Hell's Kitchen neighborhood she described as "an Irish-bordered-by-Negro slum area." They had spent a year looking for a place, guided by their good friend Hawley Truax, a lawyer who had taken over the management of his family's real estate interests following the death of his father. He showed them properties all over the city, but this brick building sandwiched between a warehouse and a tenement house was the only one that was affordable, conveniently located (near both the *Times* and Ross's magazine), and large enough to be divided into apartments, which was their plan.[14] After making a $5,000 down payment and assuming an $11,000 mortgage, they took ownership in August 1922.[15]

They were far from ready to move in, however, for they first had to carry out massive renovations, financed largely by another $6,000 mortgage provided by Truax. He was investing in his own future since they had agreed he would be a partner in the venture and live in one of the apartments. But once Woollcott learned of their plans, he browbeat the reluctant couple into letting him become another partner. On August 1, 1923, Grant and Ross sold Woollcott and Truax quarter-interests in the property.[16]

By that time the structure had been transformed. Two new top-floor apartments were rented to Woollcott's friends Bill Powell and Kate Oglebay. Woollcott and Truax moved into the two larger apartments on the third floor, while Grant and Ross occupied the sole second-floor apartment. The first floor was designed for the entertaining that Woollcott in particular assumed would be a constant activity in the house. He was, Grant noted, "a highly social but undomesticated animal." This floor held servants' quarters, a large kitchen, and—most important—a twenty-five-foot-square "community room" with a handsome tiled floor, fireplaces at both ends, and doors opening onto a huge flagstone-paved courtyard with an impressive fountain. A chronically out-of-tune concert grand piano sat in one corner of the community room.[17]

Grant's victories went beyond completion of the house. The couple's 1922 mortgage was issued in the names of "Harold W. Ross and Jane Grant, his wife," with a notary certifying that "Harold W. Ross for himself, and Jane Grant separately and independently for herself" had signed to assume the payment obligations.[18]

But her greatest triumph was at the *Times*. Around the same time she and Ross moved into their new home, she was promoted to general assignment reporter, the first woman to hold that position.[19] Her specialty was "women in the news" so she covered stories ranging from visits by presidents' wives to women pioneers in male-dominated fields, from modern trends influenced by women to Charles Lindbergh's transatlantic flights (she was assigned to get his mother's reaction).[20] She also wrote about events of wider interest.[21] *New York Herald Tribune* city editor Stanley Walker described her as a good reporter, albeit one seldom sent out on "rough night assignments."[22]

Her salary still was low—in 1925, for example, it was only $2,459—so she pursued extra work, and in 1923 she wrote four syndicated columns a week. One, on women's health, ran in fourteen newspapers and paid about one hundred dollars a month.[23] More profitable were articles sold to the *Saturday Evening Post* for four hundred or five hundred dollars. Between April and September 1924 the *Post* bought seven articles (all but one coauthored with another Lucy Stoner, Katherine Sproehnle, who later was hired by the firm of Edward L. Bernays, Counsel on Public Relations).[24] Grant had to be at the *Times* from 1 p.m. to 11 p.m. and often needed to work on her syndicated and freelance assignments at home in the morning—no easy task, given Woollcott's interruptions. "He would hear my typewriter and down he would come in his messy pajamas to gossip, needle me, cajole me, or use me as an audience for his latest work," she remembered.[25]

Most of her income went to support the operations at 412 West Forty-Seventh Street, which she supervised.[26] The size of the "family" made it possible (and, given the standards of the residents, necessary) to employ a live-in cook and butler. They hired a husband and wife, Marie and Arthur Treadwell, who adapted well to the unpredictable household and even persuaded their son to join them as a valet, "chiefly to minister to Aleck, the most demanding," Grant explained. She had to oversee the servants' work and, with Truax, determine each person's share of the household's many bills. In addition, because they frequently ate their evening meal together in the community room, it was her job to order supplies and plan menus, always assuming there would be at least five extra dinner guests.[27]

After dinner they often had still more visitors—once leading their neighbors to decide they must be operating a speakeasy and report them to the police.[28] "The house itself was situated in what was practically a slum, but certainly the cream of New York drew up at the door," wrote Edna Ferber.[29] They "drew up" to drink, eat, talk, and more. Irving Berlin sang new songs. Edna St. Vincent Millay, F. Scott Fitzgerald, and Robert Benchley read from new works. Ethel Barrymore acted out scenes from plays she was rehearsing. George Gershwin played pieces he was working on, including one he planned to call "Rhapsody in Blue."[30] These evenings typically attracted a mix of people from journalism, literature, music, and the theater, with the Round Table usually well represented.

The house also was one of the sites of the rotating Saturday-night poker games in which Ross and Woollcott had been playing since the war. Their community room had been planned with these games in mind since it provided the players with space to roam and could be closed off from the rest of the house, leaving the other residents undisturbed. That way Grant and Ross's own living room escaped the kind of damage that had been inflicted on it during games held in their apartment before they moved to the brownstone. Still, Grant and Arthur Treadwell had to clean up after the exceedingly messy players, who consumed copious amounts of her liquor and only occasionally let her (or any women) join the game.[31]

This was not an onerous restriction, for there were many other occasions for both men and women to gamble, and not only at cards. "We didn't really set out to gamble whenever we got together—we just drifted into it," Grant casually noted. "We would take any bet." Popular card games included poker, bridge, and cribbage, and since many of the men carried dice, crap games were common. They tossed coins to decide who would pick up the check at a restaurant; they bet on license plate numbers and while playing board games and anagrams; they created new wagering opportunities whenever the inspiration struck.[32]

"We turned our thoughts to our second dream—publishing"

YET GRANT AND ROSS'S BIGGEST GAMBLE was just beginning. In Paris he had told her about his hopes for starting his own publication, and they began discussing specific possibilities during their New York courtship and early in their marriage. He first was inclined toward a daily—a "high-class tabloid," an adless newspaper or one devoted to shipping news—while she favored a weekly magazine about New York, in part because it would be less time-consuming to produce. As his uncertainly undermined his confidence, she prodded and encouraged him. She also did financial research by consulting with people such as *Times* managing editor Carr Van Anda. "It was quite a responsibility," she said, "but I had the wit to seek advice from those more experienced than Ross and I were."[33]

Although they had been saving his salary to finance the project, they had to first solve their housing problem. So it was only after their brownstone renovations were complete, she explained, that "we turned our thoughts to our second dream—publishing."[34] She pressured him to draw up detailed editorial and financial outlines for what seemed to be the two best possibilities, a shipping newspaper and a metropolitan magazine. After he worked out the specifics for the two publications, the magazine won out. They then each took the fleshed-out magazine idea to several potential investors, all of whom turned them down.[35]

Nevertheless, the new venture consumed them. "Our reading was pretty much restricted to books on printing, typography, and other subjects related to magazines," Grant recalled. "Our apartment was filled with copies of *Punch, Simplici-*

mus and other foreign magazines which we studied for layout; we culled the old files of *Leslie's, Gleason's, Harper's Weekly*, and of course old and new copies of *Life, Judge, The Smart Set* and *American Mercury.*"[36]

One reason for Ross's intensified efforts was his desperation to leave the *American Legion Weekly*. His job had become even more unsatisfying since he grudgingly took it on in 1920, for he not only had little editorial control and creative opportunity but was forced to print countless dull speeches from legion executives. He was so miserable there that in March 1924 he left and took over as coeditor of *Judge*, by this time a money-losing humor magazine. Even as urban Americans had become more cosmopolitan, *Judge* had become more sophomoric, increasingly playing to the lowest common denominator. This Ross hoped to change, but the impossibility of the task quickly became clear and he quit after five months. Yet the disheartening experience strengthened his desire to publish a stylish humor magazine of his own.[37]

Equally important, *Judge's* plummeting national advertising revenues further convinced him that New York advertisers would flock to a local magazine. Writer Corey Ford described submitting a clever article on New York's snow removal problems that Ross liked but had to turn down because of its limited national appeal. "That's the trouble with this goddamn magazine," Ross exclaimed to Ford. "If it went after a local audience, it would get local advertising." He was sure "there's enough revenue right here in this city to support a smart metropolitan weekly."[38]

Still, money remained a daunting obstacle, and here Grant's initiative was crucial. They thought it would cost $50,000 to start their magazine (although Van Anda correctly estimated it would take much more) and believed they could come up with $25,000 by liquidating all their assets. But they had no luck raising the rest of the money they needed until the spring of 1924, when they went to a party at the home of Ruth and Raoul Fleischmann. They often headed there to gamble but "the only gaming that evening was bridge," Grant recalled, and since she hadn't yet learned to play, she sat with her host, telling him about their plans for a magazine.[39]

Ross had first met Fleischmann in 1921 when Franklin Pierce Adams brought him to one of their Saturday-night poker games. A General Baking Company heir who was reluctantly (and very successfully) managing the family business, Fleischmann thoroughly enjoyed the games. At the same time, the wealthy businessman's appeal to the other players went beyond his always-welcome deep pockets; he also was good company, so invitations to Algonquin lunches followed. He and his wife "saw a lot of these amusing and interesting people," he remembered, and "for ten years I had more fun than I can say."[40]

He admitted that when he got together with these friends, "I often spoke about my growing boredom with baking—it doubtless became quite boring to hear about."[41] He knew nothing about publishing but could tell that the project Grant described that night would not be boring. And with a net worth of nearly a million dollars he could well afford to put up the $25,000 she requested. He told her to send Ross over the next day to pitch his idea.[42]

When Ross met with the potential investor, though, he inexplicably tried to sell him on the shipping newspaper. "I couldn't understand why he came to me with such an dull idea," Fleischmann told Grant. "As you described it to me at the party the magazine sounded exciting." It took a week of Grant's prodding before Ross was willing to return with his proposal for a metropolitan weekly. Finding this a far more appealing gamble, Fleischmann agreed to invest $25,000 and become its publisher.[43]

"She is the one who got Fleischmann interested in promoting the magazine," Ross declared two decades later. "There would be no New Yorker today if it were not for her. She got a sucker when I failed, after a long hunt for suckers."[44] Elaborating on Grant's forcefulness in a letter to someone who knew her well, Ross revealed that he actually had gone to Fleischmann at an earlier time, asked him to fund the magazine and been refused. (This may explain why he pitched the shipping newspaper when he sat down with him again.) But, he wrote, "Jane Grant kept after Fleischmann with persistence (and I believe you now know what Jane Grant's persistence is) and got him to finance The New Yorker."[45]

Fleischmann also contributed office space in a building he owned at 25 West Forty-Fifth Street, and in August Ross and a small staff moved in. But this did not end the couple's hunt for outside financing. Grant, for example, tried to interest Bernard Baruch, a wealthy Wall Street investment banker who sometimes took her and other friends in his private railroad car to places like his South Carolina plantation and Atlantic City. On one 1924 excursion she walked with him along the Atlantic City boardwalk and made her case for investing in the magazine. He said he thought it was too risky but later offered to loan them money.[46]

Grant and Ross's home was a more convenient place to raise money. Identifying Edward L. Bernays and Doris E. Fleischmann as possible investors, they invited them to dinner and described their plans. Bernays had not liked Ross when they first met in Paris during the Versailles Peace Conference, but his negative opinion had begun to change after he got to know him better at friends' parties in New York. Unfortunately, Woollcott was in a bad mood the night of their dinner and walked back and forth through the community room insulting the guests. "Everybody was tense anyway in that household," Bernays recalled. "That strange ménage and the neurotic Ross reaffirmed my decision not to invest my time or money in *The New Yorker*."[47]

Bernays, Baruch, and several others who turned down their requests to invest in the new venture may well have seen a red flag in the couple's estimate that the magazine could be produced for $50,000. At the same time, Ross needed to better describe his plans for the publication, which he did in a fall 1924 printed prospectus. "*The New Yorker* will be a reflection in word and picture of metropolitan life," the document asserted. "It will be what is commonly called sophisticated, in that it will assume a reasonable degree of enlightenment on the part of its readers." The last line of the prospectus gave one more piece of information: "H. W. Ross, Editor."[48]

That line caused some doubts, captured well by Ross's friend, playwright Ben Hecht, who asked, "How the hell could a man who looked like a resident of the Ozarks and talked like a saloon brawler set himself up as the pilot of a sophisticated, elegant periodical?"[49] A high-school dropout who had lived in New York for only five years and loved reading dictionaries and true-detective magazines, Ross still clung to some provincial values. By 1924 it was clear that he was a talented editor with an avid curiosity, quick mind, and droll sense of humor, but he was hardly sophisticated.[50] Algonquin manager Frank Case maintained that within the Round Table group Ross was "a sort of adopted child, taken in on approval before the final papers were signed."[51]

Thanks largely to Grant's efforts and abilities, though, his home attracted the kinds of people who were influencing the city's culture and would be central to his magazine's identity. Grant's own sparse education had not kept her from being a quick learner once she left Kansas. After resolutely sharpening her social skills, she became her *Times* colleagues' dining, dancing, theater-going, and overall good-times companion. Within a few more years, she was mixing easily with wealthy people like Baruch and Fleischmann. "Few newspaper women have a wider acquaintance among the town's celebrities than Miss Grant," journalist Ishbel Ross remarked.[52]

Ross complained that he lived in a goldfish bowl, and Grant ruefully acknowledged that "he was not a relaxed host." Yet interacting with the urbane, witty, talented men and women who gathered at his West Forty-Seventh Street brownstone certainly helped prepare him to begin publishing "a sophisticated, elegant periodical" in 1925.[53]

"I have never worked harder in my life"

UNABLE TO RESIST INVOLVING himself in the *New Yorker*'s launch, Bernays offered to help publicize it. His office sent telegrams (signed by Alice Duer Miller) to area newspapers announcing the magazine's debut and noting that it coincided with the two hundredth anniversary of the publication of the city's very first weekly (a newspaper), the *New York Gazette*.[54] Some papers picked up the story, but when she and Ross anxiously checked newsstands after the first issue appeared on February 17, 1925, Grant said, "the piles of unsold *The* [*sic*] *New Yorkers* were staggering." And "as weeks passed the succeeding numbers were no better received."[55]

It was little wonder, for the *New York Gazette* surely was more satisfying to its readers in 1725 than the *New Yorker* was to those who purchased early issues and discovered weak humor, unimaginative articles, and departments that were moved and dropped at will. "It was full of *Life* and *Judge* humor and half-baked Broadway gossip," remembered early staff member Ralph McAllister Ingersoll. "And it looked like it had been made up by the office cat's knocking over the wastebasket."[56]

A key reason for the disappointing contents was that Ross had little money to pay his staff and contributors. He even cut his own weekly salary from three hundred dollars to one hundred after he and Grant liquidated their assets and netted only about $20,000 of the $25,000 they had promised to put into the magazine. Their estimate of publishing costs had been unrealistic in any case, and they had not foreseen how meager their revenues would be. They printed fifteen thousand copies of the first issue; a month later, circulation was only ten thousand; by the end of April, it was down to eight thousand. Advertising was so scarce that May issues shrank to twenty-four pages. One summer issue carried ads worth a total of $52.50 (which the magazine did not collect).[57]

The $45,000 invested by Fleischmann, Grant, and Ross lasted just six weeks, forcing Fleischmann to write personal checks to cover all subsequent printing and payroll bills. Tired of losing from $5,000 to $8,000 a week, he decided in early May to pull the plug. Only at the last minute did he agree to keep the publication going at reduced costs through the slow summer months. Ross, in turn, would stockpile the best material for the early fall issues, and $60,000 would be spent on a newspaper advertising campaign to promote the improved magazine.[58]

This new plan also obligated the couple to raise more money for their floundering enterprise, but "Ross refused to take the initiative," Grant said, so she set to work by herself. She convinced housemate Truax to invest, and, often following leads from her, he persuaded people he knew to do the same. (He had less luck when he approached Bernays, who remained resistant to buying into the magazine so passed up a chance to purchase a large block of shares for $5,000.) Grant even got a Texas oilman to agree to put up $100,000. When told about the offer, Fleischmann scrambled to raise $100,000 from family members—including his independently wealthy wife—thus making sure the Texan would not hold a major stake in the business.[59]

Earlier that spring Ross had tried to tap into another source of funds by joining a poker game at a party he and Grant attended. Though he was winning when she wanted to leave, as he rose to join her he was taunted for "being pushed around by a skirt" and dropping out when he was ahead. She went home by herself, he kept drinking and playing, and by the time the game ended he had lost nearly $30,000. "With us so completely in hock to *The New Yorker* already, this added debt gave me a feeling of utter despair," she wrote.[60]

They worked out a rough plan to slowly pay off the enormous debt, but Fleischmann, who also had been in the game, turned out to be their savior. Convinced that the other players had taken advantage of Ross's inebriated state and anxiety over the magazine's money problems, he got some of the IOUs absolved and personally paid off others. This both saved Ross and fueled his resentment, since he feared he would forever feel indebted to the publisher.[61]

The *New Yorker*'s finances were not Grant's only interest. She also helped form its staff. Probably her earliest suggestion, in January 1925, was that the art critic position be offered to theatrical press agent and art lover (and resident of Ruth Hale's second Sabine Farm house) Murdock Pemberton. She had known him for more than a decade and he had confided that he was taking drawing classes. But since he had never before written criticism, Ross was dubious about his ability to do the job, which he went on to do expertly for seven years.[62]

That summer Grant contacted another friend, Janet Flanner, whom she had visited during her 1922 trip to France. A fellow Lucy Stoner, Flanner had moved to Paris because, she said, "Americans with little private incomes, like me, who wanted to write, could afford to live on their hopes and good bistro food."[63] The two corresponded after their visit, although when Grant wrote to Flanner in June 1925 she lamented having been out of touch for many months. She and Ross had a new project, she explained, and "I have never worked harder in my life."[64]

In her letter she asked her friend to write a column for their magazine, telling her, "I think you could do it beautifully." Flanner agreed to try, and when her "Paris Letter" first ran in October it contributed to the reinvigorated *New Yorker's* more cosmopolitan image. The column continued for five decades, helping establish essay-journalism as a *New Yorker* staple and earning Flanner a reputation as a superb foreign correspondent.[65] She later told Grant, "You did more than give me an important push in 1925—You made my life and career."[66]

Grant both solicited people she knew as contributors and acted as an intermediary, recommending promising candidates who had been recommended to her. "Ross was likely to brush off all but the most persistent applicants in the early days of the magazine," she explained, so people learned to bring their suggestions to her, and she would make a case for those she thought had potential. For example, she pushed him to hire Charles Brackett, who became the publication's second drama critic; Wolcott Gibbs, a highly versatile writer and editor; and Ralph McAllister Ingersoll, hired as a reporter and subsequently named the first managing editor (despite Ross's resistance to letting anyone else do much managing).[67]

Their home became a kind of overflow office, "strewn with manuscripts, verse, drawings, dummies." There, she noted, "Ross kept me generously supplied with homework—manuscripts to read, contacts to make and keep up, which he had no time or wish for, and various other assignments."[68] One assignment that summer was to organize their first subscription campaign. Building on her *Times* society department experience and working with Ross's secretary, she wrote a sales pitch and hired "vacationing college girls" to telephone potential subscribers whose names she had culled from the *Social Register*. Their pitch was tied to newspaper ads running as part of the $60,000 promotional campaign, which Ingersoll described as "the last desperate attempt to swarm the penthouses." One ad showed fashionable apartment buildings where current subscribers (mainly the couple's friends) lived.[69]

Grant also insisted that Ross publish the article responsible for the *New Yorker's* first sold-out issue. Alice Duer Miller, another friend and Lucy Stoner, asked her to intervene in support of a manuscript submitted by her cousin, Ellin Mackey, the well-known daughter of the wealthy president of Postal Telegraph. Ross strongly resisted printing the poorly written, snobbish piece describing why young socialites preferred dancing with salesmen in cabarets to enduring men in stag lines at upper-class parties. But Grant eagerly recommended publication because she knew she could use the controversy the piece would provoke to draw attention to the magazine, especially among the elite New Yorkers Ross hoped to attract as readers.[70]

Before "Why We Go to Cabarets: A Post-Debutante Explains" ran in the November 28 issue, she leaked page proofs to the *Times*, *Tribune*, and *World*, which all ran front-page stories about the piece. Following the lead of the morning papers, the city's afternoon papers and wire services picked up on the story, and editorials and rebuttals followed. James Thurber said he first heard of the *New Yorker* when he was living in France and read a front-page *Paris Herald* story about Mackey's piece.[71] "It took Park Avenue in a storm of gossip," Ingersoll wrote, giving the magazine new visibility among "the Social (capital S) in metropolitan New York."[72] In a follow-up article two weeks later Mackey criticized upper-class hostesses for using celebrities to liven up their parties, and the *Times* responded with an article and editorial.[73]

The Park Avenue residents who wanted to read the revelations of the "post-debutante" about people like themselves were the same kinds of readers who had been targeted by Grant's summer subscription campaign and the concurrent $60,000 promotion. And during the fall, increasing numbers of ads aimed at upper-class readers could be found in the *New Yorker*, with even more appearing after Mackey's articles ran.[74] Ross's plan for luring specialized local advertisers away from the city's newspapers was beginning to succeed. As Ingersoll put it, Ross slowly was creating "a journal that could separate affluent sheep from penniless goats."[75]

At the same time, new contributors were writing substantive commentary that drew readers back each week. Flanner's column joined Morris Markey's well-reported, personal view of the city, "A Reporter at Large," while Lois Long (another Lucy Stoner) frankly reviewed nightclubs in "Tables for Two" and fashion in "On and Off the Avenue." Ross found additional writers who could provide distinctive material, and in August 1925 he hired a first-rate editor, Katharine Angell. Yet the magazine's "art"—illustrations and, especially, cartoons—always was its most popular feature, and Ross often declared, "We need to get the words like the art!"[76] That fall he was starting to get what he wanted.

By that difficult year's end, circulation had reached twenty-five thousand, and the magazine's future looked promising enough that it took over more space in Fleischmann's building. Major retailers like Saks Fifth Avenue and B. Altman's signed yearlong contracts, while advertising income, which had totaled $36,000 in 1925, rose to $389,000 the next year. In 1926 the average size of an issue grew from forty-eight pages in January to ninety-six pages in December. Even more important, by the end of 1927 Ross had hired the four people—Angell, Thurber, E. B. White, and Wolcott Gibbs—who would become the firm foundation of the magazine he envisioned. With its circulation topping seventy thousand when 1928 came to a close, the *New Yorker* announced its first profitable year.[77]

"I truly realize that I must be almost impossible"

THE MAGAZINE'S TURNAROUND was an enormous relief to Grant, "but this miracle did not happen without pain to many early participants," she admitted.[78] With what Ingersoll called "a frenzy I doubt if any of us has ever forgotten," Ross pushed his young, underpaid staff to their limits. "We thought nothing of working from early morning until nine or ten at night," said writer Marcia Davenport, noting that one reason they stayed so late was that their pieces often "had to be rewritten in whole or in part once Ross got his hooks into them." "We were badly understaffed back then," explained Thurber, who was working twelve-hour days, seven days a week. "Ross had us all thinking that the only way a magazine could get published was to work ourselves to death."[79]

Ross was still harder on himself. "He was a perfectionist, nagging, fretting, demanding, raking his fingers through his hair and pawing the air in a frantic quest of the ultimate, the issue without a flaw," observed Corey Ford, another staff writer. "He was into everything."[80] Finding it difficult to delegate any responsibilities as he ran a larger operation than he had ever before managed, he was constantly stressed.[81] Even when the workday should have been over, he dragged employees to a nearby speakeasy where, Ingersoll recalled, "we'd have five or six drinks, Ross still talking The Magazine. Some of us wanted to be home, but family life was out."[82]

Certainly Ross's own family life suffered. He brought home not only submissions he wanted to discuss with Grant but his editors, and she was expected to entertain people she disliked. Their close friend and stalwart *New Yorker* contributor Marc Connelly told Grant what Ross said to him in justification: "Well, God damn it, I've got to be nice to them—they help me all the time in my work, and I ought to be able to bring them to dinner any time, God damn it."[83] His home had become so much a part of his workplace that Ingersoll sometimes was called there for prebreakfast meetings, carried out while Ross was shaving. Notoriously, the brownstone once was the scene of a Thanksgiving-morning staff meeting.[84] "Conferences were held in our garden, the community room—any available space," Grant remembered.[85]

Worried about the extreme demands Ross was placing on himself and others, Grant tried to distract him by arranging playful trips out of town, often accompanied by other Algonks.[86] And in what she said was an effort to "keep Ross in contact with new talent and also to give the impression that we were doing fine," at least once a week she held a dinner party for up to forty people. Plus, she said, "If any of my friends wanted to throw a party I offered our house, and more and more it was regarded as the official meeting place to our crowd."[87]

She does seem to have tried to attract potential *New Yorker* contributors to these events, but mainly she was trying to brighten up her own life. She certainly could not have thought they gave Ross a reason to come home instead of working late at the office, for at the end of the day he was tired, tense, distracted, and in no mood to socialize. Thus, according to Grant, "Quite often, as a reproof, Ross would go to bed when the party was in full swing, or he was known to lie down on the floor and 'at least relax' while the startled guests climbed over him."[88]

His tolerance also weakened for the man with whom he shared what Thurber described as an "occasionally warm, always ambivalent, and often sadistic friendship." Woollcott had been difficult to live with since the day he moved in, guaranteed, for example, to hold forth at dinners in the community room whether or not he had been invited. "Ross was by no means a skillful talker" and "resented his friend's easy command of narrative," Thurber believed. "He knew and was revered or feared, liked or avoided, by almost everybody of any consequence on Broadway," and told stories that "enchanted many visitors."[89] But they were not enchanting when he felt the need to tell them late at night. Grant wrote that "Ross and I came to dread the sound of the taxicab that deposited Aleck beneath our window," for it meant Woollcott might well burst into their darkened bedroom with tales of his evening.[90]

By early 1926 it was clear that Woollcott would have to go, and since Ross hated confrontation, Grant would have to make him go. After vehemently resisting, he finally agreed to sell them his share of the property, and left in June. Their problems with him continued, however, for he remained angry, particularly at her. He pointedly invited Ross but not Grant to Broadway openings and parties at his new home, trying to set them against each other. "He played a big part in making our marriage impossible," she acknowledged.[91]

The relationship between the two men improved enough that in 1929 Woollcott began writing an exceedingly popular column for the *New Yorker*, but Ross and Grant's relationship only became more troubled. A key trigger was his irritation at her feminism. "The reason I left Jane Grant, or whatever it was, was that I never had one damned meal at home at which the discussion wasn't of women's rights and the ruthlessness of men in trampling women," he later complained. "You go through several years of that and you can't take it anymore."[92] He exaggerated, but his words show something of the depth of her concerns, how vocal she became about them, and the ways they further separated the couple.

They had married suddenly in 1920 with little chance to talk about what they wanted in their life together. He disliked hearing her called "Mrs. Ross" after the ceremony so urged her to remain Jane Grant, which initially was easy to do since their marriage was secret. By the time they moved in with Hale and Broun, Grant had kept her name for only three months, but Hale had been fighting to keep hers for three years, so she cared more about this cause. Ross could neither have anticipated the long talks the two women would have about their names, nor imagined that those talks would lead to the formation of the Lucy Stone League.

Despite the demands of life at 412 West Forty-Seventh Street, of launching the *New Yorker*, and of her *Times* and freelance writing, Grant worked vigorously for the league, demonstrating unmistakable talent as an organizer and advocate. In fact, the confidence she gained from that work probably fueled her ambition to move up at the *Times*, just as her growing knowledge of women's issues made her better qualified for the new cityside position she was offered. The league's accomplishments must have been exhilarating, just as its dissolution following her 1925 falling-out with Hale must have been heartbreaking. At that time she, too, was heavily immersed in the *New Yorker*, which may have kept her from doing all she could have done to try to patch up the wounded league and her friendship with Hale.

Nor were her efforts to patch up her marriage successful. Even with Woollcott gone, she observed, "Ross found no peace. He would lug his typewriter from one room to another in restless frenzy." Tellingly, they converted a portion of Woollcott's apartment into two new bedrooms, one for each of them. She supervised some of the remodeling from her bed in Mount Sinai Hospital, where she was taken after a nervous collapse in the fall of 1927. His added private space did not keep Ross from renting a room in a hotel across from the *New Yorker*, after which, she said, "his calls to say he wouldn't be home became more frequent."[93]

Still, she was surprised in late 1927 when he asked her to move out of the house for a three-month trial separation. She agreed to leave and to "subordinate all thought of my career and even my happiness," she explained, because she believed that "for both of our sakes—even if we were to go separate ways—*The New Yorker* must continue its new promising course—and it could not with Ross in his present state of mind." But more bad news followed. She apparently was diagnosed with colitis during her fall hospital stay, and her health did not improve afterward. Following a three-week sick leave from the *Times* to visit friends in Georgia and Florida, she returned to New York in late March 1928 and moved into a hotel.[94]

That spring she tried to be patient and understanding as she searched for ways to salvage the marriage, even enlisting the help of Marc Connelly and Ross's mother (who told her, "no wonder you had a nervous breakdown").[95] After a long talk with his friend, Connelly reported to Grant that he thought Ross was "unconsciously passing off on you (because of convenience and tangibility) the strain he feels at the magazine."[96] That strain was reflected in a letter Ross sent her immediately after her March 1928 return to New York. He called her "a disturbing and upsetting person," declared "we differ in almost everything," and asked her to let him stay in the house indefinitely since "the only real moments of placidity that I have had in several years have come during the last few weeks" when she was absent. "I truly realize that I must be almost impossible," he said, but "I simply could not live with you here."[97]

They did sometimes see each other for dinner and meet to discuss problems at the *New Yorker*. At one point he even proposed that after he solved some of those problems they try living together again, but by the end of the summer they seem to have known they could not. They agreed to divorce. The first step was to dispose of the brownstone, which they did by selling their shares to Hawley Truax, recently married and living in one of their renovated apartments.[98]

Ross rented an apartment of his own and eventually had the good fortune to find an ideal roommate: Ed McNamara, who was forced to leave the Hale/Broun brownstone (and was much missed by their son) when it was sold in the spring of 1929. The genial, considerate McNamara no doubt was immensely easier to live with than Grant had been. She moved into a small apartment at the Savoy-Plaza Hotel on Fifth Avenue and Fifty-Ninth Street.[99]

Marie Treadwell went with her as her maid. Ross was adamant about keeping Marie's husband, Arthur, with him when he moved, saying this was "one of the few things I would not consider compromise on."[100] Grant described him as having few other demands. "Breaking up our household was a shattering experience," she wrote, but "never for a moment did Ross lack consideration." He insisted that she take everything she wanted from the house and even avoided unkind words about her when he discussed their problems with his mother. "He seems to care little about himself, only work and be let alone," Ida Ross told Grant.[101]

In retrospect, his reactions are not surprising. Grant had made the *New Yorker*'s survival her first priority, had moved out of their home for him, had agreed to a divorce she did not want, had accommodated him in many other ways. Perhaps more important, they had been living apart long enough that she no longer regularly irritated him the way she had when they lived together. He now could "work and be let alone," devoting himself to what he cared about most. Indeed, around this same time he told Thurber, "I'm married to this magazine. It's all I ever think about."[102] That marriage would be a difficult, highly emotional, exceedingly rewarding one in which (despite his threats) divorce was never a real possibility.

"Wild hopefulness"

GRANT'S FEMINISM WAS A PROFOUND irritation as much because of her outspoken advocacy as because it clashed with Ross's values. "A factor in our final separation was twitting from his poker cronies that he was afraid of women, and that he allowed me to dominate him," she admitted.[103] Thurber remembered that when he first told Ross he was in love with the woman who would become his second wife, Ross asked only one question about her: "Is she quiet?"[104]

His biographer Thomas Kunkel explained that Ross was "at heart a nineteenth-century man" with "Victorian attitudes about sexuality, virtue, and women's roles." But he lived "in a time and a place where traditional attitudes and roles were being pitched out like so much bad bathtub gin. The man who emerged could appreciate the modern woman, all right, but more so intellectually than emotionally."[105] Grant knew some of Ross's Victorian attitudes well, having been turned down when she suggested that they have sex before they married. She said she never saw him nude—only in a nightshirt—during all the time of their marriage.[106]

She could have had few illusions about his values and views when she married him, but he was not prepared for the person she would become. Rather, he was drawn to the woman he met in France who had found a comfortable place for herself with the American military and at the *Times* by learning to please men. As she later wrote, "Adjusting myself to their world is one of the things at which I have been rather competent."[107]

She and Ross actually had spent only sporadic time together during the year and a half between their first meeting and their marriage. He mainly knew an exuberant, popular woman who shared his "publishing dreams." And she had other traits that must have been appealing, such as social skills he sorely lacked and a sharp financial sense rooted in her precarious and insufficient income during her early New York years. Those strengths would prove essential to the creation of the *New Yorker*.

The couple also shared a trait that goes far in explaining why two people with so many differences would marry and throw themselves into founding a magazine: they both were inveterate gamblers. They had been risk takers in their everyday lives for years before they met at a Paris poker game, while during their years together in New York, Grant remembered, "we would take any bet."

Their magazine needed a third gambler, though, and here Ross readily credited Grant's efforts. In his inelegant words, "She got a sucker when I failed." Raoul Fleischmann was not a natural match, as his *New Yorker* obituary writer noted when he compared the magazine's privileged, refined, low-key publisher with its rough-edged, abrasive, volatile editor, finally concluding, "The disparities between the two men were almost endless." Yet in describing Fleischmann's love of the racetrack the writer also observed, "His betting would often be colored by sentiment, wild hopefulness, and the most transient hunches."[108]

Surely this also was true of his innocent initial investment in the magazine and continued commitment to it. For all three of these gamblers, the thrill of playing in a game so new that both the stakes and the odds of winning were impossible to guess kept them throwing more and more into the pot. Fleischmann put approximately $700,000 (more than $8 million in today's dollars) into the *New Yorker* before it made a profit in 1928, leading Ingersoll to comment, "Although it took very nearly all the money Raoul Fleischmann had, he had enough."[109] He might have used almost the same words to characterize Grant and Ross's more arduous investment. The magazine took very nearly all they had, but they had enough.

Her meager income meant Grant could not have afforded to buy the
elegant clothes she wears in this New York studio photographer's portrait
of her at about age twenty, yet she looks comfortable and confident.
*Jane Grant Papers, Ph141, Special Collections and University Archives,
University of Oregon.*

Grant thought everything about her YMCA service uniform was ugly—including its olive-green color— but that didn't prevent her from attracting many suitors when she wore it while serving as a World War I volunteer in France. *Jane Grant Papers, Ph141, Special Collections and University Archives, University of Oregon.*

Private Harold Ross in his World War I army uniform. Although he enlisted in the engineering corps, he joined the staff of the *Stars and Stripes* soon after it was launched in February 1918, and was named managing editor nine months later. *Jane Grant Papers, Ph141, Special Collections and University Archives, University of Oregon.*

Grant with Alexander Woollcott in Belleau Wood, France. Soon
after the United States entered World War I Woollcott took a
leave from his *New York Times* drama critic position to join the
army. He was sent to France, where he much enjoyed visiting
with Ruth Hale and Heywood Broun in 1917, and introduced
Grant to Ross at a Paris poker game in 1918. *Jane Grant Papers,
Ph141, Special Collections and University Archives, University of
Oregon.*

Grant and Ross on a New Jersey outing not long after they married in March 1920. They initially kept their marriage a secret, living with roommates in separate apartments and taking weekend excursions together. *Jane Grant Papers, Ph141, Special Collections and University Archives, University of Oregon.*

Grant and Ross stand by a wall of their West Forty-Seventh Street brownstone. Despite its Hell's Kitchen location and adjacent tenement house, "the
cream of New York drew up at the door," playwright and novelist Edna
Ferber recalled. *Jane Grant Papers, Ph141, Special Collections and University
Archives, University of Oregon.*

In 1926 celebrity photographer Nickolas Muray posed Grant and Ross in old-fashioned daguerreotype style. The couple's body language and facial expressions say something about the toll that publishing the nascent *New Yorker* had taken on their marriage. *Jane Grant Papers, Ph141, Special Collections and University Archives, University of Oregon.*

Grant looks content in this photograph, probably taken in the mid- to late 1930s. *Jane Grant Papers, Ph141, Special Collections and University Archives, University of Oregon.*

Grant at her desk in her home office during the 1940s. This was her
favorite portrait of herself. *Jane Grant Papers, Ph141, Special Collections
and University Archives, University of Oregon.*

Taken around 1970 in their Litchfield home next to White Flower Farm, this photograph of Grant and William Harris captures their happy, egalitarian relationship, which lasted more than thirty years. *Jane Grant Papers, Ph141, Special Collections and University Archives, University of Oregon.*

CHAPTER 10

"I really preferred to get my financial reward from the magazine"

HER NAME ON THEIR DIVORCE PAPERS was one she had never used. Jane Grant Ross, the plaintiff, was granted a divorce from the defendant, Harold W. Ross, to take effect in early September 1929. The inaccuracy of her name was oddly consistent with the false basis for the divorce. New York State required that serious grounds be alleged and proved, so Ross—who had asked her to divorce him—agreed to be charged with adultery. He did not contest the charges, although there is no evidence that he actually was unfaithful.[1]

In any case, earlier that same year she had signed her birth name on a legal document that, unlike the divorce, was very much her idea. This one addressed her future and that of the *New Yorker*. The worst seemed to be over for the magazine, but despite all of her past efforts and sacrifices for it, once she divorced Ross she would lose her chance to share in any future financial success unless she took action.

Alimony was not a solution because she disapproved of it, while Ross had little money and was responsible for supporting his widowed mother. "I really preferred to get my financial reward from the magazine," she explained.[2] And she did. On April 1, 1929, she and Ross signed an agreement that obligated him to deposit 450 shares of his F-R Publishing Corporation stock into an escrow account for her, and to promise her $10,000 a year in dividends. If the stocks yielded less he would make up the difference himself.[3]

"Since the magazine was not certain to be over the hill, Ross objected fiercely" when her lawyer first proposed the settlement, she admitted. "We wrangled for several weeks before we reached an agreement."[4] To strengthen her position she researched the magazine's finances and stock performance. One person she asked to review its profit and loss statements was Wilbur Holleman, an Oklahoma City attorney who in late August 1929 sent her a long analysis of changes in the stocks' value, pointing out that the 1928 profit "was almost entirely wiped out by deficits for preceding years" and by a bonus the board of directors had awarded Ross. He ended by saying, "I will try to write you a personal letter before the end of the day."[5]

That letter was exceedingly personal, as were other love letters she received from him. Through those that survive it is possible to piece together a relationship that began on her trip to Europe earlier that summer and was held together in part by expensive long-distance phone calls.[6] In reality, she was the adulterer. A strong case easily can be made, however, that she well deserved whatever pleasure and financial advice the relationship brought her.

Her European trip was not primarily for pleasure, although Holleman must have made it more enjoyable than she'd anticipated, and she visited Janet Flanner in Paris to talk with her about possibly moving there. But she had time to travel because the *Times* had granted her another sick leave after a year of worsening health problems, and her ultimate destination was Châtel-Guyon, where she had an appointment to see a French doctor. After determining that her condition was more serious than the colitis her New York doctors had diagnosed, he recommended immediate surgery. "If French hospitals looked like the good doctor's office I wanted no part of one," she said, "so I returned home at once."[7]

Back in New York, additional tests showed she had cancer. She was hospitalized for two months and had two operations, the second leaving her with an open wound that did not heal for six months. By chance Ross spotted her through her taxi window when she was on her way to the hospital for the initial tests. Telling her "you look awful," he climbed into the cab and accompanied her to the hospital. He questioned the subsequent diagnosis and called in more specialists, who agreed she needed immediate surgery.[8]

When she was allowed to leave the hospital after her two operations, he summoned her sister from Missouri to help care for her, then made sure she went to Florida to recuperate (and undergo unanticipated additional surgery). He telephoned her there and sent flowers and presents. But someone else took her home. As she wrote, "One of my beau [*sic*] journeyed from Oklahoma and brought me back to New York when I was able to make the trip."[9]

Ross's solicitousness no doubt was due to genuine concern, to relief that their divorce negotiations were over, and to guilt as well. The papers finalizing the divorce were delivered to Grant in the hospital, with Ross, as she put it, "expressively absent." He had said he would bring them himself but in the end he "couldn't bear the idea," he told her friends. Similarly, he had promised to write to his mother to tell her about their final breakup but never did, so she wrote to Ida Ross herself. "I guess I never really expected he would," Grant remembered, for "he had never liked, and had rarely performed, unpleasant duties."[10]

Her *Times* editor held her job for her during her long recovery but "it took some doing," she noted, and 1930 seems to have been her last year at the paper.[11] She may have faced new health problems in 1931, for in early April Ross offered to loan her money so she could pay a doctor's bill.[12] Soon afterward she arranged to borrow against her F-R stock to cover what was described as "emergency expenses occasioned by her illness," although she canceled the paperwork following a reassessment of her options and more legal input, including from Wilbur Holleman.[13] In late September 1931, while she was continuing to explore financial alternatives, her lawyer described her as "still a semi-invalid."[14]

When Ross signed the 1929 agreement with Grant "it seemed a reasonable document," he later wrote. "The New Yorker's earnings warranted it."[15] In 1931 he could comfortably offer to loan her two $1,000 advances on her dividends because he was earning substantial income of his own from F-R stock. Notwithstanding the Depression, it continued to perform so well that even in 1934 Grant's 450 shares paid dividends in excess of $10,000.[16]

But as the Depression deepened Raoul Fleischmann decided the magazine needed to build a large cash reserve as a cushion. This reduced dividends, forcing Ross to make up the loss to Grant from his own funds. He also took on new expenses after he remarried in 1934, and the Internal Revenue Service was demanding several thousand dollars for back taxes it claimed he owed.[17] Other difficulties at the magazine and his unwise decision to sell most of his own F-R stock in 1934 and 1935 meant that his agreement with Grant, which originally had caused no hardship, was starting to become a burden.[18]

"She is both intelligent and adventurous"

INDEED, THAT 1929 DOCUMENT went on to become more important to both of them than either one could have anticipated. "The agreement was made before my illness when I thought I would be able to augment the sum agreed upon," she later emphasized in a letter to Ross's lawyer.[19] She expected to continue at the *Times*, where she had made remarkable progress since starting as a stenographer.

After recuperating from her cancer surgery, in 1930 she returned to one of the best jobs a woman could have at this prominent newspaper, and one she previously had successfully juggled with other demanding responsibilities, including those at the beleaguered *New Yorker*. Yet she left the paper sometime that year. Impossible as it is to know all the circumstances of her departure, it seems likely that she would have tried harder to hold onto her *Times* job if not for her guaranteed annual income from F-R stock equaling more than $120,000 in today's dollars. Her agreement with Ross let her gamble again, this time with her career.

The agreement also let her to do something she loved and otherwise could only have dreamed of doing. In the 1930s she took four long trips to fascinating, turbulent parts of the world. Not only did she have real adventures during each trip but she managed to socialize extensively with expatriates, diplomats, and other Americans who had found ways to live well outside the United States during the Depression. As in her YMCA travels through France and Germany immediately after the end of World War I, she did not let a country's political developments or economic privation keep her from dancing.

Her first and longest trip, in 1934, was expedited by two men. One was Ross, who loaned her a $1,000 advance on her dividends (telling her, "Have a good time in China, which I probably will never see").[20] The other was the *Times*'s managing editor, Edwin James, who agreed to consider running stories she submitted during her travels and to let her identify herself as being "associated with the *New York Times*."[21]

She called James her "faithful friend," probably based on bonding with him in Germany more than a decade earlier when he was an irrepressible *Times* foreign correspondent and she was performing for the Army of Occupation.[22] He had continued reporting from Europe until 1930 when he returned to the paper's New York offices; two years later he was promoted to managing editor.[23] She left the newsroom around the same time he returned to it, but he clearly was fond of her and valued international news coverage. So he took advantage of this opportunity to obtain more of it, while she used her *Times* connection to her own benefit.

In March 1934 she set off on a seven-month trip around the world. Her first stop was Honolulu to visit friends before boarding a steamer for Yokohama. During a ten-day stay in Japan she "was entertained at a dinner given by the foreign office," she told her father, and "did all the sight seeing trips and had a really good view of the country." She also attracted the interest of a Japanese newspaper, which identified her as a "writer for the New York Times" and "active feminist" who was studying "the woman of the crisis in Japan" and planned next to investigate "what part the modern woman of China fills in China's national life."[24]

She visited with more friends during two weeks in Shanghai, a city she declared "not particularly interesting for a tourist," then proceeded on to Beijing, which interested her more. At her next stop, Japanese-occupied Manchuria (renamed Manchukuo), she did her first reporting.[25] Among the people she interviewed were the country's prime minister and the army's commander in chief, but the sole story carried by the *Times* was her account of meeting with the recently installed puppet emperor. The first reporter ever granted an audience with him, she closely followed the instructions she had been given to wear an evening gown and restrict her questions to noncontroversial topics.[26] *Time* magazine rebuked her for writing about her subject with "utmost reverence."[27]

A seven-day journey on the Trans-Siberian Railway took her from Harbin to Moscow. She spent two months there and in Leningrad before traveling to Berlin. "Upon my arrival in Germany Hitler had just taken over and my letters of introduction turned out to be for the wrong people, for with one exception they had disappeared," she remembered.[28] (Hitler actually had been in power for more than a year.) But the director of the Nazi Foreign Press Bureau was happy to be interviewed for a *Times* story. She quoted him as informing her that "there is no more humble, modest, self-controlled person in the world today than Adolf Hitler." Less restrained than she had been in interviewing the puppet emperor, she asked about restrictions on the rights of women, including a decree prohibiting them from wearing nail polish and lipstick. He explained that these were "symbols of a modern inferiority complex on the part of the weaker sex—eternally haunted by the specter of declining attraction and under-magnetism."[29]

It had to be a relief to leave Germany for France. She probably spent time with Janet Flanner in Paris, and may have visited Gertrude Stein and Alice B. Toklas in Bellay. She had obtained a letter of introduction to the two women from a mutual friend during her stay in Beijing. "I am sure you would both enjoy meeting her, for she is both intelligent and adventurous," he wrote, adding as further recommendation that Grant had "enjoyed very much" Stein's opera *Four Saints in Three Acts*.[30]

She must have been confident of good health in early 1934 or she would not have planned such a long, strenuous trip, almost always traveling alone. At the same time, she seems to have done her best to avoid hardships. Her reservations were for first-class travel, not excluding Manchuria's Mukden-Shanhaikwan railway line, which she praised for its comfortable observation car and excellent service.[31] Since her luggage held at least one evening gown, she certainly expected to attend elegant dinners and dances. She had arranged to visit with friends in several cities and had letters introducing her to still more Westerners, helping ensure that she often would be with people whose company she enjoyed (except, apparently, in Berlin).

It is a measure of how satisfying this trip was that she took three more during the following summers, spending the most time in France, Italy, and Greece. She apparently was able to continue her claim of being "associated with the *New York Times*" during her next trip at least, for an article she wrote about the opening of an Austrian mountain road to international traffic ran in the *Times* in August 1935.[32]

Reporting, however, seems to have interested her much less than socializing with local American and British citizens and accompanying them on excursions. Her letters are full of references to drinking cocktails and eating long meals with old and new friends, dancing until dawn, and taking weekend trips to countryside villas. She even was the featured singer at one July 4 celebration held by Americans in Greece, billed on the program as the "silver tongued warbler from New York City."[33]

She did make two challenging detours, both to places where the Depression and political repression had taken a bleak toll. In 1935 she returned to the Soviet Union with an unlikely travel companion, a fashion designer. Having taken what she described as "a trip de luxe across Siberia" the previous year, this time she wanted to travel the southern route along the Black Sea—which she said had "always been one of the most glamorous places in my imagination"—to the Georgian capital of Tiflis (now known as Tbilisi). It was an exciting trip but one that involved very little glamour and almost constant difficulties. Even her typewriter stopped working.[34]

A summer 1937 trip was better planned and with a heartier companion. She and her energetic friend Marcia Davenport (formerly a *New Yorker* staff writer) rented a car and drove across Eastern Europe, with Grant judiciously using earlier contacts to help pave the way. A diplomat she knew in Greece, for example, wrote to the American minister to Albania asking him to help her when she arrived in that country. "Miss Grant is highly regarded in Athens where she visited last summer, as the personal friend of Consul General Harold Shantz," he noted, "and we all liked her directness and evident sincerity."[35]

After her August 1935 piece she apparently never again reported for the *Times*, but she did try to publish a book about that same summer's trip to the Soviet Union. It is likely that she made the trip with this in mind, for the details included in her manuscript show that she took copious notes. "Everyone who had taken the southern trip told me that it was a tough one, and that I must be prepared for the worst," she recalled, and she seems to have been glad to encounter problems that she could write about.[36] In 1936 she finished a 219-page manuscript titled "I Saw What I Could," although she had no luck finding a publisher.[37]

"All the other perfect things you do and say"

NEVERTHELESS, SHE KNEW SOMEONE who was extremely interested in her reports from her summer trips. He was William Harris, a financial analyst who almost instantly fell in love with her when they met at a cocktail party soon after she returned from traveling around the world in 1934. Harris (like Ross) had been raised in Colorado. He attended the University of Colorado for two years, worked as a *Denver Post* reporter, and held merchandising and sales positions at an electrical power company's offices in different parts of the country before he moved to New York in 1928. By the time Grant met him he was operating his own Wall Street appraisal firm, which evaluated the financial health of companies that were hoping to attract buyers or investors.[38]

He also was married. His affair with Grant was passionate but also furtive, and in September 1935 he told her, "Not that I even dare to hope that you'll ever marry me—but at least I should like to be in a position to be seen with you on the street."[39] Charming, attractive, and intelligent, he fervently wooed her in person when they were in New York and with love letters when she was traveling.

Anticipating her return from one trip, he wrote: "I want you! I want to smother your neck and breasts and arms. . . . My skin will tingle when you touch me and you will lie very still as I caress and kiss you. . . . Then we shall doze in that day-dream of ecstasy—awake, and find our love even better, fresher, riper than when it was new." He found countless ways to praise her beauty—be it her eyes, lips, walk, laugh, or "all the other perfect things you do and say." And he made sure she knew he appreciated her mind, calling "priceless" something she wrote to him about Sinclair Lewis's *Babbitt* and telling her that her written accounts of her Soviet Union adventures were so fascinating that they would make "a swell travel story."[40]

Her letters to him seldom said much about her feelings, instead describing at length her travels and the many people (including good-looking men) whose company she was enjoying. "I like your letters," he once assured her, before adding, "Of course, you're not very darned demonstrative but every once in awhile some little sweet thing is there that I jump on and take for my very own."[41]

Certainly his passion needed no encouragement, but his marital state probably was another reason she offered it only infrequently when she wrote to him. His letters reveal that he had his own New York residence apart from his wife, but they also contain references to going home to have dinner with her (and finding an excuse to leave soon afterward), her efforts to check up with him by telephone (including calling him when he was with Grant), and similar unpleasantries. At one point he wrote, "How I lived through all these years of subterfuge and evasion is more than I know."[42]

Grant had had enough of the subterfuge by July 1936. At that point Harris's wife, Pollye, apparently knew about the affair—Grant said she had "an uneasy feeling that P. will be gunning for me the moment I return"—and Harris had written to say he was delaying talking with her about divorce because she had been in a car accident. "Honestly, dear, I am trying to make no remarks about your domestic affairs," Grant wrote to him from Greece. But "you have had a long time in which to straighten this matter out and it is not my intention to fall in between. So, again I say, if you are a married man when I come home I don't want to see you."[43]

In that letter she expressed no desire to marry Harris and she sometimes even questioned whether she loved him. Yet she wrote to him three or four times a week during much of the time she was traveling in 1936 and 1937, despite problems with the mails that meant she couldn't be sure he ever would receive her letters.[44] Sometime in 1938 Harris began divorce proceedings, and in December Grant consulted with her lawyers to make sure that if she remarried she still would receive the income she had been guaranteed in her 1929 divorce agreement.[45]

By that time her situation had changed in other ways. Her father died in July 1935. In 1936, after seven years in a two-room apartment at the Savoy-Plaza, she moved into a spacious apartment in a building at 277 Park Avenue, bringing along possessions that included a red-painted bedroom set, a Baldwin concert grand electric piano, three well-traveled steamer trunks, and her Monarch typewriter. She was accompanied by her maid, Marie Treadwell, who, Grant gratefully wrote, "had seen me through illness and unhappiness."[46] Both now were well behind her.

Probably the one area of her life that disappointed her was her career. She was unable to find a publisher for her manuscript about her 1935 trip through the southern Soviet Union or for a book about weekend travel that she proposed in 1937, and she wrote about a half-dozen magazine articles that she never sold.[47] Nor did she have better luck when she turned to fiction and playwriting. She wrote at least five unpublished short stories and an equal number of unproduced plays (three in collaboration with Harris).[48]

She seems to have particularly set her sights on doing radio commentary, and one of the ways Harris showed his love was by trying to find a program sponsor. In February 1935 he cultivated an advertising agency representative by taking him to lunch, then in a letter stressing Grant's extensive reporting experience made a case for auditioning her.[49] Two months later he went directly to a possible sponsor, the American Tobacco Company. This time he met with a company executive and followed up with a sample script, which was rejected. The program looked little different from others already on the air except that the commentator would be a woman, the executive said, "and, if anything, I think the radio audience's preference is for the male voice."[50] This assumption (although it proved to be inaccurate) was widely held, and there were very few women doing radio news commentary at that time.[51]

After at least one more attempt to interest a sponsor—Procter & Gamble—for a "woman's view of the news" program, they decided on a different approach. She proposed two separate fifteen-minute music programs during which (with piano accompaniment) she would sing and discuss different kinds of songs.[52] Probably it was her hope of hosting this type of program that led her to study music with Samuel Chotzinoff, a pianist and well-known music critic.[53] He was in an excellent position to influence radio networks' music programming decisions, but there is no evidence that he recommended Grant's program ideas, and neither of them sold.

While she was facing repeated rejections, Harris's career took a promising new turn. In 1937 he was hired as the literary editor at *Fortune*, a magazine that was as unexpected a success as the *New Yorker* had been almost a decade earlier. Founded by Henry Luce at the start of the Depression in 1930, this large-format, beautifully designed magazine covering the business world sold for a dollar a copy. With a small but elite readership, it attracted luxury goods advertisers even in difficult economic times.[54]

During the previous two years Harris had held a range of jobs in advertising and finance, cobbling them together in ways that seem to have provided an adequate income but less and less security, particularly as the Depression worsened.[55] Happily, *Fortune* was an excellent fit for his talents; he would remain there or at its parent company for over two decades.[56] His more stable and promising professional life must have made it easier for him to proceed with his divorce, although he still faced the challenge of persuading Grant to marry him.

Her guaranteed income gave her little financial incentive to do so, while Harris's and her own experiences were painful testaments to potential problems of the marital state. She also had changed greatly since she had impetuously agreed to marry Ross in 1920, thanks to victories that included advancing at the *Times* while simultaneously helping create and sustain the *New Yorker*. Her travels must have changed her as well. She seems to have never lacked confidence, but now she could be even more assured of her ability to live as an independent woman—and to find pleasant male companionship wherever she went.

Still, the man who now wanted to marry her was strikingly different from the man who had insisted on a divorce a decade earlier. One friend described Harris as a gentleman and "honest charmer." Calm, gracious, well spoken, and a good listener, he could talk knowledgeably about literature, music, and art.[57] His temperament could not have been more different from that of the nervous, prickly Ross. And certainly he was far more effective in expressing his love.

Ross apparently never used that word when he wrote to Grant, coming the closest in a note that read, in its entirety, "I. L. Y. V. M."[58] In contrast, when Grant was traveling Harris seemed constantly inspired to find new ways to tell her how much he adored her and longed for her return, even as he declared his efforts inadequate. He once wrote, "If I could live a thousand years and store the wisdom and the knowledge that time would give me—even then, my darling, I wouldn't be able to express in full by deed or thought how much I love you."[59]

It was a real estate transaction, though, that tipped the matrimonial scales in his favor. In 1938 Grant was able to purchase for a very low price an acre and a third of land in Litchfield, Connecticut, a small town in the foothills of the Berkshires. On it was a hundred-year-old barn that she planned to renovate and use as a weekend and vacation retreat, accompanied by Harris. After she informed the woman who sold her the property of her plans, Harris later explained, the woman told Grant that "the neighbors would not take kindly to the fact that Miss Grant and Mr. Harris were living together without the benefit of marriage." So she agreed to marry him before the renovations were complete.[60] They wed in Maryland on June 3, 1939.[61]

"This is promotion pure and simple"

YET EVEN AS GRANT SETTLED into a satisfying relationship with
Harris, her relationship with Ross became more strained. He and his second wife
divorced in August 1939. She quickly remarried but he was financially responsible
for their young daughter, and among his many other expenses were unanticipated
federal income taxes, gambling debts, and the upkeep on a large Manhattan apartment and an even larger house the couple had built two years earlier in Stamford,
Connecticut. (Heywood Broun lived nearby and the friendship between the two
men subsequently deepened. "They had a lot in common, including old-fashioned
attitudes toward women," Broun's son remembered.)[62]

His increasingly more costly life coincided with a sharp decrease in F-R dividend payments. Fleischmann was the villain here, for in 1935 he began using the
company's revenues to subsidize *Stage*, a new magazine that not only directly com-
peted with the *New Yorker* for advertisers, contributors, and readers but drained
$750,000 from *New Yorker* profits before an enraged Ross forced Fleischmann to
pull out three years later. This fiasco, combined with a decline in advertising revenues as war broke out in Europe, meant Ross was required to write larger and
larger checks to Grant to compensate for her lower quarterly dividends.[63]

By 1939 he was falling substantially behind in these payments and within four
years his debt had climbed to more than $10,000.[64] Her lawyers sent frequent
reminders of the money he owed, while he (and his own lawyers) sent explana-
tions, reassurances, and partial payments. At a low point in 1942 he remarked,
"For many years I worked, frequently heroically, to keep this magazine going, always with the feeling that I was not working for myself but for Fleischmann, Miss
Grant, and the United States government, and the impulse to say nuts to all of
them has been strong." He also couldn't resist noting the role Grant's feminism
had played in their divorce, and the "palpable absurdity in her present dependence
on me for financial support," given her belief that "women should be themselves,
self-reliant, self-supporting, etc." He did add, "I am certain that this is a situation
that Miss Grant herself does not relish."[65]

She showed how little she relished it, and especially Fleischmann's actions,
when she led a shareholders revolt following a decision by the F-R board of directors to pay no dividends at all for the first quarter of 1942. She teamed up with the
company's second-largest shareholder, Fleischmann's ex-wife, Ruth, and with two
other shareholders, her old housemate Hawley Truax and another lawyer, Truax's
brother-in-law Lloyd Paul Stryker. After an investigation that revealed, among
other things, the extent of losses from *Stage* and how little the F-R business office
was doing to cut expenses and replace dwindling advertising revenues, they threatened to sue Fleischmann for malfeasance unless he agreed to harsh management
changes.[66]

Prior to their campaign he had seemed untroubled by the magazine's financial decline, and the board of directors, made up mainly of his friends, could be
counted on to follow his wishes.[67] Thus at the annual stockholders meeting in
1942, "Mr. Fleischmann said it is quite clear that they will operate for little or

no profit for as far ahead as he can see," an investigator sent by Grant reported, and "the meeting was then about to be adjourned without anyone's having asked any questions or made any comments of any sort." Grant's investigator did ask questions, which Fleischmann answered vaguely. Then, "after a few more general statements that everything that could be done was being done, the meeting was adjourned."[68]

Even though Fleischmann's lawyers thought he could win a malfeasance fight, he chose to compromise, but only after many months of painful negotiations. The agreement he signed in early 1943 severely reduced both his stockholder's voting rights and support on the board of directors, and placed all major management decisions in the hands of a three-member executive committee composed of Fleischmann, Stryker, and Truax. Truax became the company's treasurer and the official intermediary between Fleischmann and Ross, who by now despised the publisher.[69]

In this way Fleischmann gave up a good deal of power, some business-office practices were changed, the F-R Publishing Corporation's financial situation subsequently improved, and Grant was drawn back into the *New Yorker*. After the turmoil from these changes died down, she came forward with a proposal that initially faced strong resistance but proved to be of immense long-term benefit to the magazine.

In June 1943 she met with managing editor Ik Shuman to tell him that on a trip to Washington she had talked at length with R. L. Trautman in the War Department's Special Services Division that was responsible for obtaining reading material for soldiers overseas. She had persuaded him to consider authorizing the purchase of an advertising-free, lightweight edition of the *New Yorker* that would be made available for free in overseas commissaries. He had agreed to look at a dummy and she had specific ideas about its contents. "This is promotion pure and simple," she excitedly told Shuman. Servicemen who otherwise never would have read the *New Yorker* would pick it up and might later become subscribers. "I know that some publishers have been working on Major Trautman with no success whatever," she argued, but she had gotten him interested.[70]

Ross and Fleischmann, however, were not interested. Her idea would require more work from a staff that had been thinned by the war even as paper shortages due to rationing had forced a reduction in the print run. The magazine needed more paper, yet she wanted to use part of its allotment for an overseas edition. She convinced Shuman that she could solve the paper problem, and he persuaded Ross and Fleischmann to back the project. Shuman also agreed to handle production if Grant would handle the government hurdles—the more difficult job—and the *New Yorker*'s six-by-nine-inch "pony edition" first appeared in September 1943. Originally published monthly, its thirty-two photographically reduced pages carried mainly cartoons (often on military subjects), other humorous content, and war-related features.[71]

Yet Grant's battles had just begun. As hard as she negotiated with the War Department, it would only pay three cents per copy of the magazine. Shuman accepted the price, which was lower than their production costs, because he knew that overseas editions of even very popular magazines like *Time* and *Esquire* were not profitable. He expected to lose money on the venture. But she wanted to minimize their losses with economies of scale so devoted herself to "selling my head off to the Peexes," as she put it. One by one, she contacted purchasing officers for individual army, navy, and marine PXs, persuaded them to take the magazine, and consequently, she explained, "we got the volume up and the per unit cost down."[72]

Her greatest challenge was procuring sufficient paper. She first joined forces with representatives from other magazines to win a War Production Board ruling that overseas editions meeting certain criteria—such as being advertising-free and distributed at no charge—qualified for paper purchases beyond the publication's usual quotas. Still, locating "ex-quota" paper and getting government permission for purchases was an endless trial. At one point, for example, she tracked down paper from a defunct publisher but WPB roadblocks kept her from buying it. "They prefer to let the paper rot where it is," she wrote in disgust.[73]

The monthly edition was so popular that she promptly made a case for replacing it with a weekly to be sold to post exchanges for three-and-a-half cents per copy; they in turn would sell their copies for five cents each. This would create new risks because not only would a weekly require about four times as much paper as a monthly but the WPB had not yet decided whether overseas editions that soldiers purchased were eligible for ex-quota paper.[74]

Nevertheless, in March 1944 F-R went ahead with a weekly edition while Grant worked even harder to obtain more paper, increase distribution, and solve myriad new problems. Armed with an address book full of names and phone numbers of useful contacts, she frequently traveled to Washington for meetings with high-level government and military officials, and angled for invitations to dinner parties where she could talk with them. Back in New York, she followed up with friendly letters and phone calls. Surviving correspondence shows how well she got along with some of these men and how willing they were to help her.[75]

By early 1945 the circulation of the overseas edition rivaled that of the parent *New Yorker*. Not only did it end up making a profit of about $75,000 but it was widely viewed as helping the war effort, which created goodwill for the magazine among military leaders and the general public. Yet its greatest benefit was still to come, for it exposed hundreds of thousands of servicemen to the magazine, and when they returned home a sizable portion became subscribers. In the two years following the end of the war the *New Yorker*'s circulation almost doubled, and most of the new readers did not live in New York.[76]

"We'd do well to make a deal with her"

ONE OF THE WAYS GRANT STAYED on good terms with her high-level military contacts was by sending them gifts of bound volumes of the pony edition. In early 1946 one recipient wrote to thank and congratulate her. "I consider it heroic beyond words to have had an idea for the War Department and finally to have gotten it over. You are practically the lone woman in America in this regard," he told her.[77] If not heroic, she certainly was an expert networker and enormously energetic, determined problem solver. Her tenacity and enthusiasm for undertaking new tasks would have been familiar to those who had seen her *New Yorker* efforts in the 1920s. And the results must have been similarly satisfying to her, especially since they followed a decade of failed attempts to sell her written work and radio program ideas.

Receiving fair pay for all she was doing was another matter, however. Thus September 1943 found her negotiating not only with the WPB over paper and the military over distribution but with the F-R executive committee over compensation for her work, which included conceiving and supervising the monthly pony edition and efforts already underway to garner the necessary government support for a weekly version. She offered the committee two options: pay her a lump sum of $10,000, or, as an alternative, $2,500 plus a small percentage of the price the government paid for its copies of the magazine. Fleischmann sent her a $2,500 check but told her the additional percentage "would not be acceptable to the Board."[78]

She went to Ik Shuman, who wrote to Ross advising him to find a way to pay her more. Fleischmann's response had made her feel "that her help wasn't really wanted," he reported, and this was particularly unwise given what she had told him about her plans for a weekly. "She apparently knows her way around in this," Shuman observed. "I'd think that we'd do well to make a deal with her on some sort of sharing basis."[79] That deal was struck in October. The overseas edition could only turn a profit if it was published weekly, something Fleischmann then considered "pretty hopeless because of the printing situation." Still, if Grant could obtain the necessary paper and the magazine went weekly, she would receive a commission of half of its profits.[80]

The weekly became profitable not long after it was introduced in March 1944, but collecting all the money she believed she was owed was another matter. Her monthly commission checks increased throughout the fall, peaked at almost $2,500 in December, then shrank by almost 50 percent during the first half of 1945. Told that this was because the army had negotiated a lower per-copy price, she protested that she should have been involved in the bargaining and would have obtained a higher price. She also questioned the overall accounting and argued that she should be paid for her other work, such as developing a plan for producing six small books of material from *New Yorker* departments and selling more than a million copies to the army for overseas distribution.[81]

Fleischmann at first stonewalled her, even recalling that the monthly pony edition had lost money. Since "we did not penalize you for our losses on the monthly, but are paying you the full half on the profits of the weekly," he reasoned, "we have given you the best of the bargain."[82] This triggered a five-page response from Grant, with copies to executive committee members Stryker and Truax. Worried that "the tenor of her latest letter seems to indicate that she might be contemplating a law suit," Stryker drafted a firm retort that he said would prove that her rights "are not what she thinks they are." He had one last observation: "We must not forget that we are dealing with a woman," and "one of the best ways to get into a really difficult controversy with a lady is to leave her with a sense of affront." To avoid affront, "I have added to the proposed letter submitted herewith the suggestion that we would meet her at lunch."[83]

Fleischmann had enough sense not to send Stryker's letter. Instead he promised to pay her for her work on the six books and set up a meeting with him alone to discuss the decrease in her commissions. At that meeting in mid-July he conceded that they should have negotiated more aggressively with the army over the 1945 price of the magazine, and agreed to recalculate her commission based on a hypothetical higher price. He sent her a check for nearly $1,000 to cover what she would have made during the previous months if the army had paid more, and told her that future payments "will be based on the new arrangement."[84]

While she was bargaining with Fleischmann, Ross was reaching his own breaking point. He was exhausted from editing the wartime *New Yorker*, from dealing with what he called "the Fleischmann ring of stupid fumblers," and from fending off Grant's lawyers, who kept pressing him to pay his growing debt to her. He no sooner found a source of funds than another dividend fell short and he once again had to defend himself to the firm of Chadbourne, Wallace, Parke & Whiteside. In June 1945, with the war's end imminent, his responsibility for steering the magazine during difficult times ending, and his unhappiness acute, he announced that he planned to cancel his employment contract.[85]

This was not the first time he had threatened to quit but it was the most serious threat by far, and the F-R executive committee moved quickly to create new incentives for him to stay.[86] They knew one incentive would have to address his obligation to Grant. "This Grant hurdle tends to stop me completely," Ross pointedly told them. "To me it is a bit of underbrush concealing all the rest of the forest and it must be cleared before anything else is done." He stressed, too, that she long ago should have been paid for her crucial role in founding the magazine, something for which she "has never in any degree whatever been compensated."[87]

Bargaining continued throughout the summer and fall, with Ross emphasizing that the company owed Grant for her early work. This "is just a dandy opportunity for the corporation to clear its conscience," he argued at one point, "and thereby contribute to Jane's self-respect and to my peace of mind."[88] Although the "Grant hurdle" still loomed, by November the executive committee had shown sufficient resolve in trying to surmount it that Ross was willing to sign a new contract that increased his yearly salary to $50,000 and provided other benefits that were important to him.[89]

Grant was pleased because she had feared the magazine would collapse if he left. She also was making progress in obtaining a paid position for herself, albeit not without more bargaining. In late December Fleischmann offered her a part-time consulting job paying $5,000 a year. She wanted more. He resisted, Ross intervened, Grant and Ross met with Stryker and Truax, the haggling continued, and in late February 1946 she got what she wanted: a ten-year contract for a part-time, $7,500-a-year consulting position, renewable if she desired. Her income would be applied toward any future dividend shortfalls, thus canceling Ross's obligation to her, although he would make the back payments he still owed.[90]

Freeing Ross of that obligation mattered enormously to her. It had become far too difficult and unpleasant for both of them. As she wrote in 1945, "I dislike being a load of hay to Ross or to The New Yorker."[91] Now she no longer was financially bound to him. Equally important, she finally had an official position at the magazine she had helped found.

"Confession of a Feminist"

DURING MUCH OF 1943 she had been immersed in the male worlds of the military and the federal government. There she learned from, reasoned with, and charmed the decision makers whose help she needed to establish the pony edition. At the same time, she was working with men at the *New Yorker* to produce and distribute the magazine for servicemen.

Yet something very different also was on her mind, as she revealed in an *American Mercury* article published in December 1943. After failing to sell any work for several years, she hit the jackpot with her submission to this popular large-circulation magazine. Her article, titled "Confession of a Feminist," was an account of her lack of awareness of women's problems before she married Ross and kept her name, and the many injustices she had discovered since that time. She cited numerous restrictions on women's rights, criticized women's "protective legislation," advocated passage of an equal rights amendment, and analyzed reasons for slow progress in many areas. Interspersed throughout her arguments for women's expanded legal rights were stories and direct declarations that showed her extreme fondness for men.[92]

The magazine's summary of the piece read, "One leading Lucy Stoner who is at home in a man's world." It was an apt description of Grant, just as the choice of the word "confession" in the title was apt, for in 1943 only a tiny minority of American women identified themselves as feminists, and few of them would have announced it in a mass-circulation magazine. Grant was happy to confess and did so in a non-threatening, casual manner that no doubt broadened the appeal of her message. Yet she was not the very best spokesperson for the cause, particularly in light of her conclusion that women deserved a good portion of the blame for their lack of legal equality. "Many of them who should know better think we already have equal rights," she wrote, while others are so "confident in their personal security" that "they brush the matter aside."[93]

Whatever its failings, her article was based on a deep commitment to advancing women's equality. She was active in the National Woman's Party, which was devoted to passage of the ERA, and was a founding member of the Connecticut Committee for the Equal Rights Amendment. Her comments about women who cared too little about women's rights reflected her own frustrations, for in 1943 and 1944 she garnered little support when she wrote to powerful women asking them to use their influence to help pass the ERA. Eleanor Roosevelt, for example, politely declined.[94]

After the war she worked even more energetically for these two organizations, serving as vice chairman of the Connecticut committee and doing fundraising and other work for the NWP—until she helped organize a 1947 rebellion against its leaders, Alice Paul and Anita Pollitzer.[95] She also protested media treatment of women, not only sending letters to the editors of publications that carried articles she found objectionable but once writing to a Barnard College dean to say she hoped the college didn't "sponsor" the "policy of oppression" against women that a male Barnard sociology professor had advocated in a magazine article he wrote.[96]

Women's names were another concern, brought to light by her own passport problems. In 1932, divorced from Ross and with an expired passport, she had only been able to obtain a new one as Jane Grant by submitting affidavits from two people affirming she had never used any other name. In 1947, married to Harris, she had to work even harder to obtain a passport in her birth name. The New York Passport Bureau would not grant it under any circumstances, so she traveled to Washington and met with Ruth Shipley, the head of the State Department's Passport Division. After a great deal of correspondence between the two women, Shipley "gave a directive to the Bureaus throughout the country to accept applications from women wishing passports in their own names," Grant recalled.[97]

In reality the matter was far from settled, and women continued to be denied passports in their birth names. And despite the Lucy Stone League's earlier victories, restrictions remained in myriad other areas. Innumerable state laws still required women to take their husbands' names, local entities such as school boards often obliged employees to do the same, and in many places married women could neither vote nor own property in their birth names.[98] When Doris Fleischman declared in her 1949 *American Mercury* article that she was taking her husband's name because keeping her own had become too much trouble, she actually was not having trouble. But women might reasonably have read her piece as a warning about difficulties they would face if they chose to do what two decades earlier she had done, and now wanted to undo.

Undeterred, Grant gathered more information on women's legal rights, including their right to keep their names. For example, she wrote several letters to former secretary of labor Frances Perkins asking her to explain different government policies.[99] And she seemed always on the lookout for ways to let women know they did not have to take a husband's name. Thus in September 1948 she succeeded in making that point at length in a *Times* letter to the editor written in response to a previous letter that was, at best, peripherally related to the subject.[100]

She also engaged in a sharp exchange of personal letters with the recently married president of Wellesley College, whom she took to task for identifying herself as Mrs. Douglas Horton. "I prefer it," Mrs. Horton told her. "Having decided to merge my life with his, I like to be identified with his interests and have him identified with mine." Grant responded: "I, too, am happily married and my husband and I have similar interests but we cannot believe that our married state precludes my right to the symbol of human dignity—the name with which I was born." The college president had the last word: "Why is the name with which you were born any more a 'symbol of human dignity' than the one you have selected by marriage?"[101]

With that reference to Harris's support Grant identified a profound difference between her first and second marriages. Unlike Ross, Harris fell in love with a feminist. He would not have gotten far with her unless he supported her views, and she would not have married him unless she knew he would support her actions. Thus feminism became one of their "similar interests," and his full embrace of it was one reason their marriage would remain loving and mutually satisfying for more than three decades.

Another interest literally took root soon after their June 1939 wedding. When they moved into their renovated Litchfield barn that summer they decided Grant would be in charge of the inside of the house and Harris would handle the outside, where knee-high hay was growing on an acre of rock-strewn land. He hired a neighbor, George Luca, to help, and they spent all summer clearing the land. Grant promptly planned their first party, which required flowers, but the wildflowers she picked and arranged in water immediately wilted. "Never have flowers been cussed at so expertly," Harris wrote, describing her reaction (and explaining that she'd received a magna cum laude education in swearing at the *Times*). He had a very different response, vowing, "Next summer I'll grow some flowers for you that will be better and prettier in a bowl than any wildflower."[102]

He actually knew nothing about growing flowers and little about growing anything else, but in September he and Luca seeded a lawn, and two months later they fashioned a thirty-by-three-foot flower bed—"a very large garden for a beginner," he later realized. That winter he set out to learn about gardening. Books were not very helpful, but the manager of a Madison Avenue garden store was, and his many hours of advice (plus the seeds he sold) helped Harris successfully grow annuals for the next three years. As he learned more from the store's manager, from people he consulted at agricultural colleges, and especially from trial and error, he took on new gardening challenges, including mastering the complexities of growing perennials from seeds.[103]

The couple could only spend weekends and holidays in Litchfield, but they still managed to do most of the weeding themselves and to put in a forty-five-by-hundred-foot vegetable garden during the war. Once the war ended and they could get iron pipe, they dug the deepest well in Litchfield County. With more water, in 1946 they were able to add a twelve-by-eighty-foot perennial garden and, over their new underground garage, a large rolling lawn.[104]

The next year the woman who had sold Grant the barn and land died, leaving a will that offered them first refusal on eighteen acres of land surrounding theirs. They bought it as a buffer against development. Later in 1947 their neighbor across the road stopped by to tell them he planned to sell his farm and he, too, would give them first refusal. Even though they would not be able to take possession for more than a year, Harris said, "we shook hands on the deal on the spot." That evening, when he and Grant sat down for cocktails, she observed, "There's nothing like owning a house and one acre and protecting it with 90 acres, 2 houses, a 3-car garage, a hay barn, a horse barn, and a dog kennel. What are we going to do with them?"[105]

They pondered this as they waited for their neighbor to sell. Then on a spring night in 1949, "obviously after one more drink of bourbon than necessary," as Harris remembered it, they looked at each other and said, "Let's start a nursery."[106] Thus her second marriage, like her first, would result in a highly successful joint venture.

CHAPTER 11

"I'm Miss Grant, though married— and happily, too"

GRANT AND HARRIS QUICKLY REALIZED they had set an impossible goal in the name they'd chosen for their new business. "By that time we had become rather sophisticated gardeners, so sophisticated that we had turned the perennial border from mixed colors to pure white—what the English call a moon garden," Harris explained. This inspired their initial plan to grow only white perennials and flowering shrubs, and to call their venture White Flower Farm. Yet it was an impractical idea since few gardeners wanted to restrict themselves to white-flowering plants, and the plants' lack of stamina made them difficult to cultivate. Still, they kept this charming name (as well as the moon garden) for their nursery.[1]

Whatever name they decided on, they believed the time was ripe for a first-rate American horticulture business. Few mail-order nurseries offered either quality plants that were "true to variety" or imported plants that were not already popular and easily marketed. British nurseries, however, were selling excellent species, including new strains not available in the United States, so in 1949 they made the first of what would be many trips to England's Chelsea Flower Show to consult with nurserymen there.[2]

White Flower Farm opened for business in 1950 but was far from an immediate success, in part because they struggled to find a manager. The first one lasted just two years, replaced by a married couple who stayed for only two more. "Our unconventional approach didn't make sense to them," Harris discovered. Not until the fall of 1954 did they find someone who shared their values and had the expertise they needed. At one of England's finest nurseries they met twenty-nine-year-old David Smith, who had both—as well as an interest in moving to America. "If David had not been present in the spring of the following year when our managing couple returned to the Midwest," Harris admitted, "the chances are that Grant and I would have folded Amos Pettingill's tent and crept away."[3]

Amos Pettingill was the pseudonym they created for the manager who was featured in some of the advertisements Harris wrote for newspapers. He originally used the name of their first manager, but after he left they realized, Harris said, "that starting a nursery from scratch was not going to be in the least easy, and we'd have so many changes in personnel in the future that featuring the 'manager' (of the moment) would get us nowhere." So they settled on one unchanging fictional name that would help give the business a unique identity.[4]

Writing about White Flower Farm as Amos Pettingill, Harris created an appealing persona many customers thought existed in real life. Readers came to know Pettingill best as the author of the nursery's annual catalog, which *House & Garden* magazine called "even more a book to read and enjoy," since "over ten of its eighty-eight pages are devoted to chatty philosophical commentary, and the descriptions and prices of plants for sale are well cushioned by information on how to plant, and how not to plant." Harris was a gifted translator of specialized information into layperson's language, mixing his plant descriptions not only with straightforward practical advice and discourses on topics such as the "pH factor," but with self-deprecating accounts of his own mistakes, happy discoveries, and too-late revelations.[5]

Readers trusted Amos Pettingill, and his words persuaded more people to try growing plants not available from any other source. Grant and Harris were frequent travelers and often brought back unusual plants, looking for stock strong enough to survive the U.S. plant quarantine (sometimes none did). The hurdles of cultivating and selling these plants—such as the white forsythia they imported from South Korea in 1955 that proved a popular offering—were slowly surmounted because of the work of David Smith and Harold Calverley, another British nurseryman hired in 1955. Soon afterward they lured their head of production away from a Scottish nursery, and the enterprise's "absentee owners," as they called themselves, finally had a "horticulture core" that satisfied them.[6]

Harris admitted that during their early years they lost "more than I care to remember," but by 1960 White Flower Farm was an undisputed success. Its monthly payroll in busy seasons was $6,000, its plants were winning top honors at the country's most prestigious flower shows, and it was widely recognized as America's most innovative commercial nursery.[7]

"All civil and social rights of women"

IN AUGUST 1950 GRANT ENDED a letter to Frances Perkins with an invitation: "Bill and I are up to our ears with flowers. Have five acres of them. Won't you come up for a weekend?" They had just begun their new business, but Grant's point in writing was to tell Perkins—at that time a U.S. Civil Service commissioner—that the Lucy Stone League was being revived. "The few meetings in the spring were preliminary but in the fall we hope to really get going," Grant wrote, "and I hope you will rejoin the League and give me your wise counsel." She also asked Perkins whether she thought they should find a new name for the organization, both because it "had come in for so much ridicule" and because they now had broader goals. "It does seem to me that by whatever name the League is called it will be unpopular in certain circles," she rightly noted.[8]

Perkins had kept her birth name when she married in 1913, joining the league soon after it was founded in 1921. She then continually fought to keep using her name as she attained increasingly important New York state and federal government offices. In 1933, when President Roosevelt appointed her secretary of labor (the first woman ever to hold a cabinet post), Congress debated whether she should be allowed to receive her paycheck as Frances Perkins. Unlike all other married women working for the federal government, in the end she was allowed to use her birth name.[9] But she did not join the revived league.

Almost two dozen members from the 1920s did join. Grant started the ball rolling by inviting former members to her home on February 16, 1950, to discuss a possible resurrection. They voted to revive it, then elected four officers, including Grant as president and Doris Fleischman as vice president. A public meeting followed on March 22, and the press release account of that meeting took pains to describe members as "women and men who favor the right of married women to keep their own names, even if they themselves do not practice it." The group "will generally concern itself with all civil and social rights of women," it said.[10]

Women's names, though, were very much the focus of the March public meeting, where three of the four speakers—including Grant—addressed the topic.[11] As president she initially seems to have almost solely devoted herself to this cause. She gave speeches and wrote letters about it, investigated written and unwritten government policies related to names, and tried to get some of those policies changed. For instance, in 1950 she persuaded the Census Bureau to accept married women's birth names on census records, and the U.S. Marine Corps to permit women marines who married to continue using their birth names.[12]

Most other league members were much less concerned with names. This certainly was true of Fleischman, whose 1949 article reflected society's disapproval of women keeping their names. That same year, Frances Perkins reminded Grant, "As we have often said, you and I belong to the 'crank' element in the population."[13] Yet she apparently needed still more reminders that this was a narrow, unpopular cause. One came from member Mildred Clark, who briskly told Grant in January 1951, "I should not care to sponsor a group whose prime objective is merely or primarily to serve as a clearing house for a few eccentric females who for a variety of personal reasons want to keep their maiden names." The league, Clark said, "must never [lose] sight of its goal—*to save society, no less!*"[14]

At its first annual meeting in January 1951 members voted to form a committee to consider changing their constitution to "enable the League to exercise the greatest possible activity." Two amendments were adopted the next month. One said the organization would "serve as a center for research and for information on the status of women." The other stated: "The original object of this League to encourage women who wish to continue their own names after marriage has been amended and broadened to include activities to safeguard and extend all civil, legal, social and political rights of women."[15]

The amendments probably helped rein in the president's emphasis on names and thus accommodate the new members, most of whom had joined not out of a concern with names but because they were troubled by widespread sex discrimination in postwar America. There was hope, too, that a more general women's rights organization might help the league attract younger members. Already resistant to feminism, young women were unlikely to be drawn to the cause of keeping their names.[16] (Fleischman's daughters Doris and Anne, for example, took their husbands' names when they married in 1951 and 1954.)

Formalizing these expanded goals did not keep Grant from writing sharp but reasonably argued letters on league stationery to media outlets and governmental bodies reaffirming women's right to use their birth names. Yet she was equally alert to more serious problems and wrote letters protesting other kinds of sex discrimination to every president from Truman to Nixon, to newspapers and magazines, to private businesses and public institutions. And she gave many speeches about the league and women's rights, attaining a visibility as league president that resulted in her being asked to consult with the Women's Bureau of the U.S. Department of Labor in 1961 and the President's Commission on the Status of Women in 1962.[17]

In the 1950s the league targeted two areas where it could make a practical difference: funding scholarships for women studying in male-dominated fields and establishing small libraries honoring women's contributions to society. It also was reactive; members voted to respond to instances of sex discrimination with resolutions, letters, and other actions.[18] And Grant increasingly took to heart the league's new function as a research center, for she wrote to countless authors and organizations to gather data and studies. She drew on this information in her many speeches, and it helped the organization become known as a useful feminist resource. Its spring 1960 *Bulletin* reported that, in recent years, "We have been carrying on a lively correspondence with institutions and individuals who appeal to our research department for data on historical and present-day subjects concerning women."[19]

Ironically, its "research department" apparently had little literature related to women's names on passports, so in 1961, when Grant was trying to persuade a member of the U.S. Passport Bureau that a recent ruling by the State Department requiring women to use their husbands' surnames was improper, she could only enclose two publications to help make her case. "One of them, as you can see, is old, but no one has ever more eloquently presented the deep frustration of a woman deprived of her identity than did Ruth Hale," she wrote in explanation.[20] "The First Five Years of the Lucy Stone League"—the booklet Hale wrote in 1926 when the league was disintegrating—finally was being put to use.

In the 1960s its public meetings usually were luncheons or evening events at restaurants or clubs. By far their most distinguished guest that decade was Eleanor Roosevelt, whose talk, "The Basic Rights of Women," at the May 1962 meeting was one of her last speaking appearances. More typically, meetings featured a panel addressing a topic like women in the arts or honored women who had battled sex discrimination, such as the New York policewoman who won the right to compete with men in promotion examinations by taking her case to the state supreme court.[21] These events were occasions for socializing with like-minded women and also helped draw media attention to the league and its concerns.

Grant must have taken special pleasure in the March 1966 event honoring Janet Flanner. Speaking to a large audience of writers, editors, and many other fans, the renowned columnist announced: "I'm a charter member of the Lucy Stone League, and it's the only women's club to which I still belong. Consider that a commercial." After she was presented with a framed reproduction of her first *New Yorker* column, a league member who was a magician "mystified guests with an interlude of magic," a press release reported, "finally drawing French flags from the guest of honor's décolletage."[22]

Flanner humored Grant because they had been friends for so long and she felt she owed her—but not just for her 1925 invitation to write for the *New Yorker.* Flanner had fled France during the Nazi occupation and was in New York, eager to go home, when the country was liberated in the fall of 1944. She went to Grant for help after the best Ross could do was suggest she return on a boat transporting dynamite to Denmark. "He doesn't know the right generals," Grant told her. "You will probably leave in three or four days in an Army plane. I will phone my generals in Washington to fix things up."[23] Flanner was afraid of flying and had never flown, but she boarded the promised plane very early on a November morning and was transfixed by what she saw from the air. After landing in London she wrote to Grant, "Now I have two things, which have expanded my life, to thank you for, The New Yorker job and flying the Atlantic."[24]

The league's nonprofit IRS status meant it could not be politically active, yet its fall 1960 *Bulletin* declared, "it is impossible for us as individuals to ignore the implications of the political scene in its relation to women."[25] For Grant, passage of an equal rights amendment was key to expanding women's rights, and her ERA work intensified in the postwar period. A member since its 1943 founding of the most active state ERA committee, the Connecticut Committee for the Equal Rights Amendment, she was an officer and advisory committee member as well as good friends with its indefatigable driving force, Florence Kitchelt. After Kitchelt moved to Ohio in 1956, Grant joined the national advisory committee of the Massachusetts Committee for the Equal Rights Amendment, the most successful state committee in the 1960s.[26]

In September 1955 Grant, as vice chairman of the Connecticut committee, teamed up with Kitchelt to argue in favor of the ERA at an American Civil Liberties Union debate, making their case with the help of a written brief countering an anti-ERA argument previously submitted to the ACLU. The brief was prepared by William Harris, who was a member of the Connecticut group's national advisory committee and later joined the same committee of the Massachusetts ERA group.[27] Grant would not have been the only one who appreciated his participation, for Kitchelt worked hard to recruit male members and form a 50-percent-male advisory committee. Since 1914 she had been married to a dedicated women's rights advocate.[28]

Richard Kitchelt, though, probably endured less derision for his egalitarian marriage to a feminist than did Harris, for at least Kitchelt's wife had taken his name when they married. In postwar America Grant was even more of an anomaly for keeping her name than she was for being an outspoken feminist, and the idea was highly threatening to most men. One syndicated newspaper columnist reacted to news of the Lucy Stone League's revival by warning, "A good man is hard to find, and no girl in her right mind is going to antagonize him from the beginning by insisting on the use of her own name." Doing so "is apt to make a man tense and uneasy."[29]

In interviews Grant inevitably was asked what Harris thought of her keeping her name, and he sometimes told the interviewers himself about his approval. He was a member of the league's advisory committee and often attended its public meetings, introduced by Grant as "my husband, Mr. Harris."[30] (In private they skipped their first names and called each other Grant and Harris.) She made it clear that she found both feminism and marriage extremely satisfying. "Miss Grant is a sparkling, vivacious personality, keenly cognizant of the need for improvement in the status of women, while maintaining great interest in her husband's work," one reporter concluded. "She is an ardent advocate of equal rights, and her husband gives full support."[31] That support was one reason she was able to lead the league with confidence and enthusiasm. Harris respected her commitment and loved her for it.

"I'm bursting with ideas"

THE *NEW YORKER* SHOULD HAVE been one place where use of her birth name was routine, but in 1948 someone on his clerical staff mailed a letter from Raoul Fleischmann to Mrs. William Harris in Litchfield. In her response Grant tried to be good-natured—as she often was with people who used the wrong name on mail to her—but she stressed the possible risk of this kind of error, saying, "The post office here is aware of my proper name—you may be sure I saw to that—so any mail addressed as this letter is does not readily come to my hands." A woman named Mrs. William Harris lived in the area and was "slow about passing on communications" that she mistakenly received, Grant explained. Plus, "Mrs. Harris might be apprised of business secrets you would not want in circulation" if she decided to open letters from Fleischmann.[32]

Fleischmann and Grant often corresponded on matters related to her consulting work. He had to contact her at one of her homes because she did not have her own office at the magazine, although she had hoped for one when she began her new job in the spring of 1946. "It seems to me this is working out pretty well without your having an office," Fleischmann told her in early May. "After all, you only live eight minutes walk away and since our business can be readily handled either by your dropping over here or my dropping over to your place on my way home, I don't think we are being too hampered."[33]

She admitted she was doing fine without the office. "I put up a fight for it last year and it would have been easier for all concerned if I'd been at hand while the little [pony edition] New Yorker was booming. It's still booming even with the Army cuts but it won't be long before it just coasts to a halt and is finally liquidated." Since her new projects wouldn't require working closely with others from the magazine, "I've decided to fix up a room in the apartment as an office."[34]

In 1946 and 1947 she met with either Fleischmann or one of the other two F-R executive committee members about once a week. "I'm bursting with ideas" for large-scale promotional campaigns, she told Fleischmann soon after she'd settled in as a consultant, but he was adamant that these wait until the postwar economy stabilized. As a result, most of her early suggestions focused on ways to improve the magazine's advertising and distribution (her study of newsstand placement convinced her that the distributor was doing a poor job).[35]

For almost two decades she and the publisher worked amicably together despite the severe wounds she had helped inflict on him when she led the 1942 shareholders revolt. That revolt had left him wary of her—which likely was one reason he resisted her proposal for a pony edition—yet its enormous success both helped the magazine and explicitly demonstrated her talents. Probably more important to restoring the excellent relationship that had existed between them during the *New Yorker*'s early years, however, was her role in preventing Ross from resigning in 1945.

A gentleman through and through, Fleischmann would have had a natural preference to get along well with her, which was easier once she was a paid consultant and they were working entirely on the same side. The extensive correspondence between them shows him taking her ideas seriously, acting on some of them, and treating her with a balance of respect and affection.[36] For example, in the fall of 1947 he asked for her advice on the wording of an announcement of scheduled advertising rate increases. Because she had laryngitis and they couldn't talk, he sent a messenger to pick up her typed comments—and deliver a box of throat lozenges that he said "have done wonders for me." Along with her written thanks she warned him that "when I get my voice back good and strong my plan is to use it on you and Mr. Smith [in the business office] about newsstand representation," which she still deemed unsatisfactory.[37]

She did her work conscientiously and saw her mandate as broad. Thus in 1949 she offered many promotional ideas and put together a public relations campaign to mark the *New Yorker*'s twenty-fifth anniversary. Her 1951 activities ranged from meeting with someone interested in adapting the magazine's material for television to trying to persuade Fleischmann to let her find a paperback publisher to reprint selected contents from back issues (he told her he hated the idea).[38] She did much more during that decade, including advising on trade journal advertising, subscription price increases, and index improvements.[39] Surviving correspondence shows far less work in the early 1960s, although it was diverse. For instance, she urged that dance be covered as a separate department and had several ideas for college promotions. "With so many colleges becoming co-educational," she said, "a new attack is in order."[40]

One advantage of this kind of consulting was that she could combine it with the traveling she loved to do. She regularly reported on the magazine's availability in different parts of the country, and her last known written communication with Fleischmann, in January 1964, told him about delivery problems she had encountered in Guatemala.[41] Sometimes she planned specific tasks for the magazine around her travels. In December 1952, for example, before she and Harris set off on a long trip that would take them to several European cities, she strategized with Fleischmann about work she could do in different places. Having already arranged to meet with someone who could help solve their persistent problems collecting French copyright fees, she was hopeful that "we might get real money out of them yet."[42]

Her *New Yorker* earnings no doubt made it easier to take costly trips with Harris, to buy an additional ninety acres of land in Litchfield, and to begin a horticulture business that risked never making money and was guaranteed to initially lose large sums. In 1946 she earned the most she ever would in her life. Not only was this the first year of her consulting contract but her pony edition commissions—

which Fleischmann had reluctantly adjusted the previous year—were high, and he had agreed to pay her for her work on the six books of reprinted *New Yorker* material. Exclusive of stock dividends, she made more than $30,000 (equivalent to about $325,000 in today's dollars) from the magazine that year.[43]

Her pay would not exceed her $7,500 consultant's salary for much longer, but combined with her dividends it made for a very substantial income that was important to her beyond the lifestyle it helped support. In a 1953 newspaper interview about the Lucy Stone League she talked about financial problems women faced and admitted that as a young, poorly paid *Times* employee she had been too afraid of displeasure from her bosses to speak out against injustices. "Women need financial security to assert themselves," she argued. Concerned that women were leaving their jobs when they married, she suggested, "If women really prefer housework, let them at least get a salary so they get financial independence." The interviewer also asked about her previous marriage to Ross. It was "a casual relationship," Grant told her. "We worked hard together, but we both felt free to go off on our own."[44]

The very last time they worked hard together was in 1945 when they ended their financial entanglement and Ross signed a new contract with the magazine. He then showed how wise she and others had been to fight to keep him as its editor. By the late 1940s the *New Yorker*'s cultural influence was unmatched by any other American publication. It was prized for its essays, reporting, humor, fiction, and criticism, and for a scope that extended far beyond the city for which it was named. Many stories were filed from other parts of the country and the world. As Ross explained, only half facetiously, "We got started on the wide world during the war and can't quit. Also, the writers got in the habit of traveling." The magazine could afford to support this habit since it was so attractive to advertisers that in 1946 it made a profit of $600,000 on revenues exceeding $6 million.[45]

That same year it carried one of the most important, compelling articles ever published in a magazine: John Hersey's account of the suffering caused by the detonation of an atomic bomb over Hiroshima in August 1945. Intended as a four-part series, his 150-page manuscript was so powerful that Ross decided it should run in a single issue, even though that would mean eliminating all other articles and the cartoons. This was such a risky and unprecedented plan that it was carried out in secrecy. Most employees only learned about it when they picked up the August 31, 1946, issue and read the editor's note. "*The New Yorker* this week devotes its entire editorial space to an article on the almost complete obliteration of a city by one atomic bomb, and what happened to the people of that city," the note explained. "It does so in the conviction that few of us have yet comprehended the all but incredible destructive force of this weapon, and that everyone might well take time to consider the terrible implications of its use."[46]

Ross had feared the piece would provoke vitriolic criticism for its opposition to nuclear war, even as readers would be angry at missing regular features and cartoons. He was wrong. The issue immediately sold out; newspapers bought reprint rights (proceeds went to Red Cross relief); radio broadcasters read sections over the air; it was quickly published as a book; Albert Einstein requested a thousand copies; appreciative letters arrived constantly. Only a few weeks after it ran, Ross said, "I don't think I've ever got as much satisfaction out of anything else in my life."[47]

The postwar years were wonderful ones for the magazine, and seven hundred people gathered to celebrate it and its remarkable editor at its twenty-fifth anniversary gala in March 1950. Not everything was going well for Ross, though. His third marriage had been problematic since his 1940 wedding and in the fall of 1950 he moved into a hotel, planning on a divorce. That winter, flu brought down much of the magazine's editorial staff, and in early April he thought it finally had found him. He felt so sick that he went to Boston for a full examination at the Lahey Clinic, where he long had been successfully treated for his ulcers. Diagnosed with pleurisy, he spent May and June at his Connecticut home (without his wife), under the care of a nurse. Another examination in June revealed cancer of the windpipe. He told only his personal attorney and Hawley Truax about the diagnosis, and about the thirty-seven radiation treatments he subsequently underwent before returning to the *New Yorker* in mid-September and announcing that he was fine.[48]

In late November 1951 Grant was stranded on a pedestrian island in the middle of Park Avenue and spotted Ross striding along the sidewalk. His uncharacteristically stooped shoulders worried her. "I felt a definite urge to follow him," she said, but by the time the lights changed he was too far away, so she decided to settle for talking with him on the telephone. Calling his office, she learned he had just left for another checkup at the Lahey Clinic. She knew their old housemate Truax had gone along to help him pass the time between tests with cribbage games, but neither she nor any other friends or family members knew he was scheduled for exploratory surgery. Around midnight on December 6, her phone rang, waking her. It was Ross's secretary. When he told her Ross had died of an embolism during surgery, she cried.[49]

"Ross and the invisible me"

ONE OF ROSS'S ANNOYANCES IN late October 1951 was the publication of an invasive, superficial biography, *Ross and "The New Yorker,"* by Dale Kramer (also the author of a 1949 biography of Heywood Broun). No one on the magazine's staff had cooperated with Kramer, and Ross himself was rumored to have written the *New Yorker*'s one-paragraph review, which called the book "a conspicuously uninformed work, though a kindly intentioned one."[50]

Six years later James Thurber, by then an immensely popular humorist albeit only an occasional *New Yorker* contributor, published the first article of what was to be a ten-part series about Ross in the *Atlantic*. In preparation he had been given a secretary, an office, and access to Ross's files and the magazine's library, while dozens of people who knew or had worked for Ross were generous with information and anecdotes. The series was expanded and published as a book, *The Years with Ross*, in 1959. An immediate bestseller, it mainly received highly favorable reviews. Many people with firsthand knowledge of its subject challenged the accuracy or appropriateness of some its contents, however, and almost all reviewers pointed out that, amusing as it often was, it said much more about Thurber than about Ross.[51]

Grant, who had helped Thurber in his research by contributing her own recollections, appreciated the book's humor. But she called it "exasperating when presented as a reality" and felt it seriously underrated Ross's talents.[52] Both its deficiencies and its success may have been all the more galling because by the time it was published she had spent two years working on her own book, and it was not going well.

Her uncertainty about her precise topic was one problem. "I am writing a book about our early days, pinning it on our community house at 412 West 47th Street, but particularly going deep into the background of those of us who lived there," she wrote to a friend, before adding, "Of course, The New Yorker figures into the picture." She also admitted, "Unfortunately, I have kept practically no records."[53] She did extensive research in 1957, concentrating on learning more about Ross's life and career. For example, she wrote not only to John Winterich, Ralph Ingersoll, and Murdock Pemberton but also to secretaries at the *Sacramento Union* and Butterick Publishing for information about Ross's newspaper and *Home Sector* work. By the end of that year she had completed a manuscript and submitted it to David McKay Publishers.[54]

After it was rejected in January 1958 she substantially revised it before resubmitting it in July. "The new organization gives it a logic and flow which all of us applaud," one editor told her. Her writing, though remained a problem. "It doesn't have enough of the storytelling touch which it needs to get into the reader's heart as well as his mind." This was a critical concern because "Thurber's book is coming and covers a good deal of the same ground and no matter how deficient his facts, the book is skillfully written."[55]

That manuscript, too, was rejected, and in the midst of her next rewrite she explained to another editor that she was "changing my original concept although I am still doubtful about the wisdom of the change."[56] Harper & Row rejected that version in December 1958. "Since you returned my manuscript I have done a lot of thinking about it—with no result," Grant told her agent. She was leaving for a vacation in Mexico and would give it more thought there.[57]

Arguably the wisest decision would have been to drop the project. Different versions of her manuscript had been rejected three times in one year, and Thurber's book was due out in a few months. At that point it must have been clear that this kind of writing was not her strength and that thinking back over the details of a failed marriage to a difficult man was painful. Yet the most important person in her life wanted her to persevere with the book. As she later told an interviewer, "What finally decided me was my husband, who kept nagging me to tell my side of it."[58]

Harris adored her, wanted her to be happy, and must have hated seeing most of the work she wrote or proposed being rejected in the 1930s and 1940s. Yet he knew there was one topic she was very qualified to address and that—based on the evidence of Thurber's long, popular *Atlantic* series—could draw readers. He pushed her to write a book about her relationship with Ross and the early *New Yorker*, for this must have seemed by far her best publishing possibility. Still, the odds of publication could not have seemed high when the couple left for their Mexican vacation in late 1958. After two years of work, her project had become more of a long-shot gamble.

Her luck changed in September 1959 when Dale Kramer introduced her to Ken McCormick, the editor in chief at Doubleday & Company. If she hired the right writer to help her, McCormick said, her manuscript might well be sufficiently improved for Doubleday to publish it. The person he recommended most highly, Charles Murphy, was at first uninterested, but Grant held out for him, and after she returned from a trip to Asia in June 1960, Murphy agreed to be her collaborator. A year later, however, he wrote to say he had been too busy to start in on her book. They appear not to have corresponded again until April 1964, when she asked him if he would take up the job after four years of inactivity. "You would have heard from me before this but I have been laid up as a result of a bad motor accident Bill and I had last summer," she wrote. Now she felt well enough to get back to work.[59]

By March 1965 Murphy had dropped out completely and McCormick asked her to suggest other possible collaborators. It was a year before she found David Glixson, who began work in April 1966. McCormick was so pleased to have Glixson involved that in late May he told Grant, "I think what we need now is a general outline and then we can work out some kind of contract."[60] He changed his mind, though, after he saw the chapter Glixson reworked over the summer. "A book about Ross and The New Yorker should be sharp and witty," McCormick wrote in response, but the rewritten chapter "seems a little on the cute side." In late October 1966 Glixson quit, saying, "I simply don't have the proper kind of time to undertake the project I undertook so blithely. The book requires uninterrupted weeks and months of immersion." McCormick promptly informed Grant that because of Glixson's withdrawal, "I felt it best for me to discontinue negotiations with you on the book."[61]

By that time she must have been immensely frustrated. Having been reminded many times of her manuscript's weaknesses, she surely knew there was little she could do to remedy them on her own. Yet the woman who had defied the odds to win other battles—including obtaining financing for the nascent, unpromising *New Yorker* and launching the pony edition—was not ready for defeat. In December 1966 she sent her unchanged manuscript to Atheneum. Alfred Knopf Jr., one of the publishing company's owners and apparently a friend, wrote the rejection letter. "No manuscript has given me so much agony as yours," he began. He explained that he had tried to find larger value in what she had written, but could not. As he kindly put it, "This book really belongs to you, and to no one else."[62]

In March 1967 she did find a publisher, Reynal & Company. Eugene Reynal may have been another friend, for the letter he enclosed with her contract ended by saying, "We are looking forward to your cocktail party." He also reminded her that she had agreed to eliminate one chapter, restructure two others, and write a final "summing up" chapter. Editors would check the manuscript to eliminate duplications with Kramer's and Thurber's books, he said, "but I think on the whole it does not need a difficult editorial job."[63] That spring Grant carried out research for her final chapter by writing to numerous *New Yorker* editors and contributors, lined up Janet Flanner to write an introduction, and pondered possible titles. She had dozens of ideas, among them "Ross and the Invisible Me" and "Gluttons for Punishment."[64]

Dedicated "to William B. Harris, my husband, without whose constant prodding it would never have started," *Ross, "The New Yorker" and Me* was published in the spring of 1968. Its reception generally was tepid. Most reviewers expressed dissatisfaction at reading too little about Ross and too much about "me," and criticized her for poorly capturing a fascinating period and place. The *Christian Science Monitor* was typical in calling the book a "limp look at the wits of the 1920s." Even Bernays chimed in. His animosity toward Grant should have disqualified him as a reviewer, yet he accurately noted the book's fundamental problems when he complained that it "strings together peripheral happenings that do justice neither to Ross or The New Yorker."[65]

He could have added that they did an injustice to their author, for not only did she provide few revelations about Ross and sparsely cover the birth of the *New Yorker* but she poorly described her own contributions to the magazine. They could only be pieced together through careful, patient reading, but even then the picture presented was unimpressive, for she often portrayed herself as being not very bright, observant, or capable. This was in part because she chose to write so much about times when she did not distinguish herself. Thus, for example, she included many stories showing her naïveté during her early years at the *New York Times* but said little about how (or even exactly when) she became the paper's first woman general-assignment reporter, or about her accomplishments in that position.

Certainly the book did not demonstrate strong reporting or writing skills. Peppered with awkward phrasing, frivolous details, and errors, it cried out for tightening, polishing, and still more reorganization. Eugene Reynal did her no favor by denying that her manuscript needed serious editing. Yet his willingness to publish it may have been favor enough, for it meant the completion of a project that had gnawed at her for more than a decade.

"To Jane Grant, my partner in everything"

SOON AFTER SHE SIGNED THE Reynal & Company contract, Grant informed an assistant to the president of Harvard University that she had "assigned all the income from publishing the book (in any form) to the Harvard-Radcliffe Fund for the Study of Women."[66] She had established the fund in 1964 with Doris Stevens, the Lucy Stone League's vice president and a longtime feminist activist who had been close friends with Ruth Hale. They explained in its prospectus that they feared the paucity of serious studies of women meant "the problems of women were destined to remain unclear," so the fund would finance and promote "research and instruction in the problems of women in present and past societies anywhere."[67]

The fund was consistent with the goals of the league, which from its 1950 revival had identified itself on its stationery as "A Center for Research and Information on the Status of Women." In addition to personally collecting much of the material the league distributed, Grant saw many of the requests for information that it received, making her very aware of the need for more research. The fund also was consistent with her approach to dealing with problems. She looked for practical solutions and plunged into implementing them.

Harris plunged in with her. The couple paid $1,800 for a mailing list of do-nor "prospects," sent out a fundraising letter, and eventually collected about $35,000—a considerable accomplishment given that women's studies was not yet an academic discipline. They planned to continue raising money and later to will their estates to the fund as an endowment for a chair for the study of women. (In 1963 Grant had even drafted a will leaving her estate to any academic institution willing to set up such a chair in its sociology department.) But Harvard objected to their independent fundraising and "dragged its feet" on the fund, Harris said, so in the early 1970s, "we finished up with that institution."[68]

Their comfortable financial circumstances let them invest in this cause. After twenty years of renting a large apartment in a fashionable building at 277 Park Avenue, in 1959 they purchased a seven-room co-op apartment at 480 Park Avenue.[69] (Fleischman and Bernays lived in the same building, having begun renting an apartment there two years earlier.) By that time they were able to afford at least two full-time servants, a cook and a houseman/chauffeur. They enjoyed entertaining and did so frequently, but this seems to have put little strain on Grant. In her 1955 book, Fleischman quoted Grant as saying, "I have never bought the food. My goodness, if a cook can cook he can market, too. I can't be bothered."[70]

She unwittingly called attention to her prosperity in 1965 when she answered a letter from a young woman asking for advice on keeping her birth name after her marriage. "Some of my more conservative friends at first think I must surely use my husband's name at home, particularly with the servants," Grant wrote. She did not, nor did she answer to "Mrs. Harris" on the telephone. And if asked to explain her marital status, "I say, 'I'm Miss Grant, though married—and happily, too.'" She also noted, "I have traveled a great deal with my husband, including one trip around the world, and have never carried our marriage certificate."[71]

They took many long vacation trips and she accompanied Harris on some of his out-of-state *Fortune* assignments. He was promoted to assistant managing editor after the war, began reporting on the automotive industry in 1953, and a few years later switched to covering the burgeoning electronics industry. He left *Fortune* in 1960 to return to Wall Street, joining the Laidlaw & Company brokerage house as a general partner.[72] It was there in October 1962 that he received a typed letter with a 480 Park Avenue return address. It read: "Dear Sir: This is to notify you that I love you madly. Yours sincerely, Jane Grant."[73]

In 1968 Harris retired to devote more attention to White Flower Farm. Already thriving, it was selling more than a thousand varieties of plants "to connoisseurs all over the country," reported *House & Garden*, which called it "a horticulture enterprise probably unique in the U.S." Harris applied his managerial skills and business sense to further shape the operation, and to ensure that quality was maintained even if that meant putting the brakes on growth. "This is the kind of service business where size does not produce economies, as in manufacturing," he wrote in 1971. "Size produces confusion and a deterioration in service." He acknowledged that "it is un-American to say you are against growth" but vowed to limit the number of orders they accepted once sales exceeded a half million dollars, which he thought would happen soon.[74]

Concurrently, he took on another project for which he was exceptionally well suited: writing a gardening book based on his own experiences as a gardener and as the author of much of the copy in their yearly catalog, which was so popular that it sold for a dollar despite being illustrated only with black-and-white drawings rather than the color photographs featured in most nursery catalogues.[75] Published in 1971 under the pseudonym Amos Pettingill, *The White Flower Farm Garden Book* was dedicated "to Jane Grant, my partner in everything."

Across the road from White Flower Farm was the converted barn where the couple had been spending weekends and longer summer stretches for three decades, driven up from the city by their chauffeur. The ground floor housed the kitchen and adjacent dining room—paneled in old wood, stone-paved, with a fireplace and beamed ceiling. An open stairway led to the second floor's enormous living room with a nineteen-foot raftered ceiling, a "walk-in" fireplace on one end, and a balcony on the other. There were two bathrooms and two bedrooms on the top floor and one more bedroom off the balcony. Early American antiques and Oriental rugs were mixed with upholstered furniture arranged for easy conversation, and with objects picked up in their travels, be they English porcelains, pewter from China, Russian embroideries, or brasses from Morocco. Often tables in several rooms displayed spectacular bouquets arranged by Grant.[76]

As Harris became more involved in managing the business they kept their Manhattan co-op but spent more time in Connecticut, which may be one reason Grant stepped down as Lucy Stone League president in early 1968.[77] Litchfield also would have been an easier place for him to write his book, most of which described specific plants. "The vast majority, say 95 percent, are very friendly things. Stick them in the ground and they grow," he wrote in the same amiable tone that drew readers to the nursery's catalog. "This, of course, is the reason that gardening is not in the least difficult and why a great deal of horticultural knowledge can be acquired quickly and easily—it's the dirty thumb, not the green one, that makes plants grow."[78]

Preceding more than three hundred pages of gardening information and advice was a long foreword that gave the history of White Flower Farm. In the second paragraph Harris introduced Grant, "the other principal character in this cast," and explained that she had kept her birth name "on the grounds that it's the only thing she has so really her own it can't be taken away." He added, "I subscribe to this and object just as much to being called Mr. Grant, which sometimes happens, as I do to hearing her addressed as Mrs. Harris, which happens frequently with new friends or acquaintances who sit in the front row of traditionalism."[79]

It was a crowded front row even by the time Harris wrote his book. Grant never stopped receiving mail addressed to the wrong name, and in early 1969 letters arrived from two men who certainly should have known better. First, Howard Gotlieb, chief of special collections for the Boston University Libraries, wrote to Mrs. William Harris asking her to donate her papers to his "magnificent new library." Returning his letter to him, she declared, "I have never yet felt the need of an alias." She also enclosed Lucy Stone League brochures, saying, "It might be a good idea to file them in your library." Gotlieb thanked her for the brochures and asked her to accept his apologies. He admitted, "My only excuse, Miss Grant, is that I have been brainwashed by the exigencies of contemporary mores and habits."[80]

In February, Gene Gressley, director of the Archive of Contemporary History at the University of Wyoming Library, wrote with a different request. If she had any of Ross's papers, would she consider donating them? His letter was addressed to Mrs. Harold Ross. She informed Gressley that not only had she and Ross divorced in 1929 but she had never taken his name, "since I am a person in my own right," nor did she have his papers. After recommending that he read her recently published book to learn more about her relationship with Ross, she ended by saying, "Forgive my asperity, I am really a gentle creature, but I do find my hackles raised when people insist on using a name other than my own."[81]

Gressley was both chastened and intrigued. It was "erroneous, idiotic and obviously annoying" to call her Mrs. Harold Ross, he wrote, and he looked forward to reading her book. Perhaps she even would donate her own manuscripts related to the book. In any case, he would like to stay in touch, for "you sound to me like the kind of person I would enjoy keeping in contact with."[82]

She never met Gressley but she did continue to live happily with a man who was so secure in himself and devoted to her that he was impervious to "exigencies of contemporary mores and habits" regarding her name. One advantage of their Litchfield life was that Harris primarily worked out of their home so they were able spend most of their time near each other, which they enjoyed. She died there of cancer on March 16, 1972.[83] By that time the cofounder of the *New Yorker* was no longer as much of a New Yorker. Yet having fought passionately and successfully to keep her name, she was always Jane Grant.

CODA

"I still feel that she is looking over my shoulder"

THE DAY AFTER Doris E. Fleischman died in July 1980, Edward L. Bernays issued a press release that was as revealing of him as it was of her. It began: "Doris Fleischman Bernays, 88, pioneer counsel on public relations, author, editor, mother, honorary LLD, Lucy Stoner, musician, housewife, feminist, author of the 1955 bestseller, *A Wife Is Many Women*, died yesterday at Mount Vernon hospital in Cambridge from consequences of a stroke." The release was picked up by the PR Newswire and sent to newspaper obituary editors.[1]

Seeing beyond the baroque Bernays bombast, a *New York Times* reporter boiled down the release's information, gathered more, and wrote a nine-paragraph obituary.[2] In Los Angeles, the obituary surprised a journalism professor who had spent several years studying women in journalism history and thought she knew the names of the most accomplished ones. Like many journalism professors, she was well aware of Bernays. But she had never heard of his wife, who, according to the *Times*, had been his professional partner for more than fifty years. Who was she? Exactly what did she do?

That obituary sparked this book. I first used it in a course I was teaching on women in the media, handing out copies to my students to help them appreciate women's early success in public relations. I had no plans for doing anything more until the fall of 1985, when I was the editor of a scholarly journal, *Journalism History*, and accepted an article about Bernays that I wanted to illustrate with photographs. The author had none, but he suggested I call Bernays and ask him to lend me some of his. Although I couldn't imagine that this celebrated man would do that, the author said he had been remarkably cooperative when he'd interviewed him, so I did call.

Bernays quickly offered to help me, saying he would send several photos that sounded useful. But after waiting three weeks and not receiving them, I started to worry. I couldn't lay out the article without them and needed to get my pages to the printer soon. I apologized for calling him again and he apologized for not having found all the photos he had in mind, but he promised I'd get them shortly. They still didn't arrive. This time when I called he said he'd found them but hadn't had a chance to get copies made. He'd take care of it soon. No photos arrived, so I called once more, stressing my production deadline pressures, and he decided that rather than making me wait any longer he'd give me permission to copy any photos I wanted from his autobiography. My frustration at several delays made me glad for an easy solution, despite my disappointment at having to use previously published photos.

By this time I'd become comfortable talking with him, and he'd seemed pleased to hear from me each time I called. That gave me the confidence to do something I never would have done if our contacts had ended—as I thought they would—after one phone call. When he'd finished telling me which photos from his book he thought were most relevant to the article and we were ready to hang up, I blurted out that I'd like to study his late wife.

His voice changed. Previously businesslike, he became almost giddy as he told me that she was the first married woman to get a passport in her "maiden" name, that she was an early feminist, that she wrote a wonderful book, that she was brilliant. What about her public relations work, I asked. Hadn't she been his partner? If I studied her, I'd need to know a great deal about her contributions to his business. Would he talk with me about them? Yes, of course he would, he said. I should come to Cambridge to interview him, and stay at his home.

His efforts to ensure that my journal's article ran with photos of him had reminded me of what a virtuoso self-promoter he was, making me all the more surprised that he was so willing to discuss Fleischman's role in the achievements for which he alone had been recognized and lauded. But that wasn't the only reason I was taken aback. In addition to being immersed in another research project, I knew little about the history of public relations—and nothing at all about Fleischman, except what I'd read in her *Times* obituary. I really wasn't qualified to interview him. He had just turned ninety-four, however, and I couldn't count on him living much longer. I was afraid, too, that his acquiescence was largely based on feeling guilty about not sending me the photos he'd promised, and he might change his mind if I didn't quickly accept his offer. So I accepted, although I begged off seeing him until the spring semester was over.

After five months of cramming, in May 1986 I arrived at his door, late and in the rain. He immediately handed me a glass of sherry and two scrapbooks, which I paged through over the next week. Pasted onto the crumbling black pages of one of them were more than two hundred newspaper articles about Fleischman keeping her birth name when she married in 1922. The other scrapbook, compiled almost sixty years later, held an even larger number of condolence letters he had received after her death, arranged between sheets of plastic. The letters were as important to him as the newspaper clippings.

Bracketing her married life, those very different scrapbooks were an ideal introduction to her and his feelings about her. They also helped me decide how I should refer to her in my own work. The newspaper articles ran because she kept her name, while many condolence letters were from people who had known the couple in New York and offered Bernays their sympathies on the loss of "Miss Fleischman." When I pointed this out, he admitted that many longtime friends called her by her birth name until she died, so I have done the same.

There was much more for me to read about her on that trip because a decade earlier they had donated a small collection of her papers to the Schlesinger Library on the History of Women in America at nearby Radcliffe.[3] Those papers were a godsend, letting me ask Bernays about things I never could have known based on the extremely sparse published information I had found about Fleischman. He also made sure I met his daughters, Doris Held and Anne Bernays, who lived nearby and talked with me at length.

My first enormously productive visit was followed by two more. During each one he not only sat for many hours of interviews but offered me unfettered access to thousands of documents about their business that he had saved in neat files in his home. He was willing to answer difficult questions about any subject I raised, and to search for more information when his memory failed. Spending extended time with him also helped me understand the kind of person he was and what it must have been like to be married to him. He was unique, to say the least.

Still, I feared our good relationship would end in 1988. After visiting him in March, I finished writing a paper about Fleischman that was accepted for presentation at a national conference. I sent him a copy nervously, though, since the paper's theme was his dominance of her at home and in the office, and her lack of professional recognition. Once again he surprised me. "I have no criticisms whatsoever," he wrote to me after reading it, "except possibly one slight point." I had "overplayed" her invisibility, he thought, and not been sufficiently mindful of how their business would have suffered "if we had publicized a woman giving advice to men."[4] This was not a slight point at all, but he was willing to treat it as if it were, and to invite me back.

Eventually I better understood the motivations for his enthusiastic cooperation. First, I happened to have one qualification that was very important to him: I was a professor. By the time I rang his doorbell he had welcomed a substantial number of them to his home. As he did with me, he had settled them into the chair of the electric "inclinator" (installed for Fleischman, who had trouble climbing the long stairway) and sent it to the second floor while he trotted up the stairs beside it. He had given them the same tour he gave me of the second-floor walls where dozens of black-and-white photos showed him with famous—some of them *very* famous—clients. And he had sat with his visitors for hours, addressing the topics they were researching even as he told the stories he loved to tell. This was part of the continuous campaign to burnish his reputation that he had launched on first moving to Cambridge, although now he encouraged academics to write about him by offering them his individual attention.[5]

I had the right credentials and had come from California to listen to him. He was so pleased to be able to talk with me about himself and his past, and so confident in what he had to say, that he tried hard to accommodate me. I probably spent more time interviewing him in the last two decades of his life than any other scholar, and I may have been the only one who stayed at his home (in what had been Fleischman's office). I was exactly the kind of audience he wanted.

Of course his generosity with information and memories also was explained by his desire to control the picture of Fleischman I presented, just as he had exerted immense control over Fleischman herself. Nevertheless, he encouraged me to talk with his daughters despite the fact that (as he must have anticipated) they often were critical of him. And he paid no attention to the sometimes-uncomplimentary documents I took to copy each time I rummaged through his files. Similarly, my 1988 paper was a warning that he would not always agree with what I wrote. Yet he was happy to help me continue my research.

When I asked Anne Bernays why she thought her father was so helpful even though by telling Fleischman's story I was undermining the sole credit he had received for their work, she reminded me that one of his favorite phrases was "reflected glory." I was showing his good sense in choosing her mother as his partner, she explained. "You're flattering him."[6] I later realized that the timing of my research added to the flattery. In contrast to the antifeminism of the 1950s that made it a problematic time for Fleischman to disclose much about her career in *A Wife Is Many Women*—so she barely mentioned it—the feminism of the 1980s and 1990s made this an excellent time for Bernays to call attention to her career. He was willing to take less credit for their public relations accomplishments if he could take full credit for having been smart enough to marry and form a professional relationship with this remarkable woman.

Certainly another reason he supported my efforts was that he had admired, respected, and loved Fleischman, and now wanted to do right by her. I knew better than to take too much of what he said as the unvarnished truth, but when he repeatedly told me they had had a wonderful marriage I was convinced he really believed it, and was grateful to her for making it possible. Our long talks seemed to put her work more on his mind, and I noticed that in many of the articles written about him during the last years of his life (he lived to be 103), he took the initiative in pointing out that Fleischman had been his partner.[7]

Bernays made the most of turning one hundred in 1991. He attended events celebrating his birth in different parts of the country, gave many speeches, was interviewed often. In one of those interviews, reproduced in question-and-answer format in a public relations trade magazine, he was asked to analyze his career and the current state of the profession. The interviewer's final question was, "Do you have any regrets?" This man who had reluctantly wed in 1922 answered, "I do wish I'd married my wife sooner."[8]

RUTH HALE'S UNEXPECTED DEATH IN 1934 was widely noted. The four-deck headline of her long *New York Times* obituary nicely captured her perceived significance. "Ruth Hale Is Dead; Feminist Leader" was followed by "Founder of Lucy Stone League Was Until Recently Wife of Heywood Broun," then "Insisted on Maiden Name," and, finally, "In Conflict With Officials Over Passport—Aided Husband in Political Contest." The story's lead called her "one of the outstanding champions of women's rights in this country."[9]

But she suffered the ultimate indignity of being deprived of any part of her name by other headline writers. "Heywood Broun ex-Wife Passes" was all that ran at the top of the Associated Press story in the *Los Angeles Times*. Similarly, the *New York Journal* announced, "Heywood Broun's Ex-Wife Dies After 3 Weeks' Illness." The *Nation*'s piece (which carried no headline) was unusual in downplaying her relationship with Broun, instead trying to capture her spirit in an obituary that called her "always and without ceasing a passionate contender."[10]

Broun wrote a sad, affecting column in which he struggled to explain both her and her role in his work. He finally declared, "I suppose that for seventeen years practically every word I wrote was set down with the feeling that Ruth Hale was looking over my shoulder." Then he added, "I still feel that she is looking over my shoulder."[11] Yet however much he felt her there, it didn't keep him from falling apart. He had no trouble writing his column but drank more, slept less, stayed out very late, moved from hotel to hotel, physically deteriorated.[12]

His decline stopped four months later when he married Connie Madison. His son thought the marriage temporarily rescued his father, noting, "If Ruth had set out to improve Heywood, Connie set out to make him happy, and both were good at what they did." All the same, 1939 was a difficult year. Worn down by problems not only with his health but with Scripps-Howard and the Newspaper Guild, he died of complications of pneumonia in December.[13] More than three thousand people—including Mayor Fiorello La Guardia and Supreme Court justice Felix Frankfurter—came to his funeral, and throughout the country his readers also mourned.[14] His is remembered to this day as a gifted columnist and defender of the underdog.

By the time of Broun's death, Hale was largely forgotten. And in what she likely would have judged a worse fate, the quick actions of the woman she had fought with all her life resulted in her remains being buried in the town she most despised under a headstone with words she would have hated. Her wish had been to be cremated, with no memorial service. This gave Annie Riley Hale the chance to take possession of her daughter's ashes at the crematorium and mail them to Tennessee, where they eventually were buried in the Old Rogersville Presbyterian Cemetery under a headstone reading, "Ruth Hale, Daughter of Annie Riley and J. Richards Hale, and for 17 Years the Wife of Heywood Broun."[15]

She told no members of the Broun family about what she had done, probably because the revelation would have further endangered what she called the "monthly allowance" she had long been receiving from her daughter and that Broun continued sending to her until he died. She apparently took the secret with her to her own grave, which was dug next to her daughter's. (She would have loved the way she was identified in the headline of her 1944 *New York Times* obituary: "Writer, Lecturer, Economist Was Mother of Mrs. Heywood Broun.")[16]

About a half century later, Melissa Hale Ward, the daughter of Ruth's brother Richard, visited Tennessee in search of Hale family history and found her aunt's grave. Only when she told her cousin Heywood about her discovery did he learn that his grandmother had won her very last battle with his mother.[17] Yet she was not to have the family's last word on Hale. That would go to him.

In July 1940 Heywood Hale Broun graduated from college and joined the sports department of the new adless newspaper *PM*. Telling Broun he had hired him solely because of his admiration for his father, the managing editor gave him six months to prove himself. Broun admitted to having "no qualifications except some hard-hitting sports columns in the Swarthmore College *Phoenix*, a paper with an even smaller circulation than *PM*," but he proved up to the job since it required little beyond rewriting press releases. In the spring of 1941, though, illness reduced the size of the sports staff and he was sent to cover the opening game of the major league baseball season. With help from a sportswriter who in 1915 had broken in his father, he did sufficiently well to be kept on the beat until August, when he was drafted into the army.[18]

Discharged four and a half years later, he was surprised when Ralph McAllister Ingersoll, *PM*'s managing editor (and twenty years earlier the *New Yorker*'s managing editor), asked him to return to the paper as its sports editor. He was demoted following management changes, and *PM* folded in early 1949, but in the meantime, as "the doomed newspaper coughed away its writers and reporters," Broun's assignments multiplied. "Before we finished I was, simultaneously, a three-times-a-week sports columnist, a once-a-week humor columnist, a frequent reviewer of books, and a rewriter of much wire service material," he remembered, "in addition to covering, in person, one or two baseball games a day."[19]

He took the newspaper's demise as a sign that he should devote himself to his greatest love, acting. "I had no idea of the difficulties an actor faces, no notion of the terrible oversupply of talent and the wasting effect of long stretches of inactivity," he wrote almost two decades later as he looked back at his decision. "I just thought my daydreams were going to come true, and I must say that in a modified, scaled-down way, they have."[20] Achieving moderate success in a few films and Broadway plays but mostly in summer stock and episodic television, he had no plans for any other career until in 1966 he landed what was to be the best role of his life.

CBS Television, after broadcasting evening newscasts only on weeknights, was adding a Saturday-evening newscast that would include a sports correspondent. A CBS News executive who was in the audience when Broun amusingly hosted a sportswriters dinner asked him to audition for the job, but Broun turned him down. He explained that he had a terrific role in a soon-to-open Broadway play and critical acclaim surely would follow, for he knew "the Great Moment, for which I had waited through seventeen years of bank clerks, deputy sheriffs, and druggists, was at hand." The play closed in three days, a CBS audition was quickly scheduled, and he was hired for a four-week trial period starting with the program's February debut.[21]

The trial period was extended but he knew his work was mediocre, so early that spring he was glad to leave for Florida, where he had a part in a brief run of *The Philadelphia Story*. He offered to do sports features while he was there, although he thought his undistinguished prior work made such assignments unlikely. When he was sent to Miami for a story on the racehorse Buckpasser, his wife, Jane Lloyd-Jones, noted that horse racing was associated with loud colors, so suggested he wear the gaudy madras jacket he had worn for his role as a salesman in the Broadway production of *Send Me No Flowers*.[22]

His piece went well, helped by Buckpasser, who, "after an amazed look at my jacket, stood up in his stall and came over for closer inspection, affording me a splendid camera shot." Deciding the jacket was his "principal asset," he kept wearing it while "working and wondering whether each Saturday's piece would be the last," until in late summer he was offered a contract. Thus, he explained, his wife's costume suggestion "was to profoundly alter the course of my life and rob the theater of a man I still think of as a character actor of infinite color and variety."[23]

His weekly CBS newscast segments attracted a large, devoted audience and made him something of a journalistic icon who was known for his dry humor, gift for finding offbeat stories, and love of words. Certainly his pieces were more eloquent and literate than almost anything else on network television. Reporting on the Boston Red Sox's startling 1967 pennant victory, for example, he said of star outfielder Carl Yastrzemski: "He was not just hitting home runs but was, in fact, accomplishing the ninth labor of Hercules, bringing a championship to Boston, a city whose previous baseball idol, Ted Williams, resembled that other Greek, Achilles, who fought a great fight but spent a lot of time sulking in his tent."[24]

Shortly after he was hired by CBS, Broun wrote a charming autobiographical book mainly about the theater but also about baseball. A collection of essays about his sports reporting experiences followed in 1979. At that point he already had a very different kind of topic in mind for his next book: his life with his parents. Not only did this manuscript take much longer to write than his two previous books but it was the only one he ever rewrote.[25] *Whose Little Boy Are You? A Memoir of the Broun Family* came out in 1983, and the author's celebrity helped ensure that this very personal book was widely reviewed.

In Los Angeles, one of Broun's fans who also admired his father's work read reviews of the memoir with surprise. I had never heard of Ruth Hale. I bought a copy, began to read, and couldn't put it down once I reached this sentence about his parents on page nine: "They probably shouldn't have gotten married; they probably should never have had a child; and they probably shouldn't, after seventeen years of marriage, have gotten divorced." The story was fascinating, poignant, and beautifully told, although I didn't learn as much about Hale as I wanted to know.

A few years later, when I was researching Doris Fleischman, I returned to *Whose Little Boy Are You?* So many things about Fleischman mystified me that I was trying to identify what sociologists call a "cohort" of women who were like her and might help me better understand her. I began by looking for Lucy Stone League members who were journalists. That brought me to Hale, who, I found, Broun had even briefly compared to Fleischman in his book. So I read it again, coming away with renewed interest in—and still more questions about—Hale. But I had scant success answering them because I could find little else written about her. That dearth of information further provoked my interest.

Once Broun had retired from CBS and I was done researching Fleischman, I called him at his home in Woodstock, New York, and asked if I could talk with him about his mother. I now admit that I did this as much because I wanted to meet him as because I wanted to learn about Ruth Hale. Then again, when I first contacted him I didn't know that our interviews would be the most interesting and revealing I would ever carry out.

After years of answering questions about his famous father he was pleased that someone wanted to know about his mother, and one of the many delights of our conversations was discovering the remarkable ways his appeal to his television audiences was rooted in her values and efforts. Far more than anyone else, she resolutely nourished his mind, stimulated his curiosity, and molded him into a voracious reader and superlative talker. She died never knowing it, but she actually helped form two successful male journalists.

It was only after we became friends that I asked him a hard question about his book's subtitle, "A Memoir of the Broun Family." Why had he omitted Ruth's surname? His answer was brusquely unsatisfying: "That was the editor's idea. I didn't like it, but it's on the book, so the hell with it."[26] More to the point, I think, is that his father's accomplishments and his own made Broun a famous name that would attract readers, but almost nobody knew who Ruth Hale was. Even though the book honored her, its subtitle did not. As one reviewer who noticed the absent name remarked: "Ruth would no doubt find this as inevitable as it is painful."[27]

JANE GRANT'S MARCH 1972 *New York Times* obituary caught the eye of Ed Kemp, the acquisitions librarian for the University of Oregon Library's Special Collections. For more than a decade he had been trying to make the most of his minuscule budget to obtain significant new archival materials. More-prominent and better-endowed institutions had more to offer potential donors than his library did, so he had identified major gaps in what was being collected nationwide and concentrated on searching out the kinds of materials other archives likely would overlook. Because one particularly noticeable gap was the papers of women, this was an area of special interest. He started by soliciting the papers of women missionaries and children's book authors, which "led me to many bright and gifted women," he remembered.[28]

The *Times* was a crucial resource in his search for donors of either sex. He combed its obituaries every day, and although about 90 percent of the articles' subjects were men (and he did pursue some of their papers), he occasionally came upon the name of a promising woman. Whether his likely candidate was female or male, he assigned a graduate student in the university's library science program to research that person, then used the additional information to decide whether to go any further. "Too many emotional sessions where the death was too recent" had taught him to wait six months to a year before contacting survivors, he said.[29]

He needed only minimal research to know Grant's papers would be worth examining, but he did not write to William Harris until early November 1973—more than a year and a half after Grant's death—because he would not be able to meet with him until the following spring. Every year he packed his "blue blazer, grey flannels and appropriate ties" and took two trips to the East Coast, one in the spring and one in the fall, to collect materials from people he had been cultivating, meet new potential donors, and revisit old ones. His 1973 schedules already were so tight that he couldn't fit in an extra donor visit.[30] That initial delay, and a later unexpected one, would prove to be highly advantageous to his university.

The November letter Harris received was brief and impersonal. It stressed the value of Oregon's Special Collections and ended with boilerplate language: "Jane Grant's distinguished years of active service are recognized by many and we are writing to you in the hope that her files have been retained." Harris was not put off. He wrote back, offering to show Kemp Grant's papers and also noting that much earlier the couple had attempted "to get some of the Eastern universities interested in a chair for the study of women." Kemp responded with a much more personal letter, and by the end of December Harris had invited him to stay with him on his spring trip.[31]

They carefully worked out the details of their May meeting but budgetary problems forced Kemp to change his plans, so it was early November 1974 before he finally shook the hand of the man with whom he had been exchanging cordial letters. They met at Harris's Park Avenue apartment, where he had gathered up Grant's papers.[32]

About two-thirds of the times Kemp first looked at someone's papers he could easily dismiss them as not worth collecting, and in most of the other cases he had to examine them more closely before he could make a decision. But he instantly could tell Grant's papers were valuable, and gladly informed Harris that they were. Harris then asked if the University of Oregon had a women's studies program. Kemp replied that it had a nascent, very small one, and Harris said he would donate the papers.[33]

As the two men continued talking over a long lunch served by Harris's valet, Kemp gradually realized that his host assumed he was there to ask for more than the papers. Something that Harris had briefly mentioned in his letter a year earlier was much on his mind. As he explained to Kemp that afternoon, in the 1960s he and Grant had raised money for a chair for the study of women at Harvard and had planned to will their estates to it, but their dealings had ended very badly. Now he expected Kemp to ask for the funds originally earmarked for Harvard, perhaps for Oregon's women's studies program.[34]

Kemp was stunned. He knew nothing about raising money and had many good reasons to avoid consulting with his university's development office, which had pressured him several times for lists of Special Collections donors so it could follow up with its own solicitations. (He had not cooperated.) Meanwhile, he was paying many of his travel expenses himself and, when he obtained papers, had only two clerical assistants and student help to process them. "We had to plead for money," he said. The development office provided no financial help but wanted to take advantage of relationships he had developed with donors, and he knew sharing information might even result in actions by the office that would damage those relationships.[35]

So when he returned to Eugene he went straight to the university's president, Robert Clark. "He jumped," Kemp said, "there was no persuasion needed." Clark wasn't just excited about the prospects of a monetary donation; he also was pleased that it would go to this neglected field.[36] He promptly wrote a heartfelt letter to Harris explaining that as a dean in the 1950s he had tried and failed to establish a program focusing on women's issues. Fortunately, the 1970s were different. "Because of the courage and foresight of feminists and their supporters, we have a new perception of the role of women in our society," he wrote. And recently, "through sheer grit and dedication, the academic women of the University of Oregon convinced their colleagues that there is a vital need to create a program in Women's Studies." Work had already begun on the program, and he hoped to visit Harris to tell him more about it.[37]

This was good news to Harris, and immediately after Clark received his positive response he flew out to meet him. It was an exceptionally successful visit during which, Clark reported, Harris "spoke feelingly, and sometimes with a touch of sharpness, about the difficulties of women in our society."[38] When Clark next wrote to Harris he thanked him both for allowing him to visit and for their satisfying conversations. "In the many years I have been interested in the role of women in our society, I have not encountered any other man who could keep pace with you in a sympathetic and rational view of the issue," he said. "I should like to write to you on a personal basis within the next several weeks since I feel your interest and ours are common."[39]

The two men corresponded warmly that winter and spring, even as Clark and Kemp held meetings with the faculty running the university's small Center for the Sociological Study of Women (later renamed the Center for the Study of Women in Society). Harris planned to visit the university in March 1975 but a business emergency forced him to cancel, so instead Kemp arranged to meet him in Litchfield in early May. Just before he set off on that trip, Clark received a letter from Harris's lawyers announcing that they had prepared a new will in which "Mr. Harris intends to bequeath a very substantial portion of his estate to the 'University of Oregon Fund for the Study of Women.'"[40]

Two years later he sold White Flower Farm so that the university would not have to pay estate taxes on it. "Harris seems reconciled and even pleased with this decision," Kemp noted after visiting him.[41] The buyer was the nursery's manager, who had told Harris when he started in January 1976 that he'd like to buy it. Harris had said it was not for sale, but during the next year he became convinced that the manager would be a capable, responsible owner. Still, selling could not have been an easy decision, for the business was thriving and his interest in gardening had not waned. Indeed, he continued writing magazine articles about gardening. (And to satisfy readers, Amos Pettingill remained the voice of the White Flower Farm catalog, even though Harris stopped writing the copy at the time of the sale.)[42]

No one knew how much the university ultimately would receive, but Harris's commitment was not in doubt. Analyzing why he so quickly and wholeheartedly made that commitment, Kemp explained that one key factor was timing. Soon after Grant died, both the University of Wyoming and Boston University asked Harris for her papers, and Vassar may have too. In his grief, he was far from ready to think about what to do with materials from her past. But those institutions never contacted him again, and by the time Kemp met him more than two years after Grant's death he was somewhat desperate.[43]

Yet this was more than the right time. It also was the right place and the right people. When Robert Clark first visited in late 1974, Harris told him about the couple's bad experiences with Harvard and with other East Coast colleges and universities they subsequently approached about establishing a women's studies professorship. All had wanted to use the money for other projects already in progress. "He intruded this warning into the conversation three or four times," Clark reported. "Now he is unsure." He didn't know if a professorship was possible, but he was wary of elite institutions with their own agendas.[44] The University of Oregon was very different from the places that had disappointed him.[45]

And the men Harris came to know best from that university were impeccably qualified to gain his trust. A feminist, Clark had tried to create a program addressing women's issues in the 1950s. When they got together he and Harris talked about those kinds of issues—something Harris could not have done with most other men (and probably with no other male university president). Kemp was another feminist. He valued women's accomplishments and had long been collecting archival materials that would help keep them from being forgotten. Harris must have been pleased, as well, that Kemp was immediately impressed with Grant's papers.

The two became friends. Kemp liked the fact that Harris was confident about himself and straightforward in stating his views but also considerate of others. Kemp described him as a gentleman who "used his honesty in a diplomatic fashion." Similarly, while elegant in his bearing, he didn't take himself too seriously. Highly articulate and intellectually curious, he was the type of man Kemp would have wanted to know under any circumstances. So he was glad to be able to spend much more time with Harris after their first meeting. He visited him twice in the late spring of 1975, then returned a year later to help him pack Grant's papers into twenty-eight cartons that were shipped to Eugene. He was back for social visits on his regular collecting trips to the East Coast in May and October 1977, and in May 1978.[46]

Harris looked forward to these visits too. He was relieved to have resolved his concerns about what to do with Grant's papers, and each time Kemp came to see him he had additional materials for him. These were chances for Harris to talk about Grant with someone who knew her through her papers (which Kemp had begun cataloging as soon as they arrived in Eugene) and about other shared interests, including gardening. In all of their talks, "I never heard him say anything negative about Jane," Kemp recalled. "She walked on water."[47]

Clark retired and the president who replaced him planned to fly to New York to meet Harris in June 1978. But Harris said they'd have to find some other time because he would be in Santa Barbara, California, investigating pain clinics that he hoped could help him with some of his health problems. While he was there he had a stroke, and when Kemp visited him in September he found that his speech and reasoning abilities were severely impaired. Kemp met with the woman who was overseeing his care and with her husband, a businessman who had been investing the profits from the sale of White Flower Farm for him. He kept Kemp informed about Harris's condition, also telling him that the investments were doing well.[48]

Harris eventually was forced to move to a Massachusetts nursing home. Kemp tried to see him there in early June 1981 but instead had to track him down at a nearby hospital, where he died on June 22, not long after their visit. He left an estate even larger than Kemp and Clark had imagined—$3.5 million, including about $1 million in Grant's *New Yorker* stock. With the exception of a few small bequests to individuals, it all went to Oregon's Center for the Study of Women in Society. This tribute to Harris's love for Grant and belief in her causes was the largest donation the university had ever received.[49]

NOTES

INTRODUCTION

1. Lorine Pruette, "Why Women Fail," in *Women's Coming of Age: A Symposium*, ed. Samuel D. Schmalhausen and V. F. Calverton (New York: Horace Liveright, 1931), 257–58.
2. Stuart Ewen, *PR! A Social History of Spin* (New York: Basic Books, 1996), 3.
3. Heywood Hale Broun, *Whose Little Boy Are You? A Memoir of the Broun Family* (New York: St. Martin's, 1983), 171.
4. Letter from Harold Ross to Lloyd Stryker, Oct. 29, 1945, box 84, folder 9, *New Yorker* Records, Manuscripts and Archives Division, Astor, Lenox and Tilden Foundations, New York Public Library, New York, NY.
5. "The Married Woman's Maiden Name Again," *Philadelphia Inquirer*, Aug. 20, 1924, a clipping in Ruth Hale's Scrapbook, Schlesinger Library on the History of Women in America, Radcliffe Institute for Advanced Study, Harvard University, Cambridge, MA.
6. Ruth Hale, "Freedom in Divorce," *Forum*, Sept. 1926, 336.

CHAPTER 1

1. Author's interview with Edward L. Bernays, May 26, 1986, Cambridge, MA.
2. Notes for *A Wife Is Many Women*, Doris Fleischman Bernays Papers, box 1, folder 33, Schlesinger Library on the History of Women in America, Radcliffe Institute for Advanced Study, Harvard University, Cambridge, MA (hereafter DFB Papers). Her full name was Doris Elsa Fleischman.
3. Doris Fleischman Bernays, *A Wife Is Many Women* (New York: Crown Publishers, 1955), 167.
4. Ibid., 168; author's interview with Anne Bernays, Oct. 29, 1989, Cambridge, MA; author's telephone interview with Camille Roman, Nov. 20, 1995.
5. "Drops Dead in Park," *New York Times*, May 27, 1924, 21; *A Wife Is Many Women*, 81, 168–69. In an interview with the author on May 26, 1986, Bernays admitted that Fleischman's first job after graduating from Barnard was at a charity that "took care of women." He said he told her, "I think you're very silly to spend your life on a charity," and helped her make the contact that led to her *Tribune* job.
6. Author's interview with Edward L. Bernays, Mar. 26, 1988, Cambridge, MA; research notes for *Biography of an Idea* chapter draft titled "Doris and I," 1–4, box I:461, Edward L. Bernays Papers, Manuscript Division, Library of Congress, Washington, DC (hereafter ELB Papers).
7. Edward L. Bernays, *Biography of an Idea: Memoirs of Public Relations Counsel Edward L. Bernays* (New York: Simon & Schuster, 1965), 53–55.
8. Ibid., 57–61.
9. Transcript of Edward L. Bernays Oral History (1971), 448, Oral History Research Office, Columbia University, New York, NY.

10. Bernays described these early years at length in *Biography of an Idea*, 62–152. The quotes are on pages 102 and 75.

11. Ibid., 155–78. For a good description of the work of the CPI, see Stuart Ewen, *PR! A Social History of Spin* (New York: Basic Books, 1996), 102–27.

12. Ewen, *PR!*, 126–33; Scott Cutlip, *The Unseen Power: Public Relations. A History* (Hillsdale, NJ: Lawrence Erlbaum Associates, 1994), 105–6; Alan R. Raucher, *Public Relations and Business, 1900–1929* (Baltimore: Johns Hopkins University Press, 1968), 73–74.

13. Transcript of Edward L. Bernays Oral History, 60–62.

14. *Biography of an Idea*, 187.

15. Ibid., 187–94; transcript of Edward L. Bernays Oral History, 61–65. Specific dates are from a chronology of his activities prepared by Bernays that is in box I:498, ELB Papers.

16. Ishbel Ross, *Ladies of the Press: The Story of Women in Journalism by an Insider* (New York: Harper & Brothers, 1936), 122–25.

17. More than sixty of Fleischman's *Tribune* stories can be found in box 1, folders 2–3, DFB Papers. "Woman at the Lightweight Championship" ran on Mar. 14, 1915. Her press pass for the Panama-Pacific International Exposition is in box III:2, ELB Papers.

18. *A Wife Is Many Women*, 38, 169.

19. Her pride in her amateur theatrical acting was shown by its inclusion in the press release announcing their marriage that she and Bernays produced in September 1922. (See box I:746, ELB Papers.) Her pride in her Peace Parade participation was evident in the fact that it often was included in her later summaries of accomplishments, and it was noted in the press release Bernays sent out when she died in July 1980. (See box III:45, ELB Papers.)

20. The clipping files Fleischman donated to the Schlesinger Library contain no *Tribune* articles with her byline after March 19, 1916. Further evidence that she left that year can be found in the brief biographies she wrote to accompany her chapters in two books published in the 1920s. Both say she worked at the *Tribune* from 1914 to 1916. See Doris E. Fleischman, ed., *An Outline of Careers for Women: A Practical Guide to Achievement* (Garden City, NY: Doubleday, Doran & Co., 1928), 384, and Edward L. Bernays, ed., *An Outline of Careers: A Practical Guide to Achievement by Thirty-Eight Eminent Americans* (New York: George G. Doran Co., 1927), opposite page 423.

21. In an interview with the author (Oct. 26, 1989, Cambridge, MA), Bernays conceded that he did not hire her away from the *Tribune*, as he had always claimed.

22. Author's telephone interview with Camille Roman.

23. Fleischman told stories about her mother and father in every chapter of *A Wife Is Many Women*. Her account of attending *Damaged Goods* behind her father's back is on page 196. Her daughters described Fleischman's family and their fond memories of their grandmother Hattie in two interviews with the author: Anne Bernays on Oct. 27, 1989, and Doris Held on May 27, 1986, both in Cambridge, MA. Anne's quote about her grandfather is in Anne Bernays and Justin Kaplan, *Back Then: Two Lives in 1950s New York* (New York: William Morrow, 2002), 17.

24. Author's interview with Edward L. Bernays, May 26, 1986. Fleischman said she worked for the Baron de Hirsch Fund in her description of her career history opposite page 423 in Bernays's *An Outline of Careers*. A small amount of material related to her other work is in box 1, folder 1, and addenda, folder 1, DFB Papers.

25. Audiotape of an interview with Doris Fleischman Bernays by MaryAnn Yodelis, July 1973, Cambridge, MA, in possession of the author. A few documents about the New York Dispensary are in the addenda, folder 2, DFB Papers.

26. Fleischman's byline appears on articles about Lithuania and the servicemen's reemployment campaigns published by newspapers in April, June, and July 1919—all before Bernays opened his office. See clippings in box III:3, ELB Papers, and in the addenda, folder 1, DFB Papers.

27. *Biography of an Idea*, 188–92; "Finding My Way" (a section in Bernays's notes for *Biogra-*

phy of an Idea), 1–4, box I:461, ELB Papers; transcript of Edward L. Bernays Oral History, 61–66.

28. Edward L. Bernays, "The Emergence of the Public Relations Counsel," *Business History Review* 43 (Autumn 1971): 301.

29. The first quote is from "*Biography of an Idea* Notes, 1910–1913," 1921 section, 3, box I:460, ELB Papers. The second is from "Doris and I," 4.

30. *Biography of an Idea*, 4–11 (the quote is on page 5); *A Wife Is Many Women*, 71.

31. Bernays and Kaplan, *Back Then*, 16.

32. *Biography of an Idea*, 5–6, 84–85.

33. Author's interview with Edward L. Bernays, Mar. 29, 1988, Cambridge, MA. Also see "Miss Bernays in City Job," *New York Times*, May 13, 1934, 28.

34. Author's interview with Edward L. Bernays, Mar. 26, 1988.

35. Author's interview with Edward L. Bernays, Oct. 29, 1989, Cambridge, MA; *Biography of an Idea*, 194.

36. *A Wife Is Many Women*, 38.

37. Elizabeth Kemper Adams, *Women Professional Workers* (New York: Macmillan Company, 1921), 307.

38. Catherine Filene, ed., *Careers for Women* (Cambridge, MA: Riverside Press, 1920; reprint, New York: Arno Press, 1974), 19.

39. Transcript of Edward L. Bernays Oral History, 72.

40. Bernays described his income and some of his clients during this time in *Biography of an Idea*, 194–99. Also see chronology, box I:498, and receipt from H. P. Inman of the Lithuanian National Council for work done by Bernays, Aug. 19, 1919, box III:6, ELB Papers.

41. Walker Gilmer, *Horace Liveright: Publisher of the Twenties* (New York: David Lewis, 1970), 19; "Leon S. Fleischman, Ex-Newspaper Man," *New York Times*, July 4, 1946, 19; "Liveright" (a section of Bernays's notes for *Biography of an Idea*), 1–2, box I:458, ELB Papers. The quote is on page 1.

42. Gilmer, *Horace Liveright*, 10–20.

43. John Tebbel, *A History of Book Publishing in the United States*, vol. 3 (New York: R. R. Bowker Company, 1978), 136, 138.

44. *Biography of an Idea*, 277–78.

45. Ibid., 284; "Boni and Liveright—Book Publishers—Publicity Campaign" (a section in Bernays's notes for *Biography of an Idea*), 8–11, box I:457, ELB Papers. The quote, taken from the foreword to the First Supplementary Catalog, is on page 11.

46. "Liveright," 17.

47. Letter from Edward L. Bernays to the features editor of the *Detroit Free Press*, Nov. 13, 1919, box I:120, ELB Papers.

48. *Biography of an Idea*, 280–81; "Boni and Liveright—Book Publishers—Publicity Campaign," 21–26, 37–39.

49. Edward L. Bernays, *Crystallizing Public Opinion* (New York: Boni & Liveright, 1923; reprint, New York: Liveright Publishing Corporation, 1961), 195.

50. "Liveright," 10–11.

51. *Crystallizing Public Opinion*, 137.

52. "Boni and Liveright—Book Publishers—Publicity Campaign," 12–15; *Biography of an Idea*, 282. Some of these releases are in box I:120, ELB Papers.

53. "Boni and Liveright—Book Publishers—Publicity Campaign," 14–20.

54. Ibid., 74–75; Gilmer, *Horace Liveright*, 26, 63; *Biography of an Idea*, 282–83.

55. "Liveright," 16–17.

56. Heavy newspaper coverage of *The Swing of the Pendulum* is described in Edward L. Bernays, "Promotion Expert Urges New Sales Methods for Books," *Publisher's Weekly*, Mar. 20, 1920, 934.

57. Ibid., 933–36.

58. Ann Douglas, *Terrible Honesty: Mongrel Manhattan in the 1920s* (New York: Farrar, Straus & Giroux, 1995), 68.

59. Ibid., 67–71; *Biography of an Idea*, 286.

60. Tebbel, *History of Book Publishing*, 335–36.

61. *Biography of an Idea*, 287–88. The first quote is on page 287; the second on page 288. In many other sources, including his *Business History Review* article (pages 301–2) and in several interviews with this author, Bernays credited Fleischman with being co-creator of this new title.

62. Author's interviews with Doris Held, May 27, 1986; Anne Bernays, Oct. 27, 1989; and Edward L. Bernays, Oct. 26, 1986, and May 29, 1988.

63. Charles Flint Kellogg, *NAACP: A History of the National Association for the Advancement of Colored People*, vol. 1 (Baltimore: Johns Hopkins University Press, 1967), 137, 245–46; Mary White Ovington, *The Walls Came Tumbling Down* (New York: Harcourt, Brace & Company, 1947; reprint, New York: Arno Press, 1969), 177.

64. *Biography of an Idea*, 208–11; "The NAACP—1920" (a section in Bernays's notes for *Biography of an Idea*), 1–16, box I:459, ELB Papers.

65. "The NAACP—1920," 17.

66. Author's interview with Edward L. Bernays, Mar. 29, 1988.

67. "National Association for the Advancement of Colored People" (a section in Bernays's notes for *Biography of an Idea*), 3, box 1:459, ELB Papers.

68. "The NAACP—1920," 19–20; *Biography of an Idea*, 212–14; transcript of Edward L. Bernays Oral History, 236.

69. *Biography of an Idea*, 212–14; "The NAACP—1920," 20–22, 32–39.

70. *A Wife Is Many Women*, 170.

71. "The NAACP—1920," 18.

72. *Biography of an Idea*, 211; Camille Roman, "Profile: Doris F. Bernays," *Matrix* 59 (Summer 1974): 23.

73. "The NAACP—1920," 25A–27, 29.

74. Ovington, *Walls Came Tumbling Down*, 178.

75. "The NAACP—1920," 35–37; "National Association for the Advancement of Colored People," 4, 11, 18.

76. The press release is quoted in "The NAACP—1920," 38.

77. Ovington, *Walls Came Tumbling Down*, 178; letter from Walter White to Edward L. Bernays, July 13, 1920, box III:6, ELB Papers.

78. *Biography of an Idea*, 215.

79. Transcript of a speech by Doris Fleischman Bernays to the Radcliffe Club, Jan. 31, 1961, 11, box 1, folder 39, DFB Papers.

80. The quote is from ibid., page 11. In her interview with MaryAnn Yodelis, Fleischman estimated that she wrote fifteen to twenty stories a week. All other information is from the author's interview with Edward L. Bernays, Mar. 29, 1988.

81. Scattered information on the firm's clients during these years can be found in alphabetically arranged client files, boxes I:56–421, ELB Papers, and in *Biography of an Idea*, 187–252.

82. *Biography of an Idea*, 188; Edward L. Bernays, *Public Relations* (Norman: University of Oklahoma Press, 1952), 81. The press release is in box III:3, ELB Papers.

83. Author's interview with Edward L. Bernays, Mar. 29, 1988; "Doris and I," 7.

84. Undated (probably February 1921) memo from Fleischman to Bernays, box I:4, ELB Papers.

85. Transcript of Edward L. Bernays Oral History, 99; author's interview with Edward L. Bernays, May 28, 1986.

86. Although Bernays wrote very specifically about his 1919 staff and facilities, he had little to say about his later offices, so they cannot be described in the same kind of detail. The best evidence of the size of his 1921 staff is a memo dated January 9, 1923, which is addressed to ten employees. Significantly, one person listed on that memo is a writer (Kathleen Goldsmith), proving that another writer was working for the firm by that time. See

"Memorandum to Organization from E.L.B. and J.M.T. [T. Mitchell Thorsen]," box I:5, ELB Papers.

87. Edward L. Bernays, *Your Future in Public Relations* (New York: Richards Rose Press, 1961), 142.

88. See client files, box I:56–421, ELB Papers, and *Biography of an Idea*, 205–52.

89. "Junior League of the Cardiac Committee of the Public Education Association" and "Babies Hospital Benefit—1921" (sections in Bernays's notes for *Biography of an Idea*), box 1:461, ELB Papers.

90. The press releases are in box 1:105, ELB Papers.

91. Bernays was adamant about this whenever it came up in interviews with me. Similarly, in his memoirs, he wrote that Fleischman "has done everything in public relations, except go into direct client relationships" (*Biography of an Idea*, 220).

92. Doris E. Fleischman to Henry Morganthau Jr., May 9, 1922; Henry Morganthau Jr. to Doris E. Fleischman, May 10, 1922; plus Fleischman's follow-up notes from their May meeting, all in box II:1, ELB Papers.

93. Author's interview with Edward L. Bernays, May 24, 1986.

94. "Technical Ed." (a page in a file of Fleischman's notes for miscellaneous writing projects), box III:4, ELB Papers.

95. *A Wife Is Many Women*, 169; Fleischman's miscellaneous notes in box III:4, ELB Papers.

96. *A Wife Is Many Women*, 38.

97. Betsy Israel, *Bachelor Girl: The Secret History of Single Women in the Twentieth Century* (New York: William Morrow, 2002), 115.

98. Inez Haynes Gilmore, "Confessions of an Alien," *Harper's Bazaar*, Apr. 1912, 170.

99. Nancy Woloch, *Women and the American Experience, Volume Two: From 1860*, 2nd ed. (New York: McGraw-Hill, 1994), 395.

100. *A Wife Is Many Women*, 202; author's interview with Edward L. Bernays, May 26, 1986.

101. Doris Fleischman Bernays, "Plus Ça Change, Plus C'Est La Même Chose," *Phantasm*, Sept.–Oct. 1977, 3, possession of Edward L. Bernays.

102. *A Wife Is Many Women*, 190–92.

103. Author's interview with Anne Bernays, Oct. 27, 1989.

104. Untitled, undated press release by Doris E. Fleischman, "Boni and Liveright, 1919" file, box I:120, ELB Papers.

105. Ibid.

106. "Doris and I," 8.

107. *A Wife Is Many Women*, 199.

108. Author's interview with Anne Bernays, Oct. 27, 1989.

109. "Bridegroom Takes Name of His Bride," *New York Times*, Oct. 16, 1917, 13; "It's Come to This: Groom Takes Wife's Name," *Chicago Tribune*, Oct. 16, 1917, clipping in the possession of Edward L. Bernays. Murray and Hella Bernays divorced in 1923, but he kept the Bernays surname for the rest of his life.

110. *Biography of an Idea*, 218–19.

111. Author's interview with Anne Bernays, Oct. 27, 1989.

CHAPTER 2

1. Edward L. Bernays, *Biography of an Idea: Memoirs of Public Relations Counsel Edward L. Bernays* (New York: Simon & Schuster, 1965), 216–17. Many clippings were in a scrapbook in the possession of Edward L. Bernays in 1986, when I first examined it. Others can be found in boxes I:797 and III:6, Edward L. Bernays Papers, Manuscript Division, Library of Congress, Washington, DC (hereafter ELB Papers).

2. "Manager Carruthers has women register under their maiden names and husbands' names," *New York Times*, March 18, 1921, 15; Una Stannard, *Mrs. Man* (San Francisco: Germain Books, 1977), 191.

3. *Biography of an Idea*, 238–41, describes some of his early work for the hotel, including his plan for notifying the media of newsworthy occurrences.

4. Ibid., 217.

5. Doris E. Fleischman (Bernays), "Notes of a Retiring Feminist," *American Mercury*, February 1949, 162.

6. Research notes for *Biography of an Idea* chapter draft titled "Doris and I," 1–5, box I:461, ELB Papers. The quote is on page 5.

7. See note 1 above.

8. Doris Fleischman Bernays, *A Wife Is Many Women* (New York: Crown Publishers, 1955), 19. In *Biography of an Idea* Bernays also described her doing these tasks, and said she carried them out on the first day they lived at 44 Washington Mews (a move he didn't admit actually took place a month after they married). But it is unlikely that she waited until they moved in, since it would have taken time to hire these people and she could not have functioned in their home without help.

9. *Biography of an Idea*, 220.

10. "Doris and I," 18.

11. "*Biography of an Idea* Notes, 1920–1921," box I:461, 1, ELB Papers.

12. "Doris and I," 18; *Biography of an Idea*, 220; "Frills and Fashions," *San Francisco Bulletin*, Sept. 27, 1922 (Edward L. Bernays scrapbook).

13. Undated photograph and caption from unidentified newspaper, clippings folder, box III:2, ELB Papers.

14. Author's interview with Edward L. Bernays, Mar. 29, 1988, Cambridge, MA.

15. Letter quoted in *Biography of an Idea*, 267.

16. *A Wife Is Many Women*, 19–20, 206. The quote is on page 206.

17. Notes for *A Wife Is Many Women*, box 1, folder 33, page 24, Doris Fleischman Bernays Papers, Schlesinger Library on the History of Women in America, Radcliffe Institute for Advanced Study, Harvard University, Cambridge, MA (hereafter DFB Papers).

18. *Biography of an Idea*, 217.

19. Author's interview with Edward L. Bernays, May 24, 1986, Cambridge, MA.

20. *Biography of an Idea*, 71; *A Wife Is Many Women*, 71.

21. *Biography of an Idea*, 288–92.

22. Author's interviews with Edward L. Bernays, May 28 and May 29, 1986, and Mar. 29, 1988, Cambridge, MA; the quote is from the May 29 interview.

23. *Biography of an Idea*, 290.

24. Ibid., 289; author's interviews with Edward L. Bernays, May 26, 1986, and Mar. 27, 1988. It is difficult to determine precise starting and ending dates for *Contact* since each issue was numbered but undated, and the publication was issued irregularly. Thanks to Bernays's generosity, the author has an almost-complete run, which provides some clues to publication dates. Issue number 3, for example, contains a reference to an article appearing in the December 1922 issue of a trade journal. What seems to be the final issue is numbered 45. Alan R. Raucher, *Public Relations and Business: 1900–1929* (Baltimore: Johns Hopkins University Press, 1968), 105, states that *Contact* began in 1922 and lasted for thirteen years. But he also says forty-three issues were published, which may have caused him to underestimate its total life span.

25. *Biography of an Idea*, 289.

26. Author's interview with Edward L. Bernays, May 26, 1986.

27. *Biography of an Idea*, 221.

28. *A Wife Is Many Women*, 171.

29. Victoria Irwin, "Valentine's Day Love Stories," *Christian Science Monitor*, Feb. 14, 1980, 17.

30. Author's interview with Edward L. Bernays, Oct. 26, 1989, Cambridge, MA.

31. Author's interview with Edward L. Bernays, May 28, 1986.

32. *Biography of an Idea*, 289.

33. Richard S. Tedlow, *Keeping the Corporate Image: Public Relations and Business, 1900–1950* (Greenwich, CT: JAI Press, 1979), 42–44.

34. Since Fleischman and Bernays were spending an enormous amount of time together in 1923 and were constantly collaborating, it is probable that she helped him write the book. Other evidence can be found in two sources. Edward F. Goldman, *Two-Way Street: The Emergence of the Public Relations Counsel* (Boston: Bellman Publishing Company, 1948), 18, describes "Bernays and Doris E. Fleischman mulling over the plans for *Crystallizing Public Opinion*." Goldman was often in the Bernays firm and received Bernays's full co-operation in writing his book, so he is a good source. And in 1971 Bernays himself called *Crystallizing Public Opinion* "our first book." See transcript of Edward L. Bernays Oral History (1971), 77, Oral History Research Office, Columbia University, New York, NY.

35. Audiotape of an interview with Doris Fleischman Bernays by MaryAnn Yodelis, July 1973, Cambridge, MA, in the possession of the author.

36. Author's interview with Edward L. Bernays, May 28, 1986; the quote is from "Doris and I," 25.

37. Letter and telegrams between Fleischman and the State Department, box I:477, general correspondence folder, ELB Papers.

38. Letter to Doris E. Fleischman from Robinson Bliss, Third Assistant Secretary, Apr. 28, 1923, box I:476, general correspondence folder, ELB Papers.

39. A second scrapbook in the possession of Edward L. Bernays contained several dozen clippings related to her 1923 passport fight.

40. "Lucy Stone League Continues Passport Fight," box I:227, Lucy Stone League client folder, ELB Papers.

41. See Lucy Stone League client folder, ELB Papers, for many examples of work done for the league, and for a July 21, 1921, letter to Bernays from Jane Grant thanking him for joining the league. My conclusion that this work was done pro bono is based on an examination of the league's accounts in the Lucy Stone League Minute Book, box 10, folder 4, Jane C. Grant Papers, Special Collections, University of Oregon Library, Eugene, OR. In year-by-year listings of checks made out by the league, there are none issued to Bernays. Beyond this, the league could not have afforded to pay Bernays, particularly for the large amount of work his firm carried out.

42. Author's interview with Edward L. Bernays, May 24, 1986.

43. The letterhead on the July 21, 1921, letter to Bernays thanking him for joining the league lists five officers and twenty-eight executive committee members. More than half are easily identified as journalists or as having some connection to the theater. Bernays mentioned having known Grant for almost a decade in his research notes for *Biography of an Idea*, "Lucy Stone League" chapter draft, box I:458, ELB Papers.

44. *Biography of an Idea*, 217.

45. "Lucy Stone League" chapter draft, 4.

46. For documents related to the annual dinners and letterheads listing executive committee members for different years, see Lucy Stone League client file, ELB Papers. The media attention to the dinners is well documented in Ruth Hale's Scrapbook on the Lucy Stone League, Schlesinger Library on the History Women in America, Radcliffe Institute for Advanced Study, Harvard University, Cambridge, MA.

47. "Doris and I," 26.

48. Author's interview with Edward L. Bernays, May 28, 1986; *A Wife Is Many Women*, 155; report on Fleischman's trip (probably used as part of a press release), box I:497, undated documents folder, 1923–1989, ELB Papers.

49. "Even the Landlord Is Poor in Vienna," *Springfield (Mass.) News*, July 7, 1927, box III:2, undated documents folder, 1923–1989, ELB Papers. This interview with Fleischman, or portions of it, was carried in several other newspapers. Those articles also are in the folder.

50. Stannard, *Mrs. Man*, 204–6.

51. Ibid., 206–7.

52. Ibid., 207–8.

53. *Biography of an Idea*, 309–11.

54. "Lucy Stone League" chapter draft, 8.

55. "Heart Failure Kills Lawyer in Park," *New York Journal*, May 26, 1924, clipping in the possession of Edward L. Bernays. Also see "Drops Dead in Park," *New York Times*, May 27, 1924, 21.

56. "Notes of a Retiring Feminist," 165.

57. Ibid., 161.

58. Several newspaper stories are in Ruth Hale's Scrapbook, and many more were in a second scrapbook in the possession of Edward L. Bernays. The photograph described here also is reprinted in *Biography of an Idea* between pages 82 and 83.

59. Edward L. Bernays, "Emergence of the Public Relations Counsel: Principles and Recollections," *Business History Review* 45 (Autumn 1971): 305; *Biography of an Idea*, 356–57.

60. See, for example, letter to William B. Ward of the Ward Baking Company from Edward L. Bernays, May 20, 1925, box I:411, Ward Baking Company client folder, ELB Papers. Some of the work they carried out in Paris for a New York art-dealer client is described in *Biography of an Idea*, 335.

61. See, for example, letter from Edward L. Bernays to J. R. Weddell of the Erickson Company, Aug. 13, 1924, box I:200, Indian Refining Company client folder, ELB Papers.

62. Research notes for *Biography of an Idea*, box I:462, Edible Gelatin Manufacturers Research Society client folder, ELB Papers.

63. See client folders for these companies in boxes I:129, I:183, I:200, I:208, I:311, and I:411, ELB Papers.

64. In "Emergence of the Public Relations Counsel: Principles and Recollections" (303), Bernays wrote that during the 1920s "our normal yearly fee was between $12,000 and $15,000." Few clients were paying this much at the start of the decade, but client files show that Procter & Gamble's first contract, in 1923, was for $12,000 a year, and the Indian Refining Company paid this same amount in 1924, as did the Ward Baking Company in 1925. So this probably was the standard rate by the mid-1920s. In *Biography of an Idea* Bernays notes several higher fees in 1927, 1928, and 1929, including one of $25,000 a year (see 373, 379, 404, 438).

65. Edward L. Bernays, *Your Future in Public Relations* (New York: Richards Rosen Press, 1961), 143.

66. See, for example, 1923 disbursements of Edward L. Bernays and D. E. Fleischman, silverware inventory, June 2, 1925; Cartier delivery invoice, Dec. 24, 1927; and other records of purchases in box I:476, general correspondence folder, ELB Papers, as well as "Antiques of East Net $39,778 at Sale," *New York Times*, Nov. 15, 1926, 28.

67. "Amateur Housekeepers" (notes for *A Wife Is Many Women*), 1–2, box 19, folder 19, DFB Papers; *A Wife Is Many Women*, 19–20. The quote is on page 19.

68. "Doris and I," 32–33. "Theatre" was the preferred spelling for theatrical productions during much of the first half of the twentieth century. I have kept this spelling when quoting earlier sources that use it, but have used the current "theater" spelling in my own writing.

69. The quote is from research notes for *Biography of an Idea*, "1920–1925" folder 65, box I:462, ELB Papers.

70. *Biography of an Idea*, 233.

71. Research notes for *Biography of an Idea*, 225–26; "Doris and I," 36, 37.

72. *Biography of an Idea*, 223–30.

73. Ibid., 805.

74. Author's interview with Anne Bernays, Oct. 18, 1995.

75. Notes for *A Wife Is Many Women*, box 1, folder 19, DFB Papers.

76. Deleted portion of a manuscript draft of *A Wife is Many Women*, 61, possession of Edward L. Bernays.

77. *Biography of an Idea*, 804–5.

78. "Doris and I," 21.

79. *A Wife Is Many Women*, 175.

80. Note addressed "Dear Edward," signed "Doris," box 2, folder 44, DFB Papers. Although the note is undated, Fleischman's stationery gives their 44 Washington Mews address, indicating that it probably was written between 1922 and 1929, when they lived there.

81. Notes for *A Wife Is Many Women*, box 1, folder 32, DFB Papers.

82. *A Wife Is Many Women*, 167.

83. Ibid., 177.

84. See the following client folders: I:56, Acoustics Products Company and Aeolian Company; I:102, Ansco Photo Products; I:114, Blumenthal Company; I:151–57, Dodge Brothers Inc.; and I:227, Luggage Information Service, all ELB Papers.

85. Early draft of *Biography of an Idea*, 2–3, box I:462, 1920–1927 folder, ELB Papers.

86. Edward L. Bernays, ed., *An Outline of Careers: A Practical Guide to Achievement by Thirty-Eight Eminent Americans* (New York: George H. Doran Co., 1927).

87. *Biography of an Idea*, 295.

88. Scott M. Cutlip, *The Unseen Power: Public Relations. A History* (Hillsdale, NJ: Lawrence Erlbaum Associates, 1994), 182–84; Larry Tye, *The Father of Spin: Edward L. Bernays and the Birth of Public Relations* (New York: Crown Publishers, 1998), 96–100.

89. Doris E. Fleischman, ed., *An Outline of Careers for Women: A Practical Guide to Achievement* (Garden City, NY: Doubleday, Doran & Co., 1928).

90. See extensive correspondence to and from Fleischman during 1926 and 1927 in box I:472, ELB Papers.

91. Letter from Eleanor Roosevelt to Doris E. Fleischman, Nov. 23, 1927, and letter from Doris E. Fleischman to Eleanor Roosevelt, Nov. 25, 1927, box I:472, ELB Papers.

92. See extensive correspondence to and from Fleischman during 1927 and 1928 in box I:472, ELB Papers. For her argument about using her birth name on her contract, see letter from Doris E. Fleischman to Henry Bern, Jan. 22, 1927, box I:476, ELB Papers.

93. The publication date was announced in a letter from Doubleday, Doran & Co. to Edward L. Bernays, Nov. 2, 1928, box I:472, ELB Papers.

94. Doris E. Fleischman, "Public Relations," in *An Outline of Careers for Women*, ed. Doris E. Fleischman, 385–95. The quotes are on pages 385 and 392.

95. Doris E. Fleischman, "Concerning Women," in *An Outline of Careers*, ed. Edward L. Bernays, 426, 427.

96. Cutlip, *Unseen Power*, 169.

97. Stuart Ewen, *PR! A Social History of Spin* (New York: Basic Books, 1996), 163–72. The quote is on page 170.

98. Author's interview with Anne Bernays, Oct. 18, 1995, Cambridge, MA.

99. Scott Cutlip interview with Edward L. Bernays, March 12, 1959, quoted in Cutlip, *Unseen Power*, 169.

100. Edward L. Bernays, "Public Relations," in *An Outline of Careers*, ed. Edward L. Bernays, 296.

101. Author's interview with Anne Bernays, Oct. 27, 1989.

102. Anne Bernays and Justin Kaplan, *Back Then: Two Lives in 1950s New York* (New York: William Morrow, 2002), 142.

103. Notes for *A Wife Is Many Women*, box 1, folder 25, DFB Papers.

104. Ibid., box 1, folder 32.

105. "Doris and I," 39–41; Tye, 128.

106. *A Wife Is Many Women*, 84; "Doris and I," 38. The quote is from "Doris and I."

107. "Doris and I," 38; "Leases on Washington Square," *New York Times*, Feb. 3, 1929, 50.

108. Undated letter from Fleischman to Bernays, box I:3, ELB Papers.

CHAPTER 3

1. The quote is from a letter (addressed "Dear General") from Manny Lavine to Edward L. Bernays, Jan. 31, 1945, addenda, folder 2, Doris Fleischman Bernays Papers, Schlesinger Library on the History of Women in America, Radcliffe Institute for Advanced Study, Harvard University, Cambridge, MA (hereafter DFB Papers).
2. Walter Winchell, "Daybook for a New Yorker," *Chicago Post*, April 27, 1929, clipping in the possession of Edward L. Bernays.
3. Letter from Manny Lavine to Edward L. Bernays.
4. Letter from Edward L. Bernays to Dr. John L. Walsh, New York Department of Health, Apr. 20, 1929, box I:746, Edward L. Bernays Papers, Manuscript Division, Library of Congress, Washington, DC (hereafter ELB Papers).
5. Edward L. Bernays, *Biography of an Idea: Memoirs of Public Relations Counsel Edward L. Bernays* (New York: Simon & Schuster, 1965), 233.
6. Letter from Edward L. Bernays to City & County School, Apr. 24, 1929, box I:476, ELB Papers.
7. *Biography of an Idea*, 232.
8. Bernays's long quotes from Fleischman's notebook are in his research notes for *Biography of an Idea*, box I:461, ELB Papers.
9. Author's interview with Edward L. Bernays, Oct. 29, 1989, Cambridge, MA.
10. Ibid.
11. A scrapbook in Bernays's possession contained almost seventy clippings with this inaccurate claim about Anne's birth. Most stories came from the Associated Press and began with the quoted first sentence.
12. Anne Bernays and Justin Kaplan, *Back Then: Two Lives in 1950s New York* (New York: William Morrow, 2002), 17.
13. Author's interview with Edward L. Bernays, May 28, 1986, Cambridge, MA.
14. *Biography of an Idea*, 9, 13. The quote is on page 9.
15. Ibid., 233.
16. Ibid., 379–86. The quote is on page 386.
17. Ibid., 386–87; research notes for *Biography of an Idea* chapter draft titled "Tobacco," 53–57, box I:463, ELB Papers; Larry Tye, *The Father of Spin: Edward L. Bernays and the Birth of Public Relations* (New York: Crown Publishers, 1998), 28–30.
18. "Tobacco," 57–59; Tye, *Father of Spin*, 30–31; Allan M. Brandt, "Recruiting Women Smokers: The Engineering of Consent," *Journal of the American Medical Women's Association* 51 (Jan.–Apr. 1996): 63–66.
19. Memorandum to the American Tobacco Company, Apr. 19, 1929, box I:84, ELB Papers.
20. Memorandum to the American Tobacco Company, May 8, 1929, box I:84, ELB Papers.
21. *Biography of an Idea*, 445–47.
22. Ibid., 446–54.
23. Ibid., 448–51. The quote is on page 449.
24. Ibid., 456–59. The quote is on page 459.
25. Tye, *Father of Spin*, 65–68.
26. Ibid., 27, 37.
27. *Biography of an Idea*, 179.
28. Author's interview with Anne Bernays, Oct. 19, 1995, Cambridge, MA.
29. Scott M. Cutlip, *The Unseen Power: Public Relations. A History* (Hillsdale, NJ: Lawrence Erlbaum Associates, 1994), 127.
30. Stuart Ewen, *PR! A Social History of Spin* (New York: Basic Books, 1996), 231–33.
31. Tye, *Father of Spin*, 60.
32. Bernays and Kaplan, *Back Then*, 18.
33. "Bernays to Occupy Home at Elberon," *New York Evening Post*, undated clipping (probably spring 1930) in the possession of Edward L. Bernays.
34. Research notes for *Biography of an Idea* chapter draft titled "Doris and I," 41–43, box I:471, ELB Papers.

35. Bernays and Kaplan, *Back Then*, 19–22.

36. Ibid., 23–24; "Apartment Rentals," *New York Times*, Nov. 26, 1936, 52.

37. Bernays and Kaplan, *Back Then*, 33; Tye, *Father of Spin*, 129; "Apartment Rentals," *New York Times*, Jan. 20, 1941, 31; "E. L. Bernays Buys Home in E. 63d St.," *New York Times*, Aug. 2, 1941, C26.

38. Bernays and Kaplan, *Back Then*, 24–26; "Appraised Valuation of the Furnishings of the Apartment of Edward L. Bernays, 817 Fifth Avenue, New York City," Jan. 19, 1937, box III:75, ELB Papers. Judith Bernays's broken engagement to Elie Nadelman is mentioned in "Bridegroom Takes Name of His Bride," *New York Times*, Oct. 16, 1917, 13.

39. "Appraised Valuation."

40. Ibid.; "Doris and I," 44.

41. "Food I" (notes for *A Wife Is Many Women*), 48, box 1, folder 31, DFB Papers; "Doris and I," 46–47.

42. Author's interviews with Doris Held, May 27, 1986, and Anne Bernays, Oct. 28, 1989, both Cambridge, MA.

43. *Biography of an Idea*, 805–7. The quotes are on pages 805 and 806.

44. *A Wife Is Many Women*, 20; "Amateur Housekeepers," (notes for *A Wife Is Many Women*), 3, box 19, folder 19, DFB Papers; "Suburban Homes Rented," *New York Times*, June 9, 1932, 41; "Suburban Homes Taken," *New York Times*, June 12, 1933, 31; "Suburban Homes Rented," *New York Times*, July 11, 1936, 27.

45. Author's interview with Doris Held, Oct. 18, 1995, Cambridge, MA.

46. "Housewife" (notes for *A Wife Is Many Women*), 20, box 1, folder 27, DFB Papers.

47. "Food I," 47.

48. Author's interview with Edward L. Bernays, Oct. 29, 1989, Cambridge, MA.

49. Bernays and Kaplan, *Back Then*, 26–27 (the quote is on page 27). Evidence that they followed standard admission procedures is in *A Wife Is Many Women* (page 68), where Fleischman mentions daughter Doris being "interviewed for admission" to the school at the age of three and a half.

50. Tye, *Father of Spin*, 149; author's interview with Edward L. Bernays, Oct. 29, 1989; *Biography of an Idea*, 550, 778–79; Bernays and Kaplan, *Back Then*, 145.

51. Tye, *Father of Spin*, 141–49; author's interview with Anne Bernays, Oct. 19, 1995.

52. "Double Your Partner" (notes for *A Wife Is Many Women*), 1–2, box 1, folder 32, DFB Papers.

53. *Biography of an Idea*, 652.

54. Bernays and Kaplan, *Back Then*, 25.

55. Transcript of Edward L. Bernays Oral History (1971) , 305–9, 352–53, 371–73, Oral History Research Office, Columbia University, New York, NY; letter signed "Messersmith," Department of State, Washington, DC, to Edward L. Bernays, Apr. 18, 1938, box I:5, ELB Papers; letter from Edward L. Bernays to Lawrence S. Kubie, Mar. 11, 1941, box I:5, ELB Papers.

56. Transcript of Edward L. Bernays Oral History, 362–66.

57. Letter from Edward L. Bernays to Lawrence S. Kubie.

58. *Biography of an Idea*, 434–37, 490–622, 661–86.

59. Author's interviews with Doris Held, Oct. 18, 1995, and Anne Bernays, Oct. 27, 1989; Bernays and Kaplan, *Back Then*, 27–28.

60. Bernays and Kaplan, *Back Then*, 26–28 (the quote is on page 26); Tye, *Father of Spin*, 137; author's correspondence with Anne Bernays, Mar. 11, 1996.

61. The author photocopied more than two dozen servants' schedules, apparently from 1939, in the possession of Edward L. Bernays.

62. The cook's schedule, ibid., shows daily meetings with Fleischman; *A Wife Is Many Women*, 159.

63. Author's interview with Doris Held, Oct. 18, 1995.

64. Ibid.; author's interview with Anne Bernays, Oct. 18, 1995.

65. "Doris and I," 46.

66. Author's interview with Edward L. Bernays, Mar. 26, 1988.

67. *Biography of an Idea*, 13.

68. Author's interviews with Anne Bernays, May 27, 1986, Oct. 28, 1989, and Oct. 18, 1995, and with Doris Held, Oct. 18, 1995.

69. Author's interview with Doris Held, Oct. 18, 1995; Bernays and Kaplan, *Back Then*, 225.

70. Author's interviews with Doris Held, May 27, 1986, and Anne Bernays, May 27, 1986.

71. Author's interview with Anne Bernays, Oct. 27, 1989.

72. Author's interview with Anne Bernays, Oct. 28, 1989.

73. Author's interviews with Doris Held, May 27, 1986, and Anne Bernays, Oct. 28, 1989. The quote is from Anne Bernays, "Dear Mother," in *I've Always Meant to Tell You: An Anthology of Letters from Daughters to Mothers*, ed. Constance Warloe (New York: Pocket Books, 1997), 35.

74. Doris E. Fleischman, "Public Relations—A New Field for Women," *Independent Woman*, Feb. 1931, 58–59, 86; Doris E. Fleischman, "Keys to a Public Relations Career," *Independent Woman*, Nov. 1941, 332–33, 340.

75. Doris E. Fleischman, "Women in Business," *Ladies' Home Journal*, Jan. 1930, 16–17, 59–60, 62; Doris E. Fleischman, "Women in Business," *Ladies' Home Journal*, Mar. 1930, 24–25, 229–32; Doris E. Fleischman, "Jobs for Women," *Ladies' Home Journal*, Apr. 1930, 26–27, 230.

76. "Women in Business," Jan. 1930, 16.

77. "Women in Business," Mar. 1930, 24.

78. Doris E. Fleischman, "Women: Types and Movements," in *America as Americans See It*, ed. Fred J. Ringel (New York: Literary Guild, 1932), 105–17. The quotes are on pages 112 and 114.

79. Doris E. Fleischman, "You Can't Get Help," *McCall's*, Sept. 1946, 2, 66, 67.

80. Manuscripts and critiques of these stories are in box 1, folders 4, 7, 8, and 9, DFB Papers, and box I:475, ELB Papers. The short stories are "Perpetual Emotion" (1926), "Detective" (1931), "Dovey" (1935), "Set and Rock" (1936), "Pleasant Dreams, Dr. Gay!" (1942), "Charming Wife" (1944), "The Mother Who Lost Her No" (1946), "Last Strike" (1946), and "Heartless Melita" (1948).

81. The galley proofs of "The Last Strike," printing records, and much correspondence about it are in box I:475, ELB Papers.

82. Letter from Doris E. Fleischman to Dexter W. Masters, Oct. 30, 1937, box I:475, ELB Papers.

83. Manuscripts and correspondence related to this work are in boxes I:473 and I:474, ELB Papers, and box 1, folders 5 and 6, DFB Papers.

84. Jane Grant, "Confession of a Feminist," *American Mercury*, Dec. 1943, 684–91.

85. Letter from Edward L. Bernays to Judith Heller, July 28, 1948, quoted in Tye, *Father of Spin*, 136.

86. Doris E. Fleischman (Bernays), "Notes of a Retiring Feminist," *American Mercury*, Feb. 1949, 161–68. The quotes are on pages 161 and 163.

87. Ibid. The quotes are on pages 162, 163, and 168.

88. "Married Women with Maiden Names Have Their Troubles, Too, Says Leading Lucy Stoner in 'Mercury'" (press release), and twenty-two letters from Fleischman to readers of her article, all in addenda, folder 2, DFB Papers.

89. Author's interviews with Doris Held, May 27, 1986, and Anne Bernays, Oct. 19, 1995. The quote from "Notes of a Retiring Feminist" is on page 165.

90. Author's interviews with Anne Bernays, Oct. 19, 1995, and Edward L. Bernays, May 24, 1986.

91. Author's interview with Anne Bernays, Oct. 19, 1995.

92. Justin Kaplan and Anne Bernays, *The Language of Names* (New York: Simon & Schuster, 1997), 151.

93. "Notes of a Retiring Feminist," 161.

94. Una Stannard, *Mrs. Man* (San Francisco: Germain Books, 1977), 233–34. The quotes are on page 233.
95. Author's interview with Edward L. Bernays, May 24, 1986.

CHAPTER 4

1. Letter from Jane Grant to Doris E. Fleischman, Feb. 2, 1950; letter from Doris E. Fleischman to Jane Grant, Feb. 6, 1950; memo from Edward L. Bernays to Doris E. Fleischman, "Suggestions on the new Lucy Stone Group," Feb. 24, 1950, all in box 1, folder 39, Doris Fleischman Bernays Papers, Schlesinger Library on the History of Women in America, Radcliffe Institute for Advanced Study, Harvard University, Cambridge, MA (hereafter DFB Papers); Mary Lou Parker, "Fashioning Feminism: The Making of the Lucy Stone League by Members and Media," PhD diss., University of Oregon, 1994, 55.
2. "23 Lucy Stoners Hold Session Here," *New York Times*, March 23, 1950, 2.
3. See clippings in box 1, folder 41, DFB Papers, and in the Lucy Stone League Scrapbook, Jane C. Grant Papers, University of Oregon Special Collections, Eugene, OR (hereafter JG Papers).
4. Lucy Stone League press release, Mar. 23, 1950, box 11, folder 5, JG Papers.
5. Some of Fleischman's league activities are documented in box 1, folders 40, 41, and 42, DFB Papers. Also see minutes of the league's 1951 and 1952 annual meetings, box 10, folder 2, JG Papers.
6. Barbara Bundschu (United Press), "Lucy Stone Vets Poke Old Embers," *Hartford Times*, May 24, 1950, box 1, folder 41, DFB Papers.
7. Lucy Stone League press release, Mar. 23, 1950; Parker, "Fashioning Feminism," 72.
8. Minutes of the Lucy Stone League Annual Meeting, Jan. 18, 1951, box 10, folder 2, JG Papers.
9. Author's interview with Anne Bernays, Oct. 19, 1995, Cambridge, MA.
10. Letters from Doris E. Fleischman to Jane Grant, Nov. 3, 1952, and from Edward L. Bernays to Jane Grant, Nov. 4, 1952, box 3, folder 4, JG Papers; letter from Anne Bernays to Jane Grant, Jan. 2, 1953, box 3, folder 5, JG Papers.
11. The loan can be traced in letters from Jane Grant to Blanche Kennedy, dated Jan. 18, 1951 (but actually 1952), box 3, folder 2, JG Papers, and from Doris E. Fleischman to Jane Grant, Oct. 20, 1952, box 3, folder 4, JG Papers. Repayment is noted in the Report of the Annual Meeting of the Lucy Stone League, Oct. 30, 1952, box 10, folder 2, JG Papers. Resignation letters from four more members are in box 3, folder 4, JG Papers.
12. Letter from Eleanor Nicholes to Doris E. Fleischman, Nov. 30, 1952, box 1, folder 39, DFB Papers.
13. "Chronology: *A Wife Is Many Women*," box I:797, Edward L. Bernays Papers, Manuscript Division, Library of Congress, Washington, DC (hereafter ELB Papers); *A Wife Is Many Women* correspondence, box 1, folder 12, DFB papers.
14. Doris Fleischman Bernays, *A Wife Is Many Women* (New York: Crown Publishers, 1955), 12 and jacket copy.
15. In interviews with the author, her daughters repeatedly stated that much of what is said about them in the book is untrue. Both of them labeled the book fiction. Rereading the book in light of this knowledge and other things I have learned about Fleischman, I've come to see numerous episodes in the book—not just those involving her daughters—as unlikely to have taken place in the ways she described them. Thus in my own use of the book as a resource, I have tried to be careful to cite only information and encounters that sound plausible or are substantiated by additional sources.
16. Undated later from Wallace Brockway to Edward L. Bernays, box 1, folder 14, DFB Papers.
17. Untitled *A Wife Is Many Women* review, *Journal of Social Therapy* 2 (first quarter, 1956): 57.

18. For a record of Fleischman's research and plans of the book, see box 1, folders 12–34, and box 2, folders 53–55, DFB Papers.

19. For good summaries of these values, see Rosalind Rosenberg, *Divided Lives: American Women in the Twentieth Century* (New York: Hill & Wang, 1991), 147–57; William Chafe, *The American Woman: Her Changing Social, Economic and Political Place, 1920–1970* (New York: Oxford University Press, 1972), 199–225; and Nancy Woloch, *Women and the American Experience, Volume Two: From 1860*, 2nd ed. (New York: McGraw-Hill, 1994), 493–500.

20. Rosenberg, *Divided Lives*, 154–57; Lois Banner, *Women in America: A Brief History* (New York: Harcourt Brace Jovanovich, 1974), 211–23.

21. Leila J. Rupp and Verta Taylor, *Survival in the Doldrums: The American Women's Rights Movement, 1945 to the 1960s* (Columbus: Ohio State University Press, 1990), 18.

22. Box 1, folders 26, 30, and 34, and box 2, folders 51–55, DFB Papers, contain many research notes taken by Fleischman in preparation for her book. There are numerous notes both from books that helped define women's roles and from feminist responses to those books.

23. Doris E. Fleischman and Howard Walden Cutler, "Themes and Symbols," in *The Engineering of Consent*, ed. Edward L. Bernays (Norman: University of Oklahoma Press, 1955), 138–55. In my interviews with Bernays on May 29, 1986, and Mar. 29, 1988, he explained that the firm's office manager, Howard Cutler, shared the byline with Fleischman because she was busy with last-minute details of *A Wife Is Many Women*, so needed his help to finish the chapter on time. But he stressed that Fleischman wrote almost the entire chapter.

24. Author's interview with Anne Bernays, Oct. 28, 1989.

25. Author's telephone interview with Camille Roman, Nov. 20, 1995; Larry Tye, *The Father of Spin: Edward L. Bernays and the Birth of Public Relations* (New York: Crown Publishers, 1998), 89. (The quote is from an interview by Tye with Camille Roman.)

26. Author's interview with Anne Bernays, Oct. 19, 1995.

27. Ibid.; author's telephone interview with Camille Roman.

28. Edward L. Bernays, *Biography of an Idea: Memoirs of Public Relations Counsel Edward L. Bernays* (New York: Simon & Schuster, 1965), 815; author's interview with Anne Bernays, Oct. 18, 1995; "Whitney Buys House," *New York Times*, May 3, 1955, 52.

29. *Biography of an Idea*, 811, 815; "Doris F. Bernays Married in Home," *New York Times*, June 30, 1951, 8; Anne Bernays, "Do You? I Do. Do You? I Do," *New York Times*, June 23, 1984, 23; Anne Bernays and Justin Kaplan, *Back Then: Two Lives in 1950s New York* (New York: William Morrow, 2002), 209–10. The quote is on page 209.

30. *A Wife Is Many Women*, 2, 192–205; notes for *A Wife Is Many Women*, box 1, folders 27, 31 and 33, DFB Papers.

31. Helen W. Williams, "'A Wife Is Many Women' Said Written in Haphazard Style," *Chattanooga News Free Press*, Feb. 29, 1956, clipping in scrapbook in the possession of Edward L. Bernays.

32. Author's interviews with Doris Held, Oct. 18, 1995, and Anne Bernays, Oct. 19, 1995.

33. Anne Bernays and Justin Kaplan, "Diary of a Mad Marriage," *New Woman*, December 1989, 42–43.

34. Letter from Camille Roman to the author, May 9, 2007.

35. Ibid.; Tye, *Father of Spin*, 134–35; Anne Bernays, "Dear Mother," in *I've Always Meant to Tell You: An Anthology of Letters From Daughters to Mothers*, ed. Constance Warloe (New York: Pocket Books, 1997), 35.

36. "Chronology: *A Wife Is Many Women*."

37. Ibid., section titled "Working with Crown and Berson," 2–3.

38. *A Wife Is Many Women*, 43.

39. Ibid., 167.

40. Author's interview with Doris Held, May 27, 1986.

41. Author's interview with Anne Bernays, Oct. 18, 1995.

42. "Chronology: *A Wife Is Many Women*," section titled "DEF Speaking Engagements and Requests to Speak Stemming From Book."

43. Untitled history of the Woman Pays Club by Beulah Livingston, box 1, folder 42, DFB Papers; letter from Albertine Randall Wheelan (Woman Pays Club membership committee chairman) to Doris Fleischman, Apr. 14, 1927, box I:476, ELB Papers; "Maiden Names Voted to Be More 'Individual,'" *New York Times*, Feb. 3, 1921, 7.

44. This description is taken from numerous sources in box 1, folder 42, and box 2, folder 45, DFB Papers.

45. Ibid.

46. Letter from Doris F. Bernays to Caroline Simon, Feb. 12, 1962, box 1, folder 42, DFB Papers.

47. Author's interview with Edward L. Bernays, Mar. 29, 1988.

48. Author's interviews with Doris Held, Oct. 18, 1995, and May 27, 1986.

49. Tye, *Father of Spin*, 203; author's interview with Anne Bernays, Oct. 18, 1995; Scott Cutlip, *The Unseen Power: Public Relations. A History* (Hillsdale, NJ: Lawrence Erlbaum Associates, 1994), 214–18.

50. Author's interview with Edward L. Bernays, Oct. 26, 1989.

51. Author's interview with Anne Bernays, Oct. 19, 1995.

52. This description is based on my own observations when I stayed in the Lowell Street house, on interviews with Anne Bernays on Oct. 28, 1989, and Oct. 19, 1995, and on a collection of brief newspaper clippings about their purchase of the house in addenda, folder 3, DFB Papers.

53. Audiotape of an interview with Doris Fleischman Bernays by MaryAnn Yodelis, July 1973, Cambridge, MA, in the possession of the author.

54. Author's telephone interview with Camille Roman and Oct. 19, 1995, interview with Anne Bernays. Fleischman's driving lessons and her scheduled driving test are recorded in the couple's 1965 appointment calendar in the possession of the author.

55. Author's interviews with Edward L. Bernays, May 28, 1986, and Oct. 26, 1989.

56. Much of this work is described in box I:748–757, ELB Papers, and in the transcript of the Edward L. Bernays Oral History (1971), 158–60, 186–92, Oral History Research Office, Columbia University, New York, NY. Also see Cutlip, *Unseen Power*, 222, and Elinor Hayes, "New Job for Opinion Molder," *Oakland Tribune*, Aug. 18, 1968, and Ann Shaw, "Bernays—A Master of Human Nature," *Sunday Sun* (Lowell, MA), Sept. 25, 1977, both clippings in the possession of Edward L. Bernays.

57. Tye, *Father of Spin*, 201.

58. Ibid.; John H. Fenton, "Massachusetts Sycamore Patrol Guards Trees against Road Job," *New York Times*, Nov. 15, 1964, L29; author's interview with Edward L. Bernays, Oct. 26, 1989.

59. This work is described in about a dozen documents in box 2, folder 49, DFB Papers.

60. Author's interviews with Edward L. Bernays, May 28, 1986, and Oct. 30, 1989. The quote is from Tye, *Father of Spin*, 125 (quoting Pat Jackson).

61. Author's interview with Edward L. Bernays, Mar. 26, 1988.

62. I am grateful to Caroline Iverson Ackerman for helping me understand the reasons for Bernays's escalating involvement in public relations education once he moved to Cambridge.

63. Author's interview with Anne Bernays, Oct. 27, 1987.

64. Cutlip, *Unseen Power*, 220; author's interview with Edward L. Bernays, March 26, 1988; author's interview with Anne Bernays, Oct. 27 1989; letter from Anne Bernays to the author, Mar. 11, 1996.

65. Author's interview with Eleanor Genovese, Oct. 19, 1995, Wellesley, MA.

66. Author's interview with Doris Held, Oct. 18, 1995.

67. Author's interview with Eleanor Genovese.

68. Author's interviews with Doris Held, Oct. 19, 1995, and Anne Bernays, Oct. 19, 1995.

69. Author's interview with Caroline Iverson Ackerman, Oct. 16, 1995, South Natick, MA; letter from Caroline Iverson Ackerman to the author, Mar. 4, 1996.

70. Author's interview with Caroline Iverson Ackerman, Oct. 16, 1995.

71. Ibid.

72. Interview with Doris Fleischman Bernays by MaryAnn Yodelis.

73. Author's telephone interview with Camille Roman.

74. Letter from Camille Roman.

75. Ibid.; author's telephone interview with Camille Roman.

76. Author's interview with Anne Bernays, Oct. 28, 1989.

77. Author's interview with Eleanor Genovese.

78. Author's interviews with Doris Held, Oct. 18, 1995, and Anne Bernays, Oct. 19, 1995.

79. Bernays and Kaplan, *Back Then*, 213.

80. Author's interview with Caroline Iverson Ackerman, Oct. 15, 1995, South Natick, MA; copies of Fleischman's speech and newspaper articles about her in box 2, folders 48 and 49, DFB Papers.

81. Author's interview with Frank Genovese, Oct. 19, 1995, Wellesley, MA.

82. Keith A. Larson, *Public Relations, the Edward L. Bernayses and the American Scene: A Bibliography* (Westwood, MA: F. W. Faxon Company, 1978), 21–22; author's interview with Doris Held, Oct. 19, 1995.

83. Form letter announcing the competition from Caroline I. Ackerman, Jury of Award chairman, to journalism professors, May 9, 1974, in the possession of the author; author's interview with Caroline Iverson Ackerman, Oct. 15, 1995.

84. Two Babson College press releases—"Babson College Sponsors Edward L. Bernays Award for A Practical Program to Achieve Economic Justice for Homemakers" and "'The Truth Shall Make You Free' Applies to Homemakers"—and letter from Frank Genovese to Babson College faculty and administrators, Dec. 27, 1977, all in the possession of the author.

85. Author's interview with Caroline Iverson Ackerman, Oct. 15, 1995; "Ten-Point Plan Developed to Advance Women in Media," *Editor & Publisher*, Sept. 27, 1974, 11.

86. Author's interview with Frank Genovese.

87. Author's interviews with Eleanor Genovese, Camille Roman, and Caroline Iverson Ackerman (Oct. 16, 1995).

88. Quoted in Carol Liston, "Editor-Crusader-Housewife Now a Novelist at 74," *Boston Globe*, Dec. 15, 1965, clipping in the possession of Edward L. Bernays.

89. Undated (probably late 1973) letter from Doris Fleischman, addressed "Dear Adele," box 2, folder 43, DFB Papers.

90. Author's interview with Eleanor Genovese.

91. Author's interviews with Edward L. Bernays, Oct. 30, 1989, Anne Bernays, Oct. 19, 1995, and Caroline Iverson Ackerman, Oct. 16, 1995.

92. Doris Fleischman Bernays, "Plus Ça Change, Plus C'Est La Même Chose," *Phantasm*, Sept./Oct. 1977, in the possession of Edward L. Bernays.

93. Author's interviews with Doris Held and Anne Bernays, both Oct. 19, 1995.

94. *A Wife Is Many Women*, 31.

95. Doris Fleischman Bernays 1980 journal, box III:2, ELB Papers. The quotes are from the first entry, simply dated March, and from the April 4 entry.

96. The quotes are from the April 4 and April 19 entries, Doris Fleischman Bernays 1980 journal.

97. The quotes are from the April 16 and May 28 entries, Doris Fleischman Bernays 1980 journal.

98. Author's interviews with Caroline Iverson Ackerman, Oct. 15, 1995, and Eleanor Genovese.

99. Author's interview with Doris Held, Oct. 19, 1995.

100. Victoria Irwin, "Valentine's Day Love Stories," *Christian Science Monitor*, Feb. 14, 1980, 17.

101. The quotes are from the April 4 and April 26 entries, Doris Fleischman Bernays 1980 journal.

102. Author's interviews with Camille Roman and Eleanor Genovese; Doris Fleischman Bernays death certificate, box III:2, ELB Papers.

CHAPTER 5

1. Author's interview with Melissa Hale Ward Aug. 9, 2000, Phoenix, AZ; Hale family genealogy compiled by Melissa Hale Ward.

2. Heywood Hale Broun, *Whose Little Boy Are You? A Memoir of the Broun Family* (New York: St. Martin's, 1983), 21; author's interview with Heywood Hale Broun, June 23, 2000, Woodstock, NY. Her brothers also went on to drop their first names. The family genealogy shows that Shelton was born John Shelton Hale and Richard, named after his father, was born James Richards Hale.

3. Author's interview with Melissa Hale Ward; photograph of the Hales' Rogersville home, possession of Melissa Hale Ward; "A Backwards Glance," Richard Hale's unpublished recollections of his early years, possession of Melissa Hale Ward.

4. *Whose Little Boy*, 19; author's interview with Fiona Hale, Dec. 22, 2000, Encino, CA.

5. Author's interview with Melissa Hale Ward.

6. *Annual Register and Announcement of Hollins Institute, Session 1899–1900* (Roanoke, VA: Stone Printing & Manufacturing Co., 1900), 48, Hollins University Archives, Roanoke, VA.

7. Register of Arrivals, 1899–1900 and 1900–1901, Hollins University Archives; Grade Books, 1899–1900 and 1900–1901, Hollins University Archives.

8. "Ruth Hale Is Dead; Feminist Leader," *New York Times*, Sept. 14, 1934, 19.

9. *Whose Little Boy*, 20–21. The correct spelling actually is Culpeper.

10. "Ruth Hale Is Dead; Feminist Leader"; Ishbel Ross, *Ladies of the Press: The Story of Women in Journalism by an Insider* (New York: Harper & Brothers, 1936), 259; Dale Kramer, *Heywood Broun: A Biographical Portrait* (New York: Current Books, 1949), 58.

11. Author's interview with Heywood Hale Broun, June 23, 2000; "A Backwards Glance."

12. Kramer, *Heywood Broun*, 58; Ross, *Ladies of the Press*, 259; "Ruth Hale Is Dead; Feminist Leader."

13. Author's interview with Heywood Hale Broun, June 23, 2000.

14. Kramer, *Heywood Broun*, 58; Edna Woolman Chase and Ilka Chase, *Always in Vogue* (London: Victor Gollancz Ltd., 1954), 59–60, 257.

15. "A Backwards Glance"; author's interview with Melissa Hale Ward; author's interview with Heywood Hale Broun, June 23, 2000.

16. "Ruth Hale Is Dead; Feminist Leader."

17. *Whose Little Boy*, 21; author's interview with Heywood Hale Broun, July 31, 1999, Woodstock, NY.

18. *Whose Little Boy*, 75; author's interview with Melissa Hale Ward.

19. "A Backwards Glance"; "Mrs. Annie Riley Hale," *New York Times*, Dec. 28, 1944, 19.

20. Annie Riley Hale, "The Future of the Negro," *New York Times*, July 3, 1899, 7. Seven years later she published an article warning against a different kind of "race problem": the preference of mixed-race people to live in the North, where they had become a "yellow peril" that was worse than the threat posed by Asian immigrants. See Annie Riley Hale, "The Mulatto Negro: The Yellow Peril of the North," *National Magazine*, January 1906, 433–41.

21. I examined six of Annie Riley Hale's books in the possession of her granddaughter, Melissa. Some books note her authorship of other books not in her granddaughter's possession. The 1912 self-published Roosevelt books are *Bull Moose Tales* and *Rooseveltian Fact and Fable*. The reviews of the second book are quoted in an advertisement for it on the back page of Annie Riley Hale, *The Eden Sphinx* (New York: published by the author, 1916).

22. "Pacifists Arrested in Stormy Meeting," *New York Times*, Sept. 17, 1917, 4.

23. "Mrs. Hale Is Released," *New York Times*, Sept. 20, 1917, 8.

24. "Pacifists Arrested in Stormy Meeting."

25. Author's correspondence with Heywood Hale Broun, Feb. 26, 2000; "Shelton Hale Dead," *New York Times*, Sept. 14, 1920, 11; *Whose Little Boy*, 115.

26. Scott Messinger, "The Judge as Mentor: Oliver Wendell Homes, Jr., and His Law Clerks," *Yale Journal of Law & Humanities* 11 (Winter 1999): 119.

27. "Shelton Hale Dead."

28. Letter from Maxwell Perkins to F. Scott Fitzgerald, Aug. 8, 1924, reprinted in *Dear Scott/ Dear Max: The Fitzgerald-Perkins Correspondence*, ed. John Kuehl and Jackson R. Bryer (New York: Charles Scribner's Sons, 1971), 75.

29. Author's interviews with Fiona Hale and Melissa Hale Ward; "Beware Doctors and Food," *Los Angeles Times*, Dec. 1, 1935, 3:7.

30. *Whose Little Boy*, 115; author's interview with Melissa Hale Ward.

31. Author's interviews with Heywood Hale Broun, Aug. 1, 1999, and June 18, 2001, Woodstock, NY.

32. Congress, Senate, Committee on Woman Suffrage, *Hearings before the Committee on Woman Suffrage*, 63rd Congress, 1st sess., Apr. 19, 1913, 30–35; A. Elizabeth Taylor, *The Woman Suffrage Movement in Tennessee* (New York: Bookman Associates, 1957), 79–80; Elna C. Green, *Southern Strategies: Southern Women and the Woman Suffrage Question* (Chapel Hill: University of North Carolina Press, 1997), 106.

33. *The Eden Sphinx*, 106, 228.

34. "The Eden Sphinx," *New York Times*, Apr. 16, 1916, 64.

35. *The Eden Sphinx*, 231–32, 219.

36. Although none of the three ever specifically said they lived together during this time, I am convinced they did, based not only on the pattern that would continue for the rest of their lives but on more specific information about their New York addresses. The publishing information on Annie Riley Hale's 1912 books includes her address: 6 West Sixty-Sixth Street. An identical address is on Ruth Hale's 1917 marriage certificate. After she married, Ruth always felt obligated to provide accommodations for her mother, and this obligation logically would have been even stronger at earlier times. Richard, too, often lived with Ruth after she married, and his struggling singing career meant he could not have afforded a place of his own before that time. Additional evidence comes from Richard's reminiscences in "A Backwards Glance." He described returning to New York in 1915 after touring with a theater company, noting, "Home was an apartment in an old-fashioned brownstone near Central Park West." This sounds very much like the West Sixty-Sixth Street address.

37. She clearly was an accomplished speaker by the time she spoke in both cities, and often traveled throughout the country to speak in the 1920s. Thus it seems very likely that her travels in the previous decade went considerably beyond the newsmaking Hartford and Knoxville trips I have uncovered.

38. Author's interview with Fiona Hale.

39. *Whose Little Boy*, 76.

40. Judith Schwarz, *Radical Feminists of Heterodoxy: Greenwich Village, 1912–1940*, rev. ed. (Norwich, VT: New Victoria Publishers, 1986), 14, 17.

41. Rosalind Rosenberg, *Divided Lives: American Women in the Twentieth Century* (New York: Hill & Wang, 1992), 63.

42. Schwarz, *Radical Feminists*, 27–29. The quote is on page 29.

43. Mabel Dodge Luhan, *Movers and Shakers: Volume Three of Intimate Memories* (New York: Harcourt, Brace & Co., 1936), 143–44.

44. Schwarz, *Radical Feminists*, 1, 18–19.

45. Rheta Childe Dorr, *A Woman of Fifty* (New York: Funk & Wagnalls Company, 1924), 271.

46. See members' biographies in Schwarz, *Radical Feminists*, 116–28. I asked Heywood Hale

Broun to go through these biographies and indicate which women he remembered as being friends of his mother.

47. Schwarz, *Radical Feminists*, 18–20.

48. Ibid., 44–46.

49. "Ruth Hale is Dead; Feminist Leader"; Katharine Lyons, "The Dramatic Critic," in *Careers for Women*, ed. Catherine Filene (Cambridge, MA: Riverside Press, 1920; reprint, New York: Arno Press, 1974), 351.

50. Ross, *Ladies of the Press*, 149; Richard O'Connor, *Heywood Broun: A Biography* (New York: G. Putnam's Sons, 1975), 45.

51. Edward L. Bernays, "In the Gay Old Troubadoring Days of B'way Pressagentry," *Variety*, Fifty-Fifth Anniversary Edition, Jan. 4, 1960, 267.

52. Richard Maney, *Fanfare: The Confessions of a Press Agent* (New York: Harper & Brothers, 1957), 108–9; Allen Churchill, *The Great White Way: A Re-creation of Broadway's Golden Era of Theatrical Entertainment* (New York: E. P. Dutton & Co., 1962), 249–50; Malcolm Goldstein, *George Kaufman: His Life, His Theater* (New York: Oxford University Press, 1979), 40; author's interview with Heywood Hale Broun, July 31, 1999, Woodstock, NY.

53. Letter from Alexander Woollcott to Mrs. Charles Taber, December 1918, reprinted in *The Letters of Alexander Woollcott*, ed. Beatrice Kaufman and Joseph Hennessey (New York: Viking Press, 1944), 74.

54. Brooks Atkinson, *Broadway* (New York: Macmillan Company, 1970), 127, 128.

55. Brooks Atkinson's was among almost a dozen statements from drama critics and editors about theatrical press agents that were reprinted under the heading "Opinions from Prominent Editors" in Charles Washburn, *Press Agentry* (New York: National Library Press, 1937). The quotes are on page 143.

56. Author's interview with Heywood Hale Broun, June 22, 2001, Woodstock, NY; *Whose Little Boy*, 61. The first quote is from the interview, the second from *Whose Little Boy*.

57. Washburn, *Press Agentry*, 137; Maney, *Fanfare*, 11.

58. Author's interview with Heywood Hale Broun, June 18, 2001, Woodstock, NY.

59. *Whose Little Boy*, 18.

60. O'Connor, *Heywood Broun*, 45–46; Kramer, *Heywood Broun*, 56–57. The quote about Heterodoxy women is in Henry Wise Miller, *All Our Lives: Alice Duer Miller* (New York: Coward-McCann, 1945), 190.

61. O'Connor, *Heywood Broun*, 37; Kramer, *Heywood Broun*, 59, 67.

62. O'Connor, *Heywood Broun*, 39–41; Kramer, *Heywood Broun*, 62–64, 69–71; *Whose Little Boy*, 22.

63. "Miss Lopokova to Wed," *New York Times*, Jan. 14, 1916, 4: O'Connor, *Heywood Broun*, 41–42; Kramer, *Heywood Broun*, 72–73; Edward L. Bernays, *Biography of an Idea: Memoirs of Public Relations Counsel Edward L. Bernays* (New York: Simon & Schuster, 1965), 114–25. The quote is on page 114.

64. O'Connor, *Heywood Broun*, 47; Kramer, *Heywood Broun*, 73–76.

65. Author's interview with Heywood Hale Broun, June 21, 2000. He said his mother made it very clear to him that at the time she agreed to marry Broun she was recovering from an unsatisfactory romance. "It wasn't just hinted at." But she revealed no details that he could remember.

66. Kramer, *Heywood Broun*, 15–17; *Whose Little Boy*, 26, 64–68, 164.

67. Doris Fleischman Bernays, "Plus Ça Change, Plus C'Est La Même Chose," *Phantasm*, Sept.–Oct. 1977, 2, possession of Edward L. Bernays.

68. *Whose Little Boy*, 13–16. The quote is on page 13.

69. Ibid., 16; Kramer, *Heywood Broun*, 38–49.

70. *Whose Little Boy*, 14.

71. Author's interview with Heywood Hale Broun, June 23, 2000.

72. Author's interview with Melissa Hale Ward.

73. Kramer, *Heywood Broun*, 40, 46.

74. Author's interview with Heywood Hale Broun, June 21, 2000; *Whose Little Boy*, 163, 164.

75. *Whose Little Boy*, 75.

76. *The Eden Sphinx*, 219.

77. *Whose Little Boy*, 113.

78. Author's interview with Heywood Hale Broun, June 19, 2001.

79. *Whose Little Boy*, 68, 64.

80. Author's interview with Heywood Hale Broun, June 18, 2001.

81. Author's interview with Heywood Hale Broun, June 19, 2001.

82. *Whose Little Boy*, 23.

83. Author's interview with Heywood Hale Broun, June 19, 2001

84. O'Connor, *Heywood Broun*, 49–50; Kramer, *Heywood Broun*, 78–81; author's interview with Heywood Hale Broun, June 21, 2000.

85. Schwarz, *Radical Feminists*, 24–25, 122.

86. Hollins Institute 1900–1901 Grade Book.

87. *Whose Little Boy*, 6.

88. O'Connor, *Heywood Broun*, 49; Kramer, *Heywood Broun*, 80.

89. *Whose Little Boy*, 6–7.

90. Although all known published sources give their marriage date as June 7, both their marriage license and their certificate and record of marriage (copies of both in the author's possession) are dated June 6, 1917. In addition, the brief story about their marriage in the *New York Times*, dated June 7, says they were married "last evening." See "Heywood Broun Marries," *New York Times*, June 7, 1917, 11.

CHAPTER 6

1. Heywood Hale Broun, *Whose Little Boy Are You? A Memoir of the Broun Family* (New York: St. Martin's, 1983), 6.

2. Ibid., 6–7.

3. Ibid., 7.

4. Richard O'Connor, *Heywood Broun: A Biography* (New York: G. P. Putnam's Sons, 1975), 51–52. Broun's story is reprinted in his first book, a collection of his wartime *Tribune* pieces: Heywood Broun, *The A.E.F.: With General Pershing and the American Forces* (New York: D. Appleton & Company, 1918), 1–10. The quote is on page 3.

5. O'Connor, *Heywood Broun*, 53; *Whose Little Boy*, 62. I copied the Boulevard Raspail address from an inscription on the flyleaf of a book owned by Heywood Hale Broun that Alexander Woollcott gave to Hale as a Christmas present in 1917.

6. Joseph Gies, *The Colonel of Chicago* (New York: E. P. Dutton, 1979), 67; Robert W. Desmond, *Windows on the World: The Information Process in a Changing Society, 1900–1920* (Iowa City: University of Iowa Press, 1980), 384–85; James Melvin Lee, *History of American Journalism* (Garden City, NY: Garden City Publishing Co., 1923), 426. This assumption of Hale's involvement in launching the Army Edition is based on the likelihood that she began working there soon after she arrived in Paris. Her arrival date was determined from Broun's second newspaper report from France, filed June 28, 1917. Its first paragraph is reprinted in O'Connor, *Heywood Broun*, 83.

7. Lee, *American Journalism*, 426; Dale Kramer, *Heywood Broun: A Biographical Portrait* (New York: Current Books, 1949), 86. Little has been written about the day-to-day operations of the newspaper, but suppositions regarding Hale's responsibilities are based on knowledge of her strengths and on two additional pieces of evidence. First, in describing his own Army Edition work, which seems to have begun right after Hale left, George Seldes wrote, "I was the entire reportorial staff." See George Seldes, *Witness to a Century: Encounters with the Noted, the Notorious, and the Three SOBs* (New York: Ballantine Books, 1987), 60. Second, Hale's son thought he remembered his mother telling him that she was the editor of the Army Edition—perhaps because she sometimes was doing this

unofficially—and also recalled hearing her describe her interactions with its typesetters. See *Whose Little Boy*, 62.

The Woollcott quote is in the letter from Alexander Woollcott to Alice Hawley Truax, Dec. 4, 1917, reprinted in *The Letters of Alexander Woollcott*, ed. Beatrice Kaufman and Joseph Hennessey (New York: Viking Press, 1944), 44.

8. O'Connor, *Heywood Broun*, 53–65; Kramer, *Heywood Broun*, 82–90.

9. O'Connor, *Heywood Broun*, 59; Sally Ashley, *F.P.A.: The Life and Times of Franklin Pierce Adams* (New York: Beaufort Books, 1986), 109; letters from Alexander Woollcott to Julie Woollcott Taber, Oct. 2, 1917, and Dec. 10, 1917, and to Ruth Hale, Jan. 12, 1918, all in *The Letters of Alexander Woollcott*, 31–32, 46–47, 49. The quote is on page 46.

10. Author's interview with Heywood Hale Broun, June 21, 2000, Woodstock, NY.

11. *Whose Little Boy*, 63. Their departure date is based on information in a letter from Alexander Woollcott to Julie Woollcott Taber, Jan. 26, 1918, in *The Letters of Alexander Woollcott*, 53. Here, also, he describes his disappointment at their departure.

12. Author's interview with Heywood Hale Broun, June 21, 2000.

13. Donald Caton, *What a Blessing She Had Chloroform: The Medical and Social Response to the Pain of Childbirth from 1800 to the Present* (New Haven, CT: Yale University Press, 1999), 133–41.

14. Her son's Mar. 10, 1918, birth certificate identifies Hale as a "theatrical advertising manager," presumably the city registrar's interpretation of a theatrical press agent. A letter from Woollcott to Hale, dated Jan. 12, 1918, asks her to give his love "to Heywood and Arthur Hopkins," implying that she planned to work for Hopkins once she returned to New York. Another letter from Woollcott, this one to Mrs. Charles Taber and dated Dec. 1918, asserts that Hale was working for Hopkins at the time the letter was written. See *The Letters of Alexander Woollcott*, 50, 74.

    References to Hale as a Selwyn publicist during this time are in Margaret Case Harriman, *The Vicious Circle: The Story of the Algonquin Round Table* (New York: Rinehart & Co., 1951), 13, and Leslie Frewin, *The Late Mrs. Dorothy Parker* (New York: Macmillan Publishing, 1936), 36. In his Oct. 10, 1921, "diary" entry published in the *New York World*, F.P.A. wrote that Hale gave him her ticket to a baseball game, "she having begun this day to work for J. Golden." See Franklin Pierce Adams, *The Diary of Our Own Samuel Pepys*, vol. 1 (New York: Simon & Schuster, 1935), 293.

    For characterizations of Arthur Hopkins, Edgar Selwyn, and John Golden, see Scott Meredith, *George S. Kaufman and His Friends* (Garden City, NY: Doubleday & Company, 1974), 403, and Richard Maney, *Fanfare: The Confessions of a Press Agent* (New York: Harper & Brothers, 1957), 87, 108–9.

15. Author's interview with Heywood Hale Broun, June 22, 2000, Woodstock, NY; Alfred L. Bernheim, *The Business of the Theatre: The Economic History of the American Theatre, 1750–1932* (New York: Actors Equity Association, 1932; reprint, New York: Benjamin Blom, [1964]), 147–48; Maney, *Fanfare*, 117, 149.

16. *Whose Little Boy*, 72.

17. Maney, *Fanfare*, 346; Ann Douglas, *Terrible Honesty: Mongrel Manhattan in the 1920s* (New York: Farrar, Straus & Giroux, 1995), 60.

18. Author's interview with Heywood Hale Broun, June 19, 2001, Woodstock, NY. It is my conclusion that Hale stopped working as a publicist in 1922, and her son agreed that this seemed likely.

19. "Introducing Ruth Hale," *Judge*, Aug. 12, 1922, 15.

20. *Judge*, Feb. 24, 1923, 15.

21. George H. Douglas, *The Smart Magazines* (New York: Anchor Books, 1991), 46.

22. Kramer, *Heywood Broun*, 196–97; O'Connor, *Heywood Broun*, 15; "Noted Newspaper Man and His Wife are at Capital," *Fourth Estate*, May 4, 1925, clipping in Ruth Hale's Scrapbook, Schlesinger Library on the History of Women in America, Radcliffe Institute for Advanced Study, Harvard University, Cambridge, MA.

23. "Sophisticates," *Time*, March 3, 1923, 13.

24. These names are my best determination of the people who came to the first Algonquin Round Table luncheon and continued coming. Numerous primary and secondary sources list the group's founding members, but none give precisely the same names. And often Jane Grant and Harold Ross are included, although Grant could not have been present because she had not yet returned to New York from France, and it's very unlikely Ross was invited to early lunches on his own. It's possible a few others not listed here were at that first lunch, but I'm confident that these twelve people were indeed charter members.

25. James R. Gaines, *Wit's End: Days and Nights of the Algonquin Round Table* (New York: Harcourt Brace Jovanovich, 1977), 32–47, 194–210, 216–19; Wolcott Gibbs, *More in Sorrow* (Boston: Houghton Mifflin Company, 1964), 102–4; Malcolm Goldstein, *George S. Kaufman: His Life, His Theater* (New York: Oxford University Press, 1979), 66–74; Ashley, *F.P.A.*, 129–30.

26. Gaines, *Wit's End*, 47–54; Gibbs, *More in Sorrow*, 102–5; John Mason Brown, *The Worlds of Robert E. Sherwood: Mirror to His Times, 1896–1939* (New York: Harper & Row, 1965), 147–50.

27. Harpo Marx (with Rowland Barber), *Harpo Speaks!* (New York: Bernard Geis Associates, 1961), 175.

28. Author's interview with Heywood Hale Broun, June 24, 2000, Woodstock, NY. For an excellent analysis of women's place at the Round Table and the male Algonks' typical attitudes regarding women, see Ann Miller, *Making Love Modern* (New York: Oxford University Press, 1999), 88–96. A more benign but still useful firsthand account of men's and women's Round Table "manners" is in Harriman, *Vicious Circle*, 133–52.

29. Author's interview with Heywood Hale Broun, June 24, 2000.

30. Heywood Hale Broun, "Movies: 'Wit's End,'" *Vogue*, December 1994, 167, 170, 172, 176.

31. Author's interviews with Heywood Hale Broun, Aug. 2, 1999, and June 21, 2000, Woodstock, NY.

32. Author's interviews with Heywood Hale Broun, June 21, 2000, and June 19, 2001, Woodstock, NY.

33. Author's interviews with Heywood Hale Broun, Aug. 2, 1999, and June 21, 2000.

34. *Whose Little Boy*, 12–13.

35. Author's interviews with Heywood Hale Broun, June 21, 2000, and June 19, 2001.

36. Author's interviews with Heywood Hale Broun, July 31, 1999, June 21, 2000, and June 22, 2000.

37. Author's interviews with Heywood Hale Broun, Aug. 3, 1999, and June 24, 2000; author's interview with Melissa Hale Ward, Aug. 9, 2000, Phoenix, AZ.

38. *Whose Little Boy*, 114.

39. Author's interview with Melissa Hale Ward.

40. Author's interview with Heywood Hale Broun, Aug. 2, 1999.

41. *Whose Little Boy*, 53.

42. Ibid., 20, 194–95. The quotes are on pages 194–95.

43. The quotes are from *Whose Little Boy*, 143 and 106.

44. Ibid., 120–21.

45. Author's interviews with Heywood Hale Broun, June 18 and 21, 2001. The quote is from the June 18 interview.

46. Author's interviews with Heywood Hale Broun, June 21 and June 22, 2000, and June 19, 2001. The quote is from *Whose Little Boy*, 122.

47. *Whose Little Boy*, 9.

48. Author's interviews with Heywood Hale Broun, June 19, 2001, and June 21, 2000. The quote is from the June 21 interview.
      For an excellent description and analysis of three similar marriages, see Ellen Kay Trimberger, "Feminism, Men, and Modern Love: Greenwich Village, 1900–1925," in *Powers of Desire: The Politics of Sexuality*, ed. Ann Snitow, Christine Stansell, and Sharon Thompson (New York: Monthly Review Press, 1983), 131–52.

49. Author's interviews with Heywood Hale Broun, June 23, 2000, June 18, 2001, and June 19, 2001. The quote is from *Whose Little Boy*, 44.

50. Author's interviews with Heywood Hale Broun, June 23 and June 24, 2000, and June 18, 2001. Heywood Broun is quoted in Kramer, *Heywood Broun*, 108. The first quote from Heywood Hale Broun is from *Whose Little Boy*, 77. The second is from the June 18, 2001, interview.

51. *Whose Little Boy*, 45.

52. Author's interview with Heywood Hale Broun, June 17, 2001, Woodstock, NY.

53. Author's interview with Heywood Hale Broun, June 18, 2001.

54. *Whose Little Boy*, 44.

55. Author's interview with Heywood Hale Broun, July 31, 1999.

56. *Whose Little Boy*, 3.

57. Author's interview with Heywood Hale Broun, June 23, 2000.

58. Author's interview with Heywood Hale Broun, June 19, 2001.

59. The quote is from *Whose Little Boy*, 158.

60. O'Connor, *Heywood Broun*, 66; Kramer, *Heywood Broun*, 91–94; author's interview with Heywood Hale Broun, Aug. 3, 1999.

61. Heywood Broun, "How I Got Into This Racket," in *Collected Edition of Heywood Broun*, ed. Heywood Hale Broun (New York: Harcourt, Brace & Company, 1941), 321–22. (The column originally ran in the *New York World-Telegram* on Sept. 15, 1934.)

62. *Whose Little Boy*, 71.

63. O'Connor, *Heywood Broun*, 78–82, 126 (the quote from Swope is on page 81); E. J. Kahn Jr., *The World of Swope* (New York: Simon & Schuster, 1965), 265–69.

64. Kahn, *World of Swope*, 269; Gaines, *Wit's End*, 108.

65. Heywood Broun, "Nonsenseorship," in *Nonsenseorship*, ed. G. P. Putnam (New York: G. P. Putnam's Sons, 1922), 5–16.

66. Ruth Hale, "The Woman's Place," in *Nonsenseorship*, 33–44.

67. Ibid., 33.

68. Author's interview with Heywood Hale Broun, June 18, 2001.

69. Heywood Broun, "Ruth Hale," in *Collected Edition of Heywood Broun*, 324. (The column originally ran in the *New York World-Telegram* on Sept. 19, 1934.)

70. Ibid.

71. Author's interviews with Heywood Hale Broun, June 19 and June 22, 2001.

72. A newspaper article identified her as the coauthor of Broun's collection of *Tribune* pieces about the war, *The A.E.F.: With General Pershing and the American Forces*. (See "Miss Hale Opens Drama League Season," *Omaha Bee*, Oct. 19, 1924, clipping in Ruth Hale's Scrapbook.) Her son thought it very possible that she was sufficiently involved in his war reporting to deserve credit for coauthorship.

73. These observations about Broun's war reporting are based on an examination of the pieces collected in *The A.E.F.*

74. *Whose Little Boy*, 112.

75. Ibid., 162.

76. George Oppenheimer, *A View from the Sixties: Memories of a Spent Life* (New York: David McKay Company, 1966), 70–71.

77. Heywood Broun, "The Rabbit That Ate the Bulldog," in *Collected Edition of Heywood Broun*, 215. (The piece originally ran in *The New Yorker* on Oct. 1, 1927.)

78. Bruce Bliven, "The Man," in *Heywood Broun*, ed. M. B. Schnapper (Washington, DC: American Council on Public Affairs, 1940), 3.

79. Author's interview with Heywood Hale Broun, June 22, 2000.

80. Author's interviews with Heywood Hale Broun, Aug. 3, 1999, and June 18, 2001.

81. Author's interviews with Heywood Hale Broun, Aug. 3, 1999, and June 19, 2001.

82. Author's interviews with Heywood Hale Broun, Aug. 3, 1999, and June 23, 2000.

83. Author's interview with Heywood Hale Broun, June 19, 2001.

84. Author's interview with Heywood Hale Broun, Aug. 3, 1999.

85. Broun, "Ruth Hale," 325.

86. Una Stannard, *Mrs. Man* (San Francisco: Germain Books, 1977), 189.

87. Ibid., 188–89. See Heywood Broun, "It Seems to Me," *New York World*, May 1, 1925, clipping in Ruth Hale's Scrapbook, for a brief description of the couple's trip to Washington, DC, to obtain their passports eight years earlier.

88. Stannard, *Mrs. Man*, 190–91; "Ruth Hale or Mrs. Broun?" *New York Times*, Feb. 18, 1921, 11; undated Lucy Stone League press release reprinting letters from Charles Evans Hughes and Ruth Hale, Lucy Stone League client folder, box I:227, Edward L. Bernays Papers, Manuscript Division, Library of Congress, Washington, DC (hereafter ELB Papers).

89. Heywood Broun, "A Miss Is Even Better," *Cosmopolitan*, Feb. 1924, 44.

90. Jane Grant, *Ross, "The New Yorker" and Me* (New York: Reynal & Company, 1968), 128–29, 133; Stannard, 188.

91. Minutes of the Apr. 21 and Apr. 28, 1921, Lucy Stone League meetings, Lucy Stone League Minute Book, box 10, folder 4, Jane C. Grant Papers, Special Collections, University of Oregon Library, Eugene, OR.

92. Mary Lou Parker, "Fashioning Feminism: The Making of the Lucy Stone League by Members and Media" (PhD diss., University of Oregon, 1994), 65. Also see the listing of executive committee members in the minutes of the May 17, 1921, meeting, Lucy Stone League Minute Book.

93. "Maiden Namers Score a Victory," *New York Times*, May 15, 1921, 7. Hale's work on the Waldorf-Astoria campaign is described in Stannard, *Mrs. Man*, 191.

94. Minutes of the Apr. 28, 1921, Lucy Stone League meeting, Lucy Stone League Minute Book; Stannard, *Mrs. Man*, 192–93, 199.

95. Ruth Hale's Scrapbook contains numerous newspaper stories about these debates.

96. Stannard, *Mrs. Man*, 192–96. Clippings in Ruth Hale's Scrapbook give a good sense of the range of topics covered in articles about the league.

97. Stannard, *Mrs. Man*, 194–95.

98. Ruth Hale, "But How about the Postman?," *Bookman*, Feb. 1922, 561.

99. The Lucy Stone League client folder (box I:227, ELB Papers) contains extensive correspondence, news releases, and other materials charting Bernays's involvement in the league in the 1920s.

100. Research notes for *Biography of an Idea: Memoirs of Public Relations Counsel Edward L. Bernays*, "Lucy Stone League" chapter, 4, box I:458, ELB Papers.

101. Examples of "It Seems to Me" columns with references to the Lucy Stone League are in Ruth Hale's Scrapbook. Still more can be found in *The Collected Heywood Broun* and in two earlier collections of his columns: *Sitting on the World* (New York: G. P. Putnam's Sons, 1924), and *It Seems to Me: 1925–1935* (New York: Harcourt, Brace & Company, 1935). The scrapbook also contains numerous clippings that describe Broun speaking at league public events. His participation in the debate at its first dinner is described in "Lucy Stone League Has Clash in Views," *New York Times*, Mar. 13, 1922, 15. For his attendance at the May 17, 1921, meeting, see those minutes in the Lucy Stone League Minute Book.

102. Author's interview with Heywood Hale Broun, Aug. 3, 1999.

103. Marion Meade, *Bobbed Hair and Bathtub Gin: Writers Running Wild in the Twenties* (New York: Doubleday, 2004), 57; Adams, *Diary of Our Own Samuel Pepys*, 299; author's interview with Heywood Hale Broun, June 19, 2001.

104. *Whose Little Boy*, 146.

105. Ibid., 22.

106. Ibid., 135.

107. Author's interview with Heywood Hale Broun, June 21, 2000.

CHAPTER 7

1. Heywood Hale Broun, *Whose Little Boy Are You? A Memoir of the Broun Family* (New York: St. Martin's, 1983), 41, 44 (the quote is on page 44). Although his book gives the size of Hale's property as ninety-seven acres, in interviews Heywood Hale Broun said it actually was ninety-four acres.
2. Ibid., 42, 46–47 (the quote is on page 42); author's interview with Heywood Hale Broun, June 21, 2000, Woodstock, NY.
3. *Whose Little Boy*, 46–48; author's interview with Heywood Hale Broun, June 21, 2000.
4. Author's interview with Heywood Hale Broun, June 17, 2001, Woodstock, NY.
5. Ibid.
6. *Whose Little Boy*, 120.
7. Ibid., 132–33.
8. Ibid., 133.
9. Author's interviews with Heywood Hale Broun, Aug. 1, 1999, June 21, 2000, and July 19, 2001, Woodstock, NY.
10. Author's interviews with Heywood Hale Broun, Aug. 1, 1999, and June 21, 2000. The quote is from the Aug. 1, 1999, interview.
11. Author's interviews with Heywood Hale Broun, Aug. 1, 1999, and June 19, 2001, Woodstock, NY.
12. Author's interview with Heywood Hale Broun, June 23, 2000, Woodstock NY.
13. Letter from Maxwell Perkins to F. Scott Fitzgerald, Aug. 8, 1924, reprinted in *Dear Scott/Dear Max: The Fitzgerald-Perkins Correspondence*, ed. John Kuehl and Jackson R. Bryer (New York: Charles Scribner's Sons, 1971), 75.
14. Margaret Case Harriman, *The Vicious Circle: The Story of the Algonquin Round Table* (New York: Rinehart & Co., 1951), 129.
15. Author's interviews with Heywood Hale Broun, Aug 1, 1999, and June 23, 2000; *Whose Little Boy*, 49, 125. The quote is on page 125.
16. Author's interview with Heywood Hale Broun, June 19, 2001.
17. The following are the only magazine articles with Hale's byline that this researcher has located: Ruth Hale, "'A Personal'" (poem), *Literary Digest*, Apr. 28, 1923, 36; Ruth Hale, "As a Child Reads," *Bookman*, Nov. 1924, 257–61; Ruth Hale, "Freedom in Divorce," *Forum*, Sept. 1926, 333–38; Ruth Hale, "Why I Believe in Divorce," *Woman Citizen*, Mar. 1927, 10–11; Ruth Hale and George Jean Nathan, "Has Modern Woman Disrupted the Home? A Sparkling Dialogue Recorded by Lillian G. Genn," *Independent Woman*, Jan. 1929, 6–7.
18. *New Yorker* Profiles were unsigned, but Hale was identified as the author of "The Child Who Was Mother to a Woman" (*New Yorker*, Apr. 11, 1925, 11, 12), in *Woman of Valor: Margaret Sanger and the Birth Control Movement in America*, by Ellen Chesler (New York: Simon & Schuster, 1992), 218. Still, Chesler's footnote citing the article places Hale's byline on it, although it carried no byline. Chesler may have established that Hale was the author through some other source, then inadvertently added her name to the citation. But her evidence is never stated.

    Other confirmation can be found in box 2, folder 6, *New Yorker* Records, Manuscripts and Archives Division, Astor, Lenox and Tilden Foundations, New York Public Library, New York, NY. A "complete list of all the contributors" for 1925 includes Hale. So she wrote something for the magazine that year, and the Sanger Profile reads very much like Hale's writing.
19. Ben Yagoda, *About Town: "The New Yorker" and the World It Made* (New York: Scribner, 2000), 133.
20. Ruth Hale, "The Paper Knife," *Brooklyn Eagle*, Feb. 21, 1925, 5; Nov. 22, 1924, 5; and Apr. 4, 1925, 5.
21. Ruth Hale, "The Paper Knife," *Brooklyn Eagle*, Nov. 8, 1924, 5, and Jan. 10, 1925, 5.

22. Her final column appeared on Apr. 18, 1925. It ran every week from Nov. 1, 1924, until Mar. 21, 1925. The following Saturday, a column by another book reviewer, George Currie, ran in place of "The Paper Knife," but Hale's column returned on Apr. 4. Another Currie column ran on Apr. 11.

23. Author's telephone interview with Heywood Hale Broun, Aug. 12, 2001.

24. *Whose Little Boy*, 116.

25. Author's interviews with Heywood Hale Broun, June 23, 2000, June 18, 2001, and June 19, 2001. The quotes are from the June 18, 2001, interview.

26. Author's interview with Heywood Hale Broun, June 23, 2000.

27. *Whose Little Boy*, 171–72.

28. Ishbel Ross, *Ladies of the Press: The Story of Women in Journalism by an Insider* (New York: Harper & Brothers, 1936), 259.

29. Susan D. Becker, *The Origins of the Equal Rights Amendment: American Feminism between the Wars* (Westport, CT: Greenwood Press, 1981), 15–29, 99–101; Nancy F. Cott, *The Grounding of Modern Feminism* (New Haven, CT: Yale University Press, 1987), 75.

30. Cott, *Grounding of Modern Feminism*, 251–52 (the quote is on page 251).

31. Una Stannard, *Mrs. Man* (San Francisco: Germain Books, 1977), 196–200; Mary Lou Parker, "Fashioning Feminism: The Making of the Lucy Stone League by Members and Media" (PhD. diss., University of Oregon, 1994), 137–41, 183–84.

32. "The Married Woman's Maiden Name Again," *Philadelphia Inquirer*, Aug. 20, 1924, a clipping in Ruth Hale's Scrapbook, Schlesinger Library on the History of Women in America, Radcliffe Institute for Advanced Study, Harvard University, Cambridge, MA.

33. Stannard, *Mrs. Man*, 202–3. The quote from the Aug. 15, 1924, *World* is on page 202.

34. Ibid., 195, 203–4.

35. Ibid., 204–6.

36. Ibid., 206–7.

37. Ibid., 207–10, 214–16; Parker, "Fashioning Feminism," 183–84.

38. Stannard, *Mrs. Man*, 211–12; "Ruling that Authoress Must Copyright under Her Husband's Name Stirs Women," *New York Times*, Dec. 20, 1926, 1; "Solberg Modifies Copyright Ruling," *New York Times*, Dec. 21, 1926, 22.

39. Stannard, *Mrs. Man*, 214. Ruth Hale's Scrapbook contains no clippings after 1926, and a search of the *New York Times* index resulted in no articles about actions taken by the league after 1926.

40. Ruth Hale, "The First Five Years of the Lucy Stone League," 20, box 3, folder 2, Jane C. Grant Papers, Special Collections, University of Oregon Library, Eugene, OR (hereafter JG Papers).

41. Lucy Stone League Treasurer's Reports, box 14, folder 1, JG Papers.

42. Letter from Ruth Hale to Jane Grant, Apr. 27, 1925, box 3, folder 1, JG Papers.

43. Jane Grant, *Ross, "The New Yorker" and Me* (New York: Reynal & Company, 1968).

44. Ruth Pickering quoted in Stannard, *Mrs. Man*, 193.

45. Ella Winter, *And Not to Yield: An Autobiography* (New York: Harcourt, Brace & World, 1963), 117.

46. Author's interview with Heywood Hale Broun, June 19, 2001.

47. Philip English Mackey, ed., *Voices against Death: American Opposition to Capital Punishment, 1787–1975* (New York: Burt Franklin & Co., 1976), xxxvi–xxxviii. Although in *Whose Little Boy* Heywood Hale Broun says his mother was the league's secretary, *New York Times* stories identify her as its treasurer. See, for example, "League Opens Fight on Death Penalty," Mar. 1, 1927, 2.

48. Marc Connelly, *Voices Offstage: A Book of Memoirs* (New York: Holt, Rinehart & Winston, 1968), 96–97; *Whose Little Boy*, 39.

49. Mackey, *Voices against Death*, xxxvii–xxxix, 191.

50. Author's interviews with Heywood Hale Broun, July 31, 1999, and June 19, 2001; "A Cer-

tain City Editor" in *Collected Edition of Heywood Broun*, comp. Heywood Hale Broun (New York: Harcourt, Brace & Company, 1941), 124–25. (This is a reprint of Broun's "It Seems to Me" column from the Dec. 15, 1930, *New York World*.)

51. Mackey, *Voices against Death*, xl–xli.
52. Stannard, *Mrs. Man*, 239–61.
53. Author's interview with Heywood Hale Broun, Aug. 2, 1999.
54. "Whims," in *Collected Edition of Heywood Broun*, 69. (This is a reprint of Broun's "It Seems to Me" column from the Feb. 6, 1928, *New York World*.)
55. Percy Hammond, "Do You Use Your Husband's Name?," *Liberty*, Jan. 19, 1925, 46.
56. Author's interview with Heywood Hale Broun, Aug. 2, 1999.
57. Author's interviews with Heywood Hale Broun, Aug. 3, 1999, and June 23, 2000. The quotes are from the Aug. 3, 1999, interview.
58. Author's interview with Heywood Hale Broun, June 24, 2000.
59. "Ruth Hale," in *Collected Edition of Heywood Broun*, 324. (This is a reprint of Broun's "It Seems to Me" column from the Sept. 19, 1934, *New York World-Telegram*.)
60. James R. Gaines, *Wit's End: Days and Nights of the Algonquin Round Table* (New York: Harcourt Brace Jovanovich, 1977), 136.
61. *Whose Little Boy*, 171.
62. Janice A. Radway, *A Feeling for Books: The Book-of-the-Month Club, Literary Taste, and Middle-Class Desire* (Chapel Hill: University of North Carolina Press, 1997), 168–82.
63. Author's interview with Heywood Hale Broun, June 22, 2000.
64. *Whose Little Boy*, 78.
65. Author's interview with Heywood Hale Broun, Aug. 3, 1999.
66. Quoted in Richard Maney, *Fanfare: The Confessions of a Press Agent* (New York: Harper & Brothers, 1957), 176.
67. Radway, *Feeling for Books*, 180–81; Joan Shelley Rubin, *The Making of Middlebrow Culture* (Chapel Hill: University of North Carolina Press, 1992), 138–40; Gaines, *Wit's End*, 132.
68. John Adam Moreau, "The Often Enraged Heywood Broun: His Career and Thought Revisited," *Journalism Quarterly* 44 (Autumn 1967): 497; Richard O'Connor, *Heywood Broun: A Biography* (New York: G. P. Putnam's Sons, 1975), 151; Morris L. Ernst, *The Best Is Yet . . .* (New York: Harper & Brothers, 1945), 29.
69. Sally Ashley, *F.P.A.: The Life and Times of Franklin Pierce Adams* (New York: Beaufort Books, 1986), 201.
70. Author's interviews with Heywood Hale Broun, June 21 and 24, 2000, and June 17 and 19, 2001.
71. Hale and Nathan, "Has Modern Woman Disrupted the Home?," 6–7.
72. See note 17 above.
73. For a sampling of the causes Hale took on after 1925, including her participation in public debates, see the following: "Will Back Miss Marx," *New York Times*, Oct. 11, 1927, 6; "Debate Companion Unions," *New York Times*, May 30, 1928, 11; "Darrow Lays Crime to Curb on Liberty," *New York Times*, Feb. 18, 1929, 9; "Mrs. Dennett Inquiry by Congress Urged," *New York Times*, May 7, 1929, 23; "'Red Scare' Protest Issued by Liberals," *New York Times*, May 19, 1930, 18.
74. *Whose Little Boy*, 82.
75. Ibid., 163.
76. "Ruth Hale," 324.
77. Author's interview with Heywood Hale Broun, June 22, 2000.
78. Author's interview with Heywood Hale Broun, June 19, 2001.
79. Author's interview with Heywood Hale Broun, June 24, 2000.
80. Author's interview with Heywood Hale Broun, June 23, 2000.
81. *Whose Little Boy*, 102.
82. Author's interview with Heywood Hale Broun, June 21, 2000.

83. Author's interviews with Heywood Hale Broun, June 23 and 24, 2000. For a good description of alcoholism among members of the Algonquin Round Table, see Ashley, *F.P.A.*, 133–35.

84. Author's interviews with Heywood Hale Broun, Aug. 2, 1999, and June 24, 2000; Heywood Hale Broun, "A Full House," *American Heritage*, Dec. 1966, 66–67. The quote is from the June 24 interview.

85. Author's interview with Heywood Hale Broun, June 24, 2000.

86. Author's interview with Heywood Hale Broun, June 19, 2001.

87. *Whose Little Boy*, 77.

88. David Felix, *Sacco-Vanzetti and the Intellectuals* (Bloomington: Indiana University Press), 202–49; Dale Kramer, *Heywood Broun: A Biographical Portrait* (New York: Current Books, 1949), 171; "Arrests Check Picketing, New York Writers Are in Group of 39 Jailed in Boston," *New York Times*, Aug. 11, 1927, 1; "Boston Besieged, Scores Arrested," *New York Times*, Aug. 23, 1927, 1; "Poem by Miss Millay on Sacco and Vanzetti," *New York Times*, Aug. 22, 1927, 2; author's interview with Heywood Hale Broun, Aug. 3, 1999. The quote is from the Aug. 11 *Times* article.

89. "Preface," in *Collected Edition of Heywood Broun*, viii–ix.

90. Author's interview with Heywood Hale Broun, Aug. 3, 1999.

91. "Broun Takes Issue with World Editor," *New York Times*, Aug. 17, 1924, 5. The interview quoted was by Philip Schuyler and appeared in *Editor & Publisher*.

92. O'Connor, *Heywood Broun*, 132–40; Alfred Allen Lewis, *Man of the World. Herbert Bayard Swope: A Charmed Life of Pulitzer Prizes, Poker and Politics* (New York: Bobbs-Merrill Company, 1978), 137–43. Broun's Sacco-Vanzetti columns and the *World*'s responses are reprinted in *Collected Edition of Heywood Broun*, 197–210. The quote is on page 204.

93. O'Connor, *Heywood Broun*, 150–51.

94. Author's interview with Heywood Hale Broun, Aug. 2, 1999.

95. Author's interview with Heywood Hale Broun, June 22, 2000.

96. "Heywood Broun Sells House," *New York Times*, May 3, 1929, 50; *Whose Little Boy*, 127.

97. Author's interviews with Heywood Hale Broun, Aug. 2, 1999, and June 19, 2001. The quotes are from the June 19, 2001, interview.

98. Gaines, *Wit's End*, 222–23; "Ruth Hale to Help Broun's Campaign," *New York Times*, Sept. 3, 1930, 32.

99. "Women Oppose Mrs. Pratt," *New York Times*, Oct. 28, 1930, 6; letter from Ruth Hale to Burnita Matthews, Dec. 4, 1930, reel 44, National Woman's Party Papers microfilm.

100. "Mrs. Pratt Victor by 651 Ballots," *New York Times*, Nov. 5, 1930, 4; author's interviews with Heywood Hale Broun, Aug. 2, 1999, and June 24, 2000. The quote is from the June 24, 2000, interview.

101. Author's interview with Heywood Hale Broun, June 24, 2000; "Wardell in Senate Race in Breach with M'Adoo," *Los Angeles Times*, June 26, 1922, 1; "Fourth of Vote Wins for Tubbs," *Los Angeles Times*, Sept. 3, 1932, 4; "Annie Riley Hale Funeral Services to Be Set Today," *Los Angeles Times*, Dec. 28, 1944, 6. The quote is from the Dec. 28, 1944, article.

102. Author's interview with Heywood Hale Broun, July 31, 1999; Marion Meade, *Dorothy Parker: What Fresh Hell Is This?* (New York: Villard Books, 1988), 174–75; Judith Farr, *The Life and Death of Elinor Wylie* (Baton Rouge: Louisiana State University Press, 1963), 12–35, 102–12.

103. Maney, *Fanfare*, 10–11.

104. For this progression of events, see "Theatrical Notes," *New York Times*, Jan. 31, 1927, 13; "Intimate Opera to Depart," *New York Times*, Feb. 25, 1927, 24; J. Brooks Atkinson, "Blown in the Glass Operetta," *New York Times*, Feb. 24, 1931, 26; "'Little Opera' Withdrawn," *New York Times*, Mar. 3, 1931, 41. The quote is from the Feb. 24 review. For a more positive review, see "'Glass Nephew' Charms," *Los Angeles Times*, Mar. 1, 1931, B9.

105. O'Connor, *Heywood Broun*, 171–75; Kramer, *Heywood Broun*, 200–3, 231–32; *Whose Little Boy*, 178.

106. *Whose Little Boy*, 178–79; author's interviews with Heywood Hale Broun, Aug. 1, 1999, and June 24, 2000. The quotes are from the Aug. 1, 1999, interview.

107. Author's interview with Heywood Hale Broun, June 22, 2000.

108. Author's interview with Heywood Hale Broun, June 24, 2000; "Ruth Hale Freed in Traffic Court," *New York Times*, May 9, 1928, 2.

109. Author's interviews with Heywood Hale Broun, June 22 and 24, 2000. The quotes are from the June 24 interview.

110. Author's interview with Heywood Hale Broun, June 19, 2001.

111. Author's interview with Heywood Hale Broun, June 24, 2000.

112. Author's interviews with Heywood Hale Broun, Aug. 1, 1999, and June 19, 2001. The quote is from the Aug. 1, 1999, interview.

113. O'Connor, *Heywood Broun*, 180–85; Kramer, *Heywood Broun*, 244–51. The quote is from "A Union of Reporters," *Collected Edition of Heywood Broun*, 297. (This is a reprint of Broun's "It Seems to Me" column from the Aug. 7, 1933, *New York World-Telegram*.)

114. O'Connor, *Heywood Broun*, 186–90; Milton Kaufman, "The Labor Leader," in *Heywood Broun*, ed. M. B. Schnapper (Washington, DC: American Council on Public Affairs, 1940), 7–10. The quote is from *Whose Little Boy*, 204.

115. Author's interview with Heywood Hale Broun, June 19, 2001.

116. Author's interview with Heywood Hale Broun, June 17, 2001. (He was incorrect in saying that none of his parents' friends divorced, since Franklin Pierce Adams divorced his first wife to marry Esther Sayles Root, who then was successful in receiving a passport partially in her birth name. But Woodie only remembered the happy second marriage.)

117. *Whose Little Boy*, 150.

118. Associated Press, "Ruth Hale Divorces Broun," *Los Angeles Times*, Jan. 19, 1934, 3.

119. *Whose Little Boy*, 152–53. The quote is on page 153.

120. Ibid., 154; author's interviews with Heywood Hale Broun, June 21, 2000, and June 18 and 19, 2001. The quote is from the June 18, 2001, interview

121. "Tributes by Many to Late Mrs. Howe," *New York Times*, Mar. 26, 1934, 17.

122. Author's interviews with Heywood Hale Broun, Aug. 2, 1999, and June 24, 2000.

123. Author's interview with Heywood Hale Broun, July 31, 1999; "Ruth Hale Is Dead; Feminist Leader," *New York Times*, Sept. 19, 1934, 19.

124. Interpretation of Ruth Hale's death certificate by Reuben Beezy, a physician specializing in internal medicine. Author's telephone interview with Reuben Beezy, Jan. 23, 2001.

125. Author's interview with Heywood Hale Broun, June 24, 2000,

126. "Ruth Hale," 323.

CHAPTER 8

1. Jane Grant, *Ross, "The New Yorker" and Me* (New York: Reynal & Company, 1968), 85.

2. Ibid., 86.

3. Ibid.

4. Ibid., 70–76; "Jane Grant Dead; Aided Magazine," *New York Times*, Mar. 17, 1972, L44; "Obituary. Mrs. R. T. Grant," undated clipping, box 38, folder 1, Jane C. Grant Papers, Special Collections, University of Oregon Library, Eugene, OR (hereafter JG Papers). Grant went on to claim later birthdates. For example, when she married William Harris in 1939, her marriage license gave her age as forty-two. Her birth date on her passports is May 29, 1895. (Documents are in box 40, folder 2, and box 39, folder 1, JG Papers.) But there is little doubt that the correct year is 1892.

5. *Ross*, 70.

6. Ibid., 72–73.

7. Very early draft of *Ross, "The New Yorker" and Me*, ch. 5, 32, box 20, folder 1, JG Papers.

8. "Obituary: Mrs. R. T. Grant." Based on the information in her obituary, Sophronia Grant would seem to be a fitting role model for her daughter in adulthood. But Grant apparently was not aware of her mother's business abilities or work with her father, for when she discussed her childhood in her book she simply briefly described Sophronia Grant's background as a teacher. And she said nothing at all about how her mother's early death affected her. The obituary is filed in Grant's papers with other material gathered at the time she wrote her book, so she probably only saw it for the first time in the 1960s.

9. *Ross*, 70, 76.

10. Ibid., 76, 71.

11. Ibid., 77.

12. Letter from R. T. Grant to Jane Grant, May 27, 1910, box 1, folder 2, JG Papers.

13. *Ross*, 77–78.

14. Ibid., 77–79. The quote is on page 79.

15. Ibid., 78.

16. Early, incomplete draft of Ross, *"The New Yorker" and Me*, 119, box 28, folder 1, JG Papers.

17. *Ross*, 78, 82.

18. Jane Grant, "Confession of a Feminist," *American Mercury*, Dec. 1943, 685.

19. Letter from Anna Marcet Haldeman to Sarah Alice Haldeman, Nov. 22, 1911, quoted in Susan Van Ness, "Jane C. Grant: Co-Founder of *The New Yorker*" (master's thesis, University of Kansas, 1983), 8. Anna Marcet Haldeman, who had known Grant in Girard, by chance ended up living in the same West Eighty-Fifth Street apartment building with her and wrote a letter to her mother describing Grant's situation. Susan Van Ness found the letter in the Pittsburgh State University Library Special Collections and quoted much of it in her thesis. The date and address on the letter establish that, contrary to Grant's claim in her book, she did not take business school classes to qualify for a job at the *New York Times*, and did not move directly from the Three Arts Club to Florence Williams's home.

20. *Ross*, 77.

21. Grant is identified as working at *Collier's* from 1912 to 1914 in her entry in *Contemporary Authors, Permanent Series*, ed. Christine Nasso, vol. 2 (Detroit: Gale Research Company, 1978), 227.

   A letter to Grant (James M. Ethridge to Jane Grant, n.d., box 2, folder 16, JG Papers) from the series' editorial director explains that Grant herself supplied all of the information printed in the entry, thus making a strong argument that she was, indeed, working at the magazine during those years. Yet the entry also says that she was a "staff member," a misleading label for someone in a clerical position at best, and it gives a birth date three years later than when she actually was born.

22. *Ross*, 82.

23. Ibid.

24. Ibid., 82–83. In her book Grant gives no date (either specific or broad) for when she began at the paper. Her *New York Times* obituary says she started working there in 1912, but the information she supplied for her *Contemporary Authors* entry has her starting in 1914. Based on the available evidence, I do not believe she was at the *Times* before 1914. The mid-1914 estimate is based on a letter—sent to her by a friend in early November 1914—that asked, "You still work at the paper, do you not?" So she must have been there at least a short while by that time. (See letter from "Nettie" to Jane Grant, Nov. 1, 1914, box 31, folder 3, JG Papers.)

25. "Confession of a Feminist," 685.

26. *Ross*, 82–83.

27. Ibid., 84.

28. Ibid., 84–85.

29. Ibid., 85–86.

30. Ishbel Ross, *Ladies of the Press: The Story of Women in Journalism by an Insider* (New York: Harper & Brothers, 1936), 149.

31. *Ross*, 85–95.

32. Ibid., 89.
33. Ibid., 88–91, 95, 102–3. The quote is on page 95.
34. Ibid., 87–88; letter from Enrico Caruso to Jane Grant [ca. 1914–1915], box 1, folder 2, JG Papers. The photographs are in box 2, Photograph Collection, Special Collections, University of Oregon Library.
35. "Confession of a Feminist," 685–86.
36. *Ross*, 79–81.
37. Ibid., 31, 87, 94, 102. The quotes are on page 31.
38. Wolcott Gibbs, *More in Sorrow* (Boston: Houghton Mifflin, 1964), 95.
39. *Ross*, 100.
40. Ibid., 96–99.
41. Ibid., 99–100.
42. Early, incomplete draft of *Ross, "The New Yorker" and Me*, 272–73, box 28, folder 2.
43. *Ross*, 100, 102. The quote is on page 102.
44. Early, incomplete draft of *Ross, "The New Yorker" and Me*, 281–84, box 28, folder 2. Also see several letters recommending Grant for war work and referring to previous letters of recommendation (not included in her papers), as well as correspondence with the YMCA, box 1, folder 2, JG Papers.
45. Dorothy Schneider and Carl J. Schneider, *Into the Breach: American Women Overseas in World War I* (New York: Viking, 1991), 121–23, 155–61.
46. Contract between the YMCA and Jane Grant, Sept. 8, 1918, box 38, folder 2, JG Papers.
47. Letter from Jane Grant to Samuel Hopkins Adams [Aug. 1943], box 1, folder 13, JG Papers.
48. Early, incomplete draft of *Ross, "The New Yorker" and Me*, 283–84, 303–4, box 28, folder 2.
49. Letter from Jane Grant to Samuel Hopkins Adams; Samuel Hopkins Adams, *A. Woollcott: His Life and His World* (New York: Reynal & Hitchcock, 1945), 79–87; Alfred E. Cornebise, *The Stars and Stripes: Doughboy Journalism in World War I* (Westport, CT: Greenwood Press, 1984), 15–17.
50. Thomas Kunkel, *Genius in Disguise: Harold Ross of "The New Yorker"* (New York: Random House, 1995), 17–24.
51. Ibid., 47–62.
52. *Ross*, 19–21.
53. Ibid., 21–27. The quote is on page 27.
54. Sentences excised from the printer's copy of *Ross, "The New Yorker" and Me*, 84, box 24, folder 1, JG Papers. Letters to Grant from the aviator are in box 1, folder 2, JG Papers.
55. *Ross*, 64.
56. Letter from Harold Ross to Jane Grant (addressed "My dear dear Miss Grant"), undated, box 1, folder 2, JG Papers.
57. *Ross*, 27–28. 60–61.
58. Letter from Harold Ross to Jane Grant, Feb. 27, 1919, box 1, folder 2, JG Papers. (The letter actually is dated "Feb. 27/18," but the correct year is 1919.)
59. *Ross*, 63.
60. Ibid., 31
61. Kunkel, *Genius in Disguise*, 64–65
62. *Ross*, 64–65, 68–69.
63. YMCA Certificate of Release, July 12, 1919, box 38, folder 2, JG Papers; YMCA Motion Picture Bureau identification card, box 38, folder 2, JG Papers.
64. *Ross*, 106–8.
65. Ibid., 106–7, 114.
66. Box 1, folder 2 of Grant's papers contains half a dozen love letters written to her in 1918 and signed "Charlie," "Curtis," or "Heartbroken." Another love letter, dated Jan. 25, 1919, and signed "Jack," is in box 1, folder 3. Grant's description of her European suitors is in *Ross*, 32.

67. Harpo Marx (with Roland Barber), *Harpo Speaks!* (New York: Bernard Geis Associates, 1961), 172; Janet Flanner, "Introduction: The Unique Ross," in Grant, *Ross*, 7; research notes for *Biography of an Idea* section titled "Harold Ross—1925," 1, box I:459, Edward L. Bernays Papers, Manuscript Division, Library of Congress, Washington, DC.

68. James Thurber, *The Years with Ross* (Boston: Little, Brown & Company, 1959), vii; Flanner, "Introduction," 9; Ralph McAllister Ingersoll, *Point of Departure: An Adventure in Autobiography* (New York: Harcourt, Brace & World, 1961), 168–69.

69. *Ross*, 32–33, 251.

70. Ibid., 21.

71. Ibid., 31, 114–15. Grant's comment that "Ross was not very articulate when he tried to be romantic" (31) is borne out by a comparison of his love letters with those from some of her other suitors. See, for example, box 1, folders 2 and 3, JG Papers, for letters she received prior to her marriage to Ross, and box 1, folders 4 and 6, for letters she received from other men after her divorce.

72. *Ross*, 115.

73. Kunkel, *Genius in Disguise*, 71.

74. *Ross*, 108–9. Many sources on the Round Table place Grant and "her fiancé" Ross at the inaugural meeting. This is not true since that meeting took place before she returned to New York. Her own book is a poor source on her involvement because she remembered so little about Round Table lunches that she had to ask surviving Algonks for their recollections before she could write about the group. And she never described her own first Round Table lunch. All of this is additional evidence that she was a peripheral member of the group.

Nor was Ross present at the Round Table's inauguration, for when H. L. Mencken asked him about it, he could only recall what he had been told by Woollcott about its beginnings. See letter from Harold Ross to H. L. Mencken, July 27 (circa 1946), reprinted in *Letters from the Editor: "The New Yorker"'s Harold Ross*, ed. Thomas Kunkel (New York: Modern Library, 2000), 292–93.

75. James R. Gaines, *Wit's End: Days and Nights of the Algonquin Round Table* (New York: Harcourt Brace Jovanovich, 1977), 22–28; early, incomplete draft of *Ross, "The New Yorker" and Me*, 119, box 28, folder 1.

76. Gaines, *Wit's End*, 22–29, 47–54.

77. *Ross*, 107; Jane Grant and Katherine Sproehnle, "Hotel Beat," 1, 2, 10, 23, box 17, folder 5, JG Papers. The latter is a twenty-four-page manuscript, written around 1934 but never published. It includes facts and stories clearly based on Grant's experiences as a hotel reporter. The quote is on page 2.

78. *Ross*, 104, 122; Kunkel, *Letters*, 68, 73.

79. Franklin Pierce Adams, *The Diary of Our Own Samuel Pepys*, vol. 1 (New York: Simon & Schuster, 1935), 225. (The book is a dated, annotated compilation of some of Adams's columns.)

80. *Ross*, 116.

81. Ibid., 115–17, 123. (The quotes are on page 123.)

82. Ibid., 121–24; Kunkel, *Letters*, 72–73.

83. *Ross*, 55–57; Kunkel, *Letters*, 62–63.

84. Very early draft of *Ross, "The New Yorker" and Me*, ch. 5, 26.

85. *Ross*, 123–24.

86. Ibid., 124–29; Kunkel, *Letters*, 73.

CHAPTER 9

1. Jane Grant, *Ross, "The New Yorker" and Me* (New York: Reynal & Company, 1968), 126–28; very early draft of *Ross, "The New Yorker" and Me*, ch. 8, 26, box 20, folder 2, Jane C. Grant Papers, Special Collections, University of Oregon Library, Eugene, OR (hereafter JG Papers).

2. Ibid., 128–29.

3. Jane Grant, "Confession of a Feminist," *American Mercury*, Dec. 1943, 687.

4. *Ross*, 126–30.

5. Ibid., 124, 132.

6. Ibid., 124–25. The quotes are on page 125.

7. Ibid., 133; incomplete draft of *Ross, "The New Yorker" and Me*, 12, box 28, folder 1, JG Papers. The quote is from *Ross*.

8. Una Stannard, *Mrs. Man* (San Francisco: Germain Books, 1977), 188; minutes of the Apr. 21 and Apr. 28, 1921, Lucy Stone League meetings, Lucy Stone League Minute Book, box 10, folder 4, JG Papers.

9. "Confession of a Feminist," 686, 688.

10. Beverly G. Merrick, "Newswomen's Club of New York, 1922–Present," in *Women's Press Organizations, 1881–1999*, ed. Elizabeth V. Burt (Westport, CT: Greenwood Press, 2000), 171–76; "Mrs. Harding Honors Club," *New York Times*, Apr. 10, 1922, 21; "Newspaper Women's Dance," *New York Times*, June 6, 1925, 5; "Elected VP—Newspaper Women's Club," *New York Times*, May 8, 1927, 13; "Newspaper Women Elect," *New York Times*, May 3, 1928, 5; "Newspaper Women Pick Officers," *New York Times*, May 2, 1929, 19.

11. Quoted in Frances Herridge, "Women Need More Rights, Not Privileges," *New York Post*, Oct. 21, 1953, 74, clipping in box 11, folder 3, JG Papers.

12. Ishbel Ross, *Ladies of the Press: The Story of Women in Journalism by an Insider* (New York: Harper & Brothers, 1936), 149.

13. Ibid., 140; Edna Ferber, *A Peculiar Treasure*, 2nd ed. (Garden City, NY: Doubleday, 1960), 268.

14. *Ross*, 145–46, 150. The quote is on page 146.

15. "The House—Dates & Documents," box 28, folder 3, JG Papers. (This is a report prepared for Grant's use in writing *Ross, "The New Yorker" and Me*. A researcher summarized and quoted directly from New York City public records on the West Forty-Seventh Street property.)

16. Ibid. (quoting Aug, 1, 1923, deed of conveyance between Ross, Grant, Truax, and Woollcott); mortgage between Harold Ross, Jane Grant, and Hawley Truax, Dec. 1922, box 40, folder 1, JG Papers; *Ross*, 146–51.

17. *Ross*, 148–51, 156. The quote is on page 148.

18. Dec. 1922 mortgage document.

19. It's unclear exactly when she was promoted. She never identified a date in *Ross* or in drafts of the book, and dates cannot be determined from *Times* bylines since the paper ran bylines only infrequently. Her first byline on a cityside story appeared on Jan. 4, 1925. In 1921 and 1924 she had bylined stories in the Sunday magazine section, but these likely were extra freelance pieces. In a 1951 letter to Meyer Berger, whose *The Story of the "New York Times"* had just been published, Grant pointed out that he had neglected to describe her work and said, "For about seven years I had general assignments." Her last year at the *Times* apparently was 1930, so I've concluded that she likely began seven years earlier, in 1923. (See letter from Jane Grant to Meyer Berger, Sept. 28, 1951, box 2, folder 6, JG Papers.)

20. See *Ross*, 136–39; Jane Grant, "High Honors for a Woman Engineer," *New York Times*, Jan 10, 1926, A3; Jane Grant, "The Charleston Prances into Favor," *New York Times*, Aug. 30, 1925, SM2; Jane Grant, "Women's Influence Seen in Closed Car Comforts," *New York Times*, Jan. 4, 1925, A26.

21. Letter from Jane Grant to Meyer Berger.

22. Stanley Walker, *City Editor* (New York: Blue Ribbon Books, 1934), 259.

23. Federal Income Tax Return of Harold Ross and Jane Grant for 1925, box 117, folder 3, *New Yorker* Records, Manuscripts and Archives Division, Astor, Lenox and Tilden Foundations, New York Public Library, New York, NY (hereafter NY Records); "Statement of Syndicate Sales to November 1, 1923," box 1, folder 3, JG Papers; promotional materials for Grant's "The Beautiful Woman" column, box 40, folder 5, JG Papers; *Ross*, 134.

24. Payments are recorded in correspondence between Jane Grant and Doubleday, Page & Co., box 1, folder 3, JG Papers. The one *Saturday Evening Post* article by Grant alone was "Curtsy to the Crown," Sept. 6, 1924, 36. Those coauthored with Katherine Sproehnle were "Lead Kindly, Light," Apr. 5, 1924, 29; "To the Manner [*sic*] Born," Apr. 12, 1924, 22; "Ten Per Cent Off," May 3, 1924, 21; "Light Lady Fingers," Aug. 9, 1924, 12; "More Precious than Rubies," June 7, 1924, 24; and "Commerce in Amenities," Sept. 13, 1924, 20. Sproehnle's work for Bernays is noted in her obituary: "Katherine Sproehnle, 81, a Writer for Magazines," *New York Times*, Aug. 30, 1976, 25.

25. Incomplete draft of Ross, *"The New Yorker" and Me*, 194, 197. The quote is on page 194.

26. After Ross began working at the *New Yorker* and they no longer needed to put his salary aside for starting the magazine, it was used, along with Grant's, to help support the household.

27. *Ross*, 157, 178–80.

28. Ibid., 163–64.

29. Ferber, *Peculiar Treasure*, 287.

30. *Ross*, 179–80.

31. Ibid., 154, 166; Malcolm Goldstein, *George S. Kaufman: His Life, His Theater* (New York: Oxford University Press, 1979), 69–70. In "Women Can't Play Poker," Franklin Pierce Adams, one of the original players in the traditional Saturday-night games, described the enduring rationale for excluding women. See Adams, *Nods and Becks* (New York: McGraw-Hill, 1944), 60–64.

32. *Ross*, 116, 187. The quote is on page 187.

33. Ibid., 31, 121. The quote is on page 121.

34. Very early draft of Ross, *"The New Yorker" and Me*, ch. 5, 54.

35. *Ross*, 204–5.

36. Ibid., 212. (The correct spelling of the German magazine is *Simplicissimus*.)

37. Thomas Kunkel, *Genius in Disguise: Harold Ross of "The New Yorker"* (New York: Random House, 1995), 86–87, 90–91.

38. Corey Ford, *The Time of Laughter* (Boston: Little, Brown & Company, 1967), 112–13.

39. *Ross*, 204–6. The quote is on page 206.

40. From Raoul Fleischmann's undated, unpublished reminiscence, quoted in Ben Yagoda, *About Town: "The New Yorker" and the World It Made* (New York: Scribner, 2000), 32.

41. Ibid.

42. *Ross*, 206; Kunkel, *Genius in Disguise*, 92, 209–11.

43. *Ross*, 207.

44. Letter from Harold Ross to Lloyd Stryker, Oct. 29, 1945, box 84, folder 9, NY Records.

45. Letter from Harold Ross to Lloyd Stryker, Feb. 21, 1946, box 84, folder 9, NY Records.

46. *Ross*, 188–89, 208.

47. Edward L. Bernays, *Biography of an Idea: Memoirs of Public Relations Counsel Edward L. Bernays* (New York: Simon & Schuster, 1965), 364–65; research notes for *Biography of an Idea*, "Jane Grant," 2, box I:458, Edward L. Bernays Papers, Manuscript Division, Library of Congress, Washington, DC. The first quote is from Bernays's research notes, the second is from *Biography of an Idea*, 365.

48. "Announcing a New Weekly Magazine: *The New Yorker*," box 30, folder 1, JG Papers.

49. Ben Hecht, *Charlie: The Improbable Life and Times of Charles MacArthur* (New York: Harper & Brothers, 1957), 141.

50. Kunkel, *Genius in Disguise*, 7, 79, 89–90, 171.

51. Frank Case, *Tales of a Wayward Inn* (New York: Frederick A. Stokes Company, 1938), 65.

52. Ross, *Ladies of the Press*, 152.

53. The quote is from *Ross*, page 53. Ross's goldfish bowl complaint is on page 179.

54. Bernays, *Biography*, 365.

55. *Ross*, 220–21.

56. [Ralph McAllister Ingersoll], "*The New Yorker*," *Fortune*, May–June 1934, 82. (This article carries no byline, but in *Point of Departure* Ingersoll acknowledges being its author.)

57. Kunkel, 103–5, 110–11; Ralph McAllister Ingersoll, *Point of Departure: An Adventure in Autobiography* (New York: Harcourt, Brace & World, 1961), 187; Henry Pringle, "Harold Ross of the *New Yorker*," *'48: The Magazine of the Year*, Mar. 1948, 16.

58. Pringle, "Harold Ross," 15; Kunkel, *Genius in Disguise*, 112–13.

59. Bernays, *Biography*, 366; Kunkel, *Genius in Disguise*, 113; *Ross*, 224–26.

60. *Ross*, 187–88.

61. Ibid., 188; Kunkel, *Genius in Disguise*, 111–12.

62. *Ross*, 222–23.

63. Janet Flanner, "Introduction: The Unique Ross," in *Ross*, 8. (Flanner wrote that Grant and Neysa McMein visited her in 1923, but the correct date is 1922.)

64. Letter from Jane Grant to Janet Flanner, [June 1925], box 1, folder 3, JG Papers.

65. Yagoda, *About Town*, 76–77; Judith Yaross Lee, *Defining "New Yorker" Humor* (Jackson: University Press of Mississippi, 2000), 83–85. The quote is from Grant's letter to Flanner.

66. Postcard from Janet Flanner to Jane Grant, postmarked April 15, 1957, box 29, folder 1, JG Papers.

67. Kunkel, *Genius in Disguise*, 117–24; 151–52; *Ross*, 227–29. The quote is on page 227.

68. *Ross*, 227, 222.

69. Ibid., 226–27; Ingersoll, "The New Yorker," 82.

70. Kunkel, *Genius in Disguise*, 128–29; *Ross*, 229–30; Ingersoll, "The New Yorker," 82.

71. Kunkel, *Genius in Disguise*, 129; *Ross*, 230–31; Yagoda, *About Town*, 60–61; James Thurber, *My Years with Ross* (Boston: Little, Brown & Company, 1959), 30–31.

72. Ingersoll, "The New Yorker," 82, 85.

73. "Miss Mackay Tells How Society Plays," *New York Times*, Dec. 11, 1925, 21; "She Assumes a Certain Obligation," *New York Times*, Dec. 12, 1925, 21.

74. Lee, *Defining*, 47.

75. Ingersoll, *Point of Departure*, 192.

76. Yagoda, *About Town*, 76–77; Kunkel, *Genius in Disguise*, 105–7, 110, 116, 127–31. Ross's quote is on page 110. (Mackey's column originally was titled "In the News." Long's fashion column at first simply was called "Where to Shop.")

77. Pringle, "Harold Ross," 16; Kunkel, *Genius in Disguise*, 131, 142–52, 164; Yagoda, *About Town*, 95–97.

78. *Ross*, 251.

79. Ingersoll, *Point of Departure*, 202; Marcia Davenport, *Too Strong for Fantasy* (New York: Scribner's, 1967), 119; Thurber quoted in Harrison Kinney, *James Thurber: His Life and Times* (New York: Henry Holt & Company, 1995), 348.

80. Ford, *Time of Laughter*, 123.

81. Kunkel, *Genius in Disguise*, 135, 157.

82. Quoted in Kinney, *James Thurber*, 343.

83. Letter from Marc Connelly to Jane Grant, [February 1928], box 40, folder 2, JG Papers.

84. Kunkel, *Genius in Disguise*, 122, 158; Ingersoll, *Point of Departure*, 165.

85. Incomplete draft of *Ross, "The New Yorker" and Me*, 171.

86. *Ross*, 235–36.

87. Very early draft of *Ross, "The New Yorker" and Me*, ch. 15, 8.

88. Ibid.

89. Thurber, *My Years with Ross*, 276–77.

90. *Ross*, 156–57. The quote is on page 156.

91. Ibid., 242. Although Grant wrote that Woollcott departed in 1927, the Full Covenant Warranty Deed in which Grant and Ross agreed to pay Woollcott $4,250 for his portion of the West Forty-Seventh Street property is dated Aug. 24, 1926. See box 40, folder 1, JG Papers.

92. Letter from Harold Ross to Samuel Hopkins Adams, Thursday [1945], box 27, folder 8, NY Records.

93. *Ross*, 240–43. Both quotes are on page 243.

94. Ibid., 244–45. The quote is on page 245.

95. Letter from Ida Ross to Jane Grant, April 12, 1928, box 1, folder 4, JG Papers.
96. Letter from Marc Connelly to Jane Grant. Also see additional letters from Ida Ross to Jane Grant, and from Jane Grant to Ida Ross, box 1, folder 4, JG Papers.
97. Letter from Harold Ross to Jane Grant, [March 1928], box 1, folder 4, JG Papers.
98. *Ross*, 243–45; "The House—Dates & Documents."
99. *Ross*, 246; Heywood Hale Broun, *Whose Little Boy Are You? A Memoir of the Broun Family* (New York: St. Martin's, 1983), 128.
100. Letter from Harold Ross to Jane Grant, [March 1928].
101. *Ross*, 246; letter from Ida Ross to Jane Grant, May 16, 1928, box 1, folder 4, JG Papers.
102. Quoted in Thurber, *Years with Ross*, 16.
103. *Ross*, 252.
104. Thurber, *Years with Ross*, 189.
105. Kunkel, *Genius in Disguise*, 171.
106. Kinney, *James Thurber*, 1033.
107. "Confession of a Feminist," 685.
108. "Raoul Fleischmann," *New Yorker*, May 17, 1969, 27.
109. Kunkel, *Genius in Disguise*, 211; Ingersoll, "The New Yorker," 150.

CHAPTER 10

1. Interlocutory Judgment of Divorce, box 40, folder 2, Jane C. Grant Papers, Special Collections, University of Oregon Library, Eugene, OR (hereafter JG Papers); Thomas Kunkel, *Genius in Disguise: Harold Ross of "The New Yorker"* (New York: Random House, 1995), 162.
2. Jane Grant, *Ross, "The New Yorker" and Me* (New York: Reynal & Company, 1968), 246.
3. Kunkel, *Genius in Disguise*, 215. The Apr. 1, 1929, date was taken from later correspondence referring to the agreement, including a letter from George Whiteside (Grant's lawyer) to Jane Grant, June 20, 1929, box 1, folder 4, JG Papers.
4. *Ross*, 246.
5. Letter from Wilbur Holleman to Jane Grant, Aug. 31, 1929, box 1, folder 4, JG Papers.
6. See three handwritten, undated letters from Wilbur Holleman to Jane Grant, box 1, folder 4, JG Papers.
7. *Ross*, 245, 249. The quote is on page 249.
8. Miscellaneous pages and notes for *Ross, "The New Yorker" and Me*, 1–2, box 28, folder 3, JG Papers; *Ross*, 249–50. The quote is on page 250.
9. Miscellaneous pages and notes for *Ross, "The New Yorker" and Me*, 1–2, The quote is on page 2.

   This chronology of Grant's health problems was pieced together with difficulty because her account in *Ross, "The New Yorker" and Me* (245–46, 249) contains contradictory information. Based on all available evidence, I eventually concluded that in her book she combined two years of events into one year and that her diagnosis in France and subsequent surgery in New York took place in 1929.
10. *Ross*, 250.
11. Miscellaneous pages and notes for *Ross, "The New Yorker" and Me*, 2. Although Grant was not always accurate in her reports of when and where she worked or what she did, she gave the dates 1914 to 1930 for her *Times* employment in the information she provided for her entry in *Contemporary Authors*, Permanent Series, ed. Christine Nasso, vol. 2 (Detroit: Gale Research Company, 1978), 237. I find this information reliable when combined with the fact that her last bylined *Times* article appeared in Apr. 1929, and her papers (box 39, folder 3) contain two *Times* press passes, one expiring in June 1929, the other expiring in July 1930.
12. Letter from Harold Ross to Jane Grant, Apr. 1, 1931, box 70, folder 16, *New Yorker* Records, Manuscripts and Archives Division, Astor, Lenox and Tilden Foundations, New York Public Library, New York, NY (hereafter NY Records).

13. The quote is from a letter from Chadbourne, Stanchfield & Levy to Berkeley W. Henderson, Aug. 1, 1931, box 71, folder 13, NY Records. For related correspondence, see letter from Wilbur Holleman to Berkeley W. Henderson, July 21, 1931, box 1, folder 5, JG Papers; letter from Harold Ross to Jane Grant, June 8, 1931, box 1, folder 5, JG Papers; memorandum from "President" to D. M. Spencer, vice president, Aug. 28, 1931, box 40, folder, JG Papers; letter to Jane Grant from Chadbourne, Stanchfield & Levy, Oct. 16, 1931, box 1, folder 5, JG Papers.

14. Confidential memo from "President" to D. M. Spencer, vice president, Sept. 30, 1931, box 40, folder 2, JG Papers.

15. Letter from Harold Ross to Raoul Fleischmann, May 24, 1938, reprinted in *Letters from the Editor: The New Yorker's Harold Ross*, ed. Thomas Kunkel (New York: Modern Library, 2000), 128.

16. Letter from Harold Ross to Jane Grant, Apr. 1, 1931, box 70, folder 16, NY Records; letter from Harold Ross to Jane Grant, [undated, but probably late 1931], box 40, folder 2, JG Papers; "Dividends Paid Miss Grant on Her Stock—1934," box 72, folder 4, NY Records.

17. Kunkel, *Genius in Disguise*, 215–26; letter from Harold Ross to Raoul Fleischmann, May 24, 1938.

18. Kunkel, *Genius in Disguise*, 216–20. Kunkel actually implies that Ross's problems with these payments began in 1934, but "Dividends Paid Miss Grant on Her Stock—1934" shows that her 1934 dividends covered the $10,000 she had been guaranteed. Ross did not owe her anything that year.

19. Letter from Jane Grant to Morris Ernst, Mar. 31, 1935, box 72, folder 4, NY Records.

20. Letter from Harold Ross to Jane Grant, Mar. 5, 1934, box 1, folder 5, JG Papers.

21. In *Ross* Grant wrote that she was "armed with a few assignments given me by Edwin L. (Jimmy) James" (261). But the presence of *Times* reporters in much of the world makes it unlikely that she was given actual assignments. Much more likely, James agreed to consider stories she submitted and to identify her as affiliated with the *Times* to help her get stories. See box 1, folder 5, JG Papers for numerous letters of introduction that say Grant is "associated with the New York Times."

22. *Ross*, 64–68, 261. The quote is on page 261.

23. Gay Talese, *The Kingdom and the Power* (New York: New American Library, 1966), 38.

24. "Miss Grant in Asia: Former Girard Girl Receives Mention in Tokyo Paper. Letter to Parents Describes Experiences in China," *Girard Press*, June 7, 1934, clipping in box 40, folder 5, JG Papers. (This article quotes from Grant's letters to her father, one of which also quotes an article about Grant that she said ran in the *Japan Advertiser*.)

25. "Miss Grant in Asia."

26. Jane Grant, "Interview Finds Kang Teh Well; Manchu Ruler Cordial to American," *New York Times*, June 5, 1934, 12. "Miss Grant in Asia" describes her travels before arriving in Manchuria. She notes her other interviews in "Miss Jane Grant Given Interview," undated clipping from unidentified newspaper, box 40, folder 5, JG Papers.

27. "Manchukuo: Puppet and Visitors," *Time*, June 18, 1934, 22.

28. *Ross*, 261; travel itinerary in a letter from Edward Weinacht to Jane Grant, Mar. 13, 1934, box 1, folder 5, JG Papers.

29. Jane Grant, "Propaganda Silly, Says Hanfstaengl," *New York Times*, Aug. 26, 1934, E2.

30. Letter from George L. K. Morris to Gertrude Stein and Alice B. Toklas, May 29, 1934, box 1, folder 5, JG Papers.

31. "Miss Jane Grant Given Interview."

32. Jane Grant, "Gay Season in Austria," *New York Times*, July 21 1935, F2.

33. See numerous letters from Jane Grant to William Harris, box 1, folders 6–10, JG Papers. Her letter describing the planned July 4 celebration [July 1, 1936] is in folder 8.

34. Grant described this trip in a 219-page manuscript titled "I Saw What I Could," box 17, folder 6, JG Papers. The quotes are on page 2.

35. Letter from Laird Archer to Hugh C. Grant, July 16, 1937, box 1, folder 10, JG Papers.

36. "I Saw What I Could," 5.

37. See, for example, rejection letters from Eugene Reynal to Jane Grant, Apr. 16, 1937, box 1, folder 10, JG Papers, and from Ralph H. Graves to Jane Grant, Jan. 26, 1939, box 1, folder 11, JG Papers.

38. Edith Evans Asbury, "William Bliss Harris, Ex-Editor and Writer on Gardening Topics," *New York Times*, June 16, 1981, A17; Amos Pettingill [William Harris], *The White Flower Farm Garden Book* (New York: Alfred A. Knopf, 1971), iv; author's telephone interview with Ed Kemp, Jan. 6, 2004. Harris recalled meeting Grant at an "impossible cocktail party" in a Sept. 6, 1935, letter to her, box 1, folder 6, JG Papers.

39. Letter from William Harris to Jane Grant, Sept. 6, 1935.

40. The quotes are from Harris's letters to Grant on Sept. 15, Sept. 10, and Sept. 19, 1935, box 1, folder 6, JG Papers.

41. Letter from William Harris to Jane Grant, Sept. 17, 1935, box 1, folder 6, JG Papers.

42. Letter from William Harris to Jane Grant, Sept. 10, 1935.

43. Letter from Jane Grant to William Harris, July 20, 1936, box 1, folder 8, JG Papers.

44. Grant's 1936 letters to Harris are in box 1, folders 7, 8, and 9, JG Papers. Her 1937 letters are in box 1, folder 10, JG Papers.

45. Letter from George W. Whiteside to Jane Grant, Dec. 14, 1938, box 2, folder 11, JG Papers. Presumably Harris began divorce proceedings in 1938, as the Grant/Harris marriage license says his divorce was final in 1939. The license is in box 40, folder 2, JG Papers.

46. Kirkpatrick Funeral Home receipt, Aug. 10, 1935, box 1, folder 6, JG Papers; Appraisal of the Contents of Apartment, May 10, 1936, box 39, folder 1, JG Papers; early, incomplete draft of *Ross, "The New Yorker" and Me*, 181, box 28, folder 2, JG Papers.

47. Letter from a Reynal and Hitchcock agent (signature illegible) to Jane Grant, June 1, 1937, box 1, folder 11, JG Papers; notes, drafts, and outlines for "So, You're Going Weekending," box 31, folder 3, JG Papers. Grant's manuscripts of unpublished magazine articles are in box 15, folder 1; box 16, folder 4; box 16, folder 6; box 19, folder 4; box 17, folder 5; and box 35, folder 3, JG Papers.

48. The short stories are in box 18, folders 1–3 and 5–8, and box 35, folder 3, JG Papers. The plays are in box 15, folders 2–11; box 17, folders 1–3; box 19, folder 3; box 31, folder 2; box 31, folder 4; box 34, folder 6; and box 35, folder 4, JG papers.

49. Letter from William Harris to Dr. John Watson, Feb. 19, 1935, box 1, folder 6, JG Papers.

50. Letter from Paul M. Hahn to William Harris, May 27, 1935.

51. Donna Halper, *Invisible Stars: A Social History of Women in American Broadcasting* (Armonk, NY: M. E. Sharpe, 2001), 43–45, 65–68, 91.

52. Sample Procter & Gamble script, box 12, folder 2, JG Papers; "Home Town Songs," box 17, folder 4, JG Papers; "Your Mother's Voice," box 35, folder 5, JG Papers.

53. *Ross*, 116.

54. W. A. Swanberg, *Luce and His Empire* (New York: Charles Scribner's Sons, 1972), 122–27.

55. See Harris's letters to Grant on Sept. 6 and 18, 1935, and Grant's letter to Harris, July 1, 1936, for references to his work.

56. Asbury, "William Bliss Harris."

57. Author's telephone interview with Ed Kemp.

58. Note from Harold Ross to Jane Grant, Sept. 29, [1919], box 1, folder 2, JG Papers.

59. Letter from William Harris to Jane Grant, Sept. 10, 1935.

60. Letter from Jane Grant to Steward MacDonald, Dec. 14, 1938, box 40, folder 2, JG Papers; memo from Hope Hughes Pressman to University of Oregon President William Boyd, Sept. 26, 1978, William B. Harris Donor File, University of Oregon Archives. (The memo describes what Harris told Pressman when she visited him. The quote is from this memo.)

61. Marriage license, William B. Harris and Jane C. Grant, box 40, folder 2, JG Papers.

62. Kunkel, *Genius in Disguise*, 216–17, 231–32. Heywood Hale Broun discussed his father's

friendship with Ross in an interview with the author in Woodstock, NY, on June 19, 2001.

63. Kunkel, *Genius in Disguise*, 216, 219–22.

64. See letter from Robert Gill to Harold Ross, Nov. 6, 1939, box 76, folder 6, NY Records, and letter from Harold Ross to Chadbourne, Wallace, Parke & Whiteside, Feb. 10, 1944, box 84, folder 9, NY Records.

65. Letter from Harold Ross to Ik Shuman, Sept. 21, 1942, box 84, folder 9, NY Records.

66. Kunkel, *Genius in Disguise*, 224–25.

67. Ibid., 220–21, 224.

68. Memo from J. G. Winchester to Investment Department Research File, March 17, 1942, box 1, folder 12, JG Papers.

69. Kunkel, *Genius in Disguise*, 225–26. For more details of the negotiations, and Fleisch-mann's concerns, see letter from Lloyd Paul Stryker to Peter Vischer, July 3, 1942, box 1, folder 12, JG Papers.

70. Memo from Ik Shuman to Raoul Fleischmann, Lloyd Paul Stryker, and Hawley Truax, June 23, 1943; letter from Jane Grant to Raoul Fleischmann, June 24, 1943; and letter from Jane Grant to Ik Shuman, June 25, 1943, all in box 1, folder 13, JG Papers. The quotes are from the June 25 letter.

71. Kunkel, *Genius in Disguise*, 367; *Ross*, 262; copies of the *New Yorker* pony edition in box 36, folder 5, JG Papers.

72. See extensive correspondence regarding placing the magazine in post exchanges, box 36, folder 3, JG Papers. The quote is from a letter from Jane Grant to Raoul Fleischmann, June 18, 1945, box 1, folder 15, JG Papers.

73. See extensive correspondence regarding paper purchases in box 36, folder 3, JG Papers. The quote is from a letter in that folder from Grant addressed "Dear Al," Feb. 25, 1944. (A later letter reveals that Al is Brigadier General Albert J. Browning, director of the War Department's Purchases Division.)

74. See correspondence in box 36, folder 3, JG Papers.

75. Ibid., including letters to Secretary of the Navy James V. Forrestal, June 19, 1944, and General Douglas MacArthur, June 16, 1944. She discussed arranging dinner-party invita-tions in a speech she gave as part of a Dale Carnegie course in 1954, box 3, folder 9, JG Papers.

76. Kunkel, *Genius in Disguise*, 367; letter from Jane Grant to Raoul Fleischmann, [ca. 1947], box 2, folder 1, JG Papers.

77. Letter from Joseph V. Reed to Jane Grant, Feb. 15, 1946, box 36, folder 4, JG Papers.

78. Letter from Raoul Fleischmann to Jane Grant, Sept. 18, 1943, box 1, folder 13, JG Papers; letter from Jane Grant to Raoul Fleischmann, June 18, 1945, box 1, folder 15, JG Papers.

79. Letter from Ik Shuman to Harold Ross, Sept. 22, 1943, box 1, folder 13, JG Papers.

80. Letter from Raoul Fleischmann to Jane Grant, Oct. 7, 1943, box 1, folder 13, JG Papers; letter from Jane Grant to Raoul Fleischmann, June 18, 1945.

81. Receipts of vouchers from the *New Yorker* to Jane Grant, box 36, folder 5, JG Papers; letter from Jane Grant to R. L. Trautman, Mar. 8, 1945, box 36, folder 4, JG Papers; and several letters in box 1, folder 15, JG Papers: letter from Jane Grant to Hawley Truax, June 6, 1945; letter from Jane Grant to Raoul Fleischmann, June 19, 1945; and letter from Raoul Fleischmann to Jane Grant, July 19, 1945.

82. Letter from Raoul Fleischmann to Jane Grant, June 14, 1945, box 1, folder 15, JG Papers.

83. Letter from Lloyd Paul Stryker to Raoul Fleischmann and Hawley Truax, June 21, 1945, box 1312, folder 9, NY Records.

84. Letter from Raoul Fleischmann to Jane Grant, July 19, 1945.

85. Kunkel, *Genius in Disguise*, 375–76. The quote is on page 376. Also see voluminous correspondence between Grant's lawyers, Ross's lawyers, Grant and her lawyers, and Ross and his lawyers from 1940 to 1945 in box 76, folder 6, and box 84, folder 9, NY Records, and in box 1, folders 11 and 14, JG Papers.

86. Kunkel, *Genius in Disguise*, 376.
87. Letter from Harold Ross to Lloyd Paul Stryker, Oct. 29, 1945, box 84, folder 8, NY Records.
88. Ibid.
89. Kunkel, *Genius in Disguise*, 378.
90. Letters from Raoul Fleischmann to Jane Grant, Dec. 27, 1945, box 1, folder 16, from Lloyd Paul Stryker to Harold Ross, Feb. 13, 1946, box 2, folder 1, and from Jane Grant to Raoul Fleischmann, [ca. 1947], box 2, folder 1, all JG Papers; and from Harold Ross to Lloyd Paul Stryker, Feb. 21, 1946, box 84, folder 9, NY Records.

   The employment contract Grant signed is in box 40, folder 2, JG Papers, but the date on it—Dec. 27, 1945—is incorrect. She turned down the contract Fleischmann offered on that date. Clearly, when he offered her the new contract he simply changed the terms of the first one and neglected to change the date. Another letter from Fleischmann to Grant with the same date assures her that the contract "will be renewed, for additional ten (10) year periods as long as you live, upon the same terms and conditions." This letter is in box 1312, folder 9, NY Records.
91. Letter from Jane Grant to Lloyd Paul Stryker (marked "not sent"), [ca. 1945], box 1, folder 16, JG Papers.
92. Jane Grant, "Confession of a Feminist," *American Mercury*, Dec. 1943, 684–91.
93. Ibid., 691.
94. See the following letters, all in box 5, folder 6, JG Papers: from Jane Grant to Senator John Danaher, June 28, 1944; from Mary Anderson to Jane Grant, Aug. 14, 1943, from Eleanor Roosevelt to Jane Grant, Feb. 8, 1944, and from Henry Hazlitt to Jane Grant, Feb. 21, 1944. Box 5, folder 7, has two undated drafts, one from Jane Grant to Eleanor Roosevelt and one from Jane Grant to Freda Kirchwey. For more on the Connecticut Committee for the Equal Rights Amendment, see Leila J. Rupp and Verta Taylor, *Survival in the Doldrums: The American Women's Rights Movement, 1945 to the 1960s* (Columbus: Ohio State University Press, 1990), 32, 47, 72–75.
95. See National Woman's Party correspondence in box 11, folder 1, and Connecticut Committee for the Equal Rights Amendment correspondence in box 5, folder 6, JG Papers. See Rupp and Taylor, *Survival in the Doldrums*, 27–33, for more on the rebellion and its aftermath.
96. Rupp and Taylor, *Survival in the Doldrums*, 21; letters from Jane Grant to Jack Jessup, Feb. 1, 1945, and draft of a letter to Dean Virginia Gildersleeve, Feb. 25, 1945, both box 1, folder 15, JG Papers; letters from Jane Grant to "Mrs. Thorp," June 23, 1949, and to Agnes Meyer, Apr. 4, 1950, both box 3, folder 1, JG Papers; letters from Jane Grant to Geoffrey Parsons, Dec. 27, 1950, and to Helen Rogers Reid, both box 5, folder 6, JG Papers. The quotes are from the Feb. 25, 1945, letter to Dean Gildersleeve.
97. Letter from Jane Grant to Frances Knight, July 5, 1961, box 4, folder 4, JG Papers; letter from Robert D. Johnson to Jane Grant, July 20, 1961, box 10, folder 5, JG Papers. The quote is from the July 20 letter.
98. Una Stannard, *Mrs. Man* (San Francisco: Germain Books, 1977), 239–60.
99. Letters from Jane Grant to Frances Perkins, July 8, 1944, box 11, folder 1, JG Papers; Jan. 21, 1948, box 2, folder 3, JG Papers; and three letters in box 3, folder 1, JG Papers: Mar. 9, 1949; May 11, 1949; and May 31, 1949.
100. Jane Grant, letter to the editor headlined "Name Changes for Women," *New York Times*, Sept. 27, 1948, 22.
101. The quotes are taken, in order, from the letter from Mrs. Douglas Horton to Jane Grant, Feb. 17, 1947, from Jane Grant to Mrs. Douglas Horton, Feb. 24, 1947, and from Mrs. Douglas Horton to Jane Grant, Feb. 25, 1947, all box 3, folder 1, JG Papers. Also see the letter from Jane Grant to Dr. Mildred Horton, Feb. 11, 1947, box 3, folder 1, JG Papers. For more on Horton, see Stannard, *Mrs. Man*, 229.
102. *White Flower Farm Garden Book*, 3–9. The quotes are on pages 8 and 9.

103. Ibid., 8–20. The quote is on page 10.
104. Ibid., 20–22.
105. Ibid., 22–23. The quotes are on page 23.
106. Ibid., 23.

CHAPTER 11

1. Amos Pettingill [William Harris], *The White Flower Farm Garden Book* (New York: Alfred A. Knopf, 1971), 23; Laurie O'Neill, "A Nursery with a Flair for the Unusual," *New York Times*, May 16, 1981, CN2. The quote is from *The White Flower Farm Garden Book*.
2. *White Flower Farm Garden Book*, 24–25.
3. "Rite of Spring," *FYI* (the Time Inc. house organ), Mar. 20, 1960, box 39, folder 2, Jane C. Grant Papers, Special Collections, University of Oregon Library, Eugene, OR (hereafter JG Papers); *White Flower Farm Garden Book*, 26, 28–30. The quotes are on pages 28 and 30.
4. *White Flower Farm Garden Book*, 26.
5. Edith Evans Asbury, "William Bliss Harris, Ex-Editor and Writer on Gardening Topics," *New York Times*, June 26, 1981, A17; "White Flower Farm," *House & Garden*, Aug. 1969, 146.
6. *White Flower Farm Garden Book*, 30, 35; "White Flower Farm," 50; "Nursery with a Flair for the Unusual."
7. "Rite of Spring."
8. Letter from Jane Grant to Frances Perkins, Aug. 3, 1930, box 3, folder 1, JG Papers.
9. Una Stannard, *Mrs. Man* (San Francisco: Germain Books, 1977), 176, 187, 236.
10. Lucy Stone League press release dated Mar. 23, 1959, box 11, folder 4, JG Papers.
11. "23 Lucy Stoners Hold Session Here," *New York Times*, Mar. 23, 1950, 32.
12. See letters regarding the league to and from Grant in box 3, folders 1 and 2; box 5, folder 6; and box 10, folder 5, JG Papers. Also see Stannard, *Mrs. Man*, 262–63.
13. Letter from Frances Perkins to Jane Grant, Apr. 26, 1949, box 10, folder 5, JG Papers.
14. Letter from Mildred Clark to Jane Grant, Jan. 20, 1951, box 3, folder 2, JG Papers.
15. Minutes of the Lucy Stone League annual meeting, Jan. 18, 1951, and Revised Constitution of the Lucy Stone League, adopted Feb. 15, 1951, both box 10, folder 2, JG Papers.
16. Mary Lou Parker, "Fashioning Feminism: The Making of the Lucy Stone League by Members and Media" (PhD diss., University of Oregon, 1994), 71–73, 150–51, 169–71; Stannard, *Mrs. Man*, 264–65; Leila J. Rupp and Verta Taylor, *Survival in the Doldrums: The American Women's Rights Movement, 1945 to the 1960s* (Columbus: Ohio State University Press, 1990), 51–52.
17. Parker, "Fashioning Feminism," 56, 71, 150–51, 160–61, 187; minutes of Lucy Stone League annual meetings, Oct. 31, 1957, and Oct. 28, 1959, box 10, folder 2, JG Papers. Copies of these kinds of letters from Grant are scattered throughout her papers. Many of her published letters to the editor are in box 40, folder 5.
18. Minutes of Lucy Stone League annual meetings, Oct. 30, 1952, Oct. 28, 1954, Oct. 31, 1957, and Oct. 28, 1959, box 10, folder 2, JG Papers; Lucy Stone League *Bulletin*, Spring 1960, box 5, folder 2, JG Papers; Parker, "Fashioning Feminism," 56–57.
19. Lucy Stone League *Bulletin*, Spring 1960. Evidence of Grant's extensive efforts to gather research materials for the league during the 1950s and 1960s can be found in box 12, folders 3 and 4, JG Papers.
20. Letter from Jane Grant to Frances Knight, July 5, 1961, box 4, folder 5, JG Papers.
21. Parker, "Fashioning Feminism," 57, 104–5, 134. Also see box 9, folder 1, JG Papers, for announcements of and correspondence about these luncheons and evening meetings in the 1960s.
22. Undated press release, "Lucy Stone League Party Honors Janet Flanner at Salmagundi Club," box 11, folder 5, JG Papers. Also see the account of the event in the league's Spring 1966 *Bulletin*, box 5, folder 4, JG Papers.

23. Janet Flanner, "Introduction: The Unique Ross," in Ross, *"The New Yorker" and Me*, by Jane Grant (New York: Reynal & Company, 1968), 14–15.

24. Letter from Janet Flanner to Jane Grant, postmarked Nov. 20, 1944, box 1, folder 14, JG Papers.

25. Lucy Stone League *Bulletin*, Fall 1960, box 5, folder 2, JG Papers.

26. Rupp and Taylor, *Survival in the Doldrums*, 47, 99, 116–17. Grant's work for the ERA can be traced through box 5, folders 6 and 7, and box 6, folder 1, JG Papers. These folders include more than seventy letters from Grant to Florence Kitchelt or from Kitchelt to Grant.

27. Notes titled "ERA Meeting with ACLU," and "Brief Prepared for Presentation at the American Civil Liberties Union," both box 6, folder 1, JG Papers. For Harris's advisory committee memberships, see stationery of the Connecticut and Massachusetts ERA committees, box 4, folder 7, and box 6, folder 1, JG Papers.

28. Rupp and Taylor, *Survival in the Doldrums*, 58, 115.

29. Inez Robb, "Wives Seeking Use of Maiden Names Revive Lucy Stone League," distributed by the International News Service, Spring 1950, clipping in box 10, folder 5, JG Papers.

30. See, for example, transcript of Jane Grant radio interview, ca. 1946, box 12, folder 2, JG Papers; Frances Herridge, "Women Need More Rights, Not Privileges," *New York Post*, Oct. 21, 1953, 74; Edith Hills, "What Next!," syndicated by the Post-Hall Syndicate, Feb. 16, 1954; Joyce S. Cook, "Jane Grant, President of the Lucy Stone League, Visits Flint with Her Husband W. B. Harris, Fortune Magazine Editor," *Flint (Michigan) Journal*, July 11, 1954, all box 11, folder 5, JG Papers; McCandlish Phillips, "A Mrs. Is a Miss in Lucy Stone League," *New York Times*, Jan. 15, 1965, 17.

31. "Jane Grant, President of the Lucy Stone League, Visits Flint."

32. Letter from Jane Grant to Raoul Fleischmann, May 29, 1948, box 2, folder 3, JG Papers.

33. Letter from Raoul Fleischmann to Jane Grant, May 1, 1946, box 2, folder 1, JG Papers.

34. Letter from Jane Grant to Raoul Fleischmann, May 4, 1946, box 2, folder 1, JG Papers.

35. Letters from Jane Grant to Raoul Fleischmann, ca. 1947 and July 7, 1946, both box 2, folder 1, JG Papers. The quote is from the July 7 letter.

36. The postwar correspondence between Fleischmann and Grant fills much of box 2 of her papers, beginning with 1946 letters in folder 1 and ending with one 1964 letter in folder 12.

37. Letters from Raoul Fleischmann to Jane Grant, Oct. 16, 1947, and from Jane Grant to Raoul Fleischmann, Oct. 19, 1947, both box 2, folder 2, JG Papers.

38. See box 2, folder 4, for 1949 promotional ideas and her twenty-fifth anniversary campaign, described in a Feb. 9, 1949, letter to Fleischmann. For 1951 work, see box 2, folder 6. The cited activities are described in letters from Grant to Fleischmann on Jan. 24, 1951, and ca. Apr. 12, 1951, and from Fleischmann to Grant, Apr. 13, 1951.

39. Letter from Raoul Fleischmann to Jane Grant, Nov. 12, 1956, and letters from Jane Grant to Raoul Fleischmann, Sept. 18, 1952, and April 26, 1950, all box 2, folder 6; memo from Jane Grant to William Shawn, Feb. 20, 1958, box 2, folder 11, JG Papers.

40. Memos from Jane Grant to Raoul Fleischmann, Feb. 21, 1963, and July 16, 1962, box 2, folder 12, JG Papers. The quote is from the July 16 memo.

41. See, for example, letters from Jane Grant to Raoul Fleischmann on Sept. 18, 1952, and Oct. 2, 1952 (box 2, folder 6), and on Aug. 23, 1956, and Dec. 18, 1956 (box 2, folder 11), JG Papers. Also see the memo from Jane Grant to Raoul Fleischmann, Jan. 16, 1964, box 2, folder 13, JG Papers.

42. Letter from Jane Grant to Raoul Fleischmann, Dec. 17, 1952, box 2, folder 7, JG Papers.

43. See letters between John Ellard, Fiduciary Trust Company tax officer, and Hawley Truax, on Aug. 4, 1949, Nov. 25, 1949, Dec. 29, 1949, and Dec. 30, 1949, box 1312, folder 9, *New Yorker* Records, Manuscripts and Archives Division, Astor, Lenox and Tilden Foundations, New York Public Library, New York, NY.

44. "Women Need More Rights, Not Privileges."

45. Thomas Kunkel, *Genius in Disguise: Harold Ross of "The New Yorker"* (New York: Random House, 1995), 379, 393–98. The quote is on page 394.

46. Ibid., 370–73. The quote is on page 373.

47. Ibid., 374.

48. Ibid., 4–7, 356–57, 418, 420–23, 427.

49. *Ross*, 26–64.

50. Kunkel, *Genius in Disguise*, 426.

51. Harrison Kinney, *James Thurber: His Life and Times* (New York: Henry Holt & Company, 1995), 1025–46.

52. Letters from James Thurber to Jane Grant, Sept. 3, 1957, and from Jane Grant to James Thurber, Sept. 6, 1927, both box 29, folder 1, JG Papers; Kinney, *James Thurber*, 1048. The quote is from a letter from Grant to Kinney, Sept. 17, 1962, quoted in Kinney, *James Thurber*.

53. Letter from Jane Grant to Ann [Morrison], July 19, 1957, box 29, folder 1, JG Papers.

54. See extensive 1957 correspondence to and from Grant in box 29, folder 1, JG Papers.

55. Letter from Eleanor Rawson to Jane Grant, July 30, 1958, box 29, folder 1, JG Papers.

56. Letter from Jane Grant to Elizabeth Laurence, ca. Aug. 1958, box 29, folder 1, JG Papers.

57. Letter from Jane Grant to Phyllis Jackson, Dec. 18, 1958, box 29, folder 1, JG Papers.

58. Clipping from *Newsday*, Mar. 27, 1968, 3B, box 30, folder 1, JG Papers.

59. Grant's negotiations with McCormick and Murphy can be charted in the following letters: from Ken McCormick to Jane Grant, Sept. 21 and Dec. 28, 1959; from Jane Grant to Ken McCormick, Jan. 8, 1960, and to Dale Kramer, June 20, 1960; from Charles Murphy to Jane Grant, June 20, 1960; from Ken McCormick to Jane Grant, June 20, 1961; and from Jane Grant to Charles Murphy, Apr. 21 and June 24, 1964. All are in box 29, folder 1, JG Papers. The quote is from the June 24, 1964, letter.

60. Letters from Ken McCormick to Jane Grant, Mar. 2, 1965; from David Glixson to Jane Grant, Mar. 30 and May 30, 1966; and from Ken McCormick to Jane Grant, May 24, 1966. The quote is from the May 24, 1966, letter.

61. Letters from Ken McCormick to David Glixson (signed by McCormick's secretary, Betty Prashker), Sept. 21, 1966; from David Glixson to Jane Grant, Oct. 31, 1966; and from Ken McCormick to Jane Grant, Nov. 3, 1966, all box 29, folder 2, JG Papers.

62. Letters from Alfred Knopf Jr. to Jane Grant, Dec. 22, 1966, and Jan. 26, 1967, both box 29, folder 3, JG Papers. The quotes are from the Jan. 26 letter.

63. Letter from Eugene Reynal to Jane Grant, Mar. 27, 1967, box 29, folder 2, JG Papers.

64. See spring 1967 letters to and from, among others, Katharine White, Andy White, Peter Arno, Edna Ferber, Robert Sherwood, Philip Wylie, and Ralph Haynes, box 29, folder 2, JG Papers. Janet Flanner's manuscript and a note to Grant are in box 25, folder 1. Lists of title ideas are in box 29, folder 2.

65. See box 30, folder 1, JG Papers, for several dozen reviews of *Ross, "The New Yorker" and Me*, including the two cited. The *Christian Science Monitor* review ran on May 21, 1968. Bernays's review appeared in the *Worcester (Mass.) Telegram* on Mar. 31, 1968.

66. Letter from Jane Grant to William Betnick-Smith, Apr. 5, 1967, box 29, folder 2, JG Papers.

67. "A Prospectus," ca. 1964, box 7, folder 4, JG Papers.

68. Letter from William Harris to Edward Kemp, Nov. 28, 1973, and notes from visit by Robert Clark to William Harris, Dec. 10, 1974, both in the William B. Harris Donor File, University of Oregon Archives, Eugene, OR. The quotes are from the Nov. 28 letter. The information on Grant's 1963 draft of a will is in Rupp and Taylor, *Survival in the Doldrums*, 90.

69. The 277 Park Avenue building was described in Patricia Coffin, "Two-Seventy-Seven Park Avenue," undated clipping from an unidentified magazine, box 39, folder 2, JG Papers. The size of their 480 Park Avenue cooperative comes from the author's telephone interview with Ed Kemp, Dec. 1, 2003. The date of their move was determined from the

minutes of Lucy Stone League annual meetings—both held in Grant's apartment—in 1958 and 1959.

70. Doris Fleischman Bernays, *A Wife Is Many Women* (New York: Crown Publishers, 1955), 128.

71. Letter from Jane Grant to Elaine Derso and Louis Cutrona, Sept. 30, 1965, box 10, folder 5, JG Papers.

72. Asbury, "William Bliss Harris"; "New Partner in Laidlaw & Co., Bankers," *New York Times*, May 29, 1960, 60. The dates of Harris's different *Fortune* assignments were determined in part by searching for his bylines in the magazine. His first byline ran in Nov. 1953, the last in Aug. 1959.

73. Letter from Jane Grant to William Harris, Oct. 31, 1962, box 2, folder 12, JG Papers.

74. "White Flower Farm," 49; *White Flower Farm Garden Book*, iv, 31.

75. "White Flower Farm," 146.

76. William Pahlmann, "A Matter of Taste: A Beautiful Barn," written for the Hall Syndicate, July 2, 1967, box 2, folder 14, JG Papers; "White Flower Farm," 52, 146.

77. Author's telephone interview with Ed Kemp, Jan. 6, 2004; letter from Jane Grant to the members of the Lucy Stone League, Jan. 22, 1968, box 12, folder 3, JG Papers.

78. *White Flower Farm Garden Book*, 33.

79. Ibid., 4.

80. Letters from Howard B. Gotlieb to Mrs. William B. Harris, Jan. 9, 1969; from Jane Grant to Dr. H. B. Gotlieb, Jan 14, 1969; and from Howard B. Gotlieb to Jane Grant, Jan. 22, 1969. All are in box 2, folder 14, JG Papers.

81. Letters from Gene M. Gressley to Mrs. Harold Ross, Feb. 5, 1969, and from Jane Grant to Gene M. Gressley, Feb. 25, 1969, box 2, folder 16, JG Papers.

82. Letter from Gene M. Gressley to Jane Grant, Mar. 21, 1969, box 2, folder 16, JG Papers.

83. Author's telephone interview with Ed Kemp, Dec. 1, 2003; "Jane Grant Dead; Aided Magazine," *New York Times*, Mar. 17, 1972, L44.

CODA

1. Press release in the possession of Edward L. Bernays, Cambridge, MA; PR Newswire untitled obituary, box III:45, Edward L. Bernays Papers, Manuscript Division, Library of Congress, Washington, DC.

2. Joan Cook, "Doris Fleischman Bernays Dead; Pioneer Public Relations Counsel," *New York Times*, July 12, 1980, A22.

3. Radcliffe has since merged with Harvard University, and the Schlesinger now is identified as part of the Radcliffe Institute for Advanced Studies, Harvard University.

4. Letter from Edward L. Bernays to the author, July 19, 1988.

5. Larry Tye, *The Father of Spin: Edward L. Bernays and the Birth of Public Relations* (New York: Crown Publishers, 1998), 221, 262. For accounts by two writers who were given this tour, see Stuart Ewen, *PR! A Social History of Spin* (New York: Basic Books, 1996), 6–8, and Paul A. Holmes, "Profile: Ed Bernays—PR Founding Father and Social Scientist," *PR Week*, Mar. 14, 1985, 15.

6. Author's interview with Anne Bernays, Oct. 29, 1989, Cambridge, MA.

7. Bernays acted as his own clipping service, sending out copies of articles in which he was interviewed. He placed me on his mailing list immediately after my first visit, so I periodically received packets of clippings and noticed his increasing mention of his partnership with Fleischman.

8. Susan L. Fry, "A Conversation with Edward L. Bernays, Fellow, PRSA," *Public Relations Journal*, Nov. 1991, 31.

9. "Rule Hale Is Dead; Feminist Leader," *New York Times*, Sept. 19, 1934, 19.

10. Associated Press, "Heywood Broun Ex-Wife Passes," *Los Angeles Times*, Sept. 19, 1934, 7; *New York Journal* headline quoted in Mary Lou Parker, "Fashioning Feminism: The

Making of the Lucy Stone League by Members and Media" (PhD diss., University of Oregon, 1994), 153; untitled obituary, *Nation*, Oct. 3, 1934, 367.

11. "Ruth Hale," in *Collected Edition of Heywood Broun*, comp. Heywood Hale Broun (New York: Harcourt, Brace & Company, 1941), 325. (The column originally ran in the *New York World-Telegram* on Sept. 19, 1934.)

12. Author's interviews with Heywood Hale Broun, Aug. 3, 1999, and June 19, 2001, Woodstock, NY.

13. Heywood Hale Broun, *Whose Little Boy Are You? A Memoir of the Broun Family* (New York: St. Martin's Press, 1983), 179, 207–8. The quote is on page 179.

14. "3,000 Mourn Broun at St. Patrick Mass," *New York Times*, Dec. 21, 1939, 23.

15. Author's interview with Heywood Hale Broun, Aug. 1, 1999, Woodstock, NY. A photograph of the gravestone in the author's possession shows this inscription.

16. Duplicate of a letter from Annie Riley Hale to Morris Ernst, Feb. 14, 1940, in the possession of Melissa Hale Ward, Phoenix, AZ; "Mrs. Annie Riley Hale, Writer, Lecturer, Economist Was Mother of Mrs. Heywood Broun," *New York Times*, Dec. 28, 1944, 19.

17. Author's interviews with Heywood Hale Broun, Aug. 1, 1999, and Melissa Hale Ward, Aug. 9, 2000, Phoenix, AZ.

18. Heywood Hale Broun, *A Studied Madness* (New York: Doubleday & Company, 1965), 11–15, 252–53. The quote is on page 12.

19. Heywood Hale Broun, *Tumultuous Merriment* (New York: Richard Marek Publishers, 1979), 33–36. The quotes are on pages 35 and 36.

20. *A Studied Madness*, 19.

21. *Tumultuous Merriment*, 53–55. The quote is on page 54.

22. Ibid., 56–58.

23. Ibid., 58–61. The quotes are on pages 58 and 60.

24. Quoted in Richard Goldstein, "Heywood Hale Broun, a Sports Commentator Who Put Some Spin on the Ball, Dies at 83," *New York Times*, Sept. 8, 2001, A11.

25. Author's interview with Heywood Hale Broun, Aug. 2, 1999, Woodstock, NY.

26. Author's interview with Heywood Hale Broun, June 23, 2000, Woodstock, NY.

27. Frank Kelly, "Witty Reply to an Embarrassing Query," *Newsday*, June 7, 1983, clipping in box 1, Heywood Hale Broun Collection, Archive of Contemporary History, University of Wyoming, Laramie.

28. Author's telephone interview with Ed Kemp, Oct. 6, 2003.

29. Ibid.

30. Ibid.

31. Letters from Ed Kemp to William Harris, Nov. 9, 1973, from William Harris to Ed Kemp, Nov. 28, 1973, from Ed Kemp to William Harris, Dec. 5, 1972, and from William Harris to Ed Kemp, Dec. 26, 1973, all in the William B. Harris Donor File, University of Oregon Archives, Eugene, OR (hereafter WH Donor File).

32. Letters from Ed Kemp to William Harris, Apr. 9 and Apr. 23, 1974, WH Donor File; author's telephone interview with Ed Kemp, Oct. 6, 2003.

33. Author's telephone interview with Ed Kemp, Oct. 6, 2003.

34. Notes from Ed Kemp's Nov. 4, 1974, visit to William Harris, WH Donor File; author's telephone interview with Ed Kemp, Oct. 6, 2003.

35. Author's telephone interview with Ed Kemp, Oct. 6, 2003.

36. Ibid.

37. Letter from Robert Clark to William Harris, Nov. 21, 1974, WH Donor File.

38. Report by Robert Clark on his Dec. 10, 1974, visit with William Harris, WH Donor File.

39. Letter from Robert Clark to William Harris, Dec. 13, 1974, WH Donor File.

40. Extensive notes, memos, and letters, Dec. 1974 through Apr. 1975, WH Donor File. The quote is from a letter from Hanno D. Mott of Koenigh, Katner and Mott to Robert Clark, Apr. 10, 1975.

41. Ed Kemp's chronology of contacts with William Harris, WH Donor File.

42. Margo Miller, "He's a Blooming Success as a Planting Publisher," *Boston Globe*, Aug.

22, 1982, 1; Otile McManus, "Mail-Order Pride," *Boston Globe*, Mar. 23, 1986, 15; Edith Evans Asbury, "William Bliss Harris, Ex-Editor and Writer on Gardening Topics," *New York Times*, June 26, 1981, A17. For examples of Harris's gardening writing after the sale of White Flower Farm, see William B. Harris, "Astonishing Daylily," *Vogue*, Apr. 1978, 169–77, and William B. Harris, "Perennial Border," *Blair & Ketchums*, June 1978, 2–41.

43. Author's telephone interview with Ed Kemp, Oct. 6, 2003.

44. Report by Robert Clark on his Dec. 10, 1974, visit with William Harris.

45. Author's telephone interview with Ed Kemp, Jan. 6, 2004.

46. Ed Kemp's chronology of contacts with William Harris; author's telephone interviews with Ed Kemp, Oct. 6, 2003, and Dec. 1, 2003. The quote is from the December interview.

47. Author's telephone interview with Ed Kemp, Oct. 6, 2003.

48. Ed Kemp's chronology of contacts with William Harris.

49. Ibid.; Asbury, "William Bliss Harris"; Associated Press, "Gift to Coast Women's Center," *New York Times*, Oct. 4, 1983, A22; Mike Stahlberg, "UofO Given $3 Million," *Eugene Register Guard*, Sept. 23, 1983, 1, clipping in WH Donor File.

SELECTED BIBLIOGRAPHY

Adams, Franklin P. *The Diary of Our Own Samuel Pepys.* 2 vols. New York: Simon & Schuster, 1935.

Adams, Samuel Hopkins. *A. Woollcott: His Life and His World.* New York: Reynal & Hitchcock, 1945.

Adickes, Sandra. *To Be Young Was Very Heaven: Women in New York before the First World War.* New York: St. Martin's Press, 1997.

Alpern, Sara. *Freda Kirchwey: A Woman of "The Nation."* Cambridge, MA: Harvard University Press, 1987.

Alpern, Sara, Joyce Antler, Elisabeth Israels Perry, and Ingrid Winther Scobie. *The Challenge of Feminist Biography.* Urbana: University of Illinois Press, 1992.

Altman, Billy. *Laughter's Gentle Soul: The Life of Robert Benchley.* New York: W. W. Norton, 1997.

Ashley, Sally. *F.P.A.: The Life and Times of Franklin Pierce Adams.* New York: Beaufort, 1986.

Becker, Susan D. *The Origins of the Equal Rights Amendment: American Feminism between the Wars.* Westport, CT: Greenwood Press, 1981.

Bernays, Anne, and Justin Kaplan. *Back Then: Two Lives in 1950s New York.* New York: William Morrow, 2002.

Bernays, Doris Fleischman. *A Wife Is Many Women.* New York: Crown Publishers, 1955.

Bernays, Edward L. *Biography of an Idea: Memoirs of Public Relations Counsel Edward L. Bernays.* New York: Simon & Schuster, 1965.

———. *Crystallizing Public Opinion.* New York: Boni & Liveright, 1923; reprint, New York: Liveright Publishing, 1961.

———. Oral History. Oral History Research Office, Columbia University, New York, NY, 1971.

———, ed. *An Outline of Careers: A Practical Guide to Achievement by Thirty-Eight Eminent Americans.* New York: Doubleday, Doran & Company, 1927.

Bernheim, Alfred L. *The Business of the Theatre: The Economic History of the American Theatre, 1750–1932.* New York: Actors Equity Association, 1932; reprint, New York: Benjamin Blom, [1964].

Bernstein, Burton. *Thurber: A Biography.* New York: Dodd, Mead, 1975.

Boylan, James, ed. *"The World" and the 20's: The Best from New York's Legendary Newspaper.* New York: Dial Press, 1973.

Brazelton, Ethel M. Colson. *Writing and Editing for Women.* New York: Funk & Wagnalls Company, 1927.

Broun, Heywood. *The A.E.F.: With General Pershing and the American Forces.* New York: D. Appleton & Company, 1918.

———. *It Seems to Me: 1925–1935.* New York: Harcourt, Brace & Company, 1935.

Broun, Heywood Hale, compiler and editor. *Collected Edition of Heywood Broun.* New York: Harcourt, Brace & Company, 1941.

Broun, Heywood Hale. *Tumultuous Merriment.* New York: Richard Marek, 1979.

————. *Whose Little Boy Are You? A Memoir of the Broun Family*. New York: St. Martin's, 1983.

Brown, Dorothy M. *Setting a Course: American Women in the 1920s*. Boston: Twayne, 1987.

Brown, John Mason. *The Worlds of Robert E. Sherwood: Mirror to His Times, 1896–1939*. New York: Harper & Row, 1965.

Case, Frank. *Tales of a Wayward Inn*. New York: Frederick A. Stokes Company, 1938.

Chafe, William H. *The American Woman: Her Changing Social, Economic, and Political Roles, 1920–1970*. New York: Oxford University Press, 1972.

Coben, Stanley. *Rebellion against Victorianism: The Impetus for Cultural Change in 1920s America*. New York: Oxford University Press, 1991.

Collier, Virginia MacMakin. *Marriage and Careers: A Study of One Hundred Women Who Are Wives, Mothers, Homemakers, and Professional Workers*. New York: The Channel Bookshop [Bureau of Vocational Information], 1926.

Connelly, Marc. *Voices Offstage: A Book of Memoirs*. Chicago: Holt, Rinehart & Winston, 1968.

Cornebise, Alfred E. *The "Stars and Stripes": Doughboy Journalism of World War I*. Westport, CT: Greenwood Press, 1984.

Cott, Nancy F. *The Grounding of Modern Feminism*. New Haven, CT: Yale University Press, 1987.

Cutlip, Scott M. *The Unseen Power: Public Relations. A History*. Hillsdale, NJ: Lawrence Erlbaum, 1994.

Davis, Linda. *Onward and Upward: A Biography of Katharine S. White*. New York: Harper & Row, 1987.

Douglas, Ann. *Terrible Honesty: Mongrel Manhattan in the 1920s*. New York: Farrar, Straus & Giroux, 1995.

Douglas, George H. *The Smart Magazines*. New York: Archon Books, 1991.

Dumenil, Lynn. *The Modern Temper: American Culture and Society in the 1920s*. New York: Hill & Wang, 1995.

Erenberg, Lewis A. *Steppin' Out: New York Nightlife and the Transformation of American Culture*. Chicago: University of Chicago Press, 1984.

Ewen, Stuart. *PR! A Social History of Spin*. New York: Basic Books, 1996.

Felix, David. *Protest: Sacco-Vanzetti and the Intellectuals*. Bloomington: Indiana University Press, 1965.

Ferber, Edna. *A Peculiar Treasure*. 2nd ed. Garden City, NY: Doubleday & Co., 1960.

Filene, Catherine, ed. *Careers for Women*. New York: Houghton Mifflin, 1920; reprint, New York: Arno Press, 1974.

Fleischman, Doris E., ed. *An Outline of Careers for Women: A Practical Guide to Achievement*. New York: Doubleday, Doran & Company, 1928.

Fleischman (Bernays), Doris. "Notes of a Retiring Feminist." *American Mercury*, Feb. 1949, 161–68.

Ford, Corey. *The Time of Laughter*. Boston: Little, Brown, 1967.

Freedman, Estelle. "The New Woman: Changing Views of Women in the 1920s." *Journal of American History* 61, no. 2 (Sept. 1974): 372–93.

Frewin, Leslie. *The Late Mrs. Dorothy Parker*. New York: Macmillan, 1986.

Gaines, James R. *Wit's End: Days and Nights of the Algonquin Round Table*. New York: Harcourt Brace Jovanovich, 1977.

Gibbs, Wolcott. *More in Sorrow*. New York: Henry Holt, 1958.

Gilmer, Walker. *Horace Liveright, Publisher of the Twenties*. New York: David Lewis, 1970.

Goldstein, Malcolm. *George S. Kaufman: His Life, His Theater*. New York: Oxford University Press, 1979.

Gordon, Linda D. "Why Dorothy Thompson Lost Her Job: Political Columnists and the Press Wars of the 1930s and 1940s." *History of Education Quarterly* 34, no. 3 (Autumn 1994): 281–303.

Gottlieb, Agnes Hooper. "Grit Your Teeth, Then Learn to Swear: Women in Journalistic Careers, 1850–1926." *American Journalism* 18, no. 1 (Winter 2001): 53–71.

Grant, Jane. "Confession of a Feminist." *American Mercury*, Dec. 1943, 684–91.

———. *Ross, "The New Yorker" and Me*. New York: Reynal & Company, 1968.

Green, Elna C. *Southern Strategies: Southern Women and the Woman Suffrage Question*. Chapel Hill: University of North Carolina Press, 1997.

Hale, Annie Riley. *The Eden Sphinx*. New York: published by the author, 1916.

Harriman, Margaret Case. *Blessed Are the Debonair*. New York: Rinehart & Co., 1956.

———. *The Vicious Circle: The Story of the Algonquin Round Table*. New York: Rinehart & Co., 1951.

Heilbrun, Carolyn. *Writing a Woman's Life*. New York: W. W. Norton, 1988.

Heller, Adele, and Lois Rudnick, eds. *1915: The Cultural Moment*. New Brunswick, NJ: Rutgers University Press, 1991.

[Ingersoll, Ralph McAllister]. *"The New Yorker." Fortune*, May/June 1934, 72–97.

Ingersoll, Ralph McAllister. *Point of Departure: An Adventure in Autobiography*. New York: Harcourt, Brace & World, 1961.

Kahn, E. J., Jr. *The World of Swope*. New York: Simon & Schuster, 1965.

Kaplan, Justin, and Anne Bernays. *The Language of Names*. New York: Simon & Schuster, 1997.

Kaufman, Beatrice, and Joseph Hennessey, eds. *The Letters of Alexander Woollcott*. New York: Viking Press, 1944.

Kinney, Harrison. *James Thurber: His Life and Times*. New York: Henry Holt, 1995.

Kluger, Richard. *The Paper: The Life and Death of the "New York Herald Tribune."* New York: Alfred A. Knopf, 1986.

Kramer, Dale. *Heywood Broun: A Biographical Portrait*. New York: Current Books, 1949.

Kunkel, Thomas. *Genius in Disguise: Harold Ross of "The New Yorker."* New York: Random House, 1995.

———, ed. *Letters from the Editor: "The New Yorker"'s Harold Ross*. New York: Modern Library, 2000.

Lee, Judith Yaross. *Defining "New Yorker" Humor*. Jackson: University Press of Mississippi, 2000.

Lemons, J. Stanley. *The Woman Citizen: Social Feminism in the 1920s*. Urbana: University of Illinois Press, 1973.

Logie, Iona Robertson. *Careers for Women in Journalism*. Scranton, PA: International Textbook Company, 1938.

Lumsden, Linda. "'You're a Tough Guy, Mary—And a First-Rate Newspaperman': Gender and Women Journalists in the 1920s and 1930s." *Journalism & Mass Communication Quarterly* 72, no. 4 (Winter 1995): 913–21.

Maney, Richard. *Fanfare: The Confessions of a Press Agent*. New York: Harper & Brothers, 1957.

Marx, Harpo, with Rowland Barber. *Harpo Speaks!* New York: Bernard Geis Associates, 1961.

Matthews, Glenna. *The Rise of Public Women*. New York: Oxford University Press, 1992.

McGovern, James R. "The American Woman's Pre–World War I Freedom in Manners and Morals." *Journal of American History* 55, no. 2 (Sept. 1968): 315–33.

Meade, Marion. *Bobbed Hair and Bathtub Gin: Writers Running Wild in the Twenties*. New York: Doubleday, 2004.

Meredith, Scott. *George S. Kaufman and His Friends*. Garden City, NY: Doubleday, 1974.

Middleton, George. *These Things Are Mine: The Autobiography of a Journeyman Playwright*. New York: Macmillan, 1947.

Milford, Nancy. *Savage Beauty: The Life of Edna St. Vincent Millay*. New York: Random House, 2001.

Miller, Nina. *Making Love Modern: The Intimate Public Worlds of New York's Literary Women*. New York: Oxford University Press, 1999.

Mintz, Steven, and Susan Kellogg. *Domestic Revolutions: A Social History of American Family Life*. New York: Free Press, 1989.

O'Connor, Richard. *Heywood Broun, A Biography*. New York: G. P. Putnam's Sons, 1975.

Oppenheimer, George. *The View from the Sixties: Memories of a Spent Life*. New York: David McKay Company, 1966.

Parker, Mary Lou. "Fashioning Feminism: The Making of the Lucy Stone League by Members and Media." PhD diss., University of Oregon, 1994.

Pettingill, Amos [William Harris]. *The White Flower Farm Garden Book*. New York: Alfred A. Knopf, 1971.

Putnam, G. P., ed. *Nonsenseorship: Sundry Observations Concerning Prohibitions, Inhibitions, and Illegalities*. New York: G. P. Putnam's Sons, 1922.

Rosenberg, Rosalind. *Beyond Separate Spheres: Intellectual Roots of Modern Feminism*. New Haven, CT: Yale University Press, 1982.

———. *Divided Lives: American Women in the Twentieth Century*. New York: Hill & Wang, 1992.

Ross, Ishbel. *Ladies of the Press: The Story of Women in Journalism by an Insider*. New York: Harper & Brothers, 1936.

Rupp, Leila J. "Feminism and the Sexual Revolution in the Early Twentieth Century: The Case of Doris Stevens." *Feminist Studies* 15, no. 2 (Summer 1989): 289–309.

Rupp, Leila J., and Verta Taylor. *Survival in the Doldrums: The American Women's Rights Movement, 1945 to the 1960s*. Columbus: Ohio State University Press, 1990.

Schmalhausen, Samuel D., and V. F. Calverton, eds. *Women's Coming of Age: A Symposium*. New York: Horace Liveright, 1931.

Schneider, Dorothy, and Carl J. Schneider. *American Women in the Progressive Era, 1900–1920*. New York: Facts on File, 1993.

———. *Into the Breach: American Women Overseas in World War I*. New York: Viking Press, 1991.

Schudson, Michael. *Discovering the News: A Social History of American Newspapers*. New York: Basic Books, 1978.

Schwarz, Judith. *Radical Feminists of Heterodoxy: Greenwich Village, 1912–1940*. Rev. ed. Lebanon, NH: New Victoria Publishers, 1986.

Showalter, Elaine, ed. *These Modern Women: Autobiographical Essays from the Twenties*. New York: Feminist Press, 1978.

Simmons, Christina. "Women's Power in Sex: Radical Challenges to Marriage in the Early-Twentieth-Century United States." *Feminist Studies* 29, no. 1 (Spring 2003): 168–98.

Stannard, Una. *Mrs. Man*. San Francisco: Germain Books, 1977.

Stansell, Christine. *American Moderns: Bohemian New York and the Creation of a New Century*. New York: Henry Holt, 2000.

Steiner, Linda. "Stories of Quitting: Why Did Women Journalists Leave the Newsroom?" *American Journalism* 15, no. 3 (Summer 1998): 89–116.

Taylor, Verta. "Social Movement Continuity: The Women's Movement in Abeyance." *American Sociological Review* 54, no. 5 (Oct. 1989): 761–75.

Tebbel, John. *A History of Book Publishing in the United States*. Vol. 3. New York: R. R. Bowker, 1978.

Tedlow, Richard. *Keeping the Corporate Image: Public Relations and Business, 1900–1950*. Greenwich, CT: JAI Press, 1979.

Thurber, James. *The Years with Ross*. Boston: Little, Brown & Company, 1959.

Trigg, Mary Kathleen. "Four American Feminists, 1910–1940: Inez Haynes Irwin, Mary Ritter Beard, Doris Stevens, and Lorine Pruette." PhD diss., Brown University, 1989.

Trimberger, Ellen Kay. "Feminism, Men, and Modern Love, 1900–1925." In *Powers of Desire: The Politics of Sexuality*, edited by Ann Snitow, Christine Stansell, and Sharon Thompson, 131–52. New York: Monthly Review Press, 1983.

Tye, Larry. *The Father of Spin: Edward L. Bernays and the Birth of Public Relations*. New York: Crown Publishers, 1998.

Walker, Stanley. *City Editor*. New York: Blue Ribbon Books, 1934.

Wandersee, Winifred D. *Women's Work and Family Values, 1920–1940*. Cambridge, MA: Harvard University Press, 1981.

Washburn, Charles. *Press Agentry*. New York: National Library Press, 1937.

"White Flower Farm." *House & Garden*, Aug. 1969, 49–53, 146.

Woloch, Nancy. *Women and the American Experience, Volume Two: From 1860*. 2nd ed. New York: McGraw-Hill, 1994.

Yagoda, Ben. *About Town: "The New Yorker" and the World It Made*. New York: Scribner, 2000.

INDEX

Page numbers in **bold** indicate pictures.